D0867783

the
american
pragmatists

the american pragmatists

Selected Writings

edited by

MILTON R. KONVITZ
and
GAIL KENNEDY

Meridian Books
THE WORLD PUBLISHING COMPANY
Cleveland and New York

B.
832
. K6
1960

AN ORIGINAL MERIDIAN BOOK
Published by The World Publishing Company
2231 West 110th Street, Cleveland, Ohio 44102
First printing, October, 1960.
Sixth printing, May, 1969
Copyright © 1960 by The World Publishing Company.
All rights reserved. No part of this book may be reproduced
in any form without written permission from the publisher,
except for brief passages included in a review
appearing in a newspaper or magazine.
Library of Congress Catalog Card Number: 60-12329
Typography and Design by Elaine Lustig.
Printed in the United States of America   6WP569

JESUIT - KRAUSS - McCORMICK - LIBRARY
1100 EAST 55th STREET
CHICAGO, ILLINOIS 60615

Contents

Foreword

The word "pragmatism" is a misnomer—because it is a noun. The pragmatists as a group are not adherents to a doctrine but proponents of a method. As the contents of this book show, it is a "corridor theory": people have come to it with widely disparate backgrounds, and because of the diversity of their interests, they have interpreted and applied the theory in many different ways.

It would not be possible, therefore, to compile a fully representative selection from their writings within the limits of this volume. Other equally valid anthologies could easily be made. Our greatest difficulty—as is so often the case in editing books of this sort—has not been answering the question, What shall we include? but rather, How can we omit?

Since pragmatism is indigenous and has its roots in earlier phases of our intellectual history, we have begun with Emerson. Peirce, James, and Dewey were reared in the atmosphere of transcendentalism, and transcendentalists they remained at the core. But pragmatism has an equally strong affiliation with the American enlightenment, in particular with Jefferson, whose thought best represented the America Turgot called "the hope of the world." Perhaps most striking is the omission —though he is not an American—of F. C. S. Schiller. And though obviously necessary, it was difficult to pass over many important substantive contributions—books such as James's *Principles of Psychology, Radical Empiricism,* and *The Varieties of Religious Experience,* or Dewey's *Logic: The Theory of Inquiry, Democracy and Education,* and *The Public and Its Problems.* Fortunately, the literature is easily accessible. We hope that the incompleteness of our sample will encourage many readers to go beyond what they encounter here.

Since pragmatism is not a doctrine, not an "ism," but a method or a way of analyzing problems, our selections, exemplifying some of its applications to religion, metaphysics, science, aesthetics, ethics, education, and social philosophy, are offered in the pragmatic mood, as provocations, not definitive statements, as openers of windows and doors in the corridor.

MILTON R. KONVITZ
GAIL KENNEDY

I acknowledge gratefully the support of the Institute for Advanced Study at Princeton and the Walter E. Meyer Research Institute of Law at New Haven.

MILTON R. KONVITZ

June 1960

the american pragmatists

Ralph Waldo Emerson

1803-1882

Although Emerson is generally thought of as the leading figure in the development of American transcendentalism, his kinship with and influence on American pragmatism have been acknowledged by leading pragmatist philosophers. Preparing his "Address at the Emerson Centenary in Concord," William James wrote to his brother Henry: "The reading of the divine Emerson, volume after volume, has done me a lot of good, has thrown a strong practical light on my own path." In his essay on Emerson, written also for the centenary celebration, John Dewey said that Emerson was "the one citizen of the New World fit to have his name uttered in the same breath with that of Plato." And writing at the age of eighty-nine, Justice Holmes acknowledged the lifelong influence of Emerson. "The only firebrand of my youth," wrote Holmes to Pollock, "that burns to me as brightly as ever, is Emerson."

The aspect of Emerson's thought that probably was most attractive to pragmatists was his insistence that values must prove their worth by their relevance to present conduct. "I fancy," said Dewey, "that he reads the so-called eclecticism of Emerson wrongly who does not see that it is reduction of all the philosophers of the race, even the prophets like Plato and Proclus whom Emerson holds most dear, to the test of trial by the service rendered by the present and immediate experience."

The interactions between transcendentalism and pragmatism are quite complex. Thus, both Emerson and James believed in self-reliance and the role of great men in history; the creative function of the intelligence; the reciprocity of mind and nature, ideas and actions; "the will to believe" and the "Over-Soul" (in some sense). James, said H. G. Townsend in his PHILOSOPHICAL IDEAS IN THE UNITED STATES, *"is the central figure of what should be called neo-transcendentalism in New England." But unlike Emerson, James stressed actions more than ideas, and claimed to be a pluralist; yet with respect to these issues Charles S. Peirce stood with Emerson rather than with James.*

Challenge •

There goes in the world a notion that the scholar should be a recluse, a valetudinarian—as unfit for any handiwork or public labor as a penknife for an axe. The so-called "practical men" sneer at speculative men, as if, because they speculate or *see,* they could do nothing. I have heard it said that the clergy—who are always, more universally than any other class, the scholars of their day—are addressed as women; that the rough, spontaneous conversation of men they do not hear, but only a mincing and diluted speech. They are often virtually disfranchised; and indeed there are advocates for their celibacy. As far as this is true of the studious classes, it is not just and wise. Action is with the scholar subordinate, but it is essential. Without it he is not yet man. Without it thought can never ripen into truth. Whilst the world hangs before the eye as a cloud of beauty, we cannot even see its beauty. Inaction is cowardice, but there can be no scholar without the heroic mind. The preamble of thought, the transition through which it passes from the unconscious to the conscious, is action.

• [From: Ralph Waldo Emerson, "The American Scholar," Phi Beta Kappa Address, 1837. Concord Edition of *The Complete Works.* Boston: Houghton Mifflin Co.; 1903. Vol. I, pp. 94-100.]

Only so much do I know, as I have lived. Instantly we know whose words are loaded with life, and whose not.

The world—this shadow of the soul, or *other me*—lies wide around. Its attractions are the keys which unlock my thoughts and make me acquainted with myself. I run eagerly into this resounding tumult. I grasp the hands of those next me, and take my place in the ring to suffer and to work, taught by an instinct that so shall the dumb abyss be vocal with speech. I pierce its order; I dissipate its fear; I dispose of it within the circuit of my expanding life. So much only of life as I know by experience, so much of the wilderness have I vanquished and planted, or so far have I extended my being, my dominion. I do not see how any man can afford, for the sake of his nerves and his nap, to spare any action in which he can partake. It is pearls and rubies to his discourse. Drudgery, calamity, exasperation, want, are instructors in eloquence and wisdom. The true scholar grudges every opportunity of action past by, as a loss of power. It is the raw material out of which the intellect molds her splendid products. A strange process too, this by which experience is converted into thought, as a mulberry leaf is converted into satin. The manufacture goes forward at all hours.

The actions and events of our childhood and youth are now matters of calmest observation. They lie like fair pictures in the air. Not so with our recent actions—with the business which we now have in hand. On this we are quite unable to speculate. Our affections as yet circulate through it. We no more feel or know it than we feel the feet, or the hand, or the brain of our body. The new deed is yet a part of life—remains for a time immersed in our unconscious life. In some contemplative hour it detaches itself from the life like a ripe fruit, to become a thought of the mind. Instantly it is raised, transfigured; the corruptible has put on incorruption. Henceforth it is an object of beauty, however base its origin and neighborhood. Observe too the impossibility of antedating this act. In its grub state, it cannot fly, it cannot shine, it is a dull grub. But suddenly, without observation, the selfsame thing unfurls beautiful wings, and is an angel of wisdom. So is there no fact, no event, in our private history, which shall not, sooner or later, lose its adhesive, inert form, and astonish us by soaring from our body into the empyrean. Cradle and infancy, school and playground, the fear of boys, and dogs, and ferules, the love of little maids and berries, and many another fact that once filled the whole sky, are gone already; friend and relative, profession and party, town and country, nation and world, must also soar and sing.

Of course, he who has put forth his total strength in fit actions has the richest return of wisdom. I will not shut myself out of this globe of action, and transplant an oak into a flower-pot, there to hunger and pine; nor trust the revenue of some single faculty, and exhaust one vein of thought, much like those Savoyards, who, getting their livelihood by carving shepherds, shepherdesses, and smoking Dutchmen, for all Europe, went out one day to the mountain to find stock, and discovered that they had whittled up the last of their pine trees. Authors we have, in numbers, who have written out their vein, and who, moved by a commendable prudence, sail for Greece or Palestine, follow the trapper into the prairie, or ramble round Algiers, to replenish their merchantable stock.

If it were only for a vocabulary, the scholar would be covetous of action. Life is our dictionary. Years are well spent in country labors; in town; in the insight into trades and manufactures; in frank intercourse with many men and women; in science; in art; to the one end of mastering in all their facts a language by which to illustrate and embody our perceptions. I learn immediately from any speaker how much he has already lived, through the poverty or the splendor of his speech. Life lies behind us as the quarry from whence we get tiles and copestones for the masonry of today. This is the way to learn grammar. Colleges and books only copy the language which the field and the work-yard made.

But the final value of action, like that of books, and better than books, is that it is a resource. That great principle of Undulation in nature, that shows itself in the inspiring and expiring of the breath; in desire and satiety; in the ebb and flow of the sea; in day and night; in heat and cold; and, as yet more deeply ingrained in every atom and every fluid, is known to us under the name of Polarity—these "fits of easy transmission and reflection," as Newton called them, are the law of nature because they are the law of spirit.

The mind now thinks, now acts, and each fit reproduces the other. When the artist has exhausted his materials, when the fancy no longer paints, when thoughts are no longer apprehended and books are a weariness—he has always the resource *to live*. Character is higher than intellect. Thinking is the function. Living is the functionary. The stream retreats to its source. A great soul will be strong to live, as well as strong to think. Does he lack organ or medium to impart his truths? He can still fall back on this elemental force of living them. This is a total act. Thinking is a partial act. Let the grandeur of justice shine in his affairs. Let the beauty of affection cheer his lowly roof. Those "far from fame," who dwell and act with him, will feel the force of his constitution in the doings and passages of the day better than it can be measured by any public and designed display. Time shall teach him that the scholar loses no hour which the man lives. Herein he unfolds the sacred germ of his instinct, screened from influence. What is lost in seemliness is gained in strength. Not out of those on whom systems of education have exhausted their culture, comes the helpful giant to destroy the old or to build the new, but out of unhandselled savage nature; out of terrible Druids and Berserkers come at last Alfred and Shakespeare.

I hear therefore with joy whatever is beginning to be said of the dignity and necessity of labor to every citizen. There is virtue yet in the hoe and the spade, for learned as well as for unlearned hands. And labor is everywhere welcome; always we are invited to work; only be this limitation observed, that a man shall not for the sake of wider activity sacrifice any opinion to the popular judgments and modes of action.

Discipline •

In view of the significance of nature, we arrive at once at a new fact, that nature is a discipline. This use of the world includes the preceding uses, as parts of itself.

Space, time, society, labor, climate, food, locomotion, the animals, the mechanical forces, give us sincerest lessons, day by day, whose meaning is unlimited. They educate both the Understanding and the Reason. Every property of matter is a school for the understanding—its solidity or resistance, its inertia, its extension, its figure, its divisibility. The understanding adds, divides, combines, measures, and finds nutriment and

• [From: Ralph Waldo Emerson, *Nature*, 1836. Concord Edition of *The Complete Works*. Boston: Houghton Mifflin Co.; 1903. Vol. I., pp. 36-46.]

room for its activity in this worthy scene. Meantime, Reason transfers all these lessons into its own world of thought, by perceiving the analogy that marries Matter and Mind.

1. Nature is a discipline of the understanding in intellectual truths. Our dealing with sensible objects is a constant exercise in the necessary lessons of difference, of likeness, of order, of being and seeming, of progressive arrangement; of ascent from particular to general; of combination to one end of manifold forces. Proportioned to the importance of the organ to be formed, is the extreme care with which its tuition is provided —a care pretermitted in no single case. What tedious training, day after day, year after year, never ending, to form the common sense; what continual reproduction of annoyances, inconveniences, dilemmas; what rejoicing over us of little men; what disputing of prices, what reckoning of interest—and all to form the Hand of the mind; to instruct us that "good thoughts are no better than good dreams, unless they be executed!"

The same good office is performed by Property and its filial systems of debt and credit. Debt, grinding debt, whose iron face the widow, the orphan, and the sons of genius fear and hate; debt, which consumes so much time, which so cripples and disheartens a great spirit with cares that seem so base, is a preceptor whose lessons cannot be foregone, and is needed most by those who suffer from it most. Moreover, property, which has been well compared to snow—"if it fall level today, it will be blown into drifts tomorrow"—is the surface action of internal machinery, like the index on the face of a clock. Whilst now it is the gymnastics of the understanding, it is hiving, in the foresight of the spirit, experience in profounder laws.

The whole character and fortune of the individual are affected by the least inequalities in the culture of the understanding; for example, in the perception of differences. Therefore is Space, and therefore Time, that man may know that things are not huddled and lumped, but sundered and individual. A bell and a plough have each their use, and neither can do the office of the other. Water is good to drink, coal to burn, wool to wear; but wool cannot be drunk, nor water spun, nor coal eaten. The wise man shows his wisdom in separation, in gradation, and his scale of creatures and of merits is as wide as nature. The foolish have no range in their scale, but suppose every man is as every other man. What is not good they call the worst, and what is not hateful, they call the best.

In like manner, what good heed Nature forms in us! She pardons no mistakes. Her yea is yea, and her nay, nay.

The first steps in Agriculture, Astronomy, Zoology (those first steps which the farmer, the hunter, and sailor take), teach that Nature's dice are always loaded; that in her heaps and rubbish are concealed sure and useful results.

How calmly and genially the mind apprehends one after another the laws of physics! What noble emotions dilate the mortal as he enters into the councils of the creation, and feels by knowledge the privilege to BE! His insight refines him. The beauty of nature shines in his own breast. Man is greater that he can see this, and the universe less, because Time and Space relations vanish as laws are known.

Here again we are impressed and even daunted by the immense Universe to be explored. "What we know is a point to what we do not know." Open any recent journal of science, and weigh the problems suggested concerning Light, Heat, Electricity, Magnetism, Physiology, Geology, and judge whether the interest of natural science is likely to be soon exhausted.

Passing by many particulars of the discipline of nature, we must not omit to specify two.

The exercise of the Will, or the lesson of power, is taught in every event. From the child's successive possession of his several senses up to the hour when he saith, "Thy will be done!" he is learning the secret that he can reduce under his will not only particular events but great classes, nay, the whole series of events, and so conform all facts to his character. Nature is thoroughly mediate. It is made to serve. It receives the dominion of man as meekly as the ass on which the Saviour rode. It offers all its kingdoms to man as the raw material which he may mold into what is useful. Man is never weary of working it up. He forges the subtile and delicate air into wise and melodious words, and gives them wing as angels of persuasion and command. One after another his victorious thought comes up with and reduces all things, until the world becomes at last only a realized will—the double of the man.

2. Sensible objects conform to the premonitions of Reason and reflect the conscience. All things are moral; and in their boundless changes have an unceasing reference to spiritual nature. Therefore is nature glorious with form, color, and motion; that every globe in the remotest heaven, every chemi-

cal change from the rudest crystal up to the laws of life, every
change of vegetation from the first principle of growth in the
eye of a leaf, to the tropical forest and antediluvian coal-mine,
every animal function from the sponge up to Hercules, shall
hint or thunder to man the laws of right and wrong, and echo
the Ten Commandments. Therefore is Nature ever the ally of
Religion: lends all her pomp and riches to the religious sentiment. Prophet and priest, David, Isaiah, Jesus, have drawn
deeply from this source. This ethical character so penetrates
the bone and marrow of nature, as to seem the end for which
it was made. Whatever private purpose is answered by any
member or part, this is its public and universal function, and
is never omitted. Nothing in nature is exhausted in its first
use. When a thing has served an end to the uttermost, it is
wholly new for an ulterior service. In God, every end is converted into a new means. Thus the use of commodity, regarded
by itself, is mean and squalid. But it is to the mind an education in the doctrine of Use, namely, that a thing is good only
so far as it serves; that a conspiring of parts and efforts to the
production of an end is essential to any being. The first and
gross manifestation of this truth is our inevitable and hated
training in values and wants, in corn and meat.

It has already been illustrated, that every natural process
is a version of a moral sentence. The moral law lies at the
center of nature and radiates to the circumference. It is the
pith and marrow of every substance, every relation, and every
process. All things with which we deal, preach to us. What
is a farm but a mute gospel? The chaff and the wheat, weeds
and plants, blight, rain, insects, sun—it is a sacred emblem
from the first furrow of spring to the last stack which the
snow of winter overtakes in the fields. But the sailor, the
shepherd, the miner, the merchant, in their several resorts,
have each an experience precisely parallel, and leading to the
same conclusion: because all organizations are radically alike.
Nor can it be doubted that this moral sentiment which thus
scents the air, grows in the grain, and impregnates the waters
of the world, is caught by man and sinks into his soul. The
moral influence of nature upon every individual is that amount
of truth which it illustrates to him. Who can estimate this?
Who can guess how much firmness the sea-beaten rock has
taught the fisherman? how much tranquillity has been reflected to man from the azure sky, over whose unspotted deeps

the winds forevermore drive flocks of stormy clouds, and leave no wrinkle or stain? how much industry and providence and affection we have caught from the pantomime of brutes? What a searching preacher of self-command is the varying phenomenon of Health!

Herein is especially apprehended the unity of Nature—the unity in variety—which meets us everywhere. All the endless variety of things make an identical impression. Zenophanes complained in his old age, that, look where he would, all things hastened back to Unity. He was weary of seeing the same entity in the tedious variety of forms. The fable of Proteus has a cordial truth. A leaf, a drop, a crystal, a moment of time, is related to the whole, and partakes of the perfection of the whole. Each particle is a microcosm, and faithfully renders the likeness of the world.

Not only resemblances exist in things whose analogy is obvious, as when we detect the type of the human hand in the flipper of the fossil saurus, but also in objects wherein there is great superficial unlikeness. Thus architecture is called "frozen music," by De Staël and Goethe. Vitruvius thought an architect should be a musician. "A Gothic church," said Coleridge, "is a petrified religion." Michel Angelo maintained, that, to an architect, a knowledge of anatomy is essential. In Haydn's oratorios, the notes present to the imagination not only motions, as of the snake, the stag, and the elephant, but colors also; as the green grass. The law of harmonic sounds reappears in the harmonic colors. The granite is differenced in its laws only by the more or less of heat from the river that wears it away. The river, as it flows, resembles the air that flows over it; the air resembles the light which traverses it with more subtile currents; the light resembles the heat which rides with it through Space. Each creature is only a modification of the other; the likeness in them is more than the difference, and their radical law is one and the same. A rule of one art, or a law of one organization, holds true throughout nature. So intimate is this Unity, that, it is easily seen, it lies under the undermost garment of Nature, and betrays its source in Universal Spirit. For it pervades Thought also. Every universal truth which we express in words, implies or supposes every other truth. *Omne verum vero consonat.* It is like a great circle on a sphere, comprising all possible circles; which, however, may be drawn and comprise it in like manner. Every such truth is the absolute Ens seen from one side. But it has innumerable sides.

The central Unity is still more conspicuous in actions. Words are finite organs of the infinite mind. They cannot cover the dimensions of what is in truth. They break, chop, and impoverish it. An action is the perfection and publication of thought. A right action seems to fill the eye, and to be related to all nature. "The wise man, in doing one thing, does all; or, in the one thing he does rightly, he sees the likeness of all which is done rightly."

Words and actions are not in the attributes of brute nature. They introduce us to the human form, of which all other organizations appear to be degradations. When this appears among so many that surround it, the spirit prefers it to all others. It says, "From such as this have I drawn joy and knowledge; in such as this have I found and beheld myself; I will speak to it; it can speak again; it can yield me thought already formed and alive." In fact, the eye—the mind—is always accompanied by these forms, male and female; and these are incomparably the richest informations of the power and order that lie at the heart of things. Unfortunately every one of them bears the marks as of some injury; is marred and superficially defective. Nevertheless, far different from the deaf and dumb nature around them, these all rest like fountain-pipes on the unfathomed sea of thought and virtue whereto they alone, of all organizations, are the entrances.

It were a pleasant inquiry to follow into detail their ministry to our education, but where would it stop? We are associated in adolescent and adult life with some friends, who, like skies and waters, are coextensive with our idea; who, answering each to a certain affection of the soul, satisfy our desire on that side; whom we lack power to put at such focal distance from us, that we can mend or even analyze them. We cannot choose but love them. When much intercourse with a friend has supplied us with a standard of excellence, and has increased our respect for the resources of God who thus sends a real person to outgo our ideal; when he has, moreover, become an object of thought, and, whilst his character retains all its unconscious effect, is converted in the mind into solid and sweet wisdom—it is a sign to us that his office is closing, and he is commonly withdrawn from our sight in a short time.

Prospects •

In inquiries respecting the laws of the world and the frame of things, the highest reason is always the truest. That which seems faintly possible, it is so refined, is often faint and dim because it is deepest seated in the mind among the eternal verities. Empirical science is apt to cloud the sight, and by the very knowledge of functions and processes to bereave the student of the manly contemplation of the whole. The savant becomes unpoetic. But the best read naturalist who lends an entire and devout attention to truth, will see that there remains much to learn of his relation to the world, and that it is not to be learned by any addition or subtraction or other comparison of known quantities, but is arrived at by untaught sallies of the spirit, by a continual self-recovery, and by entire humility. He will perceive that there are far more excellent qualities in the student than preciseness and infallibility; that a guess is often more fruitful than an indisputable affirmation, and that a dream may let us deeper into the secret of nature than a hundred concerted experiments.

For the problems to be solved are precisely those which the physiologist and the naturalist omit to state. It is not so pertinent to man to know all the individuals of the animal kingdom, as it is to know whence and whereto is this tyrannizing unity in his constitution, which evermore separates and classifies things, endeavoring to reduce the most diverse to one form. When I behold a rich landscape, it is less to my purpose to recite correctly the order and superposition of the strata, than to know why all thought of multitude is lost in a tranquil sense of unity. I cannot greatly honor minuteness in details, so long as there is no hint to explain the relation between things and thoughts; no ray upon the *metaphysics* of conchology, of botany, of the arts, to show the relation of the forms of flowers, shells, animals, architecture, to the mind, and build science upon ideas. In a cabinet of natural history,

• [From: Ralph Waldo Emerson, *Nature,* 1836. Concord Edition of *The Complete Works.* Boston: Houghton Mifflin Co.; 1903. Vol. I, pp. 66-77.]

we become sensible of a certain occult recognition and sympathy in regard to the most unwieldly and eccentric forms of beast, fish, and insect. The American who has been confined, in his own country, to the sight of buildings designed after foreign models, is surprised on entering York Minster or St. Peter's at Rome, by the feeling that these structures are imitations also—faint copies of an invisible archetype. Nor has science sufficient humanity, so long as the naturalist overlooks that wonderful congruity which subsists between man and the world; of which he is lord, not because he is the most subtile inhabitant, but because he is its head and heart, and finds something of himself in every great and small thing, in every mountain stratum, in every new law of color, fact of astronomy, or atmospheric influence which observation or analysis lays open. A perception of this mystery inspires the muse of George Herbert, the beautiful psalmist of the seventeenth century. The following lines are part of his little poem on Man.

> Man is all symmetry,
> Full of proportions, one limb to another,
>   And all to all the world besides.
>   Each part may call the farthest, brother;
> For head with foot hath private amity,
>   And both with moons and tides.
>
>   Nothing hath got so far
> But man hath caught and kept it as his prey;
>   His eyes dismount the highest star:
>   He is in little all the sphere.
> Herbs gladly cure our flesh, because that they
>   Find their acquaintance there.
>
>   For us, the winds do blow,
> The earth doth rest, heaven move, and fountains flow;
>   Nothing we see, but means our good,
>   As our delight, or as our treasure;
> The whole is either our cupboard of food,
>   Or cabinet of pleasure.
>
>   The stars have us to bed:
> Night draws the curtain; which the sun withdraws.
>   Music and light attend our head.
>   All things unto our flesh are kind,
> In their descent and being; to our mind,
>   In their ascent and cause.

More servants wait on man
Than he'll take notice of. In every path,
    He treads down that which doth befriend him
    When sickness makes him pale and wan.
Oh mighty love! Man is one world, and hath
    Another to attend him.

The perception of this class of truths makes the attraction which draws men to science, but the end is lost sight of in attention to the means. In view of this half-sight of science, we accept the sentence of Plato, that "poetry comes nearer to vital truth than history." Every surmise and vaticination of the mind is entitled to a certain respect, and we learn to prefer imperfect theories, and sentences which contain glimpses of truth, to digested systems which have no one valuable suggestion. A wise writer will feel that the ends of study and composition are best answered by announcing undiscovered regions of thought, and so communicating, through hope, new activity to the torpid spirit.

I shall therefore conclude this essay with some traditions of man and nature, which a certain poet sang to me; and which, as they have always been in the world, and perhaps reappear to every bard, may be both history and prophecy.

"The foundations of man are not in matter, but in spirit. But the element of spirit is eternity. To it, therefore, the longest series of events, the oldest chronologies are young and recent. In the cycle of the universal man, from whom the known individuals proceed, centuries are points, and all history is but the epoch of one degradation.

"We distrust and deny inwardly our sympathy with nature. We own and disown our relation to it, by turns. We are like Nebuchadnezzar, dethroned, bereft of reason, and eating grass like an ox. But who can set limits to the remedial force of spirit?

"A man is a god in ruins. When men are innocent, life shall be longer, and shall pass into the immortal as gently as we awake from dreams. Now, the world would be insane and rabid, if these disorganizations should last for hundreds of years. It is kept in check by death and infancy. Infancy is the perpetual Messiah, which comes into the arms of fallen men, and pleads with them to return to paradise.

"Man is the dwarf of himself. Once he was permeated and dissolved by spirit. He filled nature with his overflowing currents. Out from him sprang the sun and moon; from man the sun, from woman the moon. The laws of his mind, the periods of his actions externized themselves into day and night, into the year and the seasons. But, having made for himself this huge shell, his waters retired; he no longer fills the veins and veinlets; he is shrunk to a drop. He sees that the structure still fits him, but fits him colossally. Say, rather, once it fitted him, now it corresponds to him from far and on high. He adores timidly his own work. Now is the man the follower of the sun, and woman the follower of the moon. Yet sometimes he starts in his slumber, and wonders at himself and his house, and muses strangely at the resemblance betwixt him and it. He perceives that if his law is still paramount, if still he have elemental power, if his word is sterling yet in nature, it is not conscious power, it is not inferior but superior to his will. It is instinct." Thus my Orphic poet sang.

At present, man applies to nature but half his force. He works on the world with his understanding alone. He lives in it and masters it by a penny-wisdom; and he that works most in it is but a half-man, and whilst his arms are strong and his digestion good, his mind is imbruted, and he is a selfish savage. His relation to nature, his power over it, is through the understanding, as by manure; the economic use of fire, wind, water, and the mariner's needle; steam, coal, chemical agriculture; the repairs of the human body by the dentist and the surgeon. This is such a resumption of power as if a banished king should buy his territories inch by inch, instead of vaulting at once into his throne. Meantime, in the thick darkness, there are not wanting gleams of a better light—occasional examples of the action of man upon nature with his entire force—with reason as well as understanding. Such examples are, the traditions of miracles in the earliest antiquity of all nations; the history of Jesus Christ; the achievements of a principle, as in religious and political revolutions, and in the abolition of the slave-trade; the miracles of enthusiasm, as those reported of Swedenborg, Hohenlohe, and the Shakers; many obscure and yet contested facts, now arranged under the name of Animal Magnetism; prayer; eloquence; self-healing; and the wisdom of children. These are examples of Reason's momentary grasp of the scepter; the exertions of a power which exists not in time or space, but an instantaneous instreaming causing power. The difference between the actual and the ideal force of man is happily figured by the schoolmen, in saying, that the knowl-

edge of man is an evening knowledge, *vespertina cognitio,* but
that of God is a morning knowledge, *matutina cognitio.*

The problem of restoring to the world original and eternal
beauty is solved by the redemption of the soul. The ruin or the
blank that we see when we look at nature, is in our own eye.
The axis of vision is not coincident with the axis of things,
and so they appear not transparent but opaque. The reason
why the world lacks unity, and lies broken and in heaps, is
because man is disunited with himself. He cannot be a
naturalist until he satisfies all the demands of the spirit. Love
is as much its demand as perception. Indeed, neither can be
perfect without the other. In the uttermost meaning of the
words, thought is devout, and devotion is thought. Deep calls
unto deep. But in actual life, the marriage is not celebrated.
There are innocent men who worship God after the tradition
of their fathers, but their sense of duty has not yet extended to
the use of all their faculties. And there are patient naturalists,
but they freeze their subject under the wintry light of the understanding. Is not prayer also a study of truth—a sally of the
soul into the unfound infinite? No man ever prayed heartily
without learning something. But when a faithful thinker,
resolute to detach every object from personal relations and see
it in the light of thought, shall, at the same time, kindle science
with the fire of the holiest affections, then will God go forth
anew into the creation.

It will not need, when the mind is prepared to study, to
search for objects. The invariable mark of wisdom is to see
the miraculous in the common. What is a day? What is a year?
What is summer? What is woman? What is a child? What is
sleep? To our blindness, these things seem unaffecting. We
make fables to hide the baldness of the fact and conform it, as
we say, to higher law of the mind. But when the fact is seen
under the light of an idea, the gaudy fable fades and shrivels.
We behold the real higher law. To the wise, therefore, a fact
is true poetry, and the most beautiful of fables. These wonders
are brought to our own door. You also are a man. Man and
woman and their social life, poverty, labor, sleep, fear, fortune, are known to you. Learn that none of these things is
superficial, but that each phenomenon has its roots in the
faculties and affections of the mind. Whilst the abstract question occupies your intellect, nature brings it in the concrete to
be solved by your hands. It were a wise inquiry for the closet,
to compare, point by point, especially at remarkable crises in

life, our daily history with the rise and progress of ideas in the mind.

So shall we come to look at the world with new eyes. It shall answer the endless inquiry of the intellect—What is truth? and of the affections—What is good? by yielding itself passive to the educated Will. Then shall come to pass what my poet said: "Nature is not fixed but fluid. Spirit alters, molds, makes it. The immobility or bruteness of nature is the absence of spirit; to pure spirit it is fluid, it is volatile, it is obedient. Every spirit builds itself a house and beyond its house a world and beyond its world a heaven. Know then that the world exists for you. For you is the phenomenon perfect. What we are, that only can we see. All that Adam had, all that Caesar could, you have and can do. Adam called his house, heaven and earth; Caesar called his house, Rome; you perhaps call yours, a cobbler's trade; a hundred acres of ploughed land; or a scholar's garret. Yet line for line and point for point your dominion is as great as theirs, though without fine names. Build therefore your own world. As fast as you conform your life to the pure idea in your mind, that will unfold its great proportions. A correspondent revolution in things will attend the influx of the spirit. So fast will disagreeable appearances, swine, spiders, snakes, pests, madhouses, prisons, enemies, vanish; they are temporary and shall be no more seen. The sordor and filths of nature, the sun shall dry up and the wind exhale. As when the summer comes from the south the snow-banks melt and the face of the earth becomes green before it, so shall the advancing spirit create its ornaments along its path, and carry with it the beauty it visits and the song which enchants it; it shall draw beautiful faces, warm hearts, wise discourse, and heroic acts, around its way, until evil is no more seen. The kingdom of man over nature, which cometh not with observation—a dominion such as now is beyond his dream of God—he shall enter without more wonder than the blind man feels who is gradually restored to perfect sight."

William James

1842-1910

When he was twenty-eight years old, James came close to suffering a breakdown. At the time, he was reading Renouvier, and following is the entry in his diary for April 30, 1870: "I think that yesterday was a crisis in my life. I finished the first part of Renouvier's second ESSAIS *and see no reason why his definition of free will—"the sustaining of a thought* BECAUSE I CHOOSE *when I might have other thoughts"—need be the definition of an illusion. At any rate, I will assume for the present . . . that it is no illusion. My first act of free will shall be to believe in free will."*

This belief in the freedom of his own will, and in the reality of that freedom, became the foundation of James's philosophy, which he called pragmatism (the origin of which he generously credited to Charles S. Peirce). It is a philosophy, James said, that is not a system, for it "has no dogmas, and no doctrine save its method." As an attitude toward philosophical questions, pragmatism, as F. C. S. Schiller has pointed out, may be traced back to the stand of Protagoras that "man is the measure."

But man's role, in the thought of James, is not merely to "measure" a world already fully planned and made; man creates and re-creates. The universe is not an Absolute; it is open, and it is full of novelty; it contains chaos, disorder, and evil. Life as it comes, said James, has an air "of being, or at least of involving, a muddle and a struggle, with an 'ever not quite' to all our formulas, and novelty and possibility forever leaking in." Rejecting absolutism or monism, James denied all inevitabilities—except the inevitability of freedom. Progress is possible but not inevitable, and it is possible because man is free to believe in ideals and to strive for their fulfillment. Man thus makes his universe—many universes. He is not merely a union reflecting a finished product: "The knower is an actor, and coefficient of the truth on one side, whilst on the other he registers the truth which he helps to create."

What Pragmatism Means •

Some years ago, being with a camping party in the mountains, I returned from a solitary ramble to find every one engaged in a ferocious metaphysical dispute. The *corpus* of the dispute was a squirrel—a live squirrel supposed to be clinging to one side of a tree-trunk; while over against the tree's opposite side a human being was imagined to stand. This human witness tries to get sight of the squirrel by moving rapidly round the tree, but no matter how fast he goes, the squirrel moves as fast in the opposite direction, and always keeps the tree between himself and the man, so that never a glimpse of him is caught. The resultant metaphysical problem now is this: *Does the man go round the squirrel or not?* He goes round the tree, sure enough, and the squirrel is on the tree; but does he go round the squirrel? In the unlimited leisure of the wilderness, discussion had been worn threadbare. Every one had taken sides, and was obstinate; and the numbers on

• [From: William James, *Pragmatism: A New Name for Some Old Ways of Thinking.* New York: Longmans, Green and Co.; 1907. Pp. 43-81. Copyright 1934 by Henry James. Reprinted by permission of Paul R. Reynolds & Son.]

both sides were even. Each side, when I appeared therefore appealed to me to make it a majority. Mindful of the scholastic adage that whenever you meet a contradiction you must make a distinction, I immediately sought and found one, as follows: "Which party is right," I said, "depends on what you *practically mean* by 'going round' the squirrel. If you mean passing from the north of him to the east, then to the south, then to the west, and then to the north of him again, obviously the man does go round him, for he occupies these successive positions. But if on the contrary you mean being first in front of him, then on the right of him, then behind him, then on his left, and finally in front again, it is quite as obvious that the man fails to go round him, for by the compensating movements the squirrel makes, he keeps his belly turned towards the man all the time, and his back turned away. Make the distinction, and there is no occasion for any farther dispute. You are both right and both wrong according as you conceive the verb 'to go round' in one practical fashion or the other."

Although one or two of the hotter disputants called my speech a shuffling evasion, saying they wanted no quibbling or scholastic hair-splitting, but meant just plain honest English "round," the majority seemed to think that the distinction has assuaged the dispute.

I tell this trivial anecdote because it is a peculiarly simple example of what I wish now to speak of as *the pragmatic method.* The pragmatic method is primarily a method of settling metaphysical disputes that otherwise might be interminable. Is the world one or many?—fated or free?—material or spiritual?—here are notions either of which may or may not hold good of the world; and disputes over such notions are unending. The pragmatic method in such cases is to try to interpret each notion by tracing its respective practical consequences. What difference would it practically make to any one if this notion rather than that notion were true? If no practical difference whatever can be traced, then the alternatives mean practically the same thing, and all dispute is idle. Whenever a dispute is serious, we ought to be able to show some practical difference that must follow from one side or the other's being right.

A glance at the history of the idea will show you still better what pragmatism means. The term is derived from the same Greek word πράγμα, meaning action, from which our words "practice" and "practical" come. It was first introduced into philosophy by Mr. Charles Peirce in 1878. In an article entitled "How to Make Our Ideas Clear," in the *Popular Science Monthly* for January of that year Mr. Peirce, after pointing out that our beliefs are really rules for action, said that, to develop a thought's meaning, we need only determine what conduct it is fitted to produce: that conduct is for us its sole significance. And the tangible fact at the root of all our thought-distinctions, however subtle, is that there is no one of them so fine as to consist in anything but a possible difference of practice. To attain perfect clearness in our thoughts of an object, then, we need only consider what conceivable effects of a practical kind the object may involve—what sensations we are to expect from it, and what reactions we must prepare. Our conception of these effects, whether immediate or remote, is then for us the whole of our conception of the object, so far as that conception has positive significance at all.

This is the principle of Peirce, the principle of pragmatism. It lay entirely unnoticed by any one for twenty years, until I, in an address before Professor Howison's philosophical union at the University of California, brought it forward again and made a special application of it to religion. By that date (1898) the times seemed ripe for its reception. The word "pragmatism" spread, and at present it fairly spots the pages of the philosophic journals. On all hands we find the "pragmatic movement" spoken of, sometimes with respect, sometimes with contumely, seldom with clear understanding. It is evident that the term applies itself conveniently to a number of tendencies that hitherto have lacked a collective name, and that it has "come to stay."

To take in the importance of Peirce's principle, one must get accustomed to applying it to concrete cases. I found a few years ago that Ostwald, the illustrious Leipzig chemist, had been making perfectly distinct use of the principle of pragmatism in his lectures on the philosophy of science, though he had not called it by that name.

"All realities influence our practice," he wrote me, "and that influence is their meaning for us. I am accustomed to put questions to my classes in this way: In what respects would the world be different if this alternative or that were true? If I can find nothing that would become different, then the alternative has no sense."

That is, the rival views mean practically the same thing, and meaning, other than practical, there is for us none. Ostwald in a published lecture gives this example of what he means. Chemists have long wrangled over the inner constitution of certain bodies called "tautomerous." Their properties seemed equally consistent with the notion that an instable hydrogen atom oscillates inside of them, or that they are instable mixtures of two bodies. Controversy raged, but never was decided. "It would never have begun," says Ostwald, "if the combatants had asked themselves what particular experimental fact could have been made different by one or the other view being correct. For it would then have appeared that no difference of fact could possibly ensue; and the quarrel was as unreal as if, theorizing in primitive times about the raising of dough by yeast, one party should have invoked a 'brownie,' while another insisted on an 'elf' as the true cause of the phenomenon."

It is astonishing to see how many philosophical disputes collapse into insignificance the moment you subject them to this simple test of tracing a concrete consequence. There can *be* no difference anywhere that doesn't *make* a difference elsewhere—no difference in abstract truth that doesn't express itself in a difference in concrete fact and in conduct consequent upon that fact, imposed on somebody, somehow, somewhere, and somewhen. The whole function of philosophy ought to be to find out what definite difference it will make to you and me, at definite instants of our life, if this world-formula or that world-formula be the true one.

There is absolutely nothing new in the pragmatic method. Socrates was an adept at it. Aristotle used it methodically. Locke, Berkeley, and Hume made momentous contributions to truth by its means. Shadworth Hodgson keeps insisting that realities are only what they are "known as." But these forerunners of pragmatism used it in fragments: they were preluders only. Not until in our time has it generalized itself, become conscious of a universal mission, pretended to a conquering destiny. I believe in that destiny, and I hope I may end by inspiring you with my belief.

Pragmatism represents a perfectly familiar attitude in philosophy, the empiricist attitude, but it represents it, as it seems to me, both in a more radical and in a less objectionable form than it has ever yet assumed. A pragmatist turns his back resolutely and once for all upon a lot of inveterate habits dear to professional philosophers. He turns away from abstraction and insufficiency, from verbal solutions, from bad *a priori* reasons, from fixed principles, closed systems, and pretended absolutes and origins. He turns towards concreteness and adequacy, towards facts, towards action and towards power. That means the empiricist temper regnant and the rationalist temper sincerely given up. It means the open air and possibilities of nature, as against dogma, artificiality, and the pretence of finality in truth.

At the same time it does not stand for any special results. It is a method only. But the general triumph of that method would mean an enormous change in what I called in my last lecture the "temperament" of philosophy. Teachers of the ultra-rationalistic type would be frozen out, much as the courtier type is frozen out in republics, as the ultramontane type of priest is frozen out in protestant lands. Science and metaphysics would come much nearer together, would in fact work absolutely hand in hand.

Metaphysics has usually followed a very primitive kind of quest. You know how men have always hankered after unlawful magic, and you know what a great part in magic *words* have always played. If you have his name, or the formula of incantation that binds him, you can control the spirit, genie, afrite, or whatever the power may be. Solomon knew the names of all the spirits, and having their names, he held them subject to his will. So the universe has always appeared to the natural mind as a kind of enigma, of which the key must be sought in the shape of some illuminating or power-bringing word or name. That word names the universe's *principle,* and to possess it is after a fashion to possess the universe itself. "God," "Matter," "Reason," "the Absolute," "Energy," are so many solving names. You can rest when you have them. You are at the end of your metaphysical quest.

But if you follow the pragmatic method, you cannot look on any such word as closing your quest. You must bring out of each word its practical cash-value, set it at work within the stream of your experience. It appears less as a solution, then, than as a program for more work, and more particularly as an indication of the ways in which existing realities may be *changed.*

Theories thus become instruments, not answers to enigmas, in which we can rest. We don't lie back upon them, we move forward, and, on occasion, make nature over again by their aid. Pragmatism unstiffens all our theories, limbers them up and sets each one at work. Being nothing essentially new, it harmonizes with many ancient philosophic tendencies. It agrees with nominalism for instance, in always appealing to particulars; with utilitarianism in emphasizing practical aspects; with positivism in its disdain for verbal solutions, useless questions and metaphysical abstractions.

All these, you see, are *anti-intellectualist* tendencies. Against rationalism as a pretension and a method pragmatism is fully armed and militant. But, at the outset, at least, it stands for no particular results. It has no dogmas, and no doctrines save its method. As the young Italian pragmatist Papini has well said, it lies in the midst of our theories, like a corridor in a hotel. Innumerable chambers open out of it. In one you may find a man writing an atheistic volume; in the next some one on his knees praying for faith and strength; in a third a chemist investigating a body's properties. In a fourth a system of idealistic metaphysics is being excogitated; in a fifth the impossibility of metaphysics is being shown. But they all own the corridor, and all must pass through it if they want a practicable way of getting into or out of their respective rooms.

No particular results then, so far, but only an attitude of orientation, is what the pragmatic method means. *The attitude of looking away from first things, principles, "categories," supposed necessities; and of looking towards last things, fruits, consequences, facts.*

So much for the pragmatic method! You may say that I have been praising it rather than explaining it to you, but I shall presently explain it abundantly enough by showing how it works on some familiar problems. Meanwhile the word pragmatism has come to be used in a still wider sense, as meaning also a certain *theory of truth*. I mean to give a whole lecture to the statement of that theory, after first paving the way, so I can be very brief now. But brevity is hard to follow, so I ask you for redoubled attention for a quarter of an hour. If much remains obscure, I hope to make it clear in the later lectures.

One of the most successfully cultivated branches of philosophy in our time is what is called inductive logic, the study of the conditions under which our sciences have evolved. Writers on this subject have begun to show a singuler unanimity as to what the laws of nature and elements of fact mean, when formulated by mathematicians, physicists and chemists. When the first mathematical, logical, and natural uniformities, the first *laws,* were discovered, men were so carried away by the clearness, beauty and simplification that resulted, that they believed themselves to have deciphered authentically the eternal thoughts of the Almighty. His mind also thundered and reverberated in syllogisms. He also thought in conic sections, squares and roots and ratios, and geometrized like Euclid. He made Kepler's laws for the planets to follow; he made velocity increase proportionally to the time in falling bodies; he made the law of the sines for light to obey when refracted; he established the classes, orders, families and genera of plants and animals, and fixed the distances between them. He thought the archetypes of all things, and devised their variations; and when we rediscover any one of these his wondrous institutions, we seize his mind in its very literal intention.

But as the sciences have developed farther the notion has gained ground that most, perhaps all, of our laws are only approximations. The laws themselves, moreover, have grown so numerous that there is no counting them; and so many rival formulations are proposed in all the branches of science that investigators have become accustomed to the notion that no theory is absolutely a transcript of reality, but that any one of them may from some point of view be useful. Their great use is to summarize old facts and to lead to new ones. They are only a man-made language, a conceptual shorthand, as some one calls them, in which we write our reports of nature; and languages, as is well known, tolerate much choice of expression and many dialects.

Thus human arbitrariness has driven divine necessity from scientific logic. If I mention the names of Sigwart, Mach, Ostwald, Pearson, Milhaud, Poincaré, Duhem, Ruyssen, those of you who are students will easily identify the tendency I speak of, and will think of additional names.

Riding now on the front of this wave of scientific logic Messrs. Schiller and Dewey appear with their pragmatistic account of what truth everywhere signifies. Everywhere, these teachers say, "truth" in our ideas and beliefs means the same thing that it means in science. It means, they say, nothing but this, *that ideas (which themselves are but parts of our experience) become true just in so far as they help us to get into satisfactory relations with other parts of our experience,* to summarize them and get about among them by conceptual short-cuts instead of following the interminable succession of particular phenomena. Any idea upon which we can ride, so to speak; any idea that will carry us prosperously from any one part of our experience to any other part, linking things satisfactorily, working securely, simplifying, saving labor; is true for just so much, true in so far forth, true *instrumentally*. This is the "instrumental" view of truth taught so successfully at Chicago, the view that truth in our ideas means their power to "work," promulgated so brilliantly at Oxford.

Messrs. Dewey, Schiller and their allies, in reaching this general conception of all truth, have only followed the example of geologists, biologists and philologists. In the establishment of these other sciences, the successful stroke was always to take some simple process actually observable in operation—as denudation by weather, say, or variation from parental type, or change of dialect by incorporation of new words and pronunciations—and then to generalize it, making it apply to all times, and produce great results by summating its effects through the ages.

The observable process which Schiller and Dewey particularly singled out for generalization is the familiar one by which any individual settles into *new opinions*. The process here is always the same. The individual has a stock of old opinions already, but he meets a new experience that puts them to a strain. Somebody contradicts them; or in a reflective moment he discovers that they contradict each other; or he hears of facts with which they are incompatible; or desires arise in him which they cease to satisfy. The result is an inward trouble to which his mind till then had been a stranger, and from which he seeks to escape by modifying his previous mass of opinions. He saves as much of it as he can, for in this matter of belief we are all extreme conservatives. So he tries to change first this opinion, and then that (for they resist change very variously), until at last some new idea comes up which he can graft upon the ancient stock with a minimum of disturbance of the latter, some idea that mediates between the stock and the new experience and runs them into one another most felicitously and expediently.

This new idea is then adopted as the true one. It preserves the older stock of truths with a minimum of modification, stretching them just enough to make them admit the novelty, but conceiving that in ways as familiar as the case leaves possible. An *outrée* explanation, violating all our preconceptions, would never pass for a true account of a novelty. We should scratch round industriously till we found something less eccentric. The most violent revolutions in an individual's beliefs leave most of his old order standing. Time and space, cause and effect, nature and history, and one's own biography remain untouched. New truth is always a go-between, a smoother-over of transitions. It marries old opinion to new fact so as ever to show a minimum of jolt, a maximum of continuity. We hold a theory true just in proportion to its success in solving this "problem of maxima and minima." But success in solving this problem is eminently a matter of approximation. We say this theory solves it on the whole more satisfactorily than that theory; but that means more satisfactorily to ourselves, and individuals will emphasize their points of satisfaction differently. To a certain degree, therefore, everything here is plastic.

The point I now urge you to observe particularly is the part played by the older truths. Failure to take account of it is the source of much of the unjust criticism levelled against pragmatism. Their influence is absolutely controlling. Loyalty to them is the first principle—in most cases it is the only principle; for by far the most usual way of handling phenomena so novel that they would make for a serious re-arrangement of our preconception is to ignore them altogether, or to abuse those who bear witness for them.

You doubtless wish examples of this process of truth's growth, and the only trouble is their superabundance. The simplest case of new truth is of course the mere numerical addition of new kinds of facts, or of new single facts of old kinds, to our experience—an addition that involves no alteration in the old beliefs. Day follows day, and its contents are simply added. The new contents themselves are not true, they simply *come* and *are*. Truth is *what we say about* them, and when we say that they have come, truth is satisfied by the plain additive formula.

But often the day's contents oblige a re-arrangement. If I should now utter piercing shrieks and act like a maniac on this platform, it would make many of you revise your ideas as to the probable worth of my philosophy. "Radium" came the other day as part of the day's content, and seemed for a moment to contradict our ideas of the whole order of nature, that order having come to be identified with what is called the conservation of energy. The mere sight of radium paying heat away indefinitely out of its own pocket seemed to violate that conservation. What to think? If the radiations from it were nothing but an escape of unsuspected "potential" en-

ergy, pre-existent inside of the atoms, the principle of conservation would be saved. The discovery of "helium" as the
radiation's outcome, opened a way to this belief. So Ramsay's
view is generally held to be true, because, although it extends
our old ideas of energy, it causes a minimum of alteration in
their nature.

I need not multiply instances. A new opinion counts as
"true" just in proportion as it gratifies the individual's desire
to assimilate the novel in his experience to his beliefs in stock.
It must both lean on old truth and grasp new fact; and its
success (as I said a moment ago) in doing this, is a matter
for the individual's appreciation. When old truth grows, then,
by new truth's addition, it is for subjective reasons. We are in
the process and obey the reasons. That new idea is truest
which performs most felicitously its function of satisfying
our double urgency. It makes itself true, gets itself classed as
true, by the way it works; grafting itself then upon the ancient
body of truth, which thus grows much as a tree grows by the
activity of a new layer of cambium.

Now Dewey and Schiller proceed to generalize this observation and to apply it to the most ancient parts of truth. They
also once were plastic. They also were called true for human
reasons. They also mediated between still earlier truths and
what in those days were novel observations. Purely objective
truth, truth in whose establishment the function of giving
human satisfaction in marrying previous parts of experience
with newer parts played no role whatever, is nowhere to be
found. The reasons why we call things true is the reason why
they *are* true, for "to be true" *means* only to perform this
marriage-function.

The trail of the human serpent is thus over everything.
Truth independent; truth that we *find* merely; truth no longer
malleable to human need; truth incorrigible, in a word; such
truth exists indeed superabundantly—or is supposed to exist by
rationalistically minded thinkers; but then it means only the
dead heart of the living tree, and its being there means only
that truth also has its paleontology, and its "prescription," and
may grow stiff with years of veteran service and petrified in
men's regard by sheer antiquity. But how plastic even the
oldest truths nevertheless really are has been vividly shown
in our day by the transformation of logical and mathematical
ideas, a transformation which seems even to be invading
physics. The ancient formulas are reinterpreted as special

expressions of much wider principles, principles that our ancestors never got a glimpse of in their present shape and formulation.

Mr. Schiller still gives to all this view of truth the name of "Humanism," but, for this doctrine too, the name of pragmatism seems fairly to be in the ascendent, so I will treat it under the name of pragmatism in these lectures.

Such then would be the scope of pragmatism—first, a method; and second, a genetic theory of what is meant by truth. And these two things must be our future topics.

What I have said of the theory of truth will, I am sure, have appeared obscure and unsatisfactory to most of you by reason of its brevity. I shall make amends for that hereafter. In a lecture on "common sense" I shall try to show what I mean by truths grown petrified by antiquity. In another lecture I shall expatiate on the idea that our thoughts become true in proportion as they successfully exert their go-between function. In a third I shall show how hard it is to discriminate subjective from objective factors in Truth's development. You may not follow me wholly in these lectures; and if you do, you may not wholly agree with me. But you will, I know, regard me at least as serious, and treat my effort with respectful consideration.

You will probably be surprised to learn, then, that Messrs. Schiller's and Dewey's theories have suffered a hailstorm of contempt and ridicule. All rationalism has risen against them. In influential quarters Mr. Schiller, in particular, has been treated like an impudent schoolboy who deserves a spanking. I should not mention this, but for the fact that it throws so much sidelight upon that rationalistic temper to which I have opposed the temper of pragmatism. Pragmatism is uncomfortable away from facts. Rationalism is comfortable only in the presence of abstractions. This pragmatist talk about truths in the plural, about their utility and satisfactoriness, about the success with which they "work," etc., suggests to the typical intellectualist mind a sort of coarse lame second-rate makeshift article of truth. Such truths are not real truth. Such tests are merely subjective. As against this, objective truth must be something non-utilitarian, haughty, refined, remote, august, exalted. It must be an absolute correspondence of our thoughts with an equally absolute reality. It must be what we *ought* to think unconditionally. The conditioned ways in which we *do* think are so much irrelevance and matter for psychology. **Down with psychology, up with logic, in all this question!**

See the exquisite contrast of the types of mind! The pragmatist clings to facts and concreteness, observes truth at its work in particular cases, and generalizes. Truth, for him, becomes a class-name for all sorts of definite working-values in experience. For the rationalist it remains a pure abstraction, to the bare name of which we must defer. When the pragmatist undertakes to show in detail just *why* we must defer, the rationalist is unable to recognize the concretes from which his own abstraction is taken. He accuses us of *denying* truth; whereas we have only sought to trace exactly why people follow it and always ought to follow it. Your typical ultra-abstractionist fairly shudders at concreteness: other things equal, he positively prefers the pale and spectral. If the two universes were offered, he would always choose the skinny outline rather than the rich thicket of reality. It is so much purer, clearer, nobler.

I hope that as these lectures go on, the concreteness and closeness to facts of the pragmatism which they advocate may be what approves itself to you as its most satisfactory peculiarity. It only follows here the example of the sister-sciences, interpreting the unobserved by the observed. It brings old and new harmoniously together. It converts the absolutely empty notion of a static relation of "correspondence" (what that may mean we must ask later) between our minds and reality, into that of a rich and active commerce (that any one may follow in detail and understand) between particular thoughts of ours, and the great universe of other experiences in which they play their parts and have their uses.

But enough of this at present? The justification of what I say must be postponed. I wish now to add a word in further explanation of the claim I made at our last meeting, that pragmatism may be a happy harmonizer of empiricist ways of thinking with the more religious demands of human beings.

Men who are strongly of the fact-loving temperament, you may remember me to have said, are liable to be kept at a distance by the small sympathy with facts which that philosophy from the present-day fashion of idealism offers them. It is far too intellectualistic. Old fashioned theism was bad enough, with its notion of God as an exalted monarch, made up of a lot of unintelligible or preposterous "attributes"; but, so long as it held strongly by the argument from design, it kept some touch with concrete realities. Since, however, darwinism has once for all displaced design from the minds of the "scientific," theism has lost that foothold; and some kind of an immanent or pantheistic deity working *in* things rather than above them is, if any, the kind recommended to our contemporary imagination. Aspirants to a philosophic religion turn, as a rule, more hopefully nowadays towards idealistic pantheism than towards the older dualistic theism, in spite of the fact that the latter still counts able defenders.

But, as I said in my first lecture, the brand of pantheism offered is hard for them to assimilate if they are lovers of facts, or empirically minded. It is the absolutistic brand, spurning the dust and reared upon pure logic. It keeps no connexion whatever with concreteness. Affirming the Absolute Mind, which is its substitute for God, to be the rational presupposition of all particulars of fact, whatever they may be, it remains supremely indifferent to what the particular facts in our world actually are. Be they what they may, the Absolute will father them. Like the sick lion in Esop's fable, all footprints lead into his den, but *nulla vestigia retrorsum.* You cannot redescend into the world of particulars by the Absolute's aid, or deduce any necessary consequences of detail important for your life from your idea of his nature. He gives you indeed the assurance that all is well with *Him,* and for his eternal way of thinking; but thereupon he leaves you to be finitely saved by your own temporal devices.

Far be it from me to deny the majesty of this conception, or its capacity to yield religious comfort to a most respectable class of minds. But from the human point of view, no one can pretend that it doesn't suffer from the faults of remoteness and abstractness. It is eminently a product of what I have ventured to call the rationalistic temper. It disdains empiricism's needs. It substitutes a pallid outline for the real world's richness. It is dapper, it is noble in the bad sense, in the sense in which to be noble is to be inapt for humble service. In this real world of sweat and dirt, it seems to me that when a view of things is "noble," that ought to count as a presumption against its truth, and as a philosophic disqualification. The prince of darkness may be a gentleman, as we are told he is, but whatever the God of earth and heaven is, he can surely be no gentleman. His menial services are needed in the dust of our human trials, even more than his dignity is needed in the empyrean.

Now pragmatism, devoted though she be to facts, has no such materialistic bias as ordinary empiricism labors under. Moreover, she has no objection whatever to the realizing of abstractions, so long as you get about among particulars with their aid and they actually carry you somewhere. Interested in no conclusions but those which our minds and our experiences work out together, she has no *a priori* prejudices against theology. *If theological ideas prove to have a value for concrete life, they will be true, for pragmatism, in the sense of being good for so much. For how much more they are true, will depend entirely on their relations to the other truths that also have to be acknowledged.*

What I said just now about the Absolute, of transcendental idealism, is a case in point. First, I called it majestic and said it yielded religious comfort to a class of minds, and then I accused it of remoteness and sterility. But so far as it affords such comfort, it surely is not sterile; it has that amount of value; it performs a concrete function. As a good pragmatist, I myself ought to call the Absolute true "in so far forth," then; and I unhesitatingly now do so.

But what does *true in so far forth* mean in this case? To answer, we need only apply the pragmatic method. What do believers in the Absolute mean by saying that their belief affords them comfort? They mean that since, in the Absolute finite evil is "overruled" already, we may, therefore, whenever we wish, treat the temporal as if it were potentially the eternal, be sure that we can trust its outcome, and, without sin, dismiss our fear and drop the worry of our finite responsibility. In short, they mean that we have a right ever and anon to take a moral holiday, to let the world wag in its own way, feeling that its issues are in better hands than ours and are none of our business.

The universe is a system of which the individual members may relax their anxieties occasionally, in which the don't-care mood is also right for men, and moral holidays in order— that, if I mistake not, is part, at least, of what the Absolute is "known-as," that is the great difference in our particular experiences which his being true makes, for us, that is his cash-value when he is pragmatically interpreted. Farther than that the ordinary lay-reader in philosophy who thinks favorably of absolute idealism does not venture to sharpen his conceptions. He can use the Absolute for so much, and so much is very precious. He is pained at hearing you speak incredulously of the Absolute, therefore, and disregards your criticisms because they deal with aspects of the conception that he fails to follow.

If the Absolute means this, and means no more than this,

who can possibly deny the truth of it? To deny it would be to insist that men should never relax, and that holidays are never in order.

I am well aware how odd it must seem to some of you to hear me say that an idea is "true" so long as to believe it is profitable to our lives. That it is *good,* for as much as it profits, you will gladly admit. If what we do by its aid is good, you will allow the idea itself to be good in so far forth, for we are the better for possessing it. But is it not a strange misuse of the word "truth," you will say, to call ideas also "true" for this reason?

To answer this difficulty fully is impossible at this stage of my account. You touch here upon the very central point of Messrs. Schiller's, Dewey's and my own doctrine of truth, which I can not discuss with detail until my sixth lecture. Let me now say only this, that truth is *one species of good,* and not, as is usually supposed, a category distinct from good, and co-ordinate with it. *The true is the name of whatever proves itself to be good in the way of belief, and good, too, for definite, assignable reasons.* Surely you must admit this, that if there were *no* good for life in true ideas, or if the knowledge of them were positively disadvantageous and false ideas the only useful ones, then the current notion that truth is divine and precious, and its pursuit a duty, could never have grown up or become a dogma. In a world like that, our duty would be to *shun* truth, rather. But in this world, just as certain foods are not only agreeable to our taste, but good for our teeth, our stomach, and our tissues; so certain ideas are not only agreeable to think about, or agreeable as supporting other ideas that we are fond of, but they are also helpful in life's practical struggles. If there be any life that it is really better we should lead, and if there be any idea which, if believed in, would help us to lead that life, then it would be really *better for us* to believe in that idea, *unless, indeed, belief in it incidentally clashed with other greater vital benefits.*

"What would be better for us to believe"! This sounds very like a definition of truth. It comes very near to saying "what we *ought* to believe": and in *that* definition none of you would find any oddity. Ought we ever not to believe what it is *better for us* to believe? And can we then keep the notion of what is better for us, and what is true for us, permanently apart?

Pragmatism says no, and I fully agree with her. Probably you also agree, so far as the abstract statement goes, but with a suspicion that if we practically did believe everything that made for good in our own personal lives, we should be found indulging all kinds of fancies about this world's affairs, and all kinds of sentimental superstitions about a world hereafter. Your suspicion here is undoubtedly well founded, and it is evident that something happens when you pass from the abstract to the concrete that complicates the situation.

I said just now that what is better for us to believe is true *unless the belief incidentally clashes with some other vital benefit*. Now in real life what vital benefits is any particular belief of ours most liable to clash with? What indeed except the vital benefits yielded by *other beliefs* when these prove incompatible with the first ones? In other words, the greatest enemy of any one of our truths may be the rest of our truths. Truths have once for all this desperate instinct of self-preservation and of desire to extinguish whatever contradicts them. My belief in the Absolute, based on the good it does me, must run the gauntlet of all my other beliefs. Grant that it may be true in giving me a moral holiday. Nevertheless, as I conceive it—and let me speak now confidentially, as it were, and merely in my own private person—it clashes with other truths of mine whose benefits I hate to give up on its account. It happens to be associated with a kind of logic of which I am the enemy, I find that it entangles me in metaphysical paradoxes that are inacceptable, etc., etc. But as I have enough trouble in life already without adding the trouble of carrying these intellectual inconsistencies, I personally just give up the Absolute. I just *take* my moral holidays; or else as a professional philosopher, I try to justify them by some other principle.

If I could restrict my notion of the Absolute to its bare holiday-giving value, it wouldn't clash with any other truths. But we can not easily thus restrict our hypotheses. They carry supernumerary features, and these it is that clash so. My disbelief in the Absolute means then disbelief in those other supernumerary features, for I fully believe in the legitimacy of taking moral holidays.

You see by this what I meant when I called pragmatism a mediator and reconciler and said, borrowing the word from Papini, that she "unstiffens" our theories. She has in fact no prejudices whatever, no obstructive dogmas, no rigid canons of what shall count as proof. She is completely genial. She will entertain any hypothesis, she will consider any evidence. It follows that in the religious field she is at a great advantage both over positivistic empiricism, with its anti-theological bias, and over religious rationalism, with its exclusive interest in the remote, the noble, the simple, and the abstract in the way of conception.

In short, she widens the field of search for God. Rationalism sticks to logic and the empyrean. Empiricism sticks to the external senses. Pragmatism is willing to take anything, to follow either logic or the senses and to count the humblest and most personal experiences. She will count mystical experiences if they have practical consequences. She will take a God who lives in the very dirt of private fact—if that should seem a likely place to find him.

Her only test of probable truth is what works best in the way of leading us, what fits every part of life best and combines with the collectivity of experience's demands, nothing being omitted. If theological ideas should do this, if the notion of God, in particular, should prove to do it, how could pragmatism possibly deny God's existence? She could see no meaning in treating as "not true" a notion that was pragmatically so successful. What other kind of truth could there be, for her, than all this agreement with concrete reality?

In my last lecture I shall return again to the relations of pragmatism with religion. But you see already how democratic she is. Her manners are as various and flexible, her resources as rich and endless, and her conclusions as friendly as those of mother nature.

Pragmatism's Conception of Truth •

When Clerk-Maxwell was a child it is written that he had a mania for having everything explained to him, and that when people put him off with vague verbal accounts of any phenomenon he would interrupt them impatiently by saying, "Yes;

• [From: William James, *Pragmatism: A New Name for Some Old Ways of Thinking*. New York: Longmans, Green and Co.; 1907. Pp. 197-236. Copyright 1934 by Henry James. Reprinted by permission of Paul R. Reynolds & Son.]

but I want you to tell me the *particular go* of it!" Had his question been about truth, only a pragmatist could have told him the particular go of it. I believe that our contemporary pragmatists, especially Messrs. Schiller and Dewey, have given the only tenable account of this subject. It is a very ticklish subject, sending subtle rootlets into all kinds of crannies, and hard to treat in the sketchy way that alone befits a public lecture. But the Schiller-Dewey view of truth has been so ferociously attacked by rationalistic philosophers, and so abominably misunderstood, that here, if anywhere, is the point where a clear and simple statement should be made.

I fully expect to see the pragmatist view of truth run through the classic stages of a theory's career. First, you know, a new theory is attacked as absurd; then it is admitted to be true, but obvious and insignificant; finally it is seen to be so important that its adversaries claim that they themselves discovered it. Our doctrine of truth is at present in the first of these three stages, with symptoms of the second stage having begun in certain quarters. I wish that this lecture might help it beyond the first stage in the eyes of many of you.

Truth, as any dictionary will tell you, is a property of certain of our ideas. It means their "agreement," as falsity means their disagreement, with "reality." Pragmatists and intellectualists both accept this definition as a matter of course. They begin to quarrel only after the question is raised as to what may precisely be meant by the term "agreement," and what by the term "reality," when reality is taken as something for our ideas to agree with.

In answering these questions the pragmatists are more analytic and painstaking, the intellectualists more offhand and irreflective. The popular notion is that a true idea must copy its reality. Like other popular views, this one follows the analogy of the most usual experience. Our true ideas of sensible things do indeed copy them. Shut your eyes and think of yonder clock on the wall, and you get just such a true picture or copy of its dial. But your idea of its "works" (unless you are a clockmaker) is much less of a copy, yet it passes muster, for it in no way clashes with the reality. Even though it should shrink to the mere word "works," that word still serves you truly; and when you speak of the "timekeeping function" of the clock, or of its spring's "elasticity," it is hard to see exactly what your ideas can copy.

You perceive that there is a problem here. Where our ideas

can not copy definitely their object, what does agreement with that object mean? Some idealists seem to say that they are true whenever they are what God means that we ought to think about that object. Others hold the copy-view all through, and speak as if our ideas possessed truth just in proportion as they approach to being copies of the Absolute's eternal way of thinking.

These views, you see, invite pragmatistic discussion. But the great assumption of the intellectualists is that truth means essentially an inert static relation. When you've got your true idea of anything, there's an end of the matter. You're in possession; you *know;* you have fulfilled your thinking destiny. You are where you ought to be mentally; you have obeyed your categorical imperative; and nothing more need follow on that climax of your rational destiny. Epistemologically you are in stable equilibrium.

Pragmatism, on the other hand, asks its usual question. "Grant an idea or belief to be true," it says, "what concrete difference will its being true make in any one's actual life? How will the truth be realized? What experiences will be different from those which would obtain if the belief were false? What, in short, is the truth's cash-value in experiential terms?"

The moment pragmatism asks this question, it sees the answer: *True ideas are those that we can assimilate, validate, corroborate and verify. False ideas are those that we can not.* That is the practical difference it makes to us to have true ideas; that, therefore, is the meaning of truth, for it is all that truth is known-as.

This thesis is what I have to defend. The truth of an idea is not a stagnant property inherent in it. Truth *happens* to an idea. It *becomes* true, is *made* true by events. Its verity *is* in fact an event, a process: the process namely of its verifying itself, its veri-*fication.* Its validity is the process of its valid-*ation.*

But what do the words verification and validation themselves pragmatically mean? They again signify certain practical consequences of the verified and validated idea. It is hard to find any one phrase that characterizes these consequences better than the ordinary agreement-formula—just such consequences being what we have in mind whenever we say that our ideas "agree" with reality. They lead us, namely, through the acts and other ideas which they instigate, into or up to, or towards, other parts of experience with which we feel all the while—such feeling being among our potentialities—that the original ideas remain in agreement. The connexions and transitions come to us from point to point as being progressive, harmonious, satisfactory. This function of agreeable leading is what we mean by an idea's verification. Such an account is vague and it sounds at first quite trivial, but it has results which it will take the rest of my hour to explain.

Let me begin by reminding you of the fact that the possession of true thoughts means everywhere the possession of invaluable instruments of action; and that our duty to gain truth, so far from being a blank command from out of the blue, or a "stunt" self-imposed by our intellect, can account for itself by excellent practical reasons.

The importance to human life of having true beliefs about matters of fact is a thing too notorious. We live in a world of realities that can be infinitely useful or infinitely harmful. Ideas that tell us which of them to expect count as the true ideas in all this primary sphere of verification, and the pursuit of such ideas is a primary human duty. The possession of truth, so far from being here an end in itself, is only a preliminary means towards other vital satisfactions. If I am lost in the woods and starved, and find what looks like a cow-path, it is of the utmost importance that I should think of a human habitation at the end of it, for if I do so and follow it, I save myself. The true thought is useful here because the house which is its object is useful. The practical value of true ideas is thus primarily derived from the practical importance of their objects to us. Their objects are, indeed, not important at all times. I may on another occasion have no use for the house; and then my idea of it, however verifiable, will be practically irrelevant, and had better remain latent. Yet since almost any object may some day become temporarily important, the advantage of having a general stock of *extra* truths, of ideas that shall be true of merely possible situations, is obvious. We store such extra truths away in our memories, and with the overflow we fill our books of reference. Whenever such an extra truth becomes practically relevant to one of our emergencies, it passes from cold-storage to do work in the world and our belief in it grows active. You can say of it then either that "it is useful because it is true" or that "it is true because it is useful." Both these phrases mean exactly the same thing, namely that here is an idea that gets fulfilled and can be verified. True is the name for whatever idea starts the verification-process, useful is the name for its completed function in experience. True ideas would never have been singled out as such, would never have acquired a class-name, least of all a name suggesting value, unless they had been useful from the outset in this way.

From this simple cue pragmatism gets her general notion of truth as something essentially bound up with the way in which one moment in our experience may lead us towards other moments which it will be worth while to have been led to. Primarily, and on the common-sense level, the truth of a state of mind means this function of *a leading that is worth while.* When a moment in our experience, of any kind whatever, inspires us with a thought that is true, that means that sooner or later we dip by that thought's guidance into the particulars of experience again and make advantageous connexion with them. This is a vague enough statement, but I beg you to retain it, for it is essential.

Our experience meanwhile is all shot through with regularities. One bit of it can warn us to get ready for another bit, can "intend" or be "significant of" that remoter object. The object's advent is the significance's verification. Truth, in these cases, meaning nothing but eventual verification, is manifestly incompatible with waywardness on our part. Woe to him whose beliefs play fast and loose with the order which realities follow in his experience; they will lead him nowhere or else make false connexions.

By "realities" or "objects" here, we mean either things of common sense, sensibly present, or else common-sense relations, such as dates, places, distances, kinds, activities. Following our mental image of a house along the cow-path, we actually come to see the house; we get the image's full verification. *Such simply and fully verified leadings are certainly the originals and prototypes of the truth-process.* Experience offers indeed other forms of truth-process, but they are all conceivable as being primary verifications arrested, multiplied or substituted one for another.

Take, for instance, yonder object on the wall. You and I consider it to be a "clock," altho no one of us has seen the hidden works that make it one. We let our notion pass for true without attempting to verify. If truths mean verification-process essentially, ought we then to call such unverified truths as this abortive? No, for they form the overwhelmingly large number of the truths we live by. Indirect as well as direct verifications pass muster. Where circumstantial evidence is sufficient, we can go without eye-witnessing. Just as we here assume Japan to exist without ever having been there, because it *works* to do so, everything we know conspiring with the belief, and nothing interfering, so we assume that thing to be a clock. We *use* it as a clock, regulating the length of our lecture by it. The verification of the assumption here means its leading to no frustration or contradiction. Verifi*ability* of wheels and weights and pendulum is as good as verification. For one truth-process completed there are a million in our lives that function in this state of nascency. They turn us *towards* direct verification; lead us into the *surroundings* of the objects they envisage; and then, if everything runs on harmoniously, we are so sure that verification is possible that we omit it, and are usually justified by all that happens.

Truth lives, in fact, for the most part on a credit system. Our thoughts and beliefs "pass," so long as nothing challenges them, just as bank-notes pass so long as nobody refuses them. But this all points to direct face-to-face verifications some-where, without which the fabric of truth collapses like a financial system with no cash-basis whatever. You accept my verification of one thing, I yours of another. We trade on each other's truth. But beliefs verified concretely by *somebody* are the posts of the whole superstructure.

Another great reason—beside economy of time—for waiving complete verification in the usual business of life is that all things exist in kinds and not singly. Our world is found once for all to have that peculiarity. So that when we have once directly verified our ideas about one specimen of a kind, we consider ourselves free to apply them to other specimens without verification. A mind that habitually discerns the kind of thing before it, and acts by the law of the kind immediately, without pausing to verify, will be a "true" mind in ninety-nine out of a hundred emergencies, proved so by its conduct fitting everything it meets, and getting no refutation.

Indirectly or only potentially verifying processes may thus be true as well as full verification-processes. They work as true processes would work, give us the same advantages, and claim our recognition for the same reasons. All this on the common-sense level of matters of fact, which we are alone considering.

But matters of fact are not our only stock in trade. *Relations among purely mental ideas* form another sphere where true and false beliefs obtain, and here the beliefs are absolute, or unconditional. When they are true they bear the name either of definitions or of principles. It is either a principle or a definition that 1 and 1 make 2, that 2 and 1 make 3, and so on; that white differs less from gray than it does from black; that when the cause begins to act the effect also commences. Such propositions hold of all possible "ones," of all conceivable "whites" and "grays" and "causes." The objects here are mental objects. Their relations are perceptually obvious at a glance, and no sense-verification is necessary. Moreover, once true, always true, of those same mental objects. Truth here has an "eternal" character. If you can find a concrete thing anywhere that is "one" or "white" or "gray" or an "effect," then your principles will everlastingly apply to it. It is but a case of ascertaining the kind, and then applying the law of its kind to the particular object. You are sure to get truth if you can but name the kind rightly, for your mental relations hold good of everything of that kind without exception. If you then, nevertheless, failed to get truth concretely, you would say that you had classed your real objects wrongly.

In this realm of mental relations, truth again is an affair of leading. We relate one abstract idea with another, framing in the end great systems of logical and mathematical truth, under the respective terms of which the sensible facts of experience eventually arrange themselves, so that our eternal truths hold good of realities also. This marriage of fact and theory is endlessly fertile. What we say is here already true in advance of special verification, *if we have subsumed our objects rightly.* Our ready-made ideal framework for all sorts of possible objects follows from the very structure of our thinking. We can no more play fast and loose with these abstract relations than we can do so with our sense-experiences. They coerce us; we must treat them consistently, whether or not we like the results. The rules of addition apply to our debts as rigorously as to our assets. The hundredth decimal of π, the ratio of the circumference to its diameter, is predetermined ideally now, tho no one may have computed it. If we should ever need the figure in our dealings with an actual circle we should need to have it given rightly, calculated by the usual rules; for it is the same kind of truth that those rules elsewhere calculate.

Between the coercions of the sensible order and those of the ideal order, our mind is thus wedged tightly. Our ideas must agree with realities, be such realities concrete or abstract, be they facts or be they principles, under penalty of endless inconsistency and frustration.

So far, intellectualists can raise no protest. They can only say that we have barely touched the skin of the matter.

Realities mean, then, either concrete facts, or abstract kinds of thing and relations perceived intuitively between them. They furthermore and thirdly mean, as things that new ideas of ours must no less take account of, the whole body of other truths already in our possession. But what now does "agreement" with such threefold realities mean?—to use again the definition that is current.

Here it is that pragmatism and intellectualism begin to part company. Primarily, no doubt, to agree means to copy, but we saw that the mere word "clock" would do instead of a mental picture of its works, and that of many realities our ideas can only be symbols and not copies. "Past time," "power," "spontaneity"—how can our mind copy such realities?

To "agree" in the widest sense with a reality *can only mean to be guided either straight up to it or into its surroundings, or to be put into such working touch with it as to handle either it or something connected with it better than if we disagreed.* Better either intellectually or practically! And often agreement will only mean the negative fact that nothing contradictory from the quarter of that reality comes to interfere with the way in which our ideas guide us elsewhere. To copy a reality is, indeed, one very important way of agreeing with it, but it is far from being essential. The essential thing is the process of being guided. Any idea that helps us to *deal*, whether practically or intellectually, with either the reality or its belongings, that doesn't entangle our progress in frustrations, that *fits*, in fact, and adapts our life to the reality's whole setting, will agree sufficiently to meet the requirement. It will hold true of that reality.

Thus, *names* are just as "true" or "false" as definite mental pictures are. They set up similar verification-processes, and lead to fully equivalent practical results.

All human thinking gets discursified; we exchange ideas; we lend and borrow verifications, get them from one another by means of social intercourse. All truth thus gets verbally built out, stored up, and made available for every one. Hence, we must *talk* consistently just as we must *think* consistently: for both in talk and thought we deal with kinds. Names are arbitrary, but once understood they must be kept to. We mustn't now call Abel "Cain" or Cain "Abel." If we do, we ungear ourselves from the whole book of Genesis, and from all its connexions with the universe of speech and fact down to the present time. We throw ourselves out of whatever truth that entire system of speech and fact may embody.

The overwhelming majority of our true ideas admit of no direct or face-to-face verification—those of past history, for example, as of Cain and Abel. The stream of time can be remounted only verbally, or verified indirectly by the present prolongations or effects of what the past harbored. Yet if they agree with these verbalities and effects, we can know that our ideas of the past are true. *As true as past time itself was,* so true was Julius Caesar, so true were antediluvian monsters, all in their proper dates and settings. That past time itself was, is guaranteed by its coherence with everything that's present. True as the present *is,* the past *was* also.

Agreement thus turns out to be essentially an affair of leading—leading that is useful because it is into quarters that contain objects that are important. True ideas lead us into useful verbal and conceptual quarters as well as directly up to useful sensible termini. They lead to consistency, stability and flowing human intercourse. They lead away from eccentricity and isolation, from foiled and barren thinking. The untrammelled flowing of the leading-process, its general freedom from clash and contradiction, passes for its indirect verification; but all roads lead to Rome, and in the end and eventually, all true processes must lead to the face of directly verifying sensible experiences *somewhere,* which somebody's ideas have copied.

Such is the large loose way in which the pragmatist interprets the word agreement. He treats it altogether practically. He lets it cover any process of conduction from a present idea to a future terminus, provided only it run prosperously. It is only thus that "scientific" ideas, flying as they do beyond common sense, can be said to agree with their realities. It is, as I have already said, *as if* reality were made of ether, atoms or electrons, but we mustn't think so literally. The term "energy" doesn't even pretend to stand for anything "objective." It is only a way of measuring the surface of phenomena so as to string their changes on a simple formula.

Yet in the choice of these man-made formulas we can not be capricious with impunity any more than we can be capricious on the common-sense practical level. We must find a theory that will *work;* and that means something extremely difficult; for our theory must mediate between all previous truths and certain new experiences. It must derange common sense and previous belief as little as possible, and it must lead to some sensible terminus or other that can be verified exactly. To "work" means both these things; and the squeeze is so tight that there is little loose play for any hypothesis. Our theories are wedged and controlled as nothing else is. Yet sometimes alternative theoretic formulas are equally compatible with all the truths we know, and then we choose between them for subjective reasons. We choose the kind of theory to which we are already partial; we follow "elegance" or "economy." Clerk-Maxwell somewhere says it would be "poor scientific taste" to choose the more complicated of two equally well-evidenced conceptions; and you will all agree with him. Truth in science is what gives us the maximum possible sum of satisfactions, taste included; but consistency both with previous truth and with novel fact is always the most imperious claimant.

I have led you through a very sandy desert. But now, if I may be allowed so vulgar an expression, we begin to taste the milk in the cocoanut. Our rationalist critics here discharge their batteries upon us, and to reply to them will take us out from all this dryness into full sight of a momentous philosophical alternative.

Our account of truth is an account of truths in the plural, of processes of leading, realized *in rebus,* and having only this quality in common, that they *pay.* They pay by guiding us into or towards some part of a system that dips at numerous points into sense-percepts, which we may copy mentally or not, but with which at any rate we are now in the kind of commerce vaguely designated as verification. Truth for us is simply a collective name for verification-processes, just as health, wealth, strength, etc., are names for other processes connected with life, and also pursued because it pays to pursue them. Truth is *made,* just as health, wealth and strength are made, in the course of experience.

Here rationalism is instantaneously up in arms against us. I can imagine a rationalist to talk as follows:

"Truth is not made," he will say; "it absolutely obtains, being a unique relation that does not wait upon any process, but shoots straight over the head of experience, and hits its reality every time. Our belief that yon thing on the wall is a clock is true already, altho no one in the whole history of the world should verify it. The bare quality of standing in that transcendent relation is what makes any thought true that possesses it, whether or not there be verification. You pragmatists put the cart before the horse in making truth's being reside in verification-processes. These are merely signs of its being, merely our lame ways of ascertaining after the fact, which of our ideas already has possessed the wondrous quality. The quality itself is timeless, like all essences and natures. Thoughts partake of it directly, as they partake of falsity or of irrelevancy. It can't be analyzed away into pragmatic consequences."

The whole plausibility of this rationalist tirade is due to the fact to which we have already paid so much attention. In our world, namely, abounding as it does in things of similar kinds and similarly associated, one verification serves for others of its kind, and one great use of knowing things is to be led not so much to them as to their associates, especially to human talk about them. The quality of truth, obtaining *ante rem*, pragmatically means, then, the fact that in such a world innumerable ideas work better by their indirect or possible than by their direct and actual verification. Truth *ante rem* means only verifiability, then; or else it is a case of the stock rationalist trick of treating the *name* of a concrete phenomenal reality as an independent prior entity, and placing it behind the reality as its explanation. Professor Mach quotes somewhere an epigram of Lessing's:

> Sagt Hänschen Schlau zu Vetter Fritz,
> "Wie kommt es, Vetter Fritzen,
> Dass grad' die Reichsten in der Welt,
> Das meiste Geld besitzen?"

Hänschen Schlau here treats the principle "wealth" as something distinct from the facts denoted by the man's being rich. It antedates them; the facts become only a sort of secondary coincidence with the rich man's essential nature.

In the case of "wealth" we all see the fallacy. We know

that wealth is but a name for concrete processes that certain men's lives play a part in, and not a natural excellence found in Messrs. Rockefeller and Carnegie, but not in the rest of us.

Like wealth, health also lives *in rebus*. It is a name for processes, as digestion, circulation, sleep, etc., that go on happily, tho in this instance we are more inclined to think of it as a principle and to say the man digests and sleeps so well *because* he is so healthy.

With "strength" we are, I think, more rationalistic still, and decidedly inclined to treat it as an excellence pre-existing in the man and explanatory of the herculean performances of his muscles.

With "truth" most people go over the border entirely, and treat the rationalistic account as self-evident. But really all these words in *th* are exactly similar. Truth exists *ante rem* just as much and as little as the other things do.

The scholastics, following Aristotle, made much of the distinction between habit and act. Health *in actu* means, among other things, good sleeping and digesting. But a healthy man need not always be sleeping, or always digesting, any more than a wealthy man need be always handling money, or a strong man always lifting weights. All such qualities sink to the status of "habits" between their times of exercise; and similarly truth becomes a habit of certain of our ideas and beliefs in their intervals of rest from their verifying activities. But those activities are the root of the whole matter, and the condition of there being any habit to exist in the intervals.

"The true," to put it very briefly, is only the expedient in the way of our thinking, just as "the right" is only the expedient in the way of our behaving. Expedient in almost any fashion; and expedient in the long run and on the whole of course; for what meets expediently all the experience in sight won't necessarily meet all farther experiences equally satisfactorily. Experience, as we know, has ways of *boiling over,* and making us correct our present formulas.

The "absolutely" true, meaning what no farther experience will ever alter, is that ideal vanishing-point towards which we imagine that all our temporary truths will some day converge. It runs on all fours with the perfectly wise man, and with the absolutely complete experience; and, if these ideals are ever realized, they will all be realized together. Meanwhile we have to live to-day by what truth we can get to-day, and be ready to-morrow to call it falsehood. Ptolemaic astronomy, euclidean space, aristotelian logic, scholastic metaphysics, were expedient for centuries, but human experience has boiled over those limits, and we now call these things only relatively true, or true within those borders of experience. "Absolutely" they are false; for we know that those limits were casual, and might have been transcended by past theorists just as they are by present thinkers.

When new experiences lead to retrospective judgments, using the past tense, what these judgments utter *was* true, even tho no past thinker had been led there. We live forwards, a Danish thinker has said, but we understand backwards. The present sheds a backward light on the world's previous processes. They may have been truth-processes for the actors in them. They are not so for one who knows the later revelations of the story.

This regulative notion of a potential better truth to be established later, possibly to be established some day absolutely, and having powers of retroactive legislation, turns its face, like all pragmatist notions, towards concreteness of fact, and towards the future. Like the half-truths, the absolute truth will have to be *made,* made as a relation incidental to the growth of a mass of verification-experience, to which the half-true ideas are all along contributing their quota.

I have already insisted on the fact that truth is made largely out of previous truths. Men's beliefs at any time are so much experience *funded.* But the beliefs are themselves parts of the sum total of the world's experience, and become matter, therefore, for the next day's funding operations. So far as reality means experienceable reality, both it and the truths men gain about it are everlastingly in process of mutation—mutation towards a definite goal, it may be—but still mutation.

Mathematicians can solve problems with two variables. On the Newtonian theory, for instance, acceleration varies with distance, but distance also varies with acceleration. In the realm of truth-processes facts come independently and determine our beliefs provisionally. But these beliefs make us act, and as fast as they do so, they bring into sight or into existence new facts which re-determine the beliefs accordingly. So the whole coil and ball of truth, as it rolls up, is the product of a double influence. Truths emerge from facts; but they dip forward into facts again and add to them; which facts again create or reveal new truth (the word is indifferent) and so on indefinitely. The "facts" themselves meanwhile are not *true.*

They simply *are*. Truth is the function of the beliefs that start and terminate among them.

The case is like a snowball's growth, due as it is to the distribution of the snow on the one hand, and to the successive pushes of the boys on the other, with these factors co-determining each other incessantly.

The most fateful point of difference between being a rationalist and being a pragmatist is now fully in sight. Experience is in mutation, and our psychological ascertainments of truth are in mutation—so much rationalism will allow; but never that either reality itself or truth itself is mutable. Reality stands complete and ready-made from all eternity, rationalism insists, and the agreement of our ideas with it is that unique unanalyzable virtue in them of which she has already told us. As that intrinsic excellence, their truth has nothing to do with our experiences. It adds nothing to the content of experience. It makes no difference to reality itself; it is supervenient, inert, static, a reflexion merely. It doesn't *exist*, it *holds* or *obtains*, it belongs to another dimension from that of either facts or fact-relations, belongs, in short, to the epistemological dimension—and with that big word rationalism closes the discussion.

Thus, just as pragmatism faces forward to the future, so does rationalism here again face backward to a past eternity. True to her inveterate habit, rationalism reverts to "principles," and thinks that when an abstraction once is named, we own an oracular solution.

The tremendous pregnancy in the way of consequences for life of this radical difference of outlook will only become apparent in my later lectures. I wish meanwhile to close this lecture by showing that rationalism's sublimity does not save it from inanity.

When, namely, you ask rationalists, instead of accusing pragmatism of desecrating the notion of truth, to define it themselves by saying exactly what *they* understand by it, the only positive attempts I can think of are these two:

1. "Truth is the system of propositions which have an unconditional claim to be recognized as valid."

2. Truth is a name for all those judgments which we find ourselves under obligation to make by a kind of imperative duty.

The first thing that strikes one in such definitions is their unutterable triviality. They are absolutely true, of course, but absolutely insignificant until you handle them pragmatically. What do you mean by "claim" here, and what do you mean by "duty"? As summary names for the concrete reasons why thinking in true ways is overwhelmingly expedient and good for mortal men, it is all right to talk of claims on reality's part to be agreed with, and of obligations on our part to agree. We feel both the claims and the obligations, and we feel them for just those reasons.

But the rationalists who talk of claim and obligation *expressly say that they have nothing to do with our practical interests or personal reasons*. Our reasons for agreeing are psychological facts, they say, relative to each thinker, and to the accidents of his life. They are his evidence merely, they are no part of the life of truth itself. That life transacts itself in a purely logical or epistemological, as distinguished from a psychological, dimension, and its claims antedate and exceed all personal motivations whatsoever. Tho neither man nor God should ever ascertain truth, the word would still have to be defined as that which *ought* to be ascertained and recognized.

There never was a more exquisite example of an idea abstracted from the concretes of experience and then used to oppose and negate what it was abstracted from.

Philosophy and common life abound in similar instances. The "sentimentalist fallacy" is to shed tears over abstract justice and generosity, beauty, etc., and never to know these qualities when you meet them in the street, because the circumstances make them vulgar. Thus I read in the privately printed biography of an eminently rationalistic mind: "It was strange that with such admiration for beauty in the abstract, my brother had no enthusiasm for fine architecture, for beautiful painting, or for flowers." And in almost the last philosophic work I have read, I find such passages as the following: "Justice is ideal, solely ideal. Reason conceives that it ought to exist, but experience shows that it can not. . . . Truth, which ought to be, can not be. . . . Reason is deformed by experience. As soon as reason enters experience it becomes contrary to reason."

The rationalist's fallacy here is exactly like the sentimentalist's. Both extract a quality from the muddy particulars of experience, and find it so pure when extracted that they con-

trast it with each and all its muddy instances as an opposite
and higher nature. All the while it is *their* nature. It is the
nature of truths to be validated, verified. It pays for our ideas
to be validated. Our obligation to seek truth is part of our
general obligation to do what pays. The payments true ideas
bring are the sole why of our duty to follow them. Identical
whys exist in the case of wealth and health.

Truth makes no other kind of claim and imposes no other
kind of ought than health and wealth do. All these claims are
conditional; the concrete benefits we gain are what we mean
by calling the pursuit a duty. In the case of truth, untrue
beliefs work as perniciously in the long run as true beliefs
work beneficially. Talking abstractly, the quality "true" may
thus be said to grow absolutely precious and the quality "untrue" absolutely damnable: the one may be called good, the
other bad, unconditionally. We ought to think the true, we
ought to shun the false, imperatively.

But if we treat all this abstraction literally and oppose it to
its mother soil in experience, see what a preposterous position
we work ourselves into.

We can not then take a step forward in our actual thinking.
When shall I acknowledge this truth and when that? Shall the
acknowledgment be loud?—or silent? If sometimes loud, sometimes silent, which *now?* When may a truth go into cold-
storage in the encyclopedia? and when shall it come out for
battle? Must I constantly be repeating the truth "twice two
are four" because of its eternal claim on recognition? or is it
sometimes irrelevant? Must my thoughts dwell night and day
on my personal sins and blemishes, because I truly have
them?—or may I sink and ignore them in order to be a decent
social unit, and not a mass of morbid melancholy and apology?

It is quite evident that our obligation to acknowledge truth,
so far from being unconditional, is tremendously conditioned.
Truth with a big T, and in the singular, claims abstractly to
be recognized, of course; but concrete truths in the plural
need be recognized only when their recognition is expedient.
A truth must always be preferred to a falsehood when both
relate to the situation; but when neither does, truth is as little
of a duty as falsehood. If you ask me what o'clock it is and I
tell you that I live at 95 Irving Street, my answer may indeed
be true, but you don't see why it is my duty to give it. A false
address would be as much to the purpose.

With this admission that there are conditions that limit the application of the abstract imperative, *the pragmatistic treatment of truth sweeps back upon us in its fulness.* Our duty to agree with reality is seen to be grounded in a perfect jungle of concrete expediencies.

When Berkeley had explained what people meant by matter, people thought that he denied matter's existence. When Messrs. Schiller and Dewey now explain what people mean by truth, they are accused of denying *its* existence. These pragmatists destroy all objective standards, critics say, and put foolishness and wisdom on one level. A favorite formula for describing Mr. Schiller's doctrines and mine is that we are persons who think that by saying whatever you find it pleasant to say and calling it truth you fulfil every pragmatistic requirement.

I leave it to you to judge whether this be not an impudent slander. Pent in, as the pragmatist more than any one else sees himself to be, between the whole body of funded truths squeezed from the past and the coercions of the world of sense about him, who so well as he feels the immense pressure of objective control under which our minds perform their operations? If any one imagines that this law is lax, let him keep its commandment one day, says Emerson. We have heard much of late of the uses of the imagination in science. It is high time to urge the use of a little imagination in philosophy. The unwillingness of some of our critics to read any but the silliest of possible meanings into our statements is as discreditable to their imaginations as anything I know in recent philosophic history. Schiller says the true is that which "works." Thereupon he is treated as one who limits verification to the lowest material utilities. Dewey says truth is what gives "satisfaction." He is treated as one who believes in calling everything true which, if it were true, would be pleasant.

Our critics certainly need more imagination of realities. I have honestly tried to stretch my own imagination and to read the best possible meaning into the rationalist conception, but I have to confess that it still completely baffles me. The notion of a reality calling on us to "agree" with it, and that for no reasons, but simply because its claim is "unconditional" or "transcendent," is one that I can make neither head nor tail of. I try to imagine myself as the sole reality in the world, and then to imagine what more I would "claim" if I were allowed to. If you suggest the possibility of my claiming that a mind should come into being from out of the void inane and stand and *copy* me, I can indeed imagine what the copying might mean, but I can conjure up no motive. What good it would do me to be copied, or what good it would do that mind to copy me, if further consequences are expressly and in principle ruled out as motives for the claim (as they are by our rationalist authorities) I can not fathom. When the Irishman's admirers ran him along to the place of banquet in a sedan chair with no bottom, he said, "Faith, if it wasn't for the honor of the thing, I might as well have come on foot." So here: but for the honor of the thing, I might as well have remained uncopied. Copying is one genuine mode of knowing (which for some strange reason our contemporary transcendentalists seem to be tumbling over each other to repudiate); but when we get beyond copying, and fall back on unnamed forms of agreeing that are expressly denied to be either copyings or leadings or fittings, or any other processes pragmatically definable, the *what* of the "agreement" claimed becomes as unintelligible as the why of it. Neither content nor motive can be imagined for it. It is an absolutely meaningless abstraction.

Surely in this field of truth it is the pragmatists and not the rationalists who are the more genuine defenders of the universe's rationality.

The Pragmatist Account of Truth and Its Misunderstanders *

The account of truth given in my volume entitled *Pragmatism*, continues to meet with such persistent misunderstanding that I am tempted to make a final brief reply. My ideas may well deserve refutation, but they can get none till they are conceived of in their proper shape. The fantastic character of the current misconceptions shows how unfamiliar is the concrete point of view which pragmatism assumes. Persons who are familiar with a conception move about so easily in it that

* [From: William James, *The Meaning of Truth: A Sequel to "Pragmatism."* New York: Longmans, Green and Co.; 1909. Pp. 180-216. Copyright 1936 by Henry James. Reprinted by permission of Paul R. Reynolds & Son.]

they understand each other at a hint, and can converse without anxiously attending to their P's and Q's. I have to admit, in view of the results, that we have assumed too ready an intelligence, and consequently in many places used a language too slipshod. We should never have spoken elliptically. The critics have boggled at every word they could boggle at, and refused to take the spirit rather than the letter of our discourse. This seems to show a genuine unfamiliarity in the whole point of view. It also shows, I think, that the second stage of opposition, which has already begun to express itself in the stock phrase that "what is new is not true, and what is true not new," in pragmatism, is insincere. If we said nothing in any degree new, why was our meaning so desperately hard to catch? The blame cannot be laid wholly upon our obscurity of speech, for in other subjects we have attained to making ourselves understood. But recriminations are tasteless; and, as far as I personally am concerned, I am sure that some of the misconception I complain of is due to my doctrine of truth being surrounded in that volume of popular lectures by a lot of other opinions not necessarily implicated with it, so that a reader may very naturally have grown confused. For this I am to blame—likewise for omitting certain explicit cautions, which the pages that follow will now in part supply.

FIRST MISUNDERSTANDING: PRAGMATISM IS ONLY
A RE-EDITING OF POSITIVISM.

This seems the commonest mistake. Scepticism, positivism, and agnosticism agree with ordinary dogmatic rationalism in presupposing that everybody knows what the word "truth" means, without further explanation. But the former doctrines then either suggest or declare that real truth, absolute truth, is inaccessible to us, and that we must fain put up with relative or phenomenal truth as its next best substitute. By scepticism this is treated as an unsatisfactory state of affairs, while positivism and agnosticism are cheerful about it, call real truth sour grapes, and consider phenomenal truth quite sufficient for all our "practical" purposes.

   In point of fact, nothing could be farther from all this than what pragmatism has to say of truth. Its thesis is an altogether previous one. It leaves off where these other theories begin, having contented itself with the word truth's *definition*. "No matter whether any mind extant in the universe possess truth or not," it asks, "what does the notion of truth signify ideally?" "What kind of things would true judgments be *in case* they existed?" The answer which pragmatism offers is intended to cover the most complete truth that can be conceived of, "absolute" truth if you like, as well as truth of the most relative and imperfect description. This question of what truth would be like if it did exist, belongs obviously to a purely speculative field of inquiry. It is not a theory about any sort of reality, or about what kind of knowledge is actually possible; it abstracts from particular terms altogether, and defines the nature of a possible relation between two of them.

As Kant's question about synthetic judgments had escaped previous philosophers, so the pragmatist question is not only so subtle as to have escaped attention hitherto, but even so subtle, it would seem, that when openly broached now, dogmatists and sceptics alike fail to apprehend it, and deem the pragmatist to be treating of something wholly different. He insists, they say (I quote an actual critic), "that the greater problems are insoluble by human intelligence, that our need of knowing truly is artificial and illusory, and that our reason, incapable of reaching the foundations of reality, must turn itself exclusively towards *action*." There could not be a worse misapprehension.

SECOND MISUNDERSTANDING: PRAGMATISM IS PRIMARILY AN APPEAL TO ACTION.

The name "pragmatism," with its suggestions of action, has been an unfortunate choice, I have to admit, and has played into the hands of this mistake. But no word could protect the doctrine from critics so blind to the nature of the inquiry that, when Dr. Schiller speaks of ideas "working" well, the only thing they think of is their immediate workings in the physical environment, their enabling us to make money, or gain some similar "practical" advantage. Ideas do work thus, of course, immediately or remotely; but they work indefinitely inside of the mental world also. Not crediting us with this rudimentary insight, our critics treat our view as offering itself exclusively to engineers, doctors, financiers, and men of action generally, who need some sort of a rough and ready *weltanschauung*, but have no time or wit to study genuine philosophy. It is usually described as a characteristically American movement, a sort of bobtailed scheme of thought, excellently fitted for the man on the street, who naturally hates theory and wants cash returns immediately.

It is quite true that, when the refined theoretic question that pragmatism begins with is once answered, secondary corollaries of a practical sort follow. Investigation shows that, in the function called truth, previous realities are not the only independent variables. To a certain extent our ideas, being realities, are also independent variables, and, just as they follow other reality and fit it, so, in a measure, does other reality follow and fit them. When they add themselves to being, they partly redetermine the existent, so that reality as a whole appears incompletely definable unless ideas also are kept account of. This pragmatist doctrine, exhibiting our ideas as complemental factors of reality, throws open (since our ideas are instigators of our action) a wide window upon human action, as well as a wide license to originality in thought. But few things could be sillier than to ignore the prior epistemological edifice in which the window is built, or to talk as if pragmatism began and ended at the window. This, nevertheless, is what our critics do almost without exception. They ignore our primary step and its motive, and make the relation to action, which is our secondary achievement, primary.

THIRD MISUNDERSTANDING: PRAGMATISTS CUT THEMSELVES OFF FROM THE RIGHT TO BELIEVE IN EJECTIVE REALITIES.

They do so, according to the critics, by making the truth of our beliefs consist in their verifiability, and their verifiability in the way in which they do work for us. Professor Stout, in his otherwise admirable and hopeful review of Schiller in *Mind* for October, 1897, considers that this ought to lead Schiller (could he sincerely realize the effects of his own doctrine) to the absurd consequence of being unable to believe genuinely in another man's headache, even were the headache there. He can only "postulate" it for the sake of the working value of the postulate to himself. The postulate guides certain of his acts and leads to advantageous consequences; but the moment he understands fully that the postulate is true *only* (!) in this sense, it ceases (or should cease) to be true for him that the other man really *has* a headache. All that makes the postulate most precious then evaporates: his interest in his fellow-man "becomes a veiled form of self-interest, and his world grows cold, dull, and heartless."

Such an objection makes a curious muddle of the pragmatist's universe of discourse. Within that universe the pragmatist finds some one with a headache or other feeling, and some one else who postulates that feeling. Asking on what condition the postulate is "true," the pragmatist replies that, for the postulator at any rate, it is true just in proportion as to believe in it works in him the fuller sum of satisfactions. What is it that is satisfactory here? Surely to *believe* in the postulated object, namely, in the really existing feeling of the other man. But how (especially if the postulator were himself a thoroughgoing pragmatist) could it ever be satisfactory to him *not* to believe in that feeling, so long as, in Professor Stout's words, disbelief "made the world seem to him cold, dull, and heartless"? Disbelief would seem, on pragmatist principles, quite out of the question under such conditions, unless the heartlessness of the world were made probable already on other grounds. And since the belief in the headache, true for the subject assumed in the pragmatist's universe of discourse, is also true for the pragmatist who for his epistemologizing purposes has assumed that entire universe, why is it not true in that universe absolutely? The headache believed in is a reality there, and no extant mind disbelieves it, neither the critic's mind nor his subject's! Have our opponents any better brand of truth in this real universe of ours that they can show us? •

• I see here a chance to forestall a criticism which some one may make on Lecture III of my *Pragmatism,* where . . . I said that "God" and "Matter" might be regarded as synonymous terms, so long as no differing future consequences were deducible from the two conceptions. The passage was transcribed from my address at the California Philosophical Union, reprinted in the *Journal of Philosophy,* vol. i, p. 673. I had no sooner given the address than I perceived a flaw in that part of it; but I have left the passage unaltered ever since, because the flaw did not spoil its illustrative value. The flaw was evident when, as a case analogous to that of a godless universe, I thought of what I called an "automatic sweetheart," meaning a soulless body which should be absolutely indistinguishable from a spiritually animated maiden, laughing, talking, blushing, nursing us, and performing all feminine offices as tactfully and sweetly as if a soul were in her. Would any one regard her as a full equivalent? Certainly not, and why? Because, framed as we are, our egoism craves above all things inward sympathy and recognition, love and admiration. The outward treatment is valued mainly as an expression, as a manifestation of the accompanying consciousness believed in. Pragmatically, then, belief in the automatic sweetheart would not *work,* and in point of fact no one treats it as a serious hypothesis. The godless universe would be exactly similar. Even if matter could do every outward thing that God does, the idea of it would not work as satisfactorily, because the chief call for a God on modern men's part is for a being who will inwardly recognize them and judge them sympathetically. Matter disappoints this craving of our ego, so God remains for most men the truer hypothesis, and indeed remains so for definite pragmatic reasons.

So much for the third misunderstanding, which is but one specification of the following still wider one.

FOURTH MISUNDERSTANDING: NO PRAGMATIST CAN BE A REALIST IN HIS EPISTEMOLOGY.

This is supposed to follow from his statement that the truth of our beliefs consists in general in their giving satisfaction. Of course satisfaction *per se* is a subjective condition; so the conclusion is drawn that truth falls wholly inside of the subject, who then may manufacture it at his pleasure. True beliefs become thus wayward affections, severed from all responsibility to other parts of experience.

It is difficult to excuse such a parody of the pragmatist's opinion, ignoring as it does every element but one of his universe of discourse. The terms of which that universe consists positively forbid any non-realistic interpretation of the function of knowledge defined there. The pragmatizing epistemologist posits there a reality and a mind with ideas. What, now, he asks, can make those ideas true of that reality? Ordinary epistemology contents itself with the vague statement that the ideas must "correspond" or "agree"; the pragmatist insists on being more concrete, and asks what such "agreement" may mean in detail. He finds first that the ideas must point to or lead towards *that* reality and no other, and then that the pointings and leadings must yield satisfaction as their result. So far the pragmatist is hardly less abstract than the ordinary slouchy epistemologist; but as he defines himself farther, he grows more concrete. The entire quarrel of the intellectualist with him is over his concreteness, intellectualism contending that the vaguer and more abstract account is here the more profound. The concrete pointing and leading are conceived by the pragmatist to be the work of other portions of the same universe to which the reality and the mind belong, intermediary verifying bits of experience with which the mind at one end, and the reality at the other, are joined. The "satisfaction," in turn, is no abstract satisfaction *uberhaupt,* felt by an unspecified being, but is assumed to consist of such satisfactions (in the plural) as concretely existing men actually do find in their beliefs. As we humans are constituted in point of fact, we find that to believe in other men's minds, in independent physical realities, in past events, in eternal logical relations, is satisfactory. We find hope satisfactory. We often find it satisfactory to cease to doubt. Above all we find *consistency* satisfactory, consistency between the present idea and the entire rest of our mental equipment, including the whole order of our sensations, and that of our intuitions of likeness and difference, and our whole stock of previously acquired truths.

The pragmatist, being himself a man, and imagining in general no contrary lines of truer belief than ours about the "reality" which he has laid at the base of his epistemological discussion, is willing to treat our satisfactions as possibly really true guides to it, not as guides true solely for *us*. It would seem here to be the duty of his critics to show with some explicitness why, being our subjective feelings, these satisfactions can *not* yield "objective" truth. The beliefs which they accompany "posit" the assumed reality, "correspond" and "agree" with it, and "fit" it in perfectly definite and assignable ways, through the sequent trains of thought and action which form their verification, so merely to insist on using these words abstractly instead of concretely is no way of driving the pragmatist from the field—his more concrete account virtually includes his critic's. If our critics have any definite idea of a truth more objectively grounded than the kind we propose, why do they not show it more articulately? As they stand, they remind one of Hegel's man who wanted "fruit," but rejected cherries, pears, and grapes, because they were not fruit in the abstract. We offer them the full quart-pot, and they cry for the empty quart-capacity.

But here I think I hear some critic retort as follows: "If satisfactions are all that is needed to make truth, how about the notorious fact that errors are so often satisfactory? And how about the equally notorious fact that certain true beliefs may cause the bitterest dissatisfaction? Isn't it clear that not the satisfaction which it gives, but the relation of the belief *to the reality* is all that makes it true? Suppose there were no such reality, and that the satisfactions yet remained: would they not then effectively work falsehood? Can they consequently be treated distinctively as the truth-builders? It is the *inherent relation to reality* of a belief that gives us that specific *truth*-satisfaction, compared with which all other satisfactions are the hollowest humbug. The satisfaction of *knowing truly* is thus the only one which the pragmatist ought to have considered. As a *psychological sentiment*, the anti-pragmatist gladly concedes it to him, but then only as a concomitant of truth, not as a constituent. What *constitutes* truth is not the sentiment, but the purely logical or objective function of rightly cognizing the reality, and the pragmatist's failure to reduce this function to lower values is patent."

Such anti-pragmatism as this seems to me a tissue of confusion. To begin with, when the pragmatist says "indispensable," it confounds this with "sufficient." The pragmatist calls satisfactions indispensable for truth-building, but I have everywhere called them insufficient unless reality be also incidentally led to. If the reality assumed were cancelled from the pragmatist's universe of discourse, he would straight-way give the name of falsehoods to the beliefs remaining, in spite of all their satisfactoriness. For him, as for his critic, there can be no truth if there is nothing to be true about. Ideas are so much flat psychological surface unless some mirrored matter gives them cognitive lustre. This is why as a pragmatist I have so carefully posited "reality" *ab initio,* and why, throughout my whole discussion, I remain an epistemological realist.●

The anti-pragmatist is guilty of the further confusion of imagining that, in undertaking to give him an account of what truth formally means, we are assuming at the same time to provide a warrant for it, trying to define the occasions when he can be sure of materially possessing it. Our making it hinge on a reality so "independent" that when it comes, truth comes, and when it goes, truth goes with it, disappoints this *naïve* expectation, so he deems our description unsatisfactory. I suspect that under this confusion lies the still deeper one of not discriminating sufficiently between the two notions, truth and reality. Realities are not *true,* they *are;* and beliefs are true *of* them. But I suspect that in the anti-pragmatist mind the two notions sometimes swap their attributes. The reality itself, I fear, is treated as if "true," and conversely. Whoso tells us of the one, it is then supposed, must also be telling us of the other; and a true idea must in a manner *be,* or at least *yield* without extraneous aid, the reality it cognitively is possessed of.

To this absolute-idealistic demand pragmatism simply opposes its *non possumus.* If there is to be truth, it says, both realities and beliefs about them must conspire to make it; but whether there ever is such a thing, or how anyone can be

● I need hardly remind the reader that both sense-percepts and percepts of ideal relation (comparisons, etc.) should be classed among the realities. The bulk of our mental "stock" consists of truths concerning these terms.

sure that his own beliefs possess it, it never pretends to determine. That truth-satisfaction *par excellence* which may tinge a belief unsatisfactory in other ways, it easily explains as the feeling of consistency with the stock of previous truths, or supposed truths, of which one's whole past experience may have left one in possession.

But are not all pragmatists sure that their own belief is right? their enemies will ask at this point; and this leads me to the

FIFTH MISUNDERSTANDING: WHAT PRAGMATISTS SAY
IS INCONSISTENT WITH THEIR SAYING SO.

A correspondent puts this objection as follows: "When you say to your audience, 'pragmatism is the truth concerning truth,' the first truth is different from the second. About the first you and they are not to be at odds; you are not giving them liberty to take or leave it according as it works satisfactorily or not for their private uses. Yet the second truth, which ought to describe and include the first, affirms this liberty. Thus the *intent* of your utterance seems to contradict the *content* of it."

General scepticism has always received this same classic refutation. "You have to dogmatize," the rationalists say to the sceptics, "whenever you express the sceptical position; so your lives keep contradicting your thesis." One would suppose that the impotence of so hoary an argument to abate in the slightest degree the amount of general scepticism in the world might have led some rationalists themselves to doubt whether these instantaneous logical refutations are such fatal ways, after all, of killing off live mental attitudes. General scepticism is the live mental attitude of refusing to conclude. It is a permanent torpor of the will, renewing itself in detail towards each successive thesis that offers, and you can no more kill it off by logic than you can kill off obstinacy or practical joking. This is why it is so irritating. Your consistent sceptic never puts his scepticism into a formal proposition—he simply chooses it as a habit. He provokingly hangs back when he might so easily join us in saying yes, but he is not illogical or stupid— on the contrary, he often impresses us by his intellectual superiority. This is the *real* scepticism that rationalists have to meet, and their logic does not even touch it.

No more can logic kill the pragmatist's behavior: his act of utterance, so far from contradicting, accurately exemplifies the matter which he utters. What is the matter which he utters? In part, it is this, that truth, concretely considered, is an attribute of our beliefs, and that these are attitudes that follow satisfactions. The ideas around which the satisfactions cluster are primarily only hypotheses that challenge or summon a belief to come and take its stand upon them. The pragmatist's idea of truth is just such a challenge. He finds it ultra-satisfactory to₋ accept it, and takes his own stand accordingly. But, being gregarious as they are, men seek to spread their beliefs, to awaken imitation, to infect others. Why should not *you* also find the same belief satisfactory? thinks the pragmatist, and forthwith endeavors to convert you. You and he will then believe similarly; you will hold up your subject-end of a truth, which will be a truth objective and irreversible if the reality holds up the object-end by being itself present simultaneously. What there is of self-contradiction in all this I confess I cannot discover. The pragmatist's conduct in his own case seems to me on the contrary admirably to illustrate his universal formula; and of all epistemologists, he is perhaps the only one who is irreproachably self-consistent.

SIXTH MISUNDERSTANDING: PRAGMATISM EXPLAINS NOT WHAT TRUTH IS, BUT ONLY HOW IT IS ARRIVED AT.

In point of fact it tells us both, tells us what it is incidentally to telling us how it is arrived at—for what *is* arrived at except just what the truth is? If I tell you how to get to the railroad station, don't I implicitly introduce you to the *what,* to the being and nature of that edifice? It is quite true that the abstract *word* "how" hasn't the same meaning as the abstract *word* "what," but in this universe of concrete facts you cannot keep hows and whats asunder. The reasons why I find it satisfactory to believe that any idea is true, the *how* of my arriving at that belief, may be among the very reasons why the idea *is* true in reality. If not, I summon the anti-pragmatist to explain the impossibility articulately.

His trouble seems to me mainly to arise from his fixed inability to understand how a concrete statement can possibly mean as much, or be as valuable, as an abstract one. I said above that the main quarrel between us and our critics was that of concreteness *versus* abstractness. This is the place to develop that point farther.

In the present question, the links of experience sequent upon an idea, which mediate between it and a reality, form and for the pragmatist indeed *are,* the *concrete* relation of truth that may obtain between the idea and that reality. They, he says, are all that we mean when we speak of the idea "pointing" to the reality, "fitting" it, "corresponding" with it, or "agreeing" with it—they or other similar mediating trains of verification. Such mediating events *make* the idea "true." The idea itself, if it exists at all, is also a concrete event: so pragmatism insists that truth in the singular is only a collective name for truths in the plural, these consisting always of series of definite events; and that what intellectualism calls *the* truth, the *inherent* truth, of any one such series is only the abstract name for its truthfulness in act, for the fact that the ideas there do lead to the supposed reality in a way that we consider satisfactory.

The pragmatist himself has no objection to abstractions. Elliptically, and "for short," he relies on them as much as any one, finding upon innumerable occasions that their comparative emptiness makes of them useful substitutes for the overfulness of the facts he meets with. But he never ascribes to them a higher grade of reality. The full reality of a truth for him is always some process of verification, in which the abstract property of connecting ideas with objects truly is workingly embodied. Meanwhile it is endlessly serviceable to be able to talk of properties abstractly and apart from their working, to find them the same in innumerable cases, to take them "out of time," and to treat of their relations to other similar abstractions. We thus form whole universes of platonic ideas *ante rem,* universes *in posse,* tho none of them exists effectively except *in rebus.* Countless relations obtain there which nobody experiences as obtaining—as, in the external universe of musical relations, for example, the notes of Aennchen von Tharau were a lovely melody long ere mortal ears ever heard them. Even so the music of the future sleeps now, to be awakened hereafter. Or, if we take the world of geometrical relations, the thousandth decimal of π sleeps there, tho no one may ever try to compute it. Or, if we take the universe of "fitting," countless coats "fit" backs, and countless boots "fit" feet, on which they are not practically *fitted;* countless stones "fit" gaps in walls into which no one seeks to fit them actually. In the same way countless opinions "fit" realities, and countless truths are valid, tho no thinker ever thinks them.

For the anti-pragmatist these prior timeless relations are the presupposition of the concrete ones, and possess the profounder dignity and value. The actual workings of our ideas in verification-processes are as naught in comparison with the "obtainings" of this discarnate truth within them.

For the pragmatist, on the contrary, all discarnate truth is static, impotent, and relatively spectral, full truth being the truth that energizes and does battle. Can any one suppose that the sleeping quality of truth would ever have been abstracted or have received a name, if truths had remained forever in that storage-vault of essential timeless "agreements" and had never been embodied in any panting struggle of men's live ideas for verification? Surely no more than the abstract property of "fitting" would have received a name, if in our world there had been no backs or feet or gaps in walls to be actually fitted. Existential truth is incidental to the actual competition of opinions. *Essential* truth, the truth of the intellectualists, the truth with no one thinking it, is like the coat that fits tho no one has ever tried it on, like the music that no ear has listened to. It is less real, not more real, than the verified article; and to attribute a superior degree of glory to it seems little more than a piece of perverse abstraction-worship. As well might a pencil insist that the outline is the essential thing in all pictorial representation, and chide the paint-brush and the camera for omitting it, forgetting that *their* pictures not only contain the whole outline, but a hundred other things in addition. Pragmatist truth contains the whole of intellectualist truth and a hundred other things in addition. Intellectualist truth is then only pragmatist truth *in posse*. That on innumerable occasions men do substitute truth *in posse* or verifiability, for verification or truth in act, is a fact to which no one attributes more importance than the pragmatist: he emphasizes the practical utility of such a habit. But he does not on that account consider truth *in posse*—truth not alive enough ever to have been asserted or questioned or contradicted—to be the metaphysically prior thing, to which truths in act are tributary and subsidiary. When intellectualists do this, pragmatism charges them with inverting the real relation. Truth in posse *means* only truths in act; and he insists that these latter take precedence in the order of logic as well as in that of being.

SEVENTH MISUNDERSTANDING: PRAGMATISM IGNORES
THE THEORETIC INTEREST.

This would seem to be an absolutely wanton slander, were not a certain excuse to be found in the linguistic affinities of the word "pragmatism," and in certain offhand habits of speech of ours which assumed too great a generosity on our reader's part. When we spoke of the meaning of ideas consisting in their "practical" consequences, or of the "practical" differences which our beliefs make to us; when we said that the truth of a belief consists in its "working" value, etc.; our language evidently was too careless, for by "practical" we were almost unanimously held to mean *opposed* to theoretical or genuinely cognitive, and the consequence was punctually drawn that a truth in our eyes could have no relation to any independent reality, or to any other truth, or to anything whatever but the acts which we might ground on it or the satisfactions they might bring. The mere existence of the idea, all by itself, if only its results were satisfactory, would give full truth to it, it was charged, in our absurd pragmatist epistemology. The solemn attribution of this rubbish to us was also encouraged by two other circumstances. First, ideas *are* practically useful in the narrow sense, false ideas sometimes, but most often ideas which we can verify by the sum total of all their leadings, and the reality of whose objects may thus be considered established beyond doubt. That these ideas should be true in advance of and apart from their utility, that, in other words, their objects should be really there, is the very condition of their having that kind of utility—the objects they connect us with are so important that the ideas which serve as the objects' substitutes grow important also. This manner of their practical working was the first thing that made truths good in the eyes of primitive men; and buried among all the other good workings by which true beliefs are characterized, this kind of subsequential utility remains.

The second misleading circumstance was the emphasis laid by Schiller and Dewey on the fact that, unless a truth be relevant to the mind's momentary predicament, unless it be germane to the "practical" situation—meaning by this the quite particular perplexity—it is no good to urge it. It doesn't meet our interests any better than a falsehood would under the same circumstances. But why our predicaments and perplexities might not be theoretical here as well as narrowly practical, I wish that our critics would explain. They simply assume that no pragmatist *can* admit a genuinely theoretic interest. Having used the phrase "cash-value" of an idea, I am implored by one correspondent to alter it, "for every one thinks you mean only pecuniary profit and loss." Having said that the true is "the expedient in our thinking," I am rebuked in this wise by another learned correspondent: "The word expedient has no other meaning than that of self-interest. The pursuit of this has ended by landing a number of officers of national banks in penitentiaries. A philosophy that leads to such results must be unsound."

But the word "practical" is so habitually loosely used that more indulgence might have been expected. When one says that a sick man has now practically recovered, or that an enterprise has practically failed, one usually means just the opposite of practically in the literal sense. One means that, altho untrue in strict practice, what one says is true in theory, true virtually, *certain to be* true. Again, by the practical one often means the distinctively concrete, the individual, particular, and effective, as opposed to the abstract, general, and inert. To speak for myself, whenever I have emphasized the practical nature of truth, this is mainly what has been in my mind. "Pragmata" are things in their plurality; and in that early California address, when I described pragmatism as holding that "the meaning of any proposition can always be brought down to some particular consequence in our future practical experience, whether passive or active," I expressly added these qualifying words: "the point lying rather in the fact that the experience must be particular than in the fact that it must be active"—by "active" meaning here "practical" in the narrow literal sense.• But particular consequences can perfectly well be of a theoretic nature. Every remote fact which we infer from an idea is a particular theoretic consequence which our mind practically works towards. The loss of every old opinion of ours which we see that we shall have to give up if a new opinion be true, is a particular theoretic as well as a particular practical consequence. After man's in-

---

• The ambiguity of the word "practical" comes out well in these words of a recent would-be reporter of our views: "Pragmatism is an Anglo-Saxon reaction against the intellectualism and rationalism of the Latin mind. . . . Man, each individual man is the measure of things. He is able to conceive none but relative truths, that is to say, illusions. What these illusions are worth is revealed to him, not by general theory, but by individual practice. Pragmatism, which consists in experiencing these illusions of the mind and obeying them by acting them out, is a *philosophy without words,* a philosophy of *gestures and of acts,* which abandons what is general and holds only to what is particular." (Bourdeau, in *Journal des Debats,* October 29, 1907.)

terest in breathing freely, the greatest of all his interests (because it never fluctuates or remits, as most of his physical interests do), is his interest in *consistency*, in feeling that what he now thinks goes with what he thinks on other occasions. We tirelessly compare truth with truth for this sole purpose. Is the present candidate for belief perhaps contradicted by principle number one? Is it compatible with fact number two? and so forth. The particular operations here are the purely logical ones of analysis, deduction, comparison, etc.; and altho general terms may be used *ad libitum,* the satisfactory *practical working* of the candidate-idea consists in the consciousness yielded by each successive theoretic consequence in particular. It is therefore simply idiotic to repeat that pragmatism takes no account of purely theoretic interests. All it insists on is that verity in act means *verifications,* and that these are always particulars. Even in exclusively theoretic matters, it insists that vagueness and generality serve to verify nothing.

EIGHTH MISUNDERSTANDING: PRAGMATISM
IS SHUT UP TO SOLIPSISM.

I have already said something about this misconception under the third and fourth heads, above, but a little more may be helpful. The objection is apt to clothe itself in words like these: "You make truth to consist in every value except the cognitive value proper; you always leave your knower at many removes (or, at the uttermost, at one remove) from his real object; the best you do is to let his ideas carry him towards it; it remains forever outside of him," etc.

I think that the leaven working here is the rooted intellectualist persuasion that, to know a reality, an idea must in some inscrutable fashion possess or be it.● For pragmatism this kind of coalescence is inessential. As a rule our cognitions are only processes of mind off their balance and in motion towards real termini; and the reality of the termini, believed in by the states of mind in question, can be *guaranteed* only by some

● Sensations may, indeed, possess their objects or coalesce with them, as common sense supposes that they do; and intuited differences between concepts may coalesce with the "eternal" objective differences; but to simplify our discussion here we can afford to abstract from these very special cases of knowing.

wider knower.● But if there is no reason extant in the universe why they should be doubted, the beliefs are true in the only sense in which anything can be true anyhow: they are practically and concretely true, namely. True in the mystical mongrel sense of an *Identitätsphilosophie* they need not be; nor is there any intelligible reason why they ever need be true otherwise than verifiably and practically. It is reality's part to possess its own existence; it is thought's part to get into "touch" with it by innumerable paths of verification.

I fear that the "humanistic" developments of pragmatism may cause a certain difficulty here. We get at one truth only through the rest of truth; and the reality, everlastingly postulated as that which all our truth must keep in touch with, may never be given to us save in the form of truth other than that which we are now testing. But since Dr. Schiller has shown that all our truths, even the most elemental, are affected by race-inheritance with a human coefficient, reality *per se* thus may appear only as a sort of limit; it may be held to shrivel to the mere *place* for an object, and what is known may be held to be only matter of our psyche that we fill the place with.

It must be confessed that pragmatism, worked in this humanistic way, is *compatible* with solipsism. It joins friendly hands with the agnostic part of kantism, with contemporary agnosticism, and with idealism generally. But worked thus, it is a metaphysical theory about the matter of reality, and flies far beyond pragmatism's own modest analysis of the nature of the knowing function, which analysis may just as harmoniously be combined with less humanistic accounts of reality.

● The transcendental idealist thinks that, in some inexplicable way, the finite states of mind are identical with the transfinite all-knower which he finds himself obliged to postulate in order to supply a *fundamentum* for the relation of knowing, as he apprehends it. Pragmatists can leave the question of identity open; but they cannot do without the wider knower any more than they can do without the reality, if they want to *prove* a case of knowing. They themselves play the part of the absolute knower for the universe of discourse which serves them as material for epistemologizing. They warrant the reality there, and the subject's true knowledge, there, of it. But whether what they themselves say about that whole universe is objectively true, i.e., whether the pragmatic theory of truth is true *really,* they cannot warrant—they can only believe it. To their hearers they can only *propose* it, as I propose it to my readers, as something to be verified *ambulando,* or by the way in which its consequences may confirm it.

One of pragmatism's merits is that it is so purely epistemological. It must assume realities; but it prejudges nothing as to their constitution, and the most diverse metaphysics can use it as their foundation. It certainly has no special affinity with solipsism.

As I look back over what I have written, much of it gives me a queer impression, as if the obvious were set forth so condescendingly that readers might well laugh at my pomposity. It may be, however, that concreteness as radical as ours is not so obvious. The whole originality of pragmatism, the whole point in it, is its use of the concrete way of seeing. It begins with concreteness, and returns and ends with it. Dr. Schiller, with his two "practical" aspects of truth, (1) relevancy to situation, and (2) subsequential utility, is only filling the cup of concreteness to the brim for us. Once seize that cup, and you cannot misunderstand pragmatism. It seems as if the power of imagining the world concretely *might* have been common enough to let our readers apprehend us better, as if they might have read between our lines, and, in spite of all our infelicities of expression, guessed a little more correctly what our thought was. But alas! this was not on fate's programme, so we can only think, with the German ditty:

> Es wär' zu schön gewesen,
> Es hat nicht sollen sein.

Charles S. Peirce

1839-1914

*Charles Sanders Peirce was the son of Benjamin Peirce, a dis-
tinguished mathematician, the professor of that subject at
Harvard College. A precocious youth, he began the study of
philosophy under his father's guidance while still in his teens.
Works of the German idealists were the first philosophical
books he read. It was his father's practice, he tells us, to rip
up the arguments of the philosophers, showing how slipshod
they really were by comparison with those of the mathematicians and physical scientists. Peirce emerged from this rigorous training with the conviction that "you may search the
whole library of modern physics from Descartes to the most
accurate metaphysical reasoners of today and hardly find a
vital argument of an elaborate and apodictic kind that does not
leave room to drive a coach and four through it."*

*There was, Peirce came to believe, a reason for this lack of
cogency. The scientist's training imbues him with "the laboratory habit of mind," but most of the philosophers are bred in
the "seminary." They seek to justify antecedently held beliefs. Having no need to discover through inquiry what may
be true, they are easily contented with specious reasons for
what they profess to know.*

Thus Peirce's thinking was given an orientation that persisted throughout his life. In his maturity, looking backward, he observed: "I was brought up in an atmosphere of scientific enquiry and all my life lived chiefly among scientific men. For the past thirty years the study which has constantly been before my mind has been upon the nature, strength and history of scientific thought." And his philosophy, he said, "may be described as the attempt of a physicist to make such conjecture as to the constitution of the universe as the methods of science may permit, with the aid of all that has been done by previous philosophers."

Yet there was in Peirce an inner instability that continually frustrated his efforts to carry out this vast enterprise. His neurotic traits prevented him from following an academic career. Aside from one period of five years at Johns Hopkins University, he was forced during most of his life to earn his living as a research scientist, chiefly by working for the U.S. Coast Survey. In 1890, having received a small legacy, he retired to a farm in Milford, Pennsylvania. Here he lived in impoverished solitude, a mere eccentric to his rural neighbors, neglected and ignored—save by a few appreciative and devoted friends like James and Royce—striving vainly to bring order out of the chaos of the manuscripts he had accumulated during his lifetime and to compose the MAGNUM OPUS *which would present to the world his finished system. This aim was never realized. All that he left was a mass of fragmentary sketches. Peirce justly characterized these writings when he said, ruefully, that he was a "mere table of contents, so abstract, a very snarl of twine." Yet, even in their unfinished form, the most essential of Peirce's writings show a remarkable consistency. And today, Peirce is recognized for what he is, a seminal mind who enunciated many of the ideas that serve as "guiding principles" for a large and increasing number of philosophers.*

The Rules of Philosophy •

Descartes is the father of modern philosophy, and the spirit of Cartesianism—that which principally distinguishes it from the scholasticism which it displaced—may be compendiously stated as follows:

1. It teaches that philosophy must begin with universal doubt; whereas scholasticism had never questioned fundamentals.

2. It teaches that the ultimate test of certainty is to be found in the individual consciousness; whereas scholasticism had rested on the testimony of sages and of the Catholic Church.

3. The multiform argumentation of the Middle Ages is replaced by a single thread of inference depending often upon inconspicuous premises.

4. Scholasticism had its mysteries of faith, but undertook to explain all created things. But there are many facts which Cartesianism not only does not explain but renders absolutely inexplicable, unless to say that "God makes them so" is to be regarded as an explanation.

In some, or all of these respects, most modern philosophers have been, in effect, Cartesians. Now without wishing to return to scholasticism, it seems to me that modern science and modern logic require us to stand upon a very different platform from this.

1. We cannot begin with complete doubt. We must begin with all the prejudices which we actually have when we enter upon the study of philosophy. These prejudices are not to be dispelled by a maxim, for they are things which it does not occur to us *can* be questioned. Hence this initial skepticism will be a mere self-deception, and not real doubt; and no one who follows the Cartesian method will ever be satisfied until

• [From: *Collected Papers of Charles Sanders Peirce,* ed. Charles Hartshorne and Paul Weiss. Cambridge, Mass.: The Belknap Press of Harvard University Press; 1934. Vol. V, pp. 156-8. Copyright 1934 by the President and Fellows of Harvard College. Reprinted by permission of the publishers. Originally published in 1868.]

he has formally recovered all those beliefs which in form he has given up. It is, therefore, as useless a preliminary as going to the North Pole would be in order to get to Constantinople by coming down regularly upon a meridian. A person may, it is true, in the course of his studies, find reason to doubt what he began by believing; but in that case he doubts because he has a positive reason for it, and not on account of the Cartesian maxim. Let us not pretend to doubt in philosophy what we do not doubt in our hearts.

2. The same formalism appears in the Cartesian criterion, which amounts to this: "Whatever I am clearly convinced of, is true." If I were really convinced, I should have done with reasoning and should require no test of certainty. But thus to make single individuals absolute judges of truth is most pernicious. The result is that metaphysicians will all agree that metaphysics has reached a pitch of certainty far beyond that of the physical sciences—only they can agree upon nothing else. In sciences in which men come to agreement, when a theory has been broached it is considered to be on probation until this agreement is reached. After it is reached, the question of certainty becomes an idle one, because there is no one left who doubts it. We individually cannot reasonably hope to attain the ultimate philosophy which we pursue; we can only seek it, therefore, for the *community* of philosophers. Hence, if disciplined and candid minds carefully examine a theory and refuse to accept it, this ought to create doubts in the mind of the author of the theory himself.

3. Philosophy ought to imitate the successful sciences in its methods, so far as to proceed only from tangible premises which can be subjected to careful scrutiny, and to trust rather to the multitude and variety of its arguments than to the conclusiveness of any one. Its reasoning should not form a chain which is no stronger than its weakest link, but a cable whose fibers may be ever so slender, provided they are sufficiently numerous and intimately connected.

4. Every unidealistic philosophy supposes some absolutely inexplicable, unanalyzable ultimate; in short, something resulting from mediation itself not susceptible of mediation. Now that anything *is* thus inexplicable can only be known by reasoning from signs. But the only justification of an inference from signs is that the conclusion explains the fact. To suppose the fact absolutely inexplicable is not to explain it, and hence this supposition is never allowable.

The Fixation
of Belief *

I

Few persons care to study logic, because everybody conceives himself to be proficient enough in the art of reasoning already. But I observe that this satisfaction is limited to one's own ratiocination, and does not extend to that of other men.

We come to the full possession of our power of drawing inferences the last of all our faculties, for it is not so much a natural gift as a long and difficult art. The history of its practice would make a grand subject for a book. The mediæval schoolman, following the Romans, made logic the earliest of a boy's studies after grammar, as being very easy. So it was as they understood it. Its fundamental principle, according to them, was that all knowledge rests on either authority or reason; but that whatever is deduced by reason depends ultimately on a premise derived from authority. Accordingly, as soon as a boy was perfect in the syllogistic procedure, his intellectual kit of tools was held to be complete.

To Roger Bacon, that remarkable mind who in the middle of the thirteenth century was almost a scientific man, the schoolmen's conception of reasoning appeared only an obstacle to truth. He saw that experience alone teaches anything —a proposition which to us seems easy to understand, because a distinct conception of experience has been handed down to us from former generations; which to him also seemed perfectly clear, because its difficulties had not yet unfolded themselves. Of all kinds of experience, the best, he thought, was interior illumination, which teaches many things about nature which the external senses could never discover, such as the transubstantiation of bread.

* [From: *Collected Papers of Charles Sanders Peirce,* ed. Charles Hartshorne and Paul Weiss. Cambridge, Mass.: The Belknap Press of Harvard University Press; 1934. Vol. V, pp. 223-47. Copyright 1934 by the President and Fellows of Harvard College. Reprinted by permission of the publishers. Originally published in 1877.]

Four centuries later, the more celebrated Bacon, in the first book of his *Novum Organum,* gave his clear account of experience as something which must be opened to verification and re-examination. But, superior as Lord Bacon's conception is to earlier notions, a modern reader who is not in awe of his grandiloquence is chiefly struck by the inadequacy of his view of scientific procedure. That we have only to make some crude experiments, to draw up briefs of the results in certain blank forms, to go through these by rule, checking off everything disproved and setting down the alternatives, and that thus in a few years physical science would be finished up— what an idea! "He wrote on science like a Lord Chancellor," • indeed, as Harvey, a genuine man of science, said.

The early scientists, Copernicus, Tycho Brahe, Kepler, Galileo, Harvey, and Gilbert, had methods more like those of their modern brethren. Kepler undertook to draw a curve through the places of Mars; •• and his greatest service to science was in impressing on men's minds that this was the thing to be done if they wished to improve astronomy; that they were not to content themselves with inquiring whether one system of epicycles was better than another but that they were to sit down by the figures and find out what the curve, in truth, was. He accomplished this by his incomparable energy and courage, blundering along in the most inconceivable way (to us), from one irrational hypothesis to another, until, after trying twenty-two of these, he fell, by the mere exhaustion of his invention, upon the orbit which a mind well furnished with the weapons of modern logic would have tried almost at the outset.

In the same way, every work of science great enough to be remembered for a few generations affords some exemplification of the defective state of the art of reasoning of the time when it was written; and each chief step in science has been a lesson in logic. It was so when Lavoisier and his contemporaries took up the study of Chemistry. The old chemist's maxim had been *Lege, lege, lege, labora, ora, et relege.* Lavoisier's method was not to read and pray, not to dream that some long and complicated chemical process would have a certain effect, to put it into practice with dull patience, after its inevitable failure to dream that with some modification it would have another result, and to end by publishing the last

• Cf. J. Aubrey's *Brief Lives.* Oxford, 1898. Vol. I, p. 299.
•• Not quite so, but as nearly as can be told in a few words.

dream as a fact: his way was to carry his mind into his laboratory, and to make of his alembics and cucurbits instruments of thought, giving a new conception of reasoning as something which was to be done with one's eyes open, by manipulating real things instead of words and fancies.

The Darwinian controversy is, in large part, a question of logic. Mr. Darwin proposed to apply the statistical method to biology.• The same thing has been done in a widely different branch of science, the theory of gases. Though unable to say what the movement of any particular molecule of gas would be on a certain hypothesis regarding the constitution of this class of bodies, Clausius and Maxwell were yet able, by the application of the doctrine of probabilities, to predict that in the long run such and such a proportion of the molecules would, under given circumstances, acquire such and such velocities; that there would take place, every second, such and such a number of collisions, etc.; and from these propositions they were able to deduce certain properties of gases, especially in regard to their heat-relations. In like manner, Darwin, while unable to say what the operation of variation and natural selection in every individual case will be, demonstrates that in the long run they will adapt animals to their circumstances. Whether or not existing animal forms are due to such action, or what position the theory ought to take, forms the subject of a discussion in which questions of fact and questions of logic are curiously interlaced.

II

The object of reasoning is to find out, from the consideration of what we already know, something else which we do not know. Consequently, reasoning is good if it be such•• as to give a true conclusion from true premises, and not otherwise. Thus, the question of validity is purely one of fact and not of thinking. A being the premises and B being the conclusion, the question is, whether these facts are really so related that if A is, B is. If so, the inference is valid; if not, not. It is not in the least the question whether, when the premises are accepted by the mind, we feel an impulse to accept the con-

• We now know what was authoritatively denied when I first suggested it, that he took a hint from Malthus' book on population. [Note added in 1903.]
•• I.e., be denominated by such a habit as generally to give. [1903.]

clusion also. It is true that we do generally reason correctly by nature. But that is an accident; the true conclusion would remain true if we had no impulse to accept it; and the false one would remain false, though we could not resist the tendency to believe in it.

We are, doubtless, in the main logical animals, but we are not perfectly so. Most of us, for example, are naturally more sanguine and hopeful than logic would justify. We seem to be so constituted that in the absence of any facts to go upon we are happy and self-satisfied; so that the effect of experience is continually to counteract our hopes and aspirations. Yet a lifetime of the application of this corrective does not usually eradicate our sanguine disposition. Where hope is unchecked by any experience, it is likely that our optimism is extravagant. Logicality in regard to practical matters is the most useful quality an animal can possess, and might, therefore, result from the action of natural selection; but outside of these it is probably of more advantage to the animal to have his mind filled with pleasing and encouraging visions, independently of their truth; and thus, upon unpractical subjects, natural selection might occasion a fallacious tendency of thought.•

That which determines us, from given premises, to draw one inference rather than another is some habit of mind, whether it be constitutional or acquired. The habit is good or otherwise, according as it produces true conclusions from true premises or not; and an inference is regarded as valid or not, without reference to the truth or falsity of its conclusion specially, but according as the habit which determines it is such as to produce true conclusions in general or not. The particular habit of mind which governs this or that inference may be formulated in a proposition whose truth depends on the validity of the inferences which the habit determines; and such a formula is called a *guiding principle* of inference. Suppose, for example, that we observe that a rotating disk of copper quickly comes to rest when placed between the poles of a magnet, and we infer that this will happen with every disk of copper. The guiding principle is that what is true of one piece of copper is true of another. Such a guiding principle with regard to copper would be much safer than with regard to many other substances—brass, for example.

A book might be written to signalize all the most important

• Let us not, however, be cocksure that natural selection is the only factor of evolution. [1903.]

of these guiding principles of reasoning. It would probably be, we must confess, of no service to a person whose thought is directed wholly to practical subjects, and whose activity moves along thoroughly beaten paths. The problems which present themselves to such a mind are matters of routine which he has learned once for all to handle in learning his business. But let a man venture into an unfamiliar field, or where his results are not continually checked by experience, and all history shows that the most masculine intellect will ofttimes lose his orientation and waste his efforts in directions which bring him no nearer to his goal, or even carry him entirely astray. He is like a ship on the open sea, with no one on board who understands the rules of navigation. And in such a case some general study of the guiding principles of reasoning would be sure to be found useful.

The subject could hardly be treated, however, without being first limited; since almost any fact may serve as a guiding principle. But it so happens that there exists a division among facts, such that in one class are all those which are absolutely essential as guiding principles, while in the other are all those which have any other interest as objects of research. This division is between those which are necessarily taken for granted in asking whether a certain conclusion follows from certain premises, and those which are not implied in that question. A moment's thought will show that a variety of facts are already assumed when the logical question is first asked. It is implied, for instance, that there are such states of mind as doubt and belief—that a passage from one to the other is possible, the object of thought remaining the same, and that this transition is subject to some rules which all minds are alike bound by. As these are facts which we must already know before we can have any clear conception of reasoning at all, it cannot be supposed to be any longer of much interest to inquire into their truth or falsity. On the other hand, it is easy to believe that those rules of reasoning which are deduced from the very idea of the process are the ones which are the most essential; and, indeed, that so long as it conforms to these it will, at least, not lead to false conclusions from true premises. In point of fact, the importance of what may be deduced from the assumptions involved in the logical question turns out to be greater than might be supposed, and this for reasons which it is difficult to exhibit at the outset. The only one which I shall here mention is that conceptions which are really products of logical reflections, without being readily seen to be so, mingle with our ordinary thoughts, and are frequently the causes of great confusion. This is the case, for example, with the conception of quality. A quality as such is never an object of observation. We can see that a thing is blue or green, but the quality of being blue and the quality of being green are not things which we see; they are products of logical reflections. The truth is that common sense, or thought as it first emerges above the level of the narrowly practical, is deeply inbued with that bad logical quality to which the epithet *metaphysical* is commonly applied; and nothing can clear it up but a severe course of logic.

III

We generally know when we wish to ask a question and when we wish to pronounce a judgment, for there is a dissimilarity between the sensation of doubting and that of believing.

But this is not all which distinguishes doubt from belief. There is a practical difference. Our beliefs guide our desires and shape our actions. The Assassins, or followers of the Old Man of the Mountain, used to rush into death at his least command, because they believed that obedience to him would insure everlasting felicity. Had they doubted this, they would not have acted as they did. So it is with every belief, according to its degree. The feeling of believing is a more or less sure indication of there being established in our nature some habit which will determine our actions. Doubt never has such an effect.

Nor must we overlook a third point of difference. Doubt is an uneasy and dissatisfied state from which we struggle to free ourselves and pass into the state of belief;● while the latter is a calm and satisfactory state which we do not wish to avoid, or to change to a belief in anything else.●● On the contrary, we cling tenaciously, not merely to believing, but to believing just what we do believe.

● In this, it is like any other stimulus. It is true that just as men may, for the sake of the pleasures of the table, like to be hungry and take means to make themselves so, although hunger always involves a desire to fill the stomach, so for the sake of the pleasures of inquiry, men may like to seek out doubts. Yet for all that, doubt essentially involves a struggle to escape it. [1903.]

●● I am not speaking of secondary effects occasionally produced by the interference of other impulses.

Thus, both doubt and belief have positive effects upon us, though very different ones. Belief does not make us act at once, but puts us into such a condition that we shall behave in a certain way, when the occasion arises. Doubt has not the least effect of this sort, but stimulates us to action until it is destroyed. This reminds us of the irritation of a nerve and the reflex action produced thereby; while for the analogue of belief, in the nervous system, we must look to what are called nervous associations—for example, to that habit of the nerves in consequence of which the smell of a peach will make the mouth water.

IV

The irritation of doubt causes a struggle to attain a state of belief.• I shall term this struggle *inquiry*, though it must be admitted that this is sometimes not a very apt designation.

The irritation of doubt is the only immediate motive for the struggle to attain belief. It is certainly best for us that our beliefs should be such as may truly guide our actions so as to satisfy our desires; and this reflection will make us reject any belief which does not seem to have been so formed as to insure this result. But it will only do so by creating a doubt in the place of that belief. With the doubt, therefore, the struggle begins, and with the cessation of doubt it ends. Hence, the sole object of inquiry is the settlement of opinion. We may fancy that this is not enough for us, and that we seek not merely an opinion, but a true opinion. But put this fancy to the test, and it proves groundless; for as soon as a firm belief is reached we are entirely satisfied, whether the belief be false or true. And it is clear that nothing out of the sphere of our knowledge can be our object, for nothing which does not affect the mind can be a motive for a mental effort. The most that can be maintained is that we seek for a belief that we

• Doubt, however, is not usually hesitancy about what is to be done then and there. It is anticipated hesitancy about what I shall do hereafter, or a feigned hesitancy about a fictitious state of things. It is the power of making believe we hesitate, together with the pregnant fact that the decision upon the make-believe dilemma goes toward forming a bona fide habit that will be operative in a real emergency. It is these two things in conjunction that constitute us intellectual beings. [Added in 1893.]

shall *think* to be true. But we think each one of our beliefs to be true, and, indeed, it is mere tautology to say so.●

That the settlement of opinion is the sole end of inquiry is a very important proposition. It sweeps away, at once, various vague and erroneous conceptions of proof. A few of these may be noticed here.

1. Some philosophers have imagined that to start an inquiry it was only necessary to utter or question or set it down on paper, and have even recommended us to begin our studies with questioning everything! But the mere putting of a proposition into the interrogative form does not stimulate the mind to any struggle after belief. There must be a real and living doubt, and without all this, discussion is idle.

2. It is a very common idea that a demonstration must rest on some ultimate and absolutely indubitable propositions. These, according to one school, are first principles of a general nature; according to another, are first sensations. But, in point of fact, an inquiry, to have that completely satisfactory result called demonstration, has only to start with propositions perfectly free from all actual doubt. If the premises are not in fact doubted at all, they cannot be more satisfactory than they are.●●

3. Some people seem to love to argue a point after all the world is fully convinced of it. But no further advance can be made. When doubt ceases, mental action on the subject comes to an end; and, if it did go on, it would be without a purpose, except that of self-criticism.

V

If the settlement of opinion is the sole object of inquiry, and if belief is of the nature of a habit, why should we not attain the desired end, by taking any answer to a question, which we may fancy, and constantly reiterating it to ourselves, dwelling on all which may conduce to that belief, and learning to turn with contempt and hatred from anything which might disturb

---

● For truth is neither more nor less than that character of a proposition which consists in this, that belief in the proposition would, with sufficient experience and reflection, lead us to such conduct as would tend to satisfy the desires we should then have. To say that truth means more than this is to say that it has no meaning at all. [1903.]

●● Doubts about them may spring up later; but we can find no propositions which are not subject to this contingency. [1903.]

it? This simple and direct method is really pursued by many men. I remember once being entreated not to read a certain newspaper lest it might change my opinion upon free-trade. "Lest I might be entrapped by its fallacies and misstatements" was the form of expression. "You are not," my friend said, "a special student of political economy. You might, therefore, easily be deceived by fallacious arguments upon the subject. You might, then, if you read this paper, be led to believe in protection. But you admit that free-trade is the true doctrine; and you do not wish to believe what is not true." I have often known this system to be deliberately adopted. Still oftener, the instinctive dislike of an undecided state of mind, exaggerated into a vague dread of doubt, makes men cling spasmodically to the views they already take. The man feels that if he only holds to his belief without wavering, it will be entirely satisfactory. Nor can it be denied that a steady and immovable faith yields great peace of mind. It may, indeed, give rise to inconveniences, as if a man should resolutely continue to believe that fire would not burn him, or that he would be eternally damned if he received his *ingesta* otherwise than through a stomach-pump. But then the man who adopts this method will not allow that its inconveniences are greater than its advantages. He will say, "I hold steadfastly to the truth and the truth is always wholesome." And in many cases it may very well be that the pleasure he derives from his calm faith overbalances any inconveniences resulting from its deceptive character. Thus, if it be true that death is annihilation, then the man who believes that he will certainly go straight to heaven when he dies, provided he have fulfilled certain simple observances in this life, has a cheap pleasure which will not be followed by the least disappointment. A similar consideration seems to have weight with many persons in religious topics, for we frequently hear it said, "Oh, I could not believe so-and-so, because I should be wretched if I did." When an ostrich buries its head in the sand as danger approaches, it very likely takes the happiest course. It hides the danger, and then calmly says there is no danger; and, if it feels perfectly sure there is none, why should it raise its head to see? A man may go through life, systematically keeping out of view all that might cause a change in his opinions, and if he only succeeds—basing his method. as he does, on two fundamental psychological laws—I do not see what can be said against his doing so. It would be an egotistical impertinence to object that his procedure is irrational, for that only amounts to saying that his method of settling belief is not ours. He does not propose to himself to be rational, and indeed, will often talk with scorn of man's weak and illusive reason. So let him think as he pleases.

But this method of fixing belief, which may be called the method of tenacity, will be unable to hold its ground in practice. The social impulse is against it. The man who adopts it will find that other men think differently from him, and it will be apt to occur to him in some saner moment that their opinions are quite as good as his own, and this will shake his confidence in his belief. This conception, that another man's thought or sentiment may be equivalent to one's own, is a distinctly new step, and a highly important one. It arises from an impulse too strong in man to be suppressed, without danger of destroying the human species. Unless we make ourselves hermits, we shall necessarily influence each other's opinions; so that the problem becomes how to fix belief, not in the individual merely, but in the community.

Let the will of the state act, then, instead of that of the individual. Let an institution be created which shall have for its object to keep correct doctrines before the attention of the people, to reiterate them perpetually, and to teach them to the young; having at the same time power to prevent contrary doctrines from being taught, advocated, or expressed. Let all possible causes of a change of mind be removed from men's apprehensions. Let them be kept ignorant, lest they should learn of some reason to think otherwise than they do. Let their passions be enlisted, so that they may regard private and unusual opinions with hatred and horror. Then, let all men who reject the established belief be terrified into silence. Let the people turn out and tar-and-feather such men, or let inquisitions be made into the manner of thinking of suspected persons, and, when they are found guilty of forbidden beliefs, let them be subjected to some signal punishment. When complete agreement could not otherwise be reached, a general massacre of all who have not thought in a certain way has proved a very effective means of settling opinion in a country. If the power to do this be wanting, let a list of opinions be drawn up, to which no man of the least independence of thought can assent, and let the faithful be required to accept all these propositions, in order to segregate them as radically as possible from the influence of the rest of the world.

This method has, from the earliest times, been one of the chief means of upholding correct theological and political doctrines, and of preserving their universal or catholic character. In Rome, especially, it has been practiced from the days of Numa Pompilius to those of Pius Nonus. This is the most perfect example in history; but wherever there is a priesthood —and no religion has been without one—this method has been more or less made use of. Wherever there is aristocracy, or a guild, or any association of a class of men whose interests depend or are supposed to depend on certain propositions, there will be inevitably found some traces of this natural product of social feeling. Cruelties always accompany this system; and when it is consistently carried out, they become atrocities of the most horrible kind in the eyes of any rational man. Nor should this occasion surprise, for the officer of a society does not feel justified in surrendering the interests of that society for the sake of mercy, as he might his own private interests. It is natural, therefore, that sympathy and fellowship should thus produce a most ruthless power.

In judging this method of fixing belief, which may be called the method of authority, we must, in the first place, allow its immeasurable mental and moral superiority to the method of tenacity. Its success is proportionally greater; and in fact it has over and over again worked the most majestic results. The mere structures of stone which it has caused to be put together—in Siam, for example, in Egypt, and in Europe—have many of them a sublimity hardly more than rivaled by the greatest works of nature. And, except the geological epochs, there are no periods of time so vast as those which are measured by some of these organized faiths. If we scrutinize the matter closely, we shall find that there has not been one of their creeds which has remained always the same; yet the change is so slow as to be imperceptible during one person's life, so that individual belief remains sensibly fixed. For the mass of mankind, then, there is perhaps no better method than this. If it is their highest impulse to be intellectual slaves, then slaves they ought to remain.

But no institution can undertake to regulate opinions upon every subject. Only the most important ones can be attended to, and on the rest men's minds must be left to the action of natural causes. This imperfection will be no source of weakness so long as men are in such a state of culture that one opinion does not influence another—that is, so long as they cannot put two and two together. But in the most priest-ridden states some individuals will be found who are raised above that condition. These men possess a wider sort of social feeling; they see that men in other countries and in other ages have held to very different doctrines from those which they themselves have been brought up to believe; and they cannot help seeing that it is the mere accident of their having been taught as they have, and of their having been surrounded with the manners and associations they have, that has caused them to believe as they do and not far differently. And their candor cannot resist the reflection that there is no reason to rate their own views at a higher value than those of other nations and other centuries; and this gives rise to doubts in their minds.

They will further perceive that such doubts as these must exist in their minds with reference to every belief which seems to be determined by the caprice either of themselves or of those who originated the popular opinions. The willful adherence to a belief, and the arbitrary forcing of it upon others, must, therefore, both be given up and a new method of settling opinions must be adopted, which shall not only produce an impulse to believe, but shall also decide what proposition it is which is to be believed. Let the action of natural preferences be unimpeded, then, and under their influence let men conversing together and regarding matters in different lights, gradually develop beliefs in harmony with natural causes. This method resembles that by which conceptions of art have been brought to maturity. The most perfect example of it is to be found in the history of metaphysical philosophy. Systems of this sort have not usually rested upon observed facts, at least not in any great degree. They have been chiefly adopted because their fundamental propositions seemed "agreeable to reason." This is an apt expression; it does not mean that which agrees with experience, but that which we find ourselves inclined to believe. Plato, for example, finds it agreeable to reason that the distances of the celestial spheres from one another should be proportional to the different lengths of strings which produce harmonious chords. Many philosophers have been led to their main conclusions by considerations like this; but this is the lowest and least developed form which the method takes, for it is clear that another man might find Kepler's [earlier] theory, that the celestial spheres are proportional to the inscribed and circumscribed spheres of the different regular solids, more agreeable to *his* reason. But the shock of opinions will soon lead men to rest on preferences of a far more universal nature. Take, for example, the doctrine that man only acts selfishly—that is, from the consideration that acting in one way will afford him more pleasure than acting in another. This rests on no fact in the world, but it has had a wide acceptance as being the only reasonable theory.

This method is far more intellectual and respectable from the point of view of reason than either of the others which we have noticed. But its failure has been the most manifest. It makes of inquiry something similar to the development of taste; but taste, unfortunately, is always more or less a matter of fashion, and accordingly, metaphysicians have never come to any fixed agreement, but the pendulum has swung backward and forward between a more material and a more spiritual philosophy, from the earliest times to the latest. And so from this, which has been called the *a priori* method, we are driven, in Lord Bacon's phrase, to a true induction. We have examined into this *a priori* method as something which promised to deliver our opinions from their accidental and capricious element. But development, while it is a process which eliminates the effect of some casual circumstances, only magnifies that of others. This method, therefore, does not differ in a very essential way from that of authority. The government may not have lifted its finger to influence my convictions; I may have been left outwardly quite free to choose, we will say, between monogamy and polygamy, and appealing to my conscience only, I may have concluded that the latter practice is in itself licentious. But when I come to see that the chief obstacle to the spread of Christianity among a people of as high culture as the Hindoos has been a conviction of the immorality of our way of treating women, I cannot help seeing that, though governments do not interfere, sentiments in their development will be very greatly determined by accidental causes. Now, there are some people, among whom I must suppose that my reader is to be found, who, when they see that any belief of theirs is determined by any circumstance extraneous to the facts, will from that moment not merely admit in words that that belief is doubtful, but will experience a real doubt of it, so that it ceases in some degree at least to be a belief.

To satisfy our doubts, therefore, it is necessary that a method should be found by which our beliefs may be caused by nothing human, but by some external permanency—by something upon which our thinking has no effect. Some mystics imagine that they have such a method in a private inspiration from on high. But that is only a form of the method of tenacity, in which the conception of truth as something public is not yet developed. Our external permanency would not be external, in our sense, if it was restricted in its influence to one individual. It must be something which affects, or might affect, every man. And, though these affections are necessarily as various as are individual conditions, yet the method must be such that the ultimate conclusion of every man shall be the same, or would be the same if inquiry were sufficiently persisted in. Such is the method of science. Its fundamental hypothesis, restated in more familiar language, is this: There are real things, whose characters are entirely independent of our opinions about them; those realities affect our senses according to regular laws, and, though our sensations are as different as our relations to the objects, yet, by taking advantage of the laws of perception, we can ascertain by reasoning how things really are, and any man, if he have sufficient experience and reason enough about it, will be led to the one true conclusion. The new conception here involved is that of reality. It may be asked how I know that there are any realities. If this hypothesis is the sole support of my method of inquiry, my method of inquiry must not be used to support my hypothesis. The reply is this: (1) If investigation cannot be regarded as proving that there are real things, it at least does not lead to a contrary conclusion; but the method and the conception on which it is based remain ever in harmony. No doubts of the method, therefore, necessarily arise from its practice, as is the case with all the others. (2) The feeling which gives rise to any method of fixing belief is a dissatisfaction at two repugnant propositions. But here already is a vague concession that there is some *one* thing to which a proposition should conform. Nobody, therefore, can really doubt that there are realities, or, if he did, doubt would not be a source of dissatisfaction. The hypothesis, therefore, is one which every mind admits. So that the social impulse does not cause men to doubt it. (3) Everybody uses the scientific method about a great many things, and only ceases to use it when he does not know how to apply it. (4) Experience of the method has not led us to doubt it, but, on the contrary, scientific investigation has had the most wonderful triumphs in the way of settling opinion. These afford the explanation of my not doubting the method or the hypothesis which it supposes; and not having any doubt, nor believing that anybody else whom I could influence has, it would be the merest babble for me to say more about it. If there be anybody with a living doubt upon the subject, let him consider it.

To describe the method of scientific investigation is the object of this series of papers. At present I have only room to notice some points of contrast between it and other methods of fixing belief.

This is the only one of the four methods which presents any distinction of a right and a wrong way. If I adopt the method of tenacity and shut myself out from all influences, whatever I think necessary to doing this is necessary according to that method. So with the method of authority: the state may try to put down heresy by means which, from a scientific point of view, seems very ill-calculated to accomplish its purposes; but the only test *on that method* is what the state thinks, so that it cannot pursue the method wrongly. So with the *a priori* method. The very essence of it is to think as one is inclined to think. All metaphysicians will be sure to do that, however they may be inclined to judge each other to be perversely wrong. The Hegelian system recognizes every natural tendency of thought as logical, although it is certain to be abolished by countertendencies. Hegel thinks there is a regular system in the succession of these tendencies, in consequence of which, after drifting one way and the other for a long time, opinion will at last go right. And it is true that metaphysicians get the right ideas at last; Hegel's system of Nature represents tolerably the science of his day; and one may be sure that whatever scientific investigation has put out of doubt will presently receive *a priori* demonstration on the part of the metaphysicians. But with the scientific method the case is different. I may start with known and observed facts to proceed to the unknown; and yet the rules which I follow in doing so may not be such as investigation would approve. The test of whether I am truly following the method is not an immediate appeal to my feelings and purposes, but, on the contrary, itself involves the application of the method. Hence it is that bad reasoning as well as good reasoning is possible; and this fact is the foundation of the practical side of logic.

It is not to be supposed that the first three methods of settling opinion present no advantage whatever over the scientific method. On the contrary, each has some peculiar con-

venience of its own. The *a priori* method is distinguished for
its comfortable conclusions. It is the nature of the process to
adopt whatever belief we are inclined to, and there are certain
flatteries to one's vanities which we all believe by nature,
until we are awakened from our pleasing dream by rough
facts. The method of authority will always govern the mass
of mankind; and those who wield the various forms of organized force in the state will never be convinced that dangerous
reasoning ought not to be suppressed in some way. If liberty
of speech is to be untrammeled from the grosser forms of
constraint, then uniformity of opinion will be secured by a
moral terrorism to which the respectability of society will
give its thorough approval. Following the method of authority is the path of peace. Certain non-conformities are permitted; certain others (considered unsafe) are forbidden.
These are different in different countries and in different
ages; but, wherever you are let it be known that you seriously
hold a tabooed belief, and you may be perfectly sure of being
treated with a cruelty no less brutal but more refined than
hunting you like a wolf. Thus, the greatest intellectual bene-
factors of mankind have never dared, and dare not now, to
utter the whole of their thought; and thus a shade of *prima
facie* doubt is cast upon every proposition which is considered
essential to the security of society. Singularly enough, the
persecution does not all come from without; but a man tor-
ments himself and is oftentimes most distressed at finding
himself believing propositions which he has been brought up
to regard with aversion. The peaceful and sympathetic man
will, therefore, find it hard to resist the temptation to submit
his opinions to authority. But most of all I admire the method
of tenacity for its strength, simplicity, and directness. Men
who pursue it are distinguished for their decision of character,
which becomes very easy with such a mental rule. They do
not waste time in trying to make up their minds to what they
want, but, fastening like lightning upon whatever alternative
comes first, they hold to it to the end, whatever happens,
without an instant's irresolution. This is one of the splendid
qualities which generally accompany brilliant, unlasting success. It is impossible not to envy the man who can dismiss
reason, although we know how it must turn out at last.

Such are the advantages which the other methods of settling
opinions have over scientific investigation. A man should consider well of them; and then he should consider that, after

all, he wishes his opinions to coincide with the fact, and that there is no reason why the results of those first three methods should do so. To bring about this effect is the prerogative of the method of science. Upon such considerations he has to make his choice—a choice which is far more than the adoption of any intellectual opinion, which is one of the ruling decisions of his life, to which when once made he is bound to adhere. The force of habit will sometimes cause a man to hold on to old beliefs after he is in a condition to see that they have no sound basis. But reflection upon the state of the case will overcome these habits, and he ought to allow reflection full weight. People sometimes shrink from doing this, having an idea that beliefs are wholesome which they cannot help feeling rest on nothing. But let such persons suppose an analogous though different case from their own. Let them ask themselves what they would say to a reformed Mussulman who should hesitate to give up his old notions in regard to the relations of the sexes; or to a reformed Catholic who should still shrink from the Bible. Would they not say that these persons ought to consider the matter fully, and clearly understand the new doctrine, and then ought to embrace it in its entirety? But, above all, let it be considered that what is more wholesome than any particular belief is integrity of belief; and that to avoid looking into the support of any belief from a fear that it may turn out rotten is quite as immoral as it is disadvantageous. The person who confesses that there is such a thing as truth, which is distinguished from falsehood simply by this, that if acted on it should, on full consideration, carry us to the point we aim at and not astray, and then, though convinced of this, dares not know the truth and seeks to avoid it, is in a sorry state of mind, indeed.

Yes, the other methods do have their merits: a clear logical conscience does cost something—just as any virtue, just as all that we cherish, costs us dear. But, we should not desire it to be otherwise. The genius of a man's logical method should be loved and reverenced as his bride, whom he has chosen from all the world. He need not condemn the others; on the contrary, he may honor them deeply, and in doing so he only honors her the more. But she is the one that he has chosen, and he knows that he was right in making that choice. And having made it, he will work and fight for her, and will not complain that there are blows to take, hoping that there may be as many and as hard to give, and will strive to be the worthy knight and champion of her from the blaze of whose splendors he draws his inspiration and his courage.

How to Make Our Ideas Clear •

I

Whoever has looked into a modern treatise on logic of the common sort, will doubtless remember the two distinctions between *clear* and *obscure* conceptions, and between *distinct* and *confused* conceptions. They have lain in the books now for nigh two centuries, unimproved and unmodified, and are generally reckoned by logicians as among the gems of their doctrine.

A clear idea is defined as one which is so apprehended that it will be recognized wherever it is met with, and so that no other will be mistaken for it. If it fails of this clearness, it is said to be obscure.

This is rather a neat bit of philosophical terminology; yet, since it is clearness that they were defining, I wish the logicians had made their definition a little more plain. Never to fail to recognize an idea, and under no circumstances to mistake another for it, let it come in how recondite a form it may, would indeed imply such prodigious force and clearness of intellect as is seldom met with in this world. On the other hand, merely to have such an acquaintance with the idea as to have become familiar with it, and to have lost all hesitancy in recognizing it in ordinary cases, hardly seems to deserve the name of clearness of apprehension, since after all it only amounts to a subjective feeling of mastery which may be

• [From: *Collected Papers of Charles Sanders Peirce,* ed. Charles Hartshorne and Paul Weiss. Cambridge, Mass.: The Belknap Press of Harvard University Press; 1934. Vol. V, pp. 248-71. Copyright 1934 by the President and Fellows of Harvard College. Reprinted by permission of the publishers. Originally published in 1878.]

entirely mistaken. I take it, however, that when the logicians speak of "clearness," they mean nothing more than such a familiarity with an idea, since they regard the quality as but a small merit, which needs to be supplemented by another, which they call *distinctness*.

A distinct idea is defined as one which contains nothing which is not clear. This is technical language; by the *contents* of an idea logicians understand whatever is contained in its definition. So that an idea is *distinctly* apprehended, according to them, when we can give a precise definition of it, in abstract terms. Here the professional logicians leave the subject; and I would not have troubled the reader with what they have to say if it were not such a striking example of how they have been slumbering through ages of intellectual activity, listlessly disregarding the enginery of modern thought, and never dreaming of applying its lessons to the improvement of logic. It is easy to show that the doctrine that familiar use and abstract distinctness make the perfection of apprehension, has its only true place in philosophies which have long been extinct; and it is now time to formulate the method of attaining to a more perfect clearness of thought, such as we see and admire in the thinkers of our own time.

When Descartes set about the reconstruction of philosophy, his first step was to (theoretically) permit skepticism and to discard the practice of the schoolmen of looking to authority as the ultimate source of truth. That done, he sought a more natural fountain of true principles, and professed to find it in the human mind; thus passing, in the directest way, from the method of authority to that of apriority, as described in my first paper. Self-consciousness was to furnish us with our fundamental truths, and to decide what was agreeable to reason. But since, evidently, not all ideas are true, he was led to note, as the first condition of infallibility, that they must be clear. The distinction between an idea *seeming* clear and really being so, never occurred to him. Trusting to introspection, as he did, even for a knowledge of external things, why should he question its testimony in respect to the contents of our own minds? But then, I suppose, seeing men, who seemed to be quite clear and positive, holding opposite opinions upon fundamental principles, he was further led to say that clearness of ideas is not sufficient, but that they need also to be distinct, i.e., to have nothing unclear about them. What he probably meant by this (for he did not explain himself with precision) was that they must sustain the test of dialectical examination; that they must not only seem clear at the outset, but that discussion must never be able to bring to light points of obscurity connected with them.

Such was the distinction of Descartes, and one sees that it was precisely on the level of his philosophy. It was somewhat developed by Leibniz. This great and singular genius was as remarkable for what he failed to see as for what he saw. That a piece of mechanism could not do work perpetually without being fed with power in some form, was a thing perfectly apparent to him; yet he did not understand that the machinery of the mind can only transform knowledge, but never originate it, unless it be fed with facts of observation. He thus missed the most essential point of the Cartesian philosophy, which is, that to accept propositions which seem perfectly evident to us is a thing which, whether it be logical or illogical, we cannot help doing. Instead of regarding the matter in this way, he sought to reduce the first principles of science to formulas which cannot be denied without self-contradiction, and was apparently unaware of the great difference between his position and that of Descartes.• So he reverted to the old formalities of logic, and, above all, abstract definitions played a great part in his philosophy. It was quite natural, therefore, that on observing that the method of Descartes labored under the difficulty that we may seem to ourselves to have clear apprehensions of ideas which in truth are very hazy, no better remedy occurred to him than to require an abstract definition of every important term. Accordingly, in adopting the distinction of *clear* and *distinct* notions, he described the latter quality as the clear apprehension of everything contained in the definition; and the books have ever since copied his words. There is no danger that his chimerical scheme will ever again be overvalued. Nothing new can ever be learned by analyzing definitions. Nevertheless, our existing beliefs can be set in order by this process, and order is an essential element of intellectual economy, as of every other. It may be acknowledged, therefore, that the books are right in making familiarity with a notion the first step toward clearness of apprehen-

---

• He was, however, above all, one of the minds that grow; while at first he was an extreme nominalist, like Hobbes, and dabbled in the nonsensical and impotent *Ars Magna* of Raymond Lully, he subsequently embraced the law of continuity and other doctrines opposed to nominalism. I speak here of his early views. [1903.]

sion, and the defining of it the second. But in omitting all mention of any higher perspicuity of thought, they simply mirror a philosophy which was exploded a hundred years ago. That much-admired "ornament of logic"—the doctrine of clearness and distinctness—may be pretty enough, but it is high time to relegate to our cabinet of curiosities the antique *bijou,* and to wear about us something better adapted to modern uses.

The very first lesson that we have a right to demand that logic shall teach us is how to make our ideas clear; and a most important one it is, depreciated only by minds who stand in need of it. To know what we think, to be masters of our own meaning, will make a solid foundation for great and weighty thought. It is most easily learned by those whose ideas are meagre and restricted; and far happier they than such as wallow helplessly in a rich mud of conceptions. A nation, it is true, may, in the course of generations, overcome the disadvantage of an excessive wealth of language and its natural concomitant, a vast, unfathomable deep of ideas. We may see it in history, slowly perfecting its literary forms, sloughing at length its metaphysics, and, by virtue of the untirable patience which is often a compensation, attaining great excellence in every branch of mental acquirement. The page of history is not yet unrolled which is to tell us whether such a people will or will not in the long run prevail over one whose ideas (like the words of their language) are few, but which possesses a wonderful mastery over those which it has. For an individual, however, there can be no question that a few clear ideas are worth more than many confused ones. A young man would hardly be persuaded to sacrifice the greater part of his thoughts to save the rest; and the muddled head is the least apt to see the necessity of such a sacrifice. Him we can usually only commiserate, as a person with a congenital defect. Time will help him, but intellectual maturity with regard to clearness comes rather late, an unfortunate arrangement of nature, inasmuch as clearness is of less use to a man settled in life, whose errors have in great measure had their effect, than it would be to one whose path lies before him. It is terrible to see how a single unclear idea, a single formula without meaning, lurking in a young man's head, will sometimes act like an obstruction of inert matter in an artery, hindering the nutrition of the brain, and condemning its victim to pine away in the fullness of his intellectual vigor and in the midst of intellectual plenty. Many a man has cherished for years as his hobby some vague shadow of an idea, too meaningless to be positively false; he has, nevertheless, passionately loved it, has made it his companion by day and by night, and has given to it his strength and his life, leaving all other occupations for its sake, and in short has lived with it and for it, until it has become, as it were, flesh of his flesh and bone of his bone; and then he has waked up some bright morning to find it gone, clean vanished away like the beautiful Melusina of the fable, and the essence of his life gone with it. I have myself known such a man; and who can tell how many histories of circle-squarers, metaphysicians, astrologers, and what not, may not be told in the old German story?

II

The principles set forth in the first of these papers lead, at once, to a method of reaching a clearness of thought of a far higher grade than the "distinctness" of the logicians. We have there found that the action of thought is excited by the irritation of doubt, and ceases when belief is attained; so that the production of belief is the sole function of thought. All these words, however, are too strong for my purpose. It is as if I had described the phenomena as they appear under a mental microscope. Doubt and Belief, as the words are commonly employed, relate to religious or other grave discussions. But here I use them to designate the starting of any question, no matter how small or how great, and the resolution of it. If, for instance, in a horsecar, I pull out my purse and find a five-cent nickel and five coppers, I decide, while my hand is going to the purse, in which way I will pay my fare. To call such a question Doubt, and my decision Belief, is certainly to use words very disproportionate to the occasion. To speak of such a doubt as causing an irritation which needs to be appeased, suggests a temper which is uncomfortable to the verge of insanity. Yet, looking at the matter minutely, it must be admitted that, if there is the least hesitation as to whether I shall pay the five coppers or the nickel (as there will be sure to be, unless I act from some previously contracted habit in the matter), though irritation is too strong a word, yet I am excited to such small mental activity as may be necessary to deciding how I shall act. Most frequently doubts arise from some indecision, however momentary, in our action. Sometimes it is not so. I have, for example, to wait in a railway-station, and to pass the time I read the advertisements on the walls, I compare the advantages of different trains and different routes which I never expect to take, merely fancying myself to be in a state of hesitancy, because I am bored with having nothing to trouble me. Feigned hesitancy, whether feigned for mere amusement or with a lofty purpose, plays a great part in the production of scientific inquiry. However the doubt may originate, it stimulates the mind to an activity which may be slight or energetic, calm or turbulent. Images pass rapidly through consciousness, one incessantly melting into another, until at last, when all is over—it may be in a fraction of a second, in an hour, or after long years—we find ourselves decided as to how we should act under such circumstances as those which occasioned our hesitation. In other words, we have attained belief.

In this process we observe two sorts of elements of consciousness, the distinction between which may best be made clear by means of an illustration. In a piece of music there are the separate notes, and there is the air. A single tone may be prolonged for an hour or a day, and it exists as perfectly in each second of that time as in the whole taken together; so that, as long as it is sounding, it might be present to a sense from which everything in the past was as completely absent as the future itself. But it is different with the air, the performance of which occupies a certain time, during the portions of which only portions of it are played. It consists in an orderliness in the succession of sounds which strike the ear at different times; and to perceive it there must be some continuity of consciousness which makes the events of a lapse of time present to us. We certainly only perceive the air by hearing the separate notes; yet we cannot be said to directly hear it, for we hear only what is present at the instant, and an orderliness of succession cannot exist in an instant. These two sorts of objects, what we are *immediately* conscious of and what we are *mediately* conscious of, are found in all consciousness. Some elements (the sensations) are completely present at every instant so long as they last, while others (like thought) are actions having beginning, middle, and end, and consist in a congruence in the succession of sensations which flow through the mind. They cannot be immediately present to us, but must cover some portion of the past or future. Thought is a thread of melody running through the succession of our sensations.

We may add that just as a piece of music may be written in

parts, each part having its own air, so various systems of relationship of succession subsist together between the same sensations. These different systems are distinguished by having different motives, ideas, or functions. Thought is only one such system; for its sole motive, idea, and function is to produce belief, and whatever does not concern that purpose belongs to some other system of relations. The action of thinking may incidentally have other results. It may serve to amuse us, for example, and among *dilettanti* it is not rare to find those who have so perverted thought to the purposes of pleasure that it seems to vex them to think that the questions upon which they delight to exercise it may ever get finally settled; and a positive discovery which takes a favorite subject out of the arena of literary debate is met with ill-concealed dislike. This disposition is the very debauchery of thought. But the soul and meaning of thought, abstracted from the other elements which accompany it, though it may be voluntarily thwarted, can never be made to direct itself toward anything but the production of belief. Thought in action has for its only possible motive the attainment of thought at rest; and whatever does not refer to belief is no part of the thought itself.

And what, then, is belief? It is the demi-cadence which closes a musical phrase in the symphony of our intellectual life. We have seen that it has just three properties: first, it is something that we are aware of; second, it appeases the irritation of doubt; and, third, it involves the establishment in our nature of a rule of action, or, say for short, a *habit*. As it appeases the irritation of doubt, which is the motive for thinking, thought relaxes, and comes to rest for a moment when belief is reached. But, since belief is a rule for action, the application of which involves further doubt and further thought, at the same time that it is a stopping-place, it is also a new starting-place for thought. That is why I have permitted myself to call it thought at rest, although thought is essentially an action. The *final* upshot of thinking is the exercise of volition, and of this thought no longer forms a part; but belief is only a stadium of mental action, an effect upon our nature due to thought, which will influence future thinking.

The essence of belief is the establishment of a habit, and different beliefs are distinguished by the different modes of action to which they give rise. If beliefs do not differ in this respect, if they appease the same doubt by producing the same rule of action, then no mere differences in the manner of consciousness of them can make them different beliefs, any more than playing a tune in different keys is playing different tunes. Imaginary distinctions are often drawn between beliefs which differ only in their mode of expression—the wrangling which ensues is real enough, however. To believe that any objects are arranged among themselves as in Fig. 1, and to believe that they are arranged as in Fig. 2, are one and the

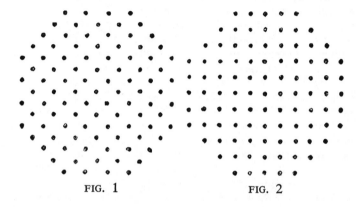

FIG. 1   FIG. 2

same belief; yet it is conceivable that a man should assert one proposition and deny the other. Such false distinctions do as much harm as the confusion of beliefs really different, and are among the pitfalls of which we ought constantly to beware, especially when we are upon metaphysical ground. One singular deception of this sort, which often occurs, is to mistake the sensation produced by our own unclearness of thought for a character of the object we are thinking. Instead of perceiving that the obscurity is purely subjective, we fancy that we contemplate a quality of the object which is essentially mysterious; and if our conception be afterward presented to us in a clear form we do not recognize it as the same, owing to the absence of the feeling of unintelligibility. So long as this deception lasts, it obviously puts an impassable barrier in the way of perspicuous thinking; so that it equally interests the opponents of rational thought to perpetuate it, and its adherents to guard against it.

Another such deception is to mistake a mere difference in the grammatical construction of two words for a distinction between the ideas they express. In this pedantic age, when the general mob of writers attend so much more to words than to things, this error is common enough. When I just said that thought is an *action,* and that it consists in a *relation,* although a person performs an action but not a relation, which can only be the result of an action, yet there was no inconsistency in what I said, but only a grammatical vagueness.

From all these sophisms we shall be perfectly safe so long as we reflect that the whole function of thought is to produce habits of action; and that whatever there is connected with a thought, but irrelevant to its purpose, is an accretion to it, but no part of it. If there be a unity among our sensations which has no reference to how we shall act on a given occasion, as when we listen to a piece of music, why, we do not call that thinking. To develop its meaning, we have, therefore, simply to determine what habits it produces, for what a thing means is simply what habits it involves. Now, the identity of a habit depends on how it might lead us to act, not merely under such circumstances as are likely to arise, but under such as might possibly occur, no matter how improbable they may be. What the habit is depends on *when* and *how* it causes us to act. As for the *when,* every stimulus to action is derived from perception; as for the *how,* every purpose of action is to produce some sensible result. Thus, we come down to what is tangible and practical as the root of every real distinction of thought, no matter how subtle it may be; and there is no distinction of meaning so fine as to consist in anything but a possible difference of practice.

To see what this principle leads to, consider in the light of it such a doctrine as that of transubstantiation. The Protestant churches generally hold that the elements of the sacrament are flesh and blood only in a tropical sense; they nourish our souls as meat and the juice of it would our bodies. But the Catholics maintain that they are literally just that, meat and blood; although they possess all the sensible qualities of wafer-cakes and diluted wine. But we can have no conception of wine except what may enter into a belief, either—

    1. That this, that, or the other, is wine; or,

    2. That wine possesses certain properties.

Such beliefs are nothing but self-notifications that we should, upon occasion, act in regard to such things as we believe to be wine according to the qualities which we believe wine to possess. The occasion of such action would be some sensible perception, the motive of it to produce some sensible result.

Thus our action has exclusive reference to what affects the senses, our habit has the same bearing as our action, our belief the same as our habit, our conception the same as our belief; and we can consequently mean nothing by wine but what has certain effects, direct or indirect, upon our senses; and to talk of something as having all the sensible characters of wine, yet being in reality blood, is senseless jargon. Now, it is not my object to pursue the theological question; and having used it as a logical example I drop it, without caring to anticipate the theologian's reply. I only desire to point out how impossible it is that we should have an idea in our minds which relates to anything but conceived sensible effects of things. Our idea of anything *is* our idea of its sensible effects; and if we fancy that we have any other we deceive ourselves, and mistake a mere sensation accompanying the thought for a part of the thought itself. It is absurd to say that thought has any meaning unrelated to its only function. It is foolish for Catholics and Protestants to fancy themselves in disagreement about the elements of the sacrament, if they agree in regard to all their sensible effects, here or hereafter.

It appears, then, that the rule for attaining the third grade of clearness of apprehension is as follows: consider what effects, which might conceivably have practical bearings, we conceive the object of our conception to have. Then, our conception of these effects is the whole of our conception of the object.

III

Let us illustrate this rule by some examples; and, to begin with the simplest one possible, let us ask what we mean by calling a thing *hard*. Evidently that it will not be scratched by many other substances. The whole conception of this quality, as of every other, lies in its conceived effects. There is absolutely no difference between a hard thing and a soft thing so long as they are not brought to the test. Suppose, then, that a diamond could be crystallized in the midst of a cushion of soft cotton, and should remain there until it was finally burned up. Would it be false to say that that diamond was soft? This seems a foolish question, and would be so, in fact, except in the realm of logic. There such questions are often of the greatest utility as serving to bring logical principles into sharper relief than real discussions ever could. In studying logic we must not put them aside with hasty answers, but must consider them with attentive care, in order to make out the principles involved. We may, in the present case, modify our question, and ask what prevents us from saying that all hard bodies remain perfectly soft until they are touched, when their hardness increases with the pressure until they are scratched. Reflection will show that the reply is this: there would be no *falsity* in such modes of speech. They would involve a modification of our present usage of speech with regard to the words "hard" and "soft," but not of their meanings. For they represent no fact to be different from what it is; only they involve arrangements of facts which would be exceedingly maladroit. This leads us to remark that the question of what would occur under circumstances which do not actually arise is not a question of fact, but only of the most perspicuous arrangement of them. For example, the question of free-will and fate in its simplest form, stripped of verbiage, is something like this: I have done something of which I am ashamed; could I, by an effort of the will, have resisted the temptation, and done otherwise? The philosophical reply is that this is not a question of fact, but only of the [possible] arrangement of facts. Arranging them so as to exhibit what is particularly pertinent to my question—namely, that I ought to blame myself for having done wrong—it is perfectly true to say that, if I had willed to do otherwise than I did, I should have done otherwise. On the other hand, arranging the facts so as to exhibit another important consideration, it is equally true that when a temptation has once been allowed to work, it will, if it has a certain force, produce its effect, let me struggle how I may. There is no objection to a contradiction in what would result from a false supposition. The *reductio ad absurdum* consists in showing that contradictory results would follow from a hypothesis which is consequently judged to be false. Many questions are involved in the free-will discussion, and I am far from desiring to say that both sides are equally right. On the contrary, I am of opinion that one side [determinism] denies important facts, and that the other does not. But what I do say is that the above single question was the origin of the whole doubt; that, had it not been for this question, the controversy would never have arisen; and that this question is perfectly solved in the manner which I have indicated.

Let us next seek a clear idea of Weight. This is another very easy case. To say that a body is heavy means simply that, in the absence of opposing force, it will fall. This (neglecting certain specifications of how it will fall, etc., which exist in the mind of the physicist who uses the word) is evidently the whole conception of weight. It is a fair question whether some particular facts may not *account* for gravity; but what we mean by the force itself is completely involved in its effects.

This leads us to undertake an account of the idea of Force in general. This is the great conception which, developed in the early part of the seventeenth century from the rude idea of a cause, and, constantly improved upon since, has shown us how to explain all the changes of motion which bodies experience, and how to think about all physical phenomena; which has given birth to modern science, and changed the face of the globe; and which, aside from its more special uses, has played a principal part in directing the course of modern thought, and in furthering modern social development. It is, therefore, worth some pains to comprehend it. According to our rule, we must begin by asking what is the immediate use of thinking about force; and the answer is that we thus account for changes of motion. If bodies were left to themselves, without the intervention of forces, every motion would continue unchanged both in velocity and in direction. Furthermore, change of motion never takes place abruptly; if its direction is changed, it is always through a curve without angles; if its velocity alters, it is by degrees. The gradual changes which are constantly taking place are conceived by geometers to be compounded together according to the rules of the parallelogram of forces. If the reader does not already know what this is, he will find it, I hope, to his advantage to endeavor to follow the following explanation; but if mathematics are insupportable to him, pray let him skip three paragraphs rather than that we should part company here.

A *path* is a line whose beginning and end are distinguished. Two paths are considered to be equivalent, which, beginning at the same point, lead to the same point. Thus the two paths, *A B C D E* and *A F G H E* (Fig. 3), are equivalent. Paths which do *not* begin at the same point are considered to be equivalent, provided that, on moving either of them without turning it, but keeping it always parallel to its original position, [so that] when its beginning coincides with that of the other path, the ends also coincide. Paths are considered as geometrically added together, when one begins where the other ends; thus the path *A E* is conceived to be a sum of

A B, B C, C D, and *D E*. In the parallelogram of Fig. 4 the diagonal *A C* is the sum of *A B* and *B C*; or, since *A D* is geometrically equivalent to *B C*, *A C* is the geometrical sum of *A B* and *A D*.

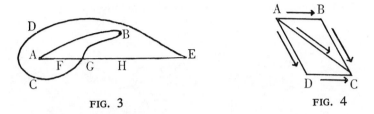

FIG. 3   FIG. 4

All this is purely conventional. It simply amounts to this: that we choose to call paths having the relations I have described equal or added. But, though it is a convention, it is a convention with a good reason. The rule for geometrical addition may be applied not only to paths, but to any other things which can be represented by paths. Now, as a path is determined by the varying direction and distance of the point which moves over it from the starting-point, it follows that anything which from its beginning to its end is determined by a varying direction and a varying magnitude is capable of being represented by a line. Accordingly, *velocities* may be represented by lines, for they have only directions and rates. The same thing is true of *accelerations,* or changes of velocities. This is evident enough in the case of velocities; and it becomes evident for accelerations if we consider that precisely what velocities are to positions—namely, states of change of them—that accelerations are to velocities.

The so-called "parallelogram of forces" is simply a rule for compounding accelerations. The rule is, to represent the accelerations by paths, and then to geometrically add the paths. The geometers, however, not only use the "parallelogram of forces" to compound different accelerations, but also to resolve one acceleration into a sum of several. Let *A B* (Fig. 5) be the path which represents a certain acceleration—say, such a change in the motion of a body that at the end of one second the body will, under the influence of that change, be in a position different from what it would have had if its motion had continued unchanged, such that a path equivalent to *A B* would lead from the latter position to the former. This acceleration may be considered as the sum of the accelerations represented by *A C* and *C B*. It may also be considered as the sum of the very different accelerations represented by *A D* and *D B*, where *A D* is almost the opposite of *A C*. And it is clear that there is an immense variety of ways in which *A B* might be resolved into the sum of two accelerations.

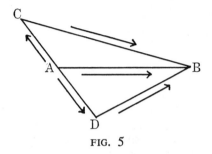

FIG. 5

After this tedious explanation, which I hope, in view of the extraordinary interest of the conception of force, may not have exhausted the reader's patience, we are prepared at last to state the grand fact which this conception embodies. This fact is that if the actual changes of motion which the different particles of bodies experience are each resolved in its appropriate way, each component acceleration is precisely such as is prescribed by a certain law of Nature, according to which bodies in the relative positions which the bodies in question actually have at the moment● always receive certain accelerations, which, being compounded by geometrical addition, give the acceleration which the body actually experiences.

This is the only fact which the idea of force represents, and whoever will take the trouble clearly to apprehend what this fact is perfectly comprehends what force is. Whether we ought to say that a force *is* an acceleration, or that it *causes* an acceleration, is a mere question of propriety of language, which has no more to do with our real meaning than the difference between the French idiom *"Il fait froid"* and its English equivalent *"It is cold."* Yet it is surprising to see how this simple affair has muddled men's minds. In how many profound treatises is not force spoken of as a "mysterious entity," which seems to be only a way of confessing that the

● Possibly the velocities also have to be taken into account.

author despairs of ever getting a clear notion of what the word means! In a recent, admired work on *Analytic Mechanics* [by Kirchhoff] it is stated that we understand precisely the effect of force, but what force itself is we do not understand! This is simply a self-contradiction. The idea which the word "force" excites in our minds has no other function than to affect our actions, and these actions can have no reference to force otherwise than through its effects. Consequently, if we know what the effects of force are, we are acquainted with every fact which is implied in saying that a force exists, and there is nothing more to know. The truth is, there is some vague notion afloat that a question may mean something which the mind cannot conceive; and when some hair-splitting philosophers have been confronted with the absurdity of such a view, they have invented an empty distinction between positive and negative conceptions, in the attempt to give their non-idea a form not obviously nonsensical. The nullity of it is sufficiently·plain from the considerations given a few pages back; and, apart from those considerations, the quibbling character of the distinction must have struck every mind accustomed to real thinking.

IV

Let us now approach the subject of logic, and consider a conception which particularly concerns it, that of *reality*. Taking clearness in the sense of familiarity, no idea could be clearer than this. Every child uses it with perfect confidence, never dreaming that he does not understand it. As for clearness in its second grade, however, it would probably puzzle most men, even among those of a reflective turn of mind, to give an abstract definition of the real. Yet such a definition may perhaps be reached by considering the points of difference between reality and its opposite, fiction. A figment is a product of somebody's imagination; it has such characters as his thought impresses upon it. That those characters are independent of how you or I think is an external reality. There are, however, phenomena within our own minds, dependent upon our thought, which are at the same time real in the sense that we really think them. But though their characters depend on how we think, they do not depend on what we think those characters to be. Thus, a dream has a real existence as a mental phenomenon, if somebody has really dreamt it; that he dreamt so and so, does not depend on what anybody thinks was dreamt, but is completely independent of all opinion on the subject. On the other hand, considering, not the fact of dreaming, but the thing dreamt, it retains its peculiarities by virtue of no other fact than that it was dreamt to possess them. Thus we may define the real as that whose characters are independent of what anybody may think them to be.

But, however satisfactory such a definition may be found, it would be a great mistake to suppose that it makes the idea of reality perfectly clear. Here, then, let us apply our rules. According to them, reality, like every other quality, consists in the peculiar, sensible effects which things partaking of it produce. The only effect which real things have is to cause belief, for all the sensations which they excite emerge into consciousness in the form of beliefs. The question, therefore, is, how is true belief (or belief in the real) distinguished from false belief (or belief in fiction). Now, as we have seen in the former paper, the ideas of truth and falsehood, in their full development, appertain exclusively to the scientific method of settling opinion. A person who arbitrarily chooses the propositions which he will adopt can use the word truth only to emphasize the expression of his determination to hold on to his choice. Of course, the method of tenacity never prevailed exclusively; reason is too natural to men for that. But in the literature of the Dark Ages we find some fine examples of it. When Scotus Erigena is commenting upon a poetical passage in which hellebore is spoken of as having caused the death of Socrates, he does not hesitate to inform the inquiring reader that Helleborus and Socrates were two eminent Greek philosophers, and that the latter having been overcome in argument by the former took the matter to heart and died of it! What sort of an idea of truth could a man have who could adopt and teach, without the qualification of a "perhaps," an opinion taken so entirely at random? The real spirit of Socrates, who I hope would have been delighted to have been "overcome in argument," because he would have learned something by it, is in curious contrast with the naïve idea of the glossist, for whom (as for the "born missionary" of today) discussion would seem to have been simply a struggle. When philosophy began to awake from its long slumber, and before theology completely dominated it, the practice seems to have been for each professor to seize upon any philosophical position he found unoccupied and which seemed a strong one, to intrench himself in it, and to sally forth from time to time to give battle to the others. Thus, even the scanty records we possess of those disputes enable us to make out a dozen or more opinions held by different teachers at one time concerning the question of nominalism and realism. Read the opening part of the *Historia Calamitatum* of Abélard, who was certainly as philosophical as any of his contemporaries, and see the spirit of combat which it breathes. For him, the truth is simply his particular stronghold. When the method of authority prevailed, the truth meant little more than the Catholic faith. All the efforts of the scholastic doctors are directed toward harmonizing their faith in Aristotle and their faith in the Church, and one may search their ponderous folios through without finding an argument which goes any further. It is noticeable that where different faiths flourish side by side, renegades are looked upon with contempt even by the party whose belief they adopt; so completely has the idea of loyalty replaced that of truth-seeking. Since the time of Descartes, the defect in the conception of truth has been less apparent. Still, it will sometimes strike a scientific man that the philosophers have been less intent on finding out what the facts are than on inquiring what belief is most in harmony with their system. It is hard to convince a follower of the *a priori* method by adducing facts; but show him that an opinion he is defending is inconsistent with what he has laid down elsewhere, and he will be very apt to retract it. These minds do not seem to believe that disputation is ever to cease; they seem to think that the opinion which is natural for one man is not so for another, and that belief will, consequently, never be settled. In contenting themselves with fixing their own opinions by a method which would lead another man to a different result, they betray their feeble hold of the conception of what truth is.

On the other hand, all the followers of science are fully persuaded that the processes of investigation, if only pushed far enough, will give one certain solution to each question to which they can be applied. One man may investigate the velocity of light by studying the transits of Venus and the aberration of the stars; another by the oppositions of Mars and the eclipses of Jupiter's satellites; a third by the method of Fizeau; a fourth by that of Foucault; a fifth by the motions of the curves of Lissajous; a sixth, a seventh, an eighth, and a ninth, may follow the different methods of comparing the measures of statical and dynamical electricity. They may at first obtain different results, but, as each perfects his method and his processes, the results will move steadily together toward a destined center. So with all scientific research. Different minds may set out with the most antagonistic views, but the progress of investigation carries them by a force outside of themselves to one and the same conclusion. This activity of thought by which we are carried, not where we wish, but to a foreordained goal, is like the operation of destiny. No modification of the point of view taken, no selection of other facts for study, no natural bent of mind even, can enable a man to escape the predestinate opinion. This great law is embodied in the conception of truth and reality. The opinion which is fated • to be ultimately agreed to by all who investigate is what we mean by the truth, and the object represented in this opinion is the real. That is the way I would explain reality.

But it may be said that this view is directly opposed to the abstract definition which we have given of reality, inasmuch as it makes the characters of the real depend on what is ultimately thought about them. But the answer to this is that, on the one hand, reality is independent, not necessarily of thought in general, but only of what you or I or any finite number of men may think about it; and that, on the other hand, though the object of the final opinion depends on what that opinion is, yet what that opinion is does not depend on what you or I or any man thinks. Our perversity and that of others may indefinitely postpone the settlement of opinion; it might even conceivably cause an arbitrary proposition to be universally accepted as long as the human race should last. Yet even that would not change the nature of the belief, which alone could be the result of investigation carried sufficiently far; and if, after the extinction of our race, another should arise with faculties and disposition for investigation, that true opinion must be the one which they would ultimately come to. "Truth crushed to earth shall rise again," and the opinion which would finally result from investigation does not depend on how anybody may actually think. But the reality of that which is real does depend on the real fact that investigation is destined to lead, at last, if continued long enough, to a belief in it.

• Fate means merely that which is sure to come true, and can nohow be avoided. It is a superstition to suppose that a certain sort of events are ever fated, and it is another to suppose that the word "fate" can never be freed from its superstitious taint. We are all fated to die.

But I may be asked what I have to say to all the minute facts of history, forgotten never to be recovered, to the lost books of the ancients, to the buried secrets.

> Full many a gem of purest ray serene
>   The dark, unfathomed caves of ocean bear;
> Full many a flower is born to blush unseen,
>   And waste its sweetness on the desert air.

Do these things not really exist because they are hopelessly beyond the reach of our knowledge? And then, after the universe is dead (according to the prediction of some scientists), and all life has ceased forever, will not the shock of atoms continue though there will be no mind to know it? To this I reply that, though in no possible state of knowledge can any number be great enough to express the relation between the amount of what rests unknown to the amount of the known, yet it is unphilosophical to suppose that, with regard to any given question (which has any clear meaning), investigation would not bring forth a solution of it, if it were carried far enough. Who would have said, a few years ago, that we could ever know of what substances stars are made whose light may have been longer in reaching us than the human race has existed? Who can be sure of what we shall not know in a few hundred years? Who can guess what would be the result of continuing the pursuit of science for ten thousand years, with the activity of the last hundred? And if it were to go on for a million, or a billion, or any number of years you please, how is it possible to say that there is any question which might not ultimately be solved?

But it may be objected, "Why make so much of these remote considerations, especially when it is your principle that only practical distinctions have a meaning?" Well, I must confess that it makes very little difference whether we say that a stone on the bottom of the ocean, in complete darkness, is brilliant or not—that is to say, that it *probably* makes no difference, remembering always that that stone *may* be fished up tomorrow. But that there are gems at the bottom of the sea, flowers in the untraveled desert, etc., are propositions which, like that about a diamond being hard when it is not pressed, concern much more the arrangement of our language than they do the meaning of our ideas.

It seems to me, however, that we have, by the application of our rule, reached so clear an apprehension of what we mean by reality, and of the fact which the idea rests on, that we should not, perhaps, be making a pretension so presumptuous as it would be singular, if we were to offer a metaphysical theory of existence for universal acceptance among those who employ the scientific method of fixing belief. However, as metaphysics is a subject much more curious than useful, the knowledge of which, like that of a sunken reef, serves chiefly to enable us to keep clear of it, I will not trouble the reader with any more Ontology at this moment. I have already been led much further into that path than I should have desired; and I have given the reader such a dose of mathematics, psychology, and all that is most abstruse, that I fear he may already have left me, and that what I am now writing is for the compositor and proofreader exclusively. I trusted to the importance of the subject. There is no royal road to logic, and really valuable ideas can only be had at the price of close attention. But I know that in the matter of ideas the public prefer the cheap and nasty; and in my next paper I am going to return to the easily intelligible, and not wander from it again. The reader who has been at the pains of wading through this paper shall be rewarded in the next one by seeing how beautifully what has been developed in this tedious way can be applied to the ascertainment of the rules of scientific reasoning.

We have, hitherto, not crossed the threshold of scientific logic. It is certainly important to know how to make our ideas clear, but they may be ever so clear without being true. How to make them so, we have next to study. How to give birth to those vital and procreative ideas which multiply into a thousand forms and diffuse themselves everywhere, advancing civilization and making the dignity of man, is an art not yet reduced to rules, but of the secret of which the history of science affords some hints.

Issues of
Pragmaticism •

Pragmaticism was originally enounced in the form of a maxim, as follows: Consider what effects that might *conceivably* have practical bearings you *conceive* the objects of your *conception* to have. Then, your *conception* of those effects is the whole of your *conception* of the object.

I will restate this in other words, since ofttimes one can thus eliminate some unsuspected source of perplexity to the reader. This time it shall be in the indicative mood, as follows: The entire intellectual purport of any symbol consists in the total of all general modes of rational conduct which, conditionally upon all the possible different circumstances and desires, would ensue upon the acceptance of the symbol.

Two doctrines that were defended by the writer about nine years before the formulation of pragmaticism may be treated as consequences of the latter belief. One of these may be called Critical Common-sensism. It is a variety of the Philosophy of Common Sense, but is marked by six distinctive characters, which had better be enumerated at once.

Character I. Critical Common-sensism admits that there not only are indubitable propositions but also that there are indubitable inferences. In one sense, anything evident is indubitable; but the propositions and inferences which Critical Common-sensism holds to be original, in the sense one cannot "go behind" them (as the lawyers say), are indubitable in the sense of being acritical. The term "reasoning" ought to be confined to such fixation of one belief by another as is reasonable, deliberate, self-controlled. A reasoning must be conscious; and this consciousness is not mere "immediate consciousness," which (as I argued in 1868) •• is simple Feeling

• [From: *Collected Papers of Charles Sanders Peirce,* ed. Charles Hartshorne and Paul Weiss. Cambridge, Mass.: The Belknap Press of Harvard University Press; 1934. Vol. V, pp. 293-6, 305-7, 309-13. Copyright 1934 by the President and Fellows of Harvard College. Reprinted by permission of the publishers. Originally published in 1905.]
•• "Questions Concerning Certain Faculties Claimed for Man," *The Journal of Speculative Philosophy* 2(1868), 103-14.

viewed from another side, but is in its ultimate nature (meaning in that characteristic element of it that is not reducible to anything simpler) a sense of taking a habit, or disposition to respond to a given kind of stimulus in a given kind of way. As to the nature of that, some *éclaircissements* will appear below and again in my third paper, on the Basis of Pragmaticism.• But the secret of rational consciousness is not so much to be sought in the study of this one peculiar nucleolus, as in the review of the process of self-control in its entirety. The machinery of logical self-control works on the same plan as does moral self-control, in multiform detail. The greatest difference, perhaps, is that the latter serves to inhibit mad puttings forth of energy, while the former most characteristically insures us against the quandary of Buridan's ass. The formation of habits under imaginary action (see the paper ["How to Make Our Ideas Clear"] of January, 1878) is one of the most essential ingredients of both; but in the logical process the imagination takes far wider flights, proportioned to the generality of the field of inquiry, being bounded in pure mathematics solely by the limits of its own powers, while in the moral process we consider only situations that may be apprehended or anticipated. For in moral life we are chiefly solicitous about our conduct and its inner springs, and the approval of conscience, while in intellectual life there is a tendency to value existence as the vehicle of forms. Certain obvious features of the phenomena of self-control (and especially of habit) can be expressed compactly and without any hypothetical addition, except what we distinctly rate as imagery, by saying that we have an occult nature of which and of its contents we can only judge by the conduct that it determines, and by phenomena of that conduct. All will assent to that (or all but the extreme nominalist), but anti-synechistic thinkers wind themselves up in a factitious snarl by falsifying the phenomena in representing consciousness to be, as it were, a skin, a separate tissue, overlying an unconscious region of the occult nature, mind, soul, or physiological basis. It appears to me that in the present state of our knowledge a sound methodeutic prescribes that, in adhesion to the appearances, the difference is only relative and the demarcation not precise.

According to the maxim of Pragmaticism, to say that determination affects our occult nature is to say that it is capable

• "Prolegomena to an Apology for Pragmaticism," *The Monist,* Vol. 16 (Oct. 1906), pp. 492-546.

of affecting deliberate conduct; and since we are conscious of what we do deliberately, we are conscious *habitualiter* of whatever hides in the depths of our nature; and it is presumable (and *only* presumable,● although curious instances are on record) that a sufficiently energetic effort of attention would bring it out. Consequently, to say that an operation of the mind is controlled is to say that it is, in a special sense, a conscious operation; and this no doubt is the consciousness of reasoning. For this theory requires that in reasoning we should be conscious, not only of the conclusion, and of our deliberate approval of it, but also of its being the result of the premise from which it does result, and furthermore that the inference is one of a possible class of inferences which conform to one guiding principle. Now in fact we find a well-marked class of mental operations, clearly of a different nature from any others which do possess just these properties. They alone deserve to be called *reasonings;* and if the reasoner is conscious, even vaguely, of what his guiding principle is, his reasoning should be called a *logical argumentation.* There are, however, cases in which we are conscious that a belief has been determined by another given belief, but are not conscious that it proceeds on any general principle. Such is St. Augustine's *"cogito, ergo sum."* Such a process should be called, not a reasoning, but an *acritical inference.* Again, there are cases in which one belief is determined by another, without our being at all aware of it. These should be called *associational suggestions of belief.*

Now the theory of Pragmaticism was originally based, as anybody will see who examines the papers of November 1877 and January 1878, upon a study of that experience of the phenomena of self-control which is common to all grown men and women; and it seems evident that to some extent, at least, it must always be so based. For it is to conceptions of deliberate conduct that Pragmaticism would trace the intellectual purport of symbols; and deliberate conduct is self-controlled conduct. Now control may itself be controlled, criticism itself subjected to criticism; and ideally there is no obvious definite limit to the sequence. But if one seriously inquires whether it is possible that a completed series of actual efforts should have been endless or beginningless (I will spare the reader

● But see the experiments of J. Jastrow and me "On Slight Differences of Sensation" in the *Memoirs of the National Academy of Sciences,* Vol. III (1884), pp. 1-11.

the discussion), I think he can only conclude that (with some vagueness as to what constitutes an effort) this must be regarded as impossible. It will be found to follow that there are, besides perceptual judgments, original (i.e., indubitable because uncriticized) beliefs of a general and recurrent kind, as well as indubitable acritical inferences.

It is important for the reader to satisfy himself that genuine doubt always has an external origin, usually from surprise; and that it is as impossible for a man to create in himself a genuine doubt by such an act of the will as would suffice to imagine the condition of a mathematical theorem, as it would be for him to give himself a genuine surprise by a simple act of the will. . . .

Another doctrine which is involved in Pragmaticism as an essential consequence of it, but which the writer defended (*North American Review,* Vol. CXIII, pp. 449-472, 1871) before he had formulated, even in his own mind, the principle of pragmaticism, is the scholastic doctrine of realism. This is usually defined as the opinion that there are real objects that are general, among the number being the modes of determination of existent singulars, if, indeed, these be not the only such objects. But the belief in this can hardly escape being accompanied by the acknowledgment that there are, besides, real *vagues,* and especially real possibilities. For possibility being the denial of a necessity, which is a kind of generality, is vague like any other contradiction of a general. Indeed, it is the reality of some possibilities that pragmaticism is most concerned to insist upon. The article of January 1878 endeavored to gloze over this point as unsuited to the exoteric public addressed; or perhaps the writer wavered in his own mind. He said that if a diamond were to be formed in a bed of cotton-wool, and were to be consumed there without ever having been pressed upon by any hard edge or point, it would be merely a question of nomenclature whether that diamond should be said to have been hard or not. No doubt this is true, except for the abominable falsehood in the word "merely," implying that symbols are unreal. Nomenclature involves classification; and classification is true or false, and the generals to which it refers are either reals in the one case, or figments in the other. For if the reader will turn to the original maxim of pragmaticism at the beginning of this article, he will see that the question is, not what *did* happen, but whether it would have been well to engage in any line of conduct whose successful issue depended upon whether that diamond *would* resist an attempt to scratch it, or whether all other logical means of determining how it ought to be classed *would* lead to the conclusion which, to quote the very words of that article, would be "the belief which alone could be the result of investigation carried *sufficiently far*." Pragmaticism makes the ultimate intellectual purport of what you please to consist in conceived conditional resolutions, or their substance; and therefore, the conditional propositions, with their hypothetical antecedents, in which such resolutions consist, being of the ultimate nature of meaning, must be capable of being true, that is, of expressing whatever there be which is such as the proposition expresses, independently of being thought to be so in any judgment, or being represented to be so in any other symbol of any man or men. But that amounts to saying that possibility is sometimes of a real kind. . . .

Let us now take up the case of that diamond which, having been crystallized upon a cushion of jeweler's cotton, was accidentally consumed by fire before the crystal of corundum that had been sent for had had time to arrive, and indeed without being subjected to any other pressure than that of the atmosphere and its own weight. The question is, was that diamond *really* hard? It is certain that no discernible *actual* fact determined it to be so. But its hardness not, nevertheless, a *real* fact? To say, as the article of January 1878 seems to intend, that it is just as an arbitrary "usage of speech" chooses to arrange its thoughts, is as much as to decide against the reality of the property, since the real is that which is such as it is regardless of how it is, at any time, thought to be. Remember that this diamond's condition is not an isolated fact. There is no such thing; and an isolated fact could hardly be real. It is an unsevered, though presciss● part of the unitary fact of nature. Being a diamond, it was a mass of pure carbon, in the form of a more or less transparent crystal (brittle, and of facile octahedral cleavage, unless it was of an unheard-of variety), which, if not trimmed after one of the fashions in which diamond may be trimmed, took the shape of an octahedron, apparently regular (I need not go into minutiæ), with grooved edges, and probably with some curved faces. Without being subjected to any considerable pressure, it could be found

● [Peirce uses this term to refer to "dissection in hypothesis," whatever may be distinguished in thought, i.e., shape from color —though not existing in isolation.]

to be insoluble, very highly refractive, showing under radium rays (and perhaps under "dark light" and X-rays) a peculiar bluish phosphorescence, having as high a specific gravity as realgar or orpiment, and giving off during its combustion less heat than any other form of carbon would have done. From some of these properties hardness is believed to be inseparable. For like it they bespeak the high polemerization of the molecule. But however this may be, how can the hardness of all other diamonds fail to bespeak *some* real relation among the diamonds without which a piece of carbon would not be a diamond? Is it not a monstrous perversion of the word and concept *real* to say that the accident of the non-arrival of the corundum prevented the hardness of the diamond from having the *reality* which it otherwise, with little doubt, would have had?

At the same time, we must dismiss the idea that the occult state of things (be it a relation among atoms or something else), which constitutes the reality of a diamond's hardness, can possibly consist in anything but in the truth of a general conditional proposition. For to what else does the entire teaching of chemistry relate except to the "behavior" of different possible kinds of material substance? And in what does that behavior consist except that if a substance of a certain kind should be exposed to an agency of a certain kind, a certain kind of sensible result *would* ensue, according to our experiences hitherto. As for the pragmaticist, it is precisely his position that nothing else than this can be so much as *meant* by saying that an object possesses a character. He is therefore obliged to subscribe to the doctrine of a real Modality, including real Necessity and real Possibility.

A good question, for the purpose of illustrating the nature of Pragmaticism, is, What is Time? It is not proposed to attack those most difficult problems connected with the psychology, the epistemology, or the metaphysics of Time, although it will be taken for granted, as it must be according to what has been said, that Time is real. The reader is only invited to the humbler question of what we mean by Time, and not of every kind of meaning attached to Past, Present, and Future either. Certain peculiar feelings are associated with the three general determinations of Time; but those are to be sedulously put out of view. That the reference of events to Time is irresistible will be recognized; but as to how it may differ from other kinds of irresistibility is a question not here to be considered. The question to be considered is simply, What is the intellectual purport of the Past, Present, and Future? It can only be treated with the utmost brevity.

That Time is a particular variety of objective Modality is too obvious for argumentation. The Past consists of the sum of *faits accomplis,* and this Accomplishment is the Existential Mode of Time. For the Past really acts upon us, and *that* it does, not at all in the way in which a Law or Principle influences us, but precisely as an Existent object acts. For instance, when a *Nova Stella* bursts out in the heavens, it acts upon one's eyes just as a light struck in the dark by one's own hands would; and yet it is an event which happened before the Pyramids were built. A neophyte may remark that its reaching the eyes, which is all we know, happens but a fraction of a second before we know it. But a moment's consideration will show him that he is losing sight of the question, which is not whether the distant Past can act upon us *immediately,* but whether it acts upon·us just as any Existent does. The instance adduced (certainly a commonplace enough fact) proves conclusively that the mode of the Past is that of Actuality. Nothing of the sort is true of the Future, to compass the understanding of which it is indispensable that the reader should divest himself of his Necessitarianism—at best, but a scientific theory—and return to the Common-sense State of Nature. Do you never say to yourself, "I *can* do this or that as well tomorrow as today"? Your Necessitarianism is a̅ theoretical pseudo-belief—a make-believe belief—that such a sentence does not express the real truth. That is only to stick to proclaiming the unreality of that Time, of which you are invited, be it reality or figment, to consider the meaning. You need not fear to compromise your darling theory by looking out at its windows. Be it true in theory or not, the unsophisticated conception is that everything in the Future is either *destined,* i.e., necessitated already, or is *undecided,* the contingent future of Aristotle. In other words, it is not Actual, since it does not act except through the idea of it, that is, as a law acts; but is either Necessary or Possible, which are of the same mode since (as remarked above) Negation being outside the category of modality cannot produce a variation in Modality. As for the Present instant, it is so inscrutable that I wonder whether no skeptic has ever attacked its reality. I can fancy one of them dipping his pen in his blackest ink to commence the assault, and then suddenly reflecting that his entire life is in the Present—the "living present," as we say, this instant when all hopes and fears concerning it come to their end, this Living Death in which we are born anew. It is plainly that Nascent State between the Determinate and the Indeterminate that was noticed above.

Pragmaticism consists in holding that the purport of any concept is its conceived bearing upon our conduct. How, then, does the Past bear upon conduct? The answer is self-evident: whenever we set out to do anything, we "go upon," we base our conduct on facts already known, and for these we can only draw upon our memory. It is true that we may institute a new investigation for the purpose; but its discoveries will only become applicable to conduct after they have been made and reduced to a memorial maxim. In short, the Past is the store-house of all our knowledge.

When we say that we know that some state of things exists, we mean that it used to exist, whether just long enough for the news to reach the brain and be retransmitted to tongue or pen, or longer ago. Thus, from whatever point of view we contemplate the Past, it appears as the Existential Mode of Time.

How does the Future bear upon conduct? The answer is that future facts are the only facts that we can, in a measure, control; and whatever there may be in the Future that is not amenable to control are the things that we *shall* be able to infer, or *should* be able to infer, under favorable circumstances. There may be questions concerning which the pendulum of opinion never would cease to oscillate, however favorable circumstances may be. But if so, those questions are *ipso facto* not *real* questions, that is to say, are questions to which there is no true answer to be given. It is natural to use the future tense (and the conditional mood is but a mollified future) in drawing a conclusion or in stating a consequence. "If two unlimited straight lines in one plane and crossed by a third making the sum . . . then these straight lines *will* meet on the side, etc." It cannot be denied that acritical inferences may refer to the Past in its capacity as past; but according to Pragmaticism, the conclusion of a Reasoning power must refer to the Future. For its meaning refers to conduct, and since it is a reasoned conclusion, must refer to deliberate conduct, which is controllable conduct. But the only controllable conduct is Future conduct. As for that part of the Past that lies beyond memory, the Pragmaticist doctrine is that the meaning of its being believed to be in connection with the Past consists in the acceptance as truth of the conception that we ought to conduct ourselves according to it (like the meaning of any other belief). Thus, a belief that Christopher Columbus discovered America really refers to the future. It is more difficult, it must be confessed, to account for beliefs that rest upon the double evidence of feeble but direct memory and upon rational inference. The difficulty does not seem insuperable; but it must be passed by. . . .

The Doctrine of Necessity Examined •

In *The Monist* for January 1891, I endeavored to show what elementary ideas ought to enter into our view of the universe. I may mention that on those considerations I had already grounded a cosmical theory, and from it had deduced a considerable number of consequences capable of being compared with experience. This comparison is now in progress, but under existing circumstances must occupy many years.

I propose here to examine the common belief that every single fact in the universe is precisely determined by law. It must not be supposed that this is a doctrine accepted everywhere and at all times by all rational men. Its first advocate appears to have been Democritus, the atomist, who was led to it, as we are informed, by reflecting upon the "impenetrability, translation, and impact of matter (*antitypia kai phora kai plege tes hyles*)." That is to say, having restricted his attention to a field where no influence other than mechanical constraint could possibly come before his notice, he straightway jumped to the conclusion that throughout the universe that was the sole principle of action—a style of reasoning so usual in our day with men not unreflecting as to be more than excusable

• [From: *Collected Papers of Charles Sanders Peirce,* ed. Charles Hartshorne and Paul Weiss. Cambridge, Mass.: The Belknap Press of Harvard University Press; 1935. Vol. VI, pp. 28-45. Copyright 1935 by the President and Fellows of Harvard College. Reprinted by permission of the publishers. Originally published in 1892.]

in the infancy of thought. But Epicurus, in revising the atomic doctrine and repairing its defenses, found himself obliged to suppose that atoms swerve from their courses by spontaneous chance; and thereby he conferred upon the theory life and entelechy. For we now see clearly that the peculiar function of the molecular hypothesis in physics is to open an entry for the calculus of probabilities. Already, the prince of philosophers [Aristotle] had repeatedly and emphatically condemned the dictum of Democritus (especially in the *Physics,* Book II, Chapters iv, v, vi), holding that events come to pass in three ways, namely (1) by external compulsion, or the action of efficient causes, (2) by virtue of an inward nature, or the influence of final causes, and (3) irregularly without definite cause, but just by absolute chance; and this doctrine is of the inmost essence of Aristotelianism. It affords, at any rate, a valuable enumeration of the possible ways in which anything can be supposed to have come about. The freedom of the will, too, was admitted both by Aristotle and by Epicurus. But the Stoa [Stoicism], which in every department seized upon the most tangible, hard, and lifeless element, and blindly denied the existence of every other, which, for example, impugned the validity of the inductive method and wished to fill its place with the *reductio ad absurdum,* very naturally became the one school of ancient philosophy to stand by a strict necessitarianism, thus returning to a single principle of Democritus that Epicurus had been unable to swallow. Necessitarianism and materialism with the Stoics went hand in hand, as by affinity they should. At the revival of learning, Stoicism met with considerable favor, partly because it departed just enough from Aristotle to give it the spice of novelty, and partly because its superficialities well adapted it for acceptance by students of literature and art who wanted their philosophy drawn mild. Afterwards, the great discoveries in mechanics inspired the hope that mechanical principles might suffice to explain the universe; and though without logical justification, this hope has since been continually stimulated by subsequent advances in physics. Nevertheless, the doctrine was in too evident conflict with the freedom of the will and with miracles to be generally acceptable, at first. But meantime there arose that most widely spread of philosophical blunders, the notion that associationalism belongs intrinsically to the materialistic family of doctrines; and thus was evolved the theory of motives; and libertarianism became weakened. At present, historical criticism has almost exploded the miracles, great and small; so that the doctrine of necessity has never been in so great vogue as now.

The proposition in question is that the state of things existing at any time, together with certain immutable laws, completely determine the state of things at every other time (for a limitation to *future* time is indefensible). Thus, given the state of the universe in the original nebula, and given the laws of mechanics, a sufficiently powerful mind could deduce from these data the precise form of every curlicue of every letter I am now writing.

Whoever holds that every act of the will as well as every idea of the mind is under the rigid governance of a necessity co-ordinated with that of the physical world, will logically be carried to the proposition that minds are part of the physical world in such a sense that the laws of mechanics determine everything that happens according to immutable attractions and repulsions. In that case, that instantaneous state of things from which every other state of things is calculable consists in the positions and velocities of all the particles at any instant. This, the usual and most logical form of necessitarianism, is called the mechanical philosophy.

When I have asked thinking men what reason they had to believe that every fact in the universe is precisely determined by law, the first answer has usually been that the proposition is a "presupposition" or postulate of scientific reasoning. Well, if that is the best that can be said for it, the belief is doomed. Suppose it be "postulated": that does not make it true, nor so much as afford the slightest rational motive for yielding it any credence. It is as if a man should come to borrow money, and when asked for his security, should reply he "postulated" the loan. To "postulate" a proposition is no more than to hope it is true. There are, indeed, practical emergencies in which we act upon assumptions of certain propositions as true, because if they are not so, it can make no difference how we act. But all such propositions I take to be hypotheses of individual facts. For it is manifest that no universal principle can in its universality be comprised in a special case or can be requisite for the validity of any ordinary inference. To say, for instance, that the demonstration by Archimedes of the property of the lever would fall to the ground if men were endowed with free-will, is extravagant; yet this is implied by those who make a proposition incompatible with the freedom of the will the postulate of all inference. Considering, too, that the conclusions of science make no pretense to being more than probable, and considering that a probable inference can at most only suppose something to be most frequently, or otherwise approximately, true, but never that anything is precisely true without exception throughout the universe, we see how far this proposition in truth is from being so postulated.

But the whole notion of a postulate being involved in reasoning appertains to a by-gone and false conception of logic. Non-deductive, or ampliative inference, is of three kinds: induction, hypothesis, and analogy. If there be any other modes, they must be extremely unusual and highly complicated, and may be assumed with little doubt to be of the same nature as those enumerated. For induction, hypothesis, and analogy, as far as their ampliative character goes, that is, so far as they conclude something not implied in the premises, depend upon one principle and involve the same procedure. All are essentially inferences from sampling. Suppose a ship arrives at Liverpool laden with wheat in bulk. Suppose that by some machinery the whole cargo be stirred up with great thoroughness. Suppose that twenty-seven thimblefuls be taken equally from the forward, midships, and aft parts, from the starboard, center, and larboard parts, and from the top, half depth, and lower parts of her hold, and that these being mixed and the grains counted, four-fifths of the latter are found to be of quality A. Then we infer, experientially and provisionally, that approximately four-fifths of all the grain in the cargo is of the same quality. I say we infer this *experientially* and *provisionally*. By saying that we infer it *experientially*, I mean that our conclusion makes no pretension to knowledge of wheat-in-itself, our *alétheia*, as the derivation of that word implies, has nothing to do with *latent* wheat. We are dealing only with the matter of possible experience—experience in the full acceptation of the term as something not merely affecting the senses but also as the subject of thought. If there be any wheat hidden on the ship, so that it can neither turn up in the sample nor be heard of subsequently from purchasers—or if it be half-hidden, so that it may, indeed, turn up, but is less likely to do so than the rest—or if it can affect our senses and our pockets, but from some strange cause or causelessness cannot be reasoned about—all such wheat is to be excluded (or have only its proportional weight) in calculating that true proportion of quality A, to which our inference seeks to approximate. By saying that we draw the inference *provisionally*, I mean that we do not hold that we have reached any assigned degree of approximation as yet, but only hold that if our experience be indefinitely extended, and if every fact of whatever nature, as fast as it presents itself, be duly applied, according to the inductive method, in correcting the inferred ratio, then our approximation will become indefinitely close in the long run; that is to say, close to the experience *to come* (not merely close by the exhaustion of a finite collection) so that if experience in general is to fluctuate irregularly to and fro, in a manner to deprive the ratio sought of all definite value, we shall be able to find out approximately within what limits it fluctuates, and if, after having one definite value, it changes and assumes another, we shall be able to find that out, and in short, whatever may be the variations of this ratio in experience, experience indefinitely extended will enable us to detect them, so as to predict rightly, at last, what its ultimate value may be, if it have any ultimate value, or what the ultimate law of succession of values may be, if there be any such ultimate law, or that it ultimately fluctuates irregularly within certain limits, if it do so ultimately fluctuate. Now our inference, claiming to be no more than thus experiential and provisional, manifestly involves no postulate whatever.

For what is a postulate? It is the formulation of a material fact which we are not entitled to assume as a premise, but the truth of which is requisite to the validity of an inference. Any fact, then, which might be supposed postulated, must either be such that it would ultimately present itself in experience, or not. If it will present itself, we need not postulate it now in our provisional inference, since we shall ultimately be entitled to use it as a premise. But if it never would present itself in experience, our conclusion is valid but for the possibility of this fact being otherwise than assumed, that is, it is valid as far as possible experience goes, and that is all that we claim. Thus, every postulate is cut off, either by the provisionality or by the experientiality of our inference. For instance, it has been said that induction postulates that if an indefinite succession of samples be drawn, examined, and thrown back each before the next is drawn, then in the long run every grain will be drawn as often as any other, that is to say, postulates that the ratio of the numbers of times in which any two are drawn will indefinitely approximate to unity. But no such postulate is made; for if, on the one hand, we are to have no other experience of the wheat than from such drawings, it is the ratio that presents itself in those drawings and not the ratio which belongs to the wheat in its latent existence that we are endeavoring to determine; while if, on the other hand, there is some other mode by which the wheat is to come under our knowledge, equivalent to another kind of sampling, so that after all our care in stirring up the wheat, some experiential grains will present themselves in the first sampling operation more often than others in the long run, this very singular fact will be sure to get discovered by the inductive method, which must avail itself of every sort of experience; and our inference, which was only provisional, corrects itself at last. Again, it has been said, that induction postulates that under like circumstances like events will happen, and that this postulate is at bottom the same as the principle of universal causation. But this is a blunder, or *bévue,* due to thinking exclusively of inductions where the concluded ratio is either 1 or 0. If any such proposition were postulated, it would be that under like circumstances (the circumstances of drawing the different samples) different events occur in the same proportions in all the different sets—a proposition which is false and even absurd. But in truth no such thing is postulated, the experiential character of the inference reducing the condition of validity to this, that if a certain result does not occur, the opposite result will be manifested, a condition assured by the provisionality of the inference. But it may be asked whether it is not conceivable that every instance of a certain class destined to be ever employed as a datum of induction should have one character, while every instance destined not to be so employed should have the opposite character. The answer is that in that case, the instances excluded from being subjects of reasoning would not be experienced in the full sense of the word, but would be among these *latent* individuals of which our conclusion does not pretend to speak.

To this account of the rationale of induction I know of but one objection worth mention: it is that I thus fail to deduce the full degree of force which this mode of inference in fact possesses; that according to my view, no matter how thorough and elaborate the stirring and mixing process had been, the examination of a single handful of grain would not give me any assurance, sufficient to risk money upon, that the next handful would not greatly modify the concluded value of the ratio under inquiry, while, in fact, the assurance would be very high that this ratio was not greatly in error. If the true ratio of grains of quality *A* were 0.80 and the handful contained a thousand grains, nine such handfuls out of every ten would contain from 780 to 820 grains of quality *A*. The answer to this is that the calculation given is correct when we know that the units of this handful and the quality inquired into have the normal independence of one another, if for instance the stirring has been complete and the character sampled for has been settled upon in advance of the examination of the sample. But in so far as these conditions are not known to be complied with, the above figures cease to be applicable. Random sampling and predesignation of the character sampled for should always be striven after in inductive reasoning, but when they cannot be attained, so long as it is conducted honestly, the inference retains some value. When we cannot ascertain how the sampling has been done or the sample-character selected, induction still has the essential validity which my present account of it shows it to have.

I do not think a man who combines a willingness to be convinced with a power of appreciating an argument upon a difficult subject can resist the reasons which have been given to show that the principle of universal necessity cannot be defended as being a postulate of reasoning. But then the question immediately arises whether it is not proved to be true, or at least rendered highly probable, by observation of nature.

Still, this question ought not long to arrest a person accustomed to reflect upon the force of scientific reasoning. For the essence of the necessitarian position is that certain continuous quantities have certain exact values. Now, how can observation determine the value of such a quantity with a probable error absolutely *nil?* To one who is behind the scenes, and knows that the most refined comparisons of masses, lengths, and angles, far surpassing in precision all other measurements, yet fall behind the accuracy of bank accounts, and that the ordinary determinations of physical constants, such as appear from month to month in the journals, are about on a par with an upholsterer's measurements of carpets and curtains, the idea of mathematical exactitude being demonstrated in the laboratory will appear simply ridiculous. There is a recognized method of estimating the probable magnitudes of errors in physics—the method of least squares. It is universally admitted that this method makes the errors smaller than they really are; yet even according to that theory an error indefinitely small is indefinitely improbable; so that any statement to the effect that a certain continuous quantity has a certain exact value, if well-founded at all, must be founded on something other than observation.

Still, I am obliged to admit that this rule is subject to a certain qualification. Namely, it only applies to continuous• quantity. Now, certain kinds of continuous quantity are discontinuous at one or at two limits, and for such limits the rule must be modified. Thus, the length of a line cannot be less than zero. Suppose, then, the question arises how long a line a certain person had drawn from a marked point on a piece of paper. If no line at all can be seen, the observed length is zero; and the only conclusion this observation warrants is that the length of the line is less than the smallest length visible with the optical power employed. But indirect observations—for example, that the person supposed to have drawn the line was never within fifty feet of the paper—may make it probable that no line at all was made, so that the concluded length will be strictly zero. In like manner, experience no doubt would warrant the conclusion that there is absolutely *no* indigo in a given ear of wheat, and absolutely *no* attar in a given lichen. But such inferences can only be rendered valid by positive experiential evidence, direct or remote, and cannot rest upon a mere inability to detect the quantity in question. We have reason to think there is no indigo in the wheat, because we have remarked that wherever indigo is produced it is produced in considerable quantities, to mention only one argument. We have reason to think there is no attar in the lichen, because essential oils seem to be in general peculiar to single species. If the question had been whether there was iron in the wheat or the lichen, though chemical analysis should fail to detect its presence, we should think some of it probably was there, since iron is almost everywhere. Without any such information, one way or the other, we could only abstain from any opinion as to the presence of the substance in question. It cannot, I conceive, be maintained that we are in any *better* position than this in regard to the presence of the element of chance or spontaneous departures from law in nature.

Those observations which are generally adduced in favor of mechanical causation simply prove that there is an element

---

• *Continuous* is not exactly the right word, but I let it go to avoid a long and irrelevant discussion.

of regularity in nature, and have no bearing whatever upon the question of whether such regularity is exact and universal, or not. Nay, in regard to this *exactitude,* all observation is directly *opposed* to it; and the most that can be said is that a good deal of this observation can be explained away. Try to verify any law of nature, and you will find that the more precise your observations, the more certain they will be to show irregular departures from the law. We are accustomed to ascribe these, and I do not say wrongly, to errors of observation; yet we cannot usually account for such errors in any antecedently probable way. Trace their causes back far enough, and you will be forced to admit they are always due to arbitrary determination, or chance.

But it may be asked whether if there were an element of real chance in the universe it must not occasionally be productive of signal effects such as could not pass unobserved. In answer to this question, without stopping to point out that there is an abundance of great events which one might be tempted to suppose were of that nature, it will be simplest to remark that physicists hold that the particles of gases are moving about irregularly, substantially as if by real chance, and that by the principles of probabilities there must occasionally happen to be concentrations of heat in the gases contrary to the second law of thermodynamics, and these concentrations, occurring in explosive mixtures, must sometimes have tremendous effects. Here, then, is in substance the very situation supposed; yet no phenomena ever have resulted which we are forced to attribute to such chance concentration of heat, or which anybody, wise or foolish, has ever dreamed of accounting for in that manner.

In view of all these considerations, I do not believe that anybody, not in a state of case-hardened ignorance respecting the logic of science, can maintain that the precise and universal conformity of facts to law is clearly proved, or even rendered particularly probable, by any observations hitherto made. In this way, the determined advocate of exact regularity will soon find himself driven to *a priori* reasons to support his thesis. These received such a socdolager from Stuart Mill in his Examination of Hamilton, that holding to them now seems to me to denote a high degree of imperviousness to reason; so that I shall pass them by with little notice.

To say that we cannot help believing a given proposition is no argument, but it is a conclusive fact if it be true; and with the substitution of "I" for "we," it is true in the mouths of several classes of minds, the blindly passionate, the unreflecting and ignorant, and the person who has overwhelming evidence before his eyes. But that which has been inconceivable today has often turned out indisputable on the morrow. Inability to conceive is only a stage through which every man must pass in regard to a number of beliefs—unless endowed with extraordinary obstinacy and obtuseness. His understanding is enslaved to some blind compulsion which a vigorous mind is pretty sure soon to cast off.

Some seek to back up the *a priori* position with empirical arguments. They say that the exact regularity of the world is a natural belief, and that natural beliefs have generally been confirmed by experience. There is some reason in this. Natural beliefs, however, if they generally have a foundation of truth, also require correction and purification from natural illusions. The principles of mechanics are undoubtedly natural beliefs; but, for all that, the early formulations of them were exceedingly erroneous. The general approximation to truth in natural beliefs is, in fact, a case of the general adaptation of genetic products to recognizable utilities or ends. Now, the adaptations of nature, beautiful and often marvelous as they verily are, are never found to be quite perfect; so that the argument is quite *against* the absolute exactitude of any natural belief, including that of the principle of causation.

Another argument, or convenient commonplace, is that absolute chance is *inconceivable*. (This word has eight current significations. The *Century Dictionary* enumerates six.) Those who talk like this will hardly be persuaded to say in what sense they mean that chance is inconceivable. Should they do so, it would easily be shown either that they have no sufficient reason for the statement or that the inconceivability is of a kind which does not prove that chance is non-existent.

Another *a priori* argument is that chance is unintelligible; that is to say, while it may perhaps be conceivable, it does not disclose to the eye of reason the how or why of things; and since a hypothesis can only be justified so far as it renders some phenomenon intelligible, we never can have any right to suppose absolute chance to enter into the production of anything in nature. This argument may be considered in connection with two others. Namely, instead of going so far as to say that the supposition of chance can *never* properly be used to explain any observed fact, it may be alleged merely that no facts are known which such a supposition could in any way help in explaining. Or again, the allegation being still further weakened, it may be said that since departures from law are not unmistakably observed, chance is not a *vera causa,* and ought not unnecessarily to be introduced into a hypothesis.

These are no mean arguments, and require us to examine the matter a little more closely. Come, my superior opponent, let me learn from your wisdom. It seems to me that every throw of sixes with a pair of dice is a manifest instance of chance.

"While you would hold a throw of deuce-ace to be brought about by necessity?" (The opponent's supposed remarks are placed in quotation marks.)

Clearly one throw is as much chance as another.

"Do you think throws of dice are of a different nature from other events?"

I see that I must say that *all* the diversity and specificalness of events is attributable to chance.

"Would you, then, deny that there is any regularity in the world?"

That is clearly undeniable. I must acknowledge there is an approximate regularity, and that every event is influenced by it. But the diversification, specificalness, and irregularity of things I suppose is chance. A throw of sixes appears to me a case in which this element is particularly obtrusive.

"If you reflect more deeply, you will come to see that *chance* is only a name for a cause that is unknown to us."

Do you mean that we have no idea whatever what kind of causes could bring about a throw of sixes?

"On the contrary, each die moves under the influence of precise mechanical laws."

But it appears to me that it is not these *laws* which made the die turn up sixes; for these laws act just the same when other throws come up. The chance lies in the diversity of throws; and this diversity cannot be due to laws which are immutable.

"The diversity is due to the diverse circumstances under which the laws act. The dice lie differently in the box, and the motion given to the box is different. These are the unknown causes which produce the throws, and to which we give the name of chance; not the mechanical law which regulates the operation of these causes. You see you are already beginning to think more clearly about this subject."

Does the operation of mechanical law not increase the diversity?

"Properly not. You must know that the instantaneous state of a system of particles is defined by six times as many numbers as there are particles, three for the co-ordinates of each particle's position, and three more for the components of its velocity. This number of numbers, which expresses the amount of diversity in the system, remains the same at all times. There may be, to be sure, some kind of relation between the co-ordinates and component velocities of the different particles, by means of which the state of the system might be expressed by a smaller number of numbers. But, if this is the case, a precisely corresponding relationship must exist between the co-ordinates and component velocities at any other time, though it may doubtless be a relation less obvious to us. Thus, the intrinsic complexity of the system is the same at all times."

Very well, my obliging opponent, we have now reached an issue. You think all the arbitrary specifications of the universe were introduced in one dose, in the beginning, if there was a beginning, and that the variety and complication of nature has always been just as much as it is now. But I, for my part, think that the diversification, the specification, has been continually taking place. Should you condescend to ask me why I so think, I should give my reasons as follows:

(1) Question any science which deals with the course of time. Consider the life of an individual animal or plant, or of a mind. Glance at the history of states, of institutions, of language, of ideas. Examine the successions of forms shown by paleontology, the history of the globe as set forth in geology, of what the astronomer is able to make out concerning the changes of stellar systems. Everywhere the main fact is growth and increasing complexity. Death and corruption are mere accidents or secondary phenomena. Among some of the lower organisms, it is a moot point with biologists whether there be anything which ought to be called death. Races, at any rate, do not die out except under unfavorable circumstances. From these broad and ubiquitous facts we may fairly infer, by the most unexceptionable logic, that there is probably in nature some agency by which the complexity and diversity of things can be increased; and that consequently the rule of mechanical necessity meets in some way with interference.

(2) By thus admitting pure spontaneity or life as a character of the universe, acting always and everywhere though restrained within narrow bounds by law, producing infinitesimal departures from law continually, and great ones with infinite infrequency, I account for all the variety and diversity of the universe, in the only sense in which the really *sui generis* and new can be said to be accounted for. The ordinary view has to admit the inexhaustible multitudinous variety of the world, has to admit that its mechanical law cannot account for this in the least, that variety can spring only from spontaneity, and yet denies without any evidence or reason the existence of this spontaneity, or else shoves it back to the beginning of time and supposes it dead ever since. The superior logic of my view appears to me not easily controverted.

(3) When I ask the necessitarian how he would explain the diversity and irregularity of the universe, he replies to me out of the treasury of his wisdom that irregularity is something which from the nature of things we must not seek to explain. Abashed at this, I seek to cover my confusion by asking how he would explain the uniformity and regularity of the universe, whereupon he tells me that the laws of nature are immutable and ultimate facts, and no account is to be given of them. But my hypothesis of spontaneity does explain irregularity, in a certain sense; that is, it explains the general fact of irregularity, though not, of course, what each lawless event is to be. At the same time, by thus loosening the bond of necessity, it gives room for the influence of another kind of causation, such as seems to be operative in the mind in the formation of associations, and enables us to understand how the uniformity of nature could have been brought about. That single events should be hard and unintelligible, logic will permit without difficulty: we do not expect to make the shock of a personally experienced earthquake appear natural and reasonable by any amount of cogitation. But logic does expect things *general* to be understandable. To say that there is a universal law, and that it is a hard, ultimate, unintelligible fact, the why and wherefore of which can never be inquired into, at this a sound logic will revolt; and will pass over at once to a method of philosophizing which does not thus barricade the road of discovery.

(4) Necessitarianism cannot logically stop short of making the whole action of the mind a part of the physical universe. Our notion that we decide what we are going to do, if as the

necessitarian says, it has been calculable since the earliest times, is reduced to illusion. Indeed, consciousness in general thus becomes a mere illusory aspect of a material system. What we call red, green, and violet are in reality only different rates of vibration. The sole reality is the distribution of qualities of matter in space and time. Brain-matter is protoplasm in a certain degree and kind of complication—a certain arrangement of mechanical particles. Its feeling is but an inward aspect, a phantom. For, from the positions and velocities of the particles at any one instant, and the knowledge of the immutable forces, the positions at all other times are calculable; so that the universe of space, time, and matter is a rounded system uninterfered with from elsewhere. But from the state of feeling at any instant, there is no reason to suppose the states of feeling at all other instants are thus exactly calculable; so that feeling is, as I said, a mere fragmentary and illusive aspect of the universe. This is the way, then, that necessitarianism has to make up its accounts. It enters consciousness under the head of sundries, as a forgotten trifle; its scheme of the universe would be more satisfactory if this little fact could be dropped out of sight. On the other hand, by supposing the rigid exactitude of causation to yield, I care not how little—be it but by a strictly infinitesimal amount—we gain room to insert mind into our scheme, and to put it into the place where it is needed, into the position which, as the sole self-intelligible thing, it is entitled to occupy, that of the fountain of existence; and in so doing we resolve the problem of the connection of soul and body.

(5) But I must leave undeveloped the chief of my reasons, and can only adumbrate it. The hypothesis of chance-spontaneity is one whose inevitable consequences are capable of being traced out with mathematical precision into considerable detail. Much of this I have done and find the consequences to agree with observed facts to an extent which seems to me remarkable. But the matter and methods of reasoning are novel, and I have no right to promise that other mathematicians shall find my deductions as satisfactory as I myself do, so that the strongest reason for my belief must for the present remain a private reason of my own, and cannot influence others. I mention it to explain my own position; and partly to indicate to future mathematical speculators a veritable gold mine, should time and circumstances and the abridger of all joys prevent my opening it to the world.

If now I, in my turn, inquire of the necessitarian why he prefers to suppose that all specification goes back to the beginning of things, he will answer me with one of those last three arguments which I left unanswered.

First, he may say that chance is a thing absolutely unintelligible, and, therefore, that we never can be entitled to make such a supposition. But does not this objection smack of naïve impudence? It is not mine, it is his own conception of the universe which leads abruptly up to hard, ultimate, inexplicable, immutable law, on the one hand, and to inexplicable specification and diversification of circumstances on the other. My view, on the contrary, hypothetizes nothing at all, unless it be hypothesis to say that all specification came about in some sense, and is not to be accepted as unaccountable. To undertake to account for anything by saying boldly that it is due to chance would, indeed, be futile. But this I do not do. I make use of chance chiefly to make room for a principle of generalization, or tendency to form habits, which I hold has produced all regularities. The mechanical philosopher leaves the whole specification of the world utterly unaccounted for, which is pretty nearly as bad as to boldly attribute it to chance. I attribute it altogether to chance, it is true, but to chance in the form of a spontaneity which is to some degree regular. It seems to me clear at any rate that one of these two positions must be taken, or else specification must be supposed due to a spontaneity which develops itself in a certain and not in a chance way, by an objective logic like that of Hegel. This last way I leave as an open possibility, for the present; for it is as much opposed to the necessitarian scheme of existence as my own theory is.

Secondly, the necessitarian may say there are, at any rate, no observed phenomena which the hypothesis of chance could aid in explaining. In reply, I point first to the phenomenon of growth and developing complexity, which appears to be universal, and which though it may possibly be an affair of mechanism perhaps, certainly presents all the appearance of increasing diversification. Then, there is variety itself, beyond comparison the most obtrusive character of the universe: no mechanism can account for this. Then, there is the very fact the necessitarian most insists upon, the regularity of the universe which for him serves only to block the road of inquiry. Then, there are the regular relationships between the laws of nature—similarities and comparative characters, which appeal to our intelligence as its cousins, and call upon us for a reason. Finally, there is consciousness, feeling, a patent fact enough, but a very inconvenient one to the mechanical philosopher.

Thirdly, the necessitarian may say that chance is not a *vera causa,* that we cannot know positively there is any such element in the universe. But the doctrine of the *vera causa* has nothing to do with elementary conceptions. Pushed to that extreme, it at once cuts off belief in the existence of a material universe; and without that necessitarianism could hardly maintain its ground. Besides, variety is a fact which must be admitted; and the theory of chance merely consists in supposing this diversification does not antedate all time. Moreover, the avoidance of hypotheses involving causes nowhere positively known to act—is only a recommendation of logic, not a positive command. It cannot be formulated in any precise terms without at once betraying its untenable character—I mean as rigid rule, for as a recommendation it is wholesome enough.

I believe I have thus subjected to fair examination all the important reasons for adhering to the theory of universal necessity, and have shown their nullity. I earnestly beg that whoever may detect any flaw in my reasoning will point it out to me, either privately or publicly; for if I am wrong, it much concerns me to be set right speedily. If my argument remains unrefuted, it will be time, I think, to doubt the absolute truth of the principle of universal law; and when once such a doubt has obtained a living root in any man's mind, my cause with him, I am persuaded, is gained.

Oliver Wendell Holmes, Jr.

1841-1935

Although as a young man in Boston Holmes had spent many pleasant evenings with William James and Charles S. Peirce, his expressed opinion of pragmatism was not complimentary. "I think pragmatism an amusing humbug," Holmes wrote to Pollock. James's books, he said, seemed to him "to belong on the side of art and belles lettres rather than to the opposite pole, philosophy." He did not think that James was strong "in logic or in that kind of abstract thinking that needs it." He felt his own philosophy to be closer to that of Santayana than of James or Royce.

Yet when James died in 1910, Holmes wrote that the event cut one of his roots "that went far into the past."

While Holmes himself may not have seen how close he was to James, others have had no difficulty in seeing in Holmes the application of pragmatic principles to legal thought and institutions. In his Lowell Institute lectures, later published as THE COMMON LAW *(1882), Holmes contended that "the life of the law has not been logic, it has been experience. The felt necessities of the time, the prevalent moral and political theories, intuitions of public policy, avowed or unconscious, even the prejudices which judges share with their fellow men, have a good deal more to do than the syllogism in determining the rules by which men shall be governed."*

As a justice of the United States Supreme Court (1902-1932) he often argued that the courts must not stand in the way of social experiments projected by legislative enactments of Congress or state legislatures; yet at the same time courts must be vigilant and quick to strike down, as unconstitutional, invasions of basic civil liberties—without which social and personal experimentation becomes impossible. With Dewey, Holmes stood for freedom of the quest for experience and the novel and against a quest for certainty and the unchanging. Just as James did not reject abstract ideas, concepts, so Holmes did not reject precedents—ideas, concepts, precedents could be useful as summaries of past events and experiences, and thus might be helpful as guides, as tools; but the emphasis must be on the fact that the "Constitution is an experiment, as all life is an experiment."

The Path of the Law •

When we study law we are not studying a mystery but a well-known profession. We are studying what we shall want in order to appear before judges, or to advise people in such a way as to keep them out of court. The reason why it is a profession, why people will pay lawyers to argue for them or to advise them, is that in societies like ours the command of the public force is intrusted to the judges in certain cases, and the whole power of the state will be put forth, if necessary, to carry out their judgments and decrees. People want to know under what circumstances and how far they will run the risk of coming against what is so much stronger than themselves, and hence it becomes a business to find out when this danger is to be feared. The object of our study, then, is prediction, the prediction of the incidence of the public force through the instrumentality of the courts.

• [From: Oliver Wendell Holmes, *Collected Legal Papers.* New York: Harcourt, Brace and Company; 1920. Pp. 167-202. Copyright 1920 by Harcourt, Brace and Company, Inc.; copyright renewed 1948 by Edward J. Holmes. Reprinted by permission of the publishers. This essay was originally an address delivered in 1897.]

The means of the study are a body of reports, of treatises, and of statutes, in this country and in England, extending back for six hundred years, and now increasing annually by hundreds. In these sibylline leaves are gathered the scattered prophecies of the past upon the cases in which the axe will fall. These are what properly have been called the oracles of the law. Far the most important and pretty nearly the whole meaning of every new effort of legal thought is to make these prophecies more precise, and to generalize them into a thoroughly connected system. The process is one, from a lawyer's statement of a case, eliminating as it does all the dramatic elements with which his client's story has clothed it, and retaining only the facts of legal import, up to the final analyses and abstract universals of theoretic jurisprudence. The reason why a lawyer does not mention that his client wore a white hat when he made a contract, while Mrs. Quickly would be sure to dwell upon it along with the parcel gilt goblet and the sea-coal fire, is that he foresees that the public force will act in the same way whatever his client had upon his head. It is to make the prophecies easier to be remembered and to be understood that the teachings of the decisions of the past are put into general propositions and gathered into text-books, or that statutes are passed in a general form. The primary rights and duties with which jurisprudence busies itself again are nothing but prophecies. One of the many evil effects of the confusion between legal and moral ideas, about which I shall have something to say in a moment, is that theory is apt to get the cart before the horse, and to consider the right or the duty as something existing apart from and independent of the consequences of its breach, to which certain sanctions are added afterward. But, as I shall try to show, a legal duty so called is nothing but a prediction that if a man does or omits certain things he will be made to suffer in this or that way by judgment of the court; and so of a legal right.

The number of predictions when generalized and reduced to a system is not unmanageably large. They present themselves as a finite body of dogma which may be mastered within a reasonable time. It is a great mistake to be frightened by the ever-increasing number of reports. The reports of a given jurisdiction in the course of a generation take up pretty much the whole body of the law, and restate it from the present point of view. We could reconstruct the corpus from them if all that went before were burned. The use of the earlier reports is mainly historical, a use about which I shall have something to say before I have finished.

I wish, if I can, to lay down some first principles for the study of this body of dogma or systematized prediction which we call the law, for men who want to use it as the instrument of their business to enable them to prophesy in their turn, and, as bearing upon the study, I wish to point out an ideal which as yet our law has not attained.

The first thing for a business-like understanding of the matter is to understand its limits, and therefore I think it desirable at once to point out and dispel a confusion between morality and law, which sometimes rises to the height of conscious theory, and more often and indeed constantly is making trouble in detail without reaching the point of consciousness. You can see very plainly that a bad man has as much reason as a good one for wishing to avoid an encounter with the public force, and therefore you can see the practical importance of the distinction between morality and law. A man who cares nothing for an ethical rule which is believed and practised by his neighbors is likely nevertheless to care a good deal to avoid being made to pay money, and will want to keep out of jail if he can.

I take it for granted that no hearer of mine will misinterpret what I have to say as the language of cynicism. The law is the witness and external deposit of our moral life. Its history is the history of the moral development of the race. The practice of it, in spite of popular jests, tends to make good citizens and good men. When I emphasize the difference between law and morals I do so with reference to a single end, that of learning and understanding the law. For that purpose you must definitely master its specific marks, and it is for that I ask you for the moment to imagine yourselves indifferent to other and greater things.

I do not say that there is not a wider point of view from which the distinction between law and morals becomes a secondary or no importance, as all mathematical distinctions vanish in presence of the infinite. But I do say that that distinction is of the first importance for the object which we are here to consider—a right study and mastery of the law as a business with well understood limits, a body of dogma enclosed within definite lines. I have just shown the practical reason for saying so. If you want to know the law and nothing else, you must look at it as a bad man, who cares only for the material consequences which such knowledge enables him to predict, not as a good one, who finds his reasons for conduct, whether inside the law or outside of it, in the vaguer sanctions of conscience. The theoretical importance of the distinction is no less, if you would reason on your subject aright. The law is full of phraseology drawn from morals, and by the mere force of language continually invites us to pass from one domain to the other without perceiving it, as we are sure to do unless we have the boundary constantly before our minds. The law talks about rights, and duties, and malice, and intent, and negligence, and so forth, and nothing is easier, or, I may say, more common in legal reasoning, than to take these words in their moral sense, at some stage of the argument, and so to drop into fallacy. For instance, when we speak of the rights of man in a moral sense, we mean to mark the limits of interference with individual freedom which we think are prescribed by conscience, or by our ideal, however reached. Yet it is certain that many laws have been enforced in the past, and it is likely that some are enforced now, which are condemned by the most enlightened opinion of the time, or which at all events pass the limit of interference as many consciences would draw it. Manifestly, therefore, nothing but confusion of thought can result from assuming that the rights of man in a moral sense are equally rights in the sense of the Constitution and the law. No doubt simple and extreme cases can be put of imaginable laws which the statute-making power would not dare to enact, even in the absence of written constitutional prohibitions, because the community would rise in rebellion and fight; and this gives some plausibility to the proposition that the law, if not a part of morality, is limited by it. But this limit of power is not coextensive with any system of morals. For the most part it falls far within the lines of any such system, and in some cases may extend beyond them, for reasons drawn from the habits of a particular people at a particular time. I once heard the late Professor Agassiz say that a German population would rise if you added two cents to the price of a glass of beer. A statute in such a case would be empty words, not because it was wrong, but because it could not be enforced. No one will deny that wrong statutes can be and are enforced, and we should not all agree as to which were the wrong ones.

The confusion with which I am dealing besets confessedly

legal conceptions. Take the fundamental question, What constitutes the law? You will find some text writers telling you that it is something different from what is decided by the courts of Massachusetts or England, that it is a system of reason, that it is a deduction from principles of ethics or admitted axioms or what not, which may or may not coincide with the decisions. But if we take the view of our friend the bad man we shall find that he does not care two straws for the axioms or deductions, but that he does want to know what the Massachusetts or English courts are likely to do in fact. I am much of his mind. The prophecies of what the courts will do in fact, and nothing more pretentious, are what I mean by the law.

Take again a notion which as popularly understood is the widest conception which the law contains—the notion of legal duty, to which already I have referred. We fill the word with all the content which we draw from morals. But what does it mean to a bad man? Mainly, and in the first place, a prophecy that if he does certain things he will be subjected to disagreeable consequences by way of imprisonment or compulsory payment of money. But from his point of view, what is the difference between being fined and being taxed a certain sum for doing a certain thing? That his point of view is the test of legal principles is shown by the many discussions which have arisen in the courts on the very question whether a given statutory liability is a penalty or a tax. On the answer to this question depends the decision whether conduct is legally wrong or right, and also whether a man is under compulsion or free. Leaving the criminal law on one side, what is the difference between the liability under the mill acts or statutes authorizing a taking by eminent domain and the liability for what we call a wrongful conversion of property where restoration is out of the question. In both cases the party taking another man's property has to pay its fair value as assessed by a jury, and no more. What significance is there in calling one taking right and another wrong from the point of view of the law? It does not matter, so far as the given consequence, the compulsory payment, is concerned, whether the act to which it is attached is described in terms of praise or in terms of blame, or whether the law purports to prohibit it or to allow it. If it matters at all, still speaking from the bad man's point of view, it must be because in one case and not in the other some further disadvantages, or at least some further consequences, are attached to the act by the law. The only other disadvantages thus attached to it which I ever have been able to think of are to be found in two somewhat insignificant legal doctrines, both of which might be abolished without disturbance. One is, that a contract to do a prohibited act is unlawful, and the other, that, if one of two or more joint wrongdoers has to pay all the damages, he cannot recover contribution from his fellows. And that I believe is all. You see how the vague circumference of the notion of duty shrinks and at the same time grows more precise when we wash it with cynical acid and expel everything except the object of our study, the operations of the law.

Nowhere is the confusion between legal and moral ideas more manifest than in the law of contract. Among other things, here again the so called primary rights and duties are invested with a mystic significance beyond what can be assigned and explained. The duty to keep a contract at common law means a prediction that you must pay damages if you do not keep it—and nothing else. If you commit a tort, you are liable to pay a compensatory sum. If you commit a contract, you are liable to pay a compensatory sum unless the promised event comes to pass, and that is all the difference. But such a mode of looking at the matter stinks in the nostrils of those who think it advantageous to get as much ethics into the law as they can. It was good enough for Lord Coke, however, and here, as in many other cases, I am content to abide with him. In Bromage v. Genning,• a prohibition was sought in the King's Bench against a suit in the marches of Wales for the specific performance of a covenant to grant a lease, and Coke said that it would subvert the intention of the covenantor, since he intends it to be at his election either to lose the damages or to make the lease. Sergeant Harris for the plaintiff confessed that he moved the matter against his conscience, and a prohibition was granted. This goes further than we should go now, but it shows what I venture to say has been the common law point of view from the beginning, although Mr. Harriman, in his very able little book upon Contracts has been misled, as I humbly think, to a different conclusion.

I have spoken only of the common law, because there are some cases in which a logical justification can be found for speaking of civil liabilities as imposing duties in an intelligible

• Roll. Rep. 368.

sense. These are the relatively few in which equity will grant an injunction, and will enforce it by putting the defendant in prison or otherwise punishing him unless he complies with the order of the court. But I hardly think it advisable to shape general theory from the exception, and I think it would be better to cease troubling ourselves about primary rights and sanctions altogether, than to describe our prophecies concerning the liabilities commonly imposed by the law in those inappropriate terms.

I mentioned, as other examples of the use by the law of words drawn from morals, malice, intent, and negligence. It is enough to take malice as it is used in the law of civil liability for wrongs—what we lawyers call the law of torts—to show that it means something different in law from what it means in morals, and also to show how the difference has been obscured by giving to principles which have little or nothing to do with each other the same name. Three hundred years ago a parson preached a sermon and told a story out of Fox's *Book of Martyrs* of a man who had assisted at the torture of one of the saints, and afterward died, suffering compensatory inward torment. It happened that Fox was wrong. The man was alive and chanced to hear the sermon, and thereupon he sued the parson. Chief Justice Wray instructed the jury that the defendant was not liable, because the story was told innocently, without malice. He took malice in the moral sense, as importing a malevolent motive. But nowadays no one doubts that a man may be liable, without any malevolent motive at all, for false statements manifestly calculated to inflict temporal damage. In stating the case in pleading, we still should call the defendant's conduct malicious; but, in my opinion at least, the word means nothing about motives, or even about the defendant's attitude toward the future, but only signifies that the tendency of his conduct under the known circumstances was very plainly to cause the plaintiff temporal harm.•

In the law of contract the use of moral phraseology has led to equal confusion, as I have shown in part already, but only in part. Morals deal with the actual internal state of the individual's mind, what he actually intends. From the time of the Romans down to now, this mode of dealing has affected the language of the law as to contract, and the language used has reacted upon the thought. We talk about a contract

• See Hanson v. Globe Newspaper Co., 159 Mass. 293, 302.

as a meeting of the minds of the parties, and thence it is inferred in various cases that there is no contract because their minds have not met; that is, because they have intended different things or because one party has not known of the assent of the other. Yet nothing is more certain than that parties may be bound by a contract to things which neither of them intended, and when one does not know of the other's assent. Suppose a contract is executed in due form and in writing to deliver a lecture, mentioning no time. One of the parties thinks that the promise will be construed to mean at once, within a week. The other thinks that it means when he is ready. The court says that it means within a reasonable time. The parties are bound by the contract as it is interpreted by the court, yet neither of them meant what the court declares that they have said. In my opinion no one will understand the true theory of contract or be able even to discuss some fundamental questions intelligently until he has understood that all contracts are formal, that the making of a contract depends not on the agreement of two minds in one intention, but on the agreement of two sets of external signs —not on the parties' having *meant* the same thing but on their having said the same thing. Furthermore, as the signs may be addressed to one sense or another—to sight or to hearing— on the nature of the sign will depend the moment when the contract is made. If the sign is tangible, for instance, a letter, the contract is made when the letter of acceptance is delivered. If it is necessary that the minds of the parties meet, there will be no contract until the acceptance can be read—none, for example, if the acceptance be snatched from the hand of the offerer by a third person.

This is not the time to work out a theory in detail, or to answer many obvious doubts and questions which are suggested by these general views. I know of none which are not easy to answer, but what I am trying to do now is only by a series of hints to throw some light on the narrow path of legal doctrine, and upon two pitfalls which, as it seems to me, lie perilously near to it. Of the first of these I have said enough. I hope that my illustrations have shown the danger, both to speculation and to practice, of confounding morality with law, and the trap which legal language lays for us on that side of our way. For my own part, I often doubt whether it would not be a gain if every word of moral significance could be banished from the law altogether, and other words adopted which should convey legal ideas uncolored by anything outside the law. We should lose the fossil records of a good deal of history and the majesty got from ethical associations, but by ridding ourselves of an unnecessary confusion we should gain very much in the clearness of our thought.

So much for the limits of the law. The next thing which I wish to consider is what are the forces which determine its content and its growth. You may assume, with Hobbes and Bentham and Austin, that all law emanates from the sovereign, even when the first human beings to enunciate it are the judges, or you may think that law is the voice of the Zeitgeist, or what you like. It is all one to my present purpose. Even if every decision required the sanction of an emperor with despotic power and a whimsical turn of mind, we should be interested none the less, still with a view to prediction, in discovering some order, some rational explanation, and some principle of growth for the rules which he laid down. In every system there are such explanations and principles to be found. It is with regard to them that a second fallacy comes in, which I think it important to expose. The fallacy to which I refer is the notion that the only force at work in the development of the law is logic. In the broadest sense, indeed, that notion would be true. The postulate on which we think about the universe is that there is a fixed quantitative relation between every phenomenon and its antecedents and consequents. If there is such a thing as a phenomenon without these fixed quantitative relations, it is a miracle. It is outside the law of cause and effect, and as such transcends our power of thought, or at least is something to or from which we cannot reason. The condition of our thinking about the universe is that it is capable of being thought about rationally, or, in other words, that every part of it is effect and cause in the same sense in which those parts are with which we are most familiar. So in the broadest sense it is true that the law is a logical development, like everything else. The danger of which I speak is not the admission that the principles governing other phenomena also govern the law, but the notion that a given system, ours, for instance, can be worked out like mathematics from some general axioms of conduct. This is the natural error of the schools, but it is not confined to them. I once heard a very eminent judge say that he never let a decision go until he was absolutely sure that it was right. So judicial dissent often is blamed, as if it meant simply that one side or the other were not doing their sums right, and, if they would take more trouble, agreement inevitably would come.

This mode of thinking is entirely natural. The training of lawyers is a training in logic. The processes of analogy, discrimination, and deduction are those in which they are most at home. The language of judicial decision is mainly the language of logic. And the logical method and form flatter that longing for certainty and for repose which is in every human mind. But certainty generally is illusion, and repose is not the destiny of man. Behind the logical form lies a judgment as to the relative worth and importance of competing legislative grounds, often an inarticulate and unconscious judgment, it is true, and yet the very root and nerve of the whole proceeding. You can give any conclusion a logical form. You always can imply a condition in a contract. But why do you imply it? It is because of some belief as to the practice of the community or of a class, or because of some attitude of yours upon a matter not capable of exact quantitative measurement, and therefore not capable of founding exact logical conclusions. Such matters really are battle grounds where the means do not exist for determinations that shall be good for all time, and where the decision can do no more than embody the preference of a given body in a given time and place. We do not realize how large a part of our law is open to reconsideration upon a slight change in the habit of the public mind. No concrete proposition is self evident, no matter how ready we may be to accept it, not even Mr. Herbert Spencer's "Every man has a right to do what he wills, provided he interferes not with a like right on the part of his neighbors."

Why is a false and injurious statement privileged, if it is made honestly in giving information about a servant? It is because it has been thought more important that information should be given freely, than that a man should be protected from what under other circumstances would be an actionable wrong. Why is a man at liberty to set up a business which he knows will ruin his neighbor? It is because the public good is supposed to be best subserved by free competition. Obviously such judgments of relative importance may vary in different times and places. Why does a judge instruct a jury that an employer is not liable to an employee for an injury received in the course of his employment unless he is negligent, and why do the jury generally find for the plaintiff if the case is allowed to go to them? It is because the traditional policy of our law is to confine liability to cases where a prudent man might have foreseen the injury, or at least the danger, while the inclination of a very large part of the community is to make certain classes of persons insure the safety of those with whom they deal. Since the last words were written, I have seen the requirement of such insurance put forth as part of the programme of one of the best known labor organizations. There is a concealed, half conscious battle on the question of legislative policy, and if any one thinks that it can be settled deductively, or once for all, I only can say that I think he is theoretically wrong, and that I am certain that his conclusion will not be accepted in practice *semper ubique et ab omnibus*.

Indeed, I think that even now our theory upon this matter is open to reconsideration, although I am not prepared to say how I should decide if a reconsideration were proposed. Our law of torts comes from the old days of isolated, ungeneralized wrongs, assaults, slanders, and the like, where the damages might be taken to lie where they fell by legal judgment. But the torts with which our courts are kept busy to-day are mainly the incidents of certain well known businesses. They are injuries to person or property by railroads, factories, and the like. The liability for them is estimated, and sooner or later goes into the price paid by the public. The public really pays the damages, and the question of liability, if pressed far enough, is really the question how far it is desirable that the public should insure the safety of those whose work it uses. It might be said that in such cases the chance of a jury finding for the defendant is merely a chance, once in a while rather arbitrarily interrupting the regular course of recovery, most likely in the case of an unusually conscientious plaintiff, and therefore better done away with. On the other hand, the economic value even of a life to the community can be estimated, and no recovery, it may be said, ought to go beyond that amount. It is conceivable that some day in certain cases we may find ourselves imitating, on a higher plane, the tariff for life and limb which we see in the *Leges Barbarorum*.

I think that the judges themselves have failed adequately to recognize their duty of weighing considerations of social advantage. The duty is inevitable, and the result of the often proclaimed judicial aversion to deal with such considerations is simply to leave the very ground and foundation of judgments inarticulate, and often unconscious, as I have said. When socialism first began to be talked about, the comfortable classes of the community were a good deal frightened. I suspect that this fear has influenced judicial action both here and in England, yet it is certain that it is not a conscious factor in the decisions to which I refer. I think that something similar has led people who no longer hope to control the legislatures to look to the courts as expounders of the Constitutions, and that in some courts new principles have been discovered outside the bodies of those instruments, which may be generalized into acceptance of the economic doctrines which prevailed about fifty years ago, and a wholesale prohibition of what a tribunal of lawyers does not think about right. I cannot but believe that if the training of lawyers led them habitually to consider more definitely and explicitly the social advantage on which the rule they lay down must be justified, they sometimes would hesitate where now they are confident, and see that really they were taking sides upon debatable and often burning questions.

So much for the fallacy of logical form. Now let us consider the present condition of the law as a subject for study, and the ideal toward which it tends. We still are far from the point of view which I desire to see reached. No one has reached it or can reach it as yet. We are only at the beginning of a philosophical reaction, and of a reconsideration of the worth of doctrines which for the most part still are taken for granted without any deliberate, conscious, and systematic questioning of their grounds. The development of our law has gone on for nearly a thousand years, like the development of a plant, each generation taking the inevitable next step, mind, like matter, simply obeying a law of spontaneous growth. It is perfectly natural and right that it should have been so. Imitation is a necessity of human nature, as has been illustrated by a remarkable French writer, M. Tarde, in an admirable book, *Les Lois de l'Imitation*. Most of the things we do, we do for no better reason than that our fathers have done them or that our neighbors do them, and the same is true of a larger part than we suspect of what we think. The reason is a good one, because our short life gives us no time for a better, but it is not the best. It does not follow, because we all are compelled to take on faith at second hand most of the rules on which we base our action and our thought, that each of us may not try to set some corner of his world in the order of reason, or that all of us collectively should not aspire to carry reason as far as it will go throughout the whole domain. In regard to the law, it is true, no doubt, that an evolutionist will hesitate to affirm universal validity for his social ideals, or for the principles which he thinks should be embodied in legislation. He is content if he can prove them best for here and now. He may be ready to admit that he knows nothing about an absolute best in the cosmos, and even that he knows next to nothing about a permanent best for men. Still it is true that a body of law is more rational and more civilized when every rule it contains is referred articulately and definitely to an end which it subserves, and when the grounds for desiring that end are stated or are ready to be stated in words.

At present, in very many cases, if we want to know why a rule of law has taken its particular shape, and more or less if we want to know why it exists at all, we go to tradition. We follow it into the Year Books, and perhaps beyond them to the customs of the Salian Franks, and somewhere in the past, in the German forests, in the needs of Norman kings, in the assumptions of a dominant class, in the absence of generalized ideas, we find out the practical motive for what now best is justified by the mere fact of its acceptance and that men are accustomed to it. The rational study of law is still to a large extent the study of history. History must be a part of the study, because without it we cannot know the precise scope of rules which it is our business to know. It is a part of the rational study, because it is the first step toward an enlightened scepticism, that is, towards a deliberate reconsideration of the worth of those rules. When you get the dragon out of his cave on to the plain and in the daylight, you can count his teeth and claws, and see just what is his strength. But to get him out is only the first step. The next is either to kill him, or to tame him and make him a useful animal. For the rational study of the law the black-letter man may be the man of the present, but the man of the future is the man of statistics and the master of economics. It is revolting to have no better reason for a rule of law than that so it was laid down in the time of Henry IV. It is still more revolting if the grounds upon which it was laid down have vanished long since, and the rule simply persists from blind imitation of the past. I am thinking of the technical rule as to trespass *ab initio,* as it is called, which I attempted to explain in a recent Massachusetts case.•

• Commonwealth v. Rubin, 165 Mass. 453.

Let me take an illustration, which can be stated in a few words, to show how the social end which is aimed at by a rule of law is obscured and only partially attained in consequence of the fact that the rule owes its form to a gradual historical development, instead of being reshaped as a whole, with conscious articulate reference to the end in view. We think it desirable to prevent one man's property being misappropriated by another, and so we make larceny a crime. The evil is the same whether the misappropriation is made by a man into whose hands the owner has put the property, or by one who wrongfully takes it away. But primitive law in its weakness did not get much beyond an effort to prevent violence, and very naturally made a wrongful taking, a trespass, part of its definition of the crime. In modern times the judges enlarged the definition a little by holding that, if the wrongdoer gets possession by a trick or device, the crime is committed. This really was giving up the requirement of a trespass, and it would have been more logical, as well as truer to the present object of the law, to abandon the requirement altogether. That, however, would have seemed too bold, and was left to statute. Statutes were passed making embezzlement a crime. But the force of tradition caused the crime of embezzlement to be regarded as so far distinct from larceny that to this day, in some jurisdictions at least, a slip corner is kept open for thieves to contend, if indicted for larceny, that they should have been indicted for embezzlement, and if indicted for embezzlement, that they should have been indicted for larceny, and to escape on that ground.

Far more fundamental questions still await a better answer than that we do as our fathers have done. What have we better than a blind guess to show that the criminal law in its present form does more good than harm? I do not stop to refer to the effect which it has had in degrading prisoners and in plunging them further into crime, or to the question whether fine and imprisonment do not fall more heavily on a criminal's wife and children than on himself. I have in mind more far-reaching questions. Does punishment deter? Do we deal with criminals on proper principles? A modern school of Continental criminalists plumes itself on the formula, first suggested, it is said, by Gall, that we must consider the criminal rather than the crime. The formula does not carry us very far, but the inquiries which have been started look toward an answer of my questions based on science for the first time. If the typical criminal is a degenerate, bound to swindle or to murder by as deep seated and organic necessity as that which makes the rattlesnake bite, it is idle to talk of deterring him by the classical method of imprisonment. He must be got rid of; he cannot be improved, or frightened out of his structural reaction. If, on the other hand, crime, like normal human conduct, is mainly a matter of imitation, punishment fairly may be expected to help to keep it out of fashion. The study of criminals has been thought by some well known men of science to sustain the former hypothesis. The statistics of the relative increase of crime in crowded places like large cities, where example has the greatest chance to work, and in less populated parts, where the contagion spreads more slowly, have been used with great force in favor of the latter view. But there is weighty authority for the belief that, however this may be, "not the nature of the crime, but the dangerousness of the criminal, constitutes the only reasonable legal criterion to guide the inevitable social reaction against the criminal." •

The impediments to rational generalization, which I illustrated from the law of larceny, are shown in the other branches of the law, as well as in that of crime. Take the law of tort or civil liability for damages apart from contract and the like. Is there any general theory of such liability, or are the cases in which it exists simply to be enumerated, and to be explained each on its special ground, as is easy to believe from the fact that the right of action for certain well known classes of wrongs like trespass or slander has its special history for each class? I think that there is a general theory to be discovered, although resting in tendency rather than established and accepted. I think that the law regards the infliction of temporal damage by a responsible person as actionable, if under the circumstances known to him the danger of his act is manifest according to common experience, or according to his own experience if it is more than common, except in cases where upon special grounds of policy the law refuses to protect the plaintiff or grants a privilege to the defendant.•• I think

• Havelock Ellis, *The Criminal,* 41, citing Garofalo. See also Ferri, *Sociologie Criminelle, passim.* Compare Tarde, *La Philosophie Pénale.*

•• An example of the law's refusing to protect the plaintiff is when he is interrupted by a stranger in the use of a valuable way, which he has travelled adversely for a week less than the period of prescription. A week later he will have gained a right, but now he is only a trespasser. Example of privilege I have given already. One of the best is competition in business.

that commonly malice, intent, and negligence mean only that the danger was manifest to a greater or less degree, under the circumstances known to the actor, although in some cases of privilege malice may mean an actual malevolent motive, and such a motive may take away a permission knowingly to inflict harm, which otherwise would be granted on this or that ground of dominant public good. But when I stated my view to a very eminent English judge the other day, he said: "You are discussing what the law ought to be; as the law is, you must show a right. A man is not liable for negligence unless he is subject to a duty." If our difference was more than a difference in words, or with regard to the proportion between the exceptions and the rule, then, in his opinion, liability for an act cannot be referred to the manifest tendency of the act to cause temporal damage in general as a sufficient explanation, but must be referred to the special nature of the damage, or must be derived from some special circumstances outside of the tendency of the act, for which no generalized explanation exists. I think that such a view is wrong, but it is familiar, and I dare say generally is accepted in England.

Everywhere the basis of principle is tradition, to such an extent that we even are in danger of making the role of history more important than it is. The other day Professor Ames wrote a learned article to show, among other things, that the common law did not recognize the defence of fraud in actions upon specialties, and the moral might seem to be that the personal character of that defence is due to its equitable origin. But if, as I have said, all contracts are formal, the difference is not merely historical, but theoretic, between defects of form which prevent a contract from being made, and mistaken motives which manifestly could not be considered in any system that we should call rational except against one who was privy to those motives. It is not confined to specialties, but is of universal application. I ought to add that I do not suppose that Mr. Ames would disagree with what I suggest.

However, if we consider the law of contract, we find it full of history. The distinctions between debt, covenant, and assumpsit are merely historical. The classification of certain obligations to pay money, imposed by the law irrespective of any bargain as quasi contracts, is merely historical. The doctrine of consideration is merely historical. The effect given to a seal is to be explained by history alone. Consideration is a mere form. Is it a useful form? If so, why should it not be required in all contracts? A seal is a mere form, and is vanishing in the scroll and in enactments that a consideration must be given, seal or no seal. Why should any merely historical distinction be allowed to affect the rights and obligations of business men?

Since I wrote this discourse I have come on a very good example of the way in which tradition not only overrides rational policy, but overrides it after first having been misunderstood and having been given a new and broader scope than it had when it had a meaning. It is the settled law of England that a material alteration of a written contract by a party avoids it as against him. The doctrine is contrary to the general tendency of the law. We do not tell a jury that if a man ever has lied in one particular he is to be presumed to lie in all. Even if a man has tried to defraud, it seems no sufficient reason for preventing him from proving the truth. Objections of like nature in general go to the weight, not to the admissibility, of evidence. Moreover, this rule is irrespective of fraud, and is not confined to evidence. It is not merely that you cannot use the writing, but that the contract is at an end. What does this mean? The existence of a written contract depends on the fact that the offerer and offeree have interchanged their written expressions, not on the continued existence of those expressions. But in the case of a bond, the primitive notion was different. The contract was inseparable from the parchment. If a stranger destroyed it, or tore off the seal, or altered it, the obligee could not recover, however free from fault, because the defendant's contract, that is, the actual tangible bond which he had sealed, could not be produced in the form in which it bound him. About a hundred years ago Lord Kenyon undertook to use his reason on this tradition, as he sometimes did to the detriment of the law, and, not understanding it, said he could see no reason why what was true of a bond should not be true of other contracts. His decision happened to be right, as it concerned a promissory note, where again the common law regarded the contract as inseparable from the paper on which it was written, but the reasoning was general, and soon was extended to other written contracts, and various absurd and unreal grounds of policy were invented to account for the enlarged rule.

I trust that no one will understand me to be speaking with disrespect of the law, because I criticise it so freely. I venerate the law, and especially our system of law, as one of the vastest products of the human mind. No one knows better than I do the countless number of great intellects that have spent themselves in making some addition or improvement, the greatest of which is trifling when compared with the mighty whole. It has the final title to respect that it exists, that it is not a Hegelian dream, but a part of the lives of men. But one may criticise even what one reveres. Law is the business to which my life is devoted, and I should show less than devotion if I did not do what in me lies to improve it, and, when I perceive what seems to me the ideal of its future, if I hesitated to point it out and to press toward it with all my heart.

Perhaps I have said enough to show the part which the study of history necessarily plays in the intelligent study of the law as it is to-day. In the teaching of this school and at Cambridge it is in no danger of being undervalued. Mr. Bigelow here and Mr. Ames and Mr. Thayer there have made important contributions which will not be forgotten, and in England the recent history of early English law by Sir Frederick Pollock and Mr. Maitland has lent the subject an almost deceptive charm. We must beware of the pitfall of antiquarianism, and must remember that for our purposes our only interest in the past is for the light it throws upon the present. I look forward to a time when the part played by history in the explanation of dogma shall be very small, and instead of ingenious research we shall spend our energy on a study of the ends sought to be attained and the reasons for desiring them. As a step toward that ideal it seems to me that every lawyer ought to seek an understanding of economics. The present divorce between the schools of political economy and law seems to me an evidence of how much progress in philosophical study still remains to be made. In the present state of political economy, indeed, we come again upon history on a larger scale, but there we are called on to consider and weigh the ends of legislation, the means of attaining them, and the cost. We learn that for everything we have we give up something else, and we are taught to set the advantage we gain against the other advantage we lose, and to know what we are doing when we elect.

There is another study which sometimes is undervalued by the practical minded, for which I wish to say a good word, although I think a good deal of pretty poor stuff goes under that name. I mean the study of what is called jurisprudence. Jurisprudence, as I look at it, is simply law in its most generalized part. Every effort to reduce a case to a rule is an effort of jurisprudence, although the name as used in English is confined to the broadest rules and most fundamental conceptions. One mark of a great lawyer is that he sees the application of the broadest rules. There is a story of a Vermont justice of the peace before whom a suit was brought by one farmer against another for breaking a churn. The justice took time to consider, and then said that he had looked through the statutes and could find nothing about churns, and gave judgment for the defendant. The same state of mind is shown in all our common digests and text-books. Applications of rudimentary rules of contract or tort are tucked away under the head of Railroads or Telegraphs or go to swell treatises on historical subdivisions, such as Shipping or Equity, or are gathered under an arbitrary title which is thought likely to appeal to the practical mind, such as Mercantile Law. If a man goes into law it pays to be a master of it, and to be a master of it means to look straight through all the dramatic incidents and to discern the true basis for prophecy. Therefore, it is well to have an accurate notion of what you mean by law, by a right, by a duty, by malice, intent, and negligence, by ownership, by possession, and so forth. I have in mind cases in which the highest courts seem to me to have floundered because they had no clear ideas on some of these themes. I have illustrated their importance already. If a further illustration is wished, it may be found by reading the Appendix to Sir James Stephen's *Criminal Law* on the subject of possession, and then turning to Pollock and Wright's enlightened book. Sir James Stephen is not the only writer whose attempts to analyze legal ideas have been confused by striving for a useless quintessence of all systems, instead of an accurate anatomy of one. The trouble with Austin was that he did not know enough English law. But still it is a practical advantage to master Austin, and his predecessors, Hobbes and Bentham, and his worthy successors, Holland and Pollock. Sir Frederick Pollock's recent little book is touched with the felicity which marks all his works, and is wholly free from the perverting influence of Roman models.

The advice of the elders to young men is very apt to be as unreal as a list of the hundred best books. At least in my day I had my share of such counsels, and high among the unrealities I place the recommendation to study the Roman law. I assume that such advice means more than collecting a few Latin maxims with which to ornament the discourse—the purpose for which Lord Coke recommended Bracton. If that is all that is wanted, the title *De Regulis Juris Antiqui* can be read in an hour. I assume that, if it is well to study the Roman Law, it is well to study it as a working system. That means mastering a set of technicalities more difficult and less understood than our own, and studying another course of history by which even more than our own the Roman law must be explained. If any one doubts me, let him read Keller's *Der Romische Civil Process und die Actionen,* a treatise on the praetor's edict, Muirhead's most interesting *Historical Introduction to the Private Law of Rome,* and, to give him the best chance, Sohm's admirable *Institutes.* No. The way to gain a liberal view of your subject is not to read something else, but to get to the bottom of the subject itself. The means of doing that are, in the first place, to follow the existing body of dogma into its highest generalizations by the help of jurisprudence; next, to discover from history how it has come to be what it is; and, finally, so far as you can, to consider the ends which the several rules seek to accomplish, the reasons why those ends are desired, what is given up to gain them, and whether they are worth the price.

We have too little theory in the law rather than too much, especially on this final branch of study. When I was speaking of history, I mentioned larceny as an example to show how the law suffered from not having embodied in a clear form a rule which will accomplish its manifest purpose. In that case the trouble was due to the survival of forms coming from a time when a more limited purpose was entertained. Let me now give an example to show the practical importance, for the decision of actual cases of understanding the reasons of the law, by taking an example from rules which, so far as I know, never have been explained or theorized about in any adequate way. I refer to statutes of limitation and the law of prescription. The end of such rules is obvious, but what is the justification for depriving a man of his rights, a pure evil as far as it goes, in consequence of the lapse of time? Sometimes the loss of evidence is referred to, but that is a secondary matter. Sometimes the desirability of peace, but why is peace more desirable after twenty years than before? It is increasingly likely to come without the aid of legislation. Sometimes it is said that, if a man neglects to enforce his rights, he cannot complain if, after a while, the law follows his example. Now if this is all that can be said about it, you probably will decide a case I am going to put, for the plaintiff; if you take the view which I shall suggest, you possibly will decide it for the defendant. A man is sued for trespass upon land, and justifies under a right of way. He proves that he has used the way openly and adversely for twenty years, but it turns out that the plaintiff had granted a license to a person whom he reasonably supposed to be the defendant's agent, although not so in fact, and therefore had assumed that the use of the way was permissive, in which case no right would be gained. Has the defendant gained a right or not? If his gaining it stands on the fault and neglect of the landowner in the ordinary sense, as seems commonly to be supposed, there has been no such neglect, and the right of way has not been acquired. But if I were the defendant's counsel, I should suggest that the foundation of the acquisition of rights by lapse of time is to be looked for in the position of the person who gains them, not in that of the loser. Sir Henry Maine has made it fashionable to connect the archaic notion of property with prescription. But the connection is further back than the first recorded history. It is in the nature of man's mind. A thing which you have enjoyed and used as your own for a long time, whether property or an opinion, takes root in your being and cannot be torn away without your resenting the act and trying to defend yourself, however you came by it. The law can ask no better justification than the deepest instincts of man. It is only by way of reply to the suggestion that you are disappointing the former owner, that you refer to his neglect having allowed the gradual dissociation between himself and what he claims, and the gradual association of it with another. If he knows that another is doing acts which on their face show that he is on the way toward establishing such an association, I should argue that in justice to that other he was bound at his peril to find out whether the other was acting under his permission, to see that he was warned, and if necessary, stopped.

I have been speaking about the study of the law, and I have said next to nothing of what commonly is talked about in that connection—text-books and the case system, and all the machinery with which a student comes most immediately in contact. Nor shall I say anything about them. Theory is my subject, not practical details. The modes of teaching have been improved since my time, no doubt, but ability and industry will master the raw material with any mode. Theory is the most important part of the dogma of the law, as the architect is the most important man who takes part in the building of a house. The most important improvements of the last twenty-five years are improvements in theory. It is not to be feared as unpractical, for, to the competent, it simply means going to the bottom of the subject. For the incompetent, it sometimes is true, as has been said, that an interest in general ideas means an absence of particular knowledge. I remember in army days reading of a youth who, being examined for the lowest grade and being asked a question about squadron drill, answered that he never had considered the evolutions of less than ten thousand men. But the weak and foolish must be left to their folly. The danger is that the able and practical minded should look with indifference or distrust upon ideas the connection of which with their business is remote. I heard a story, the other day, of a man who had a valet to whom he paid high wages, subject to deduction for faults. One of his deductions was, "For lack of imagination, five dollars." The lack is not confined to valets. The object of ambition, power, generally presents itself nowadays in the form of money alone. Money is the most immediate form, and is a proper object of desire. "The fortune," said Rachel, "is the measure of the intelligence." That is a good text to waken people out of a fool's paradise. But, as Hegel says,● "It is in the end not the appetite, but the opinion, which has to be satisfied." To an imagination of any scope the most far-reaching form of power is not money, it is the command of ideas. If you want great examples, read Mr. Leslie Stephen's *History of English Thought in the Eighteenth Century,* and see how a hundred years after his death the abstract speculations of Descartes had become a practical force controlling the conduct of men. Read the works of the great German jurists, and see how much more the world is governed to-day by Kant than by Bonaparte. We cannot all be Descartes or Kant, but we all want happiness. And happiness, I am sure from having known many successful men, cannot be won simply by being counsel for great corporations and having an income of fifty thousand dollars. An intellect great enough to win the prize needs other food besides success. The remoter and more general aspects of the law are those which give it universal interest. It is through them that you not only become a great master in your calling, but con-

● *Phil. des Rechts,* §190.

nect your subject with the universe and catch an echo of the infinite, a glimpse of its unfathomable process, a hint of the universal law.

"The Best
Test of
Truth . . ." •

This indictment is founded wholly upon the publication of two leaflets which I shall describe in a moment. The first count charges a conspiracy pending the war with Germany to publish abusive language about the form of government of the United States, laying the preparation and publishing of the first leaflet as overt acts. The second count charges a conspiracy pending the war to publish language intended to bring the form of government into contempt, laying the preparations and publishing of the two leaflets as overt acts. The third count alleges a conspiracy to encourage resistance to the United States in the same war and to attempt to effectuate the purpose by publishing the same leaflets. The fourth count lays a conspiracy to incite curtailment of production of things necessary to the prosecution of the war and to attempt to accomplish it by publishing the second leaflet to which I have referred.

The first of these leaflets says that the President's cowardly silence about the intervention in Russia reveals the hypocrisy of the plutocratic gang in Washington. It intimates that "German militarism combined with Allied capitalism to crush the Russian revolution," goes on that the tyrants of the world fight each other until they see a common enemy—working-class enlightenment—when they combine to crush it; and that now militarism and capitalism combined, though not openly, to crush the Russian revolution. It says that there is only one enemy of the workers of the world and that is capitalism; that it is a crime for workers of America, &c., to fight the workers' republic of Russia, and ends "Awake! Awake, you workers of the world!" Signed "Revolutionists." A note adds,

• [From: Dissenting opinion of Justice Holmes in Abrams v. United States, 250 U.S. 616 (1919).]

"It is absurd to call us pro-German. We hate and despise German militarism more than do you hypocritical tyrants. We have more reasons for denouncing German militarism than has the coward of the White House."

The other leaflet, headed "Workers—Wake up," with abusive language says that America together with the Allies will march for Russia to help the Czecho-Slovaks in their struggle against the Bolsheviki, and that this time the hypocrites shall not fool the Russian emigrants and friends of Russia in America. It tells the Russian emigrants that they now must spit in the face of false military propaganda by which their sympathy and help to the prosecution of the war have been called forth and says that with the money they have lent or are going to lend "they will make bullets not only for the Germans but also for the Workers' Soviets of Russia," and further, "Workers in the ammunition factories, you are producing bullets, bayonets, cannon, to murder not only the Germans but also your dearest, best, who are in Russia fighting for freedom." It then appeals to the same Russian emigrants at some length not to consent to the "inquisitionary expedition to Russia," and says that the destruction of the Russian revolution is "the politics of the march on Russia." The leaflet winds up by saying "Workers, our reply to this barbaric intervention has to be a general strike!" and after a few words on the spirit of revolution, exhortations not to be afraid, and some usual tall talk, ends "Woe unto those who will be in the way of progress. Let solidarity live! The Rebels."

No argument seems to me necessary to show that these pronunciamentos in no way attack the form of government of the United States, or that they do not support either of the first two counts. What little I have to say about the third count may be postponed until I have considered the fourth. With regard to that it seems too plain to be denied that the suggestion to workers in ammunition factories that they are producing bullets to murder their dearest, and the further advocacy of a general strike, both in the second leaflet, do urge curtailment of production of things necessary to the prosecution of the war within the meaning of the Act of May 16, 1918 . . . amending § 3 of the earlier Act of 1917. But to make the conduct criminal that statute requires that it should be "with intent by such curtailment to cripple or hinder the United States in the prosecution of the war." It seems to me that no such intent is proved.

I am aware of course that the word intent as vaguely used

in ordinary legal discussion means no more than knowledge at the time of the act that the consequences said to be intended will ensue. Even less than that will satisfy the general principle of civil and criminal liability. A man may have to pay damages, may be sent to prison, at common law might be hanged, if at the time of his act he knew facts from which common experience showed that the consequences would follow, whether he individually could foresee them or not. But, when words are used exactly, a deed is not done with intent to produce a consequence unless that consequence is the aim of the deed. It may be obvious, and obvious to the actor, that the consequence will follow, and he may be liable for it even if he forgets it, but he does not do the act with intent to produce it unless the aim to produce it is the proximate motive of the specific act, although there may be some deeper motive behind.

It seems to me that this statute must be taken to use its words in a strict and accurate sense. They would be absurd in any other. A patriot might think that we were wasting money on aeroplanes, or making more cannon of a certain kind than we needed, and might advocate curtailment with success, yet even if it turned out that the curtailment hindered and was thought by other minds to have been obviously likely to hinder the United States in the prosecution of the war, no one would hold such conduct a crime. I admit that my illustration does not answer all that might be said but it is enough to show what I think and to let me pass to a more important aspect of the case. I refer to the First Amendment to the Constitution that Congress shall make no law abridging the freedom of speech.

I never have seen any reason to doubt that the questions of law that alone were before this Court in the cases of *Schenck, Frohwerk* and *Debs,*• were rightly decided. I do not doubt for a moment that by the same reasoning that would justify punishing persuasion to murder, the United States constitutionally may punish speech that produces or is intended to produce a clear and imminent danger that it will bring about forthwith certain substantive evils that the United States constitutionally may seek to prevent. The power undoubtedly is greater in time of war than in time of peace because war opens dangers that do not exist at other times.

• [Schenck v. U.S., 249 U.S. 47 (1919); Frohwerk v. U.S., 249 U.S. 204 (1919); Debs v. U.S., 249 U.S. 211 (1919).]

But as against dangers peculiar to war, as against others, the principle of the right to free speech is always the same. It is only the present danger of immediate evil or an intent to bring it about that warrants Congress in setting a limit to the expression of opinion where private rights are not concerned. Congress certainly cannot forbid all effort to change the mind of the country. Now nobody can suppose that the surreptitious publishing of a silly leaflet by an unknown man, without more, would present any immediate danger that its opinions would hinder the success of the Government arms or have any appreciable tendency to do so. Publishing these opinions for the very purpose of obstructing, however, might indicate a greater danger and at any rate would have the quality of an attempt. So I assume that the second leaflet, if published for the purpose alleged in the fourth count, might be punishable. But it seems pretty clear to me that nothing less than that would bring these papers within the scope of this law.

An actual intent in the sense that I have explained is necessary to constitute an attempt, where a further act of the same individual is required to complete the substantive crime, for reasons given in *Swift & Co.* v. *United States,* 196 U.S. 375. It is necessary where the success of the attempt depends upon others, because if that intent is not present the actor's aim may be accomplished without bringing about the evils sought to be checked. An intent to prevent interference with the revolution in Russia might have been satisfied without any hindrance to carrying on the war in which we were engaged.

I do not see how anyone can find the intent required by the statute in any of the defendants' words. The second leaflet is the only one that affords even a foundation for the charge, and there, without invoking the hatred of German militarism expressed in the former one, it is evident from the beginning to the end that the only object of the paper is to help Russia and stop American intervention there against the popular government—not to impede the United States in the war that it was carrying on. To say that two phrases taken literally might import a suggestion of conduct that would have interference with the war as an indirect and probably undesired effect seems to me by no means enough to show an attempt to produce that effect.

I return for a moment to the third count. That charges an intent to provoke resistance to the United States in its war with Germany. Taking the clause in the statute that deals with that in connection with the other elaborate provisions of the Act, I think that resistance to the United States means some forcible act of opposition to some proceeding of the United States in pursuance of the war. I think the intent must be the specific intent that I have described and for the reasons that I have given. I think that no such intent was proved or existed in fact. I also think that there is no hint at resistance to the United States as I construe the phrase.

In this case sentences of twenty years' imprisonment have been imposed for the publishing of two leaflets that I believe the defendants had as much right to publish as the Government has to publish the Constitution of the United States now vainly invoked by them. Even if I am technically wrong and enough can be squeezed from these poor and puny anonymities to turn the color of legal litmus paper—I will add, even if what I think the necessary intent were shown—the most nominal punishment seems to me all that possibly could be inflicted, unless the defendants are to be made to suffer not for what the indictment alleges but for the creed that they avow —a creed that I believe to be the creed of ignorance and immaturity when honestly held, as I see no reason to doubt that it was held here, but which, although made the subject of examination at the trial, no one has a right even to consider in dealing with the charges before the Court.

Persecution for the expression of opinions seems to me perfectly logical. If you have no doubt of your premises or your power and want a certain result with all your heart you naturally express your wishes in law and sweep away all opposition. To allow opposition by speech seems to indicate that you think the speech impotent, as when a man says that he has squared the circle, or that you do not care wholeheartedly for the result, or that you doubt either your power or your premises.

But when men have realized that time has upset many fighting faiths, they may come to believe even more than they believe the very foundations of their own conduct that the ultimate good desired is better reached by free trade in ideas—that the best test of truth is the power of the thought to get itself accepted in the competition of the market, and that truth is the only ground upon which their wishes safely can be carried out. That, at any rate, is the theory of our Constitution. It is an experiment, as all life is an experiment. Every year if not every day we have to wager our salvation upon some prophecy based upon imperfect knowledge. While that experiment is part of our system I think that we should be eternally vigilant against attempts to check the expression of opinions that we loathe and believe to be fraught with death, unless they so imminently threaten immediate interference with the lawful and pressing purposes of the law that an immediate check is required to save the country.

I wholly disagree with the argument of the Government that the First Amendment left the common law as to seditious libel in force. History seems to me against the notion. I had conceived that the United States through many years had shown its repentance for the Sedition Act of 1798 by repaying fines that it imposed. Only the emergency that makes it immediately dangerous to leave the correction of evil counsels to time warrants making any exception to the sweeping command, "Congress shall make no law . . . abridging the freedom of speech." Of course I am speaking only of expressions of opinion and exhortations, which were all that were uttered here, but I regret that I cannot put into more impressive words my belief that in their conviction upon this indictment the defendants were deprived of their rights under the Constitution of the United States.

Words That Create *"A Clear and Present Danger"* •

Mr. Justice Brandeis and I are of opinion that this judgment should be reversed. The general principle of free speech, it seems to me, must be taken to be included in the Fourteenth Amendment, in view of the scope that has been given to the word "liberty" as there used, although perhaps it may be accepted with a somewhat larger latitude of interpretation than is allowed to Congress by the sweeping language that governs or ought to govern the laws of the United States.

If I am right, then I think that the criterion sanctioned by

• [From: Dissenting opinion of Justice Holmes in Gitlow v. New York, 268 U.S. 652 (1925).]

the full Court in *Schenck* v. *United States* [249 U.S. 47] applies. "The question in every case is whether the words used are used in such circumstances and are of such a nature as to create a clear and present danger that will bring about the substantive evils that [the State] has a right to prevent."

It is true that in my opinion this criterion was departed from in *Abrams* v. *United States* [250 U.S. 616], but the convictions that I expressed in that case are too deep for it to be possible for me as yet to believe that it and *Schaefer* v. *United States,* 251 U.S. 466, have settled the law. If what I think the correct test is applied, it is manifest that there was no present danger of an attempt to overthrow the Government by force on the part of the admittedly small minority who shared the defendant's views.

It is said that this manifesto is more than a theory, that it was an incitement. Every idea is an incitement. It offers itself for belief and if believed it is acted on unless some other belief outweighs it or some failure of energy stifles the movement at its birth. The only difference between the expression of an opinion and an incitement in the narrower sense is the speaker's enthusiasm for the result. Eloquence may set fire to reason. But whatever may be thought of the redundant discourse before us it had no chance of starting a present conflagration.

If in the long run the beliefs expressed in proletarian dictatorship are destined to be accepted by the dominant forces of the community, the only meaning of free speech is that they should be given their chance and have their way.

If the publication of this document had been laid as an attempt to induce an uprising against government at once and not at some indefinite time in the future, it would have presented a different question. The object would have been one with which the law might deal, subject to the doubt whether there was any danger that the publication could produce any result, or in other words, whether it was not futile and too remote from possible consequences. But the indictment alleges the publication and nothing more.

John Dewey

1859-1952

Dewey grew up during the post-Civil War decades in the New England town of Burlington, Vermont. He attended the state university, where in philosophy he was taught the prevalent Scotch realism. In 1882 he entered the recently founded Johns Hopkins University, to undertake that new thing in America, graduate study. Here Dewey was subjected to the two sets of antagonistic influences, scientific positivism and post-Kantian idealism.

During the ensuing period of about fifteen years, first at the University of Michigan and then at Chicago, he endeavored to incorporate the results of science within a neo-Hegelian framework. He was interested in a unified interpretation of human experience which would show in detail how human beings subsist within society and how society subsists within nature. As T. H. Green had stated the question, What is the relation between the "spiritual principle in knowledge" and the "spiritual principle in nature"? Dewey tried to bring them together by demonstrating that the first of these gradually produces the second. But to show how they are related in this way is to attempt to transform a THEORETICAL into a PRACTICAL idealism. And this means that the crucial issue is how *to make science an instrument for the realization of values. At this stage of his development Dewey, like Marx, was a "left-wing Hegelian." He would have subscribed, had he known of it, to Marx's dictum: "The philosophers have only 'interpreted' the world in various ways; the point, however, is to change it." But for Dewey, unlike Marx, the focal point at which to attack this problem of translating a theoretical into a practical idealism was an analysis of the moral act—since it is in terms of specifically human purposes that social institutions are transformed.*

While Dewey was reviewing the problems of ethics in the light of these considerations, James's PRINCIPLES OF PSYCHOLOGY *appeared. This book provided the reorientation of his thinking which he needed. In it he found the basis for his "instrumentalism": the fusion of an evolutionary conception of the function of intelligence with the Hegelian view (which he already held) that the workings of the mind are objectively expressed in social traditions and institutions. This is the matrix out of which Dewey's subsequent philosophy develops. In its origins, then, intelligence is inherently practical. One side of James's book was a brave beginning in the working out of a behavioral psychology. What would happen if the problems of logic and ethics were put into this naturalistic setting?*

Dewey had long realized that "the problem of restoring integration and cooperation between man's beliefs about the world in which he lives and his beliefs about the values and purposes that should direct his conduct is the deepest problem of modern life." And he believed that it is the philosopher's duty to do what HE *can to restore this integration. But he now saw more clearly than before that in making this attempt the philosopher is confronted by two basic tasks. One of these is to establish a relation between "common-sense objects" and "scientific objects" which will not relegate either to the realm of "appearances"; the other is to do away with the pathological segregation of "fact" and "value." These two problems are inseparable; both are results of the "bifurcation of nature." For if "scientific objects" alone are real and the objects of our ordinary experience mere appearances, then all that is valuable has become "subjective" and illusory. Science then will have nothing to say about values; it can merely tell us* HOW *things occur. Descriptive statements may be "true," but prescriptive statements will merely "evince" interests and desires.*

During a long and fruitful life, Dewey thoroughly and extensively developed the pragmatic method, applying it in a wide variety of fields—to the problems of logic, of the philosophy of science and of metaphysics, to ethics, the philosophy of education and social philosophy, to aesthetics, and to the philosophy of religion. Because Dewey always conceived of philosophy as dealing primarily with the problems generated by conflicts within one's own culture, it was he who made of "pragmatism" a comprehensive system of thought which is now identified by critics, sympathetic and hostile alike, as THE *philosophy of American civilization.*

Philosophy and Civilization •

Volumes have been written about each term of our theme. What *is* civilization? philosophy? Yet time passes, and ambiguities and complexities cannot be eliminated by definition; we can only circumvent them by begging questions. But as to one of the terms at least, namely, philosophy, we shall frankly make what is begged explicit. A statement of the relations of philosophy to civilization will, after all, only expound, in some indirect manner, the view of philosophy to which one is already committed. Unless this fact is faced, we shall not only beg the issue, but we shall deceive ourselves into thinking that we are setting forth the conclusions of an original inquiry, undertaken and executed independently of our own philosophical conceptions.

As for myself, then, the discussion is approached with the antecedent idea that philosophy, like politics, literature and the plastic arts, is itself a phenomenon of human culture. Its connection with social history, with civilization, is intrinsic. There is current among those who philosophize the conviction that, while past thinkers have reflected in their systems the conditions and perplexities of their own day, present-day

• [From: John Dewey, *Philosophy and Civilization*. New York: Minton, Balch and Co.; 1931. Pp. 3-12. Copyright 1931 by John Dewey; copyright renewed 1959 by Roberta L. Dewey. Reprinted by permission of G. P. Putnam's Sons.]

philosophy in general, and one's own philosophy in particular, is emancipated from the influence of that complex of institutions which forms culture. Bacon, Descartes, Kant each thought with fervor that he was founding philosophy anew because he was placing it securely upon an exclusive intellectual basis, exclusive, that is, of everything but intellect. The movement of time has revealed the illusion; it exhibits as the work of philosophy the old and ever new undertaking of adjusting that body of traditions which constitute the actual mind of man to scientific tendencies and political aspirations which are novel and incompatible with received authorities. Philosophers are parts of history, caught in its movement; creators perhaps in some measure of its future, but also assuredly creatures of its past.

Those who assert in the abstract definition of philosophy that it deals with eternal truth or reality, untouched by local time and place, are forced to admit that philosophy as a concrete existence is historical, having temporal passage and a diversity of local habitations. Open your histories of philosophy, and you find written throughout them the same periods of time and the same geographical distributions which provide the intellectual scheme of histories of politics, industry or the fine arts. I cannot imagine a history of philosophy which did not partition its material between the occident and the orient; which did not find the former falling into ancient, medieval and modern epochs; which, in setting forth Greek thought, did not specify Asiatic and Italian colonies and Athens. On the other hand, those who express contempt for the enterprise of philosophy as a sterile and monotonous preoccupation with unsolvable or unreal problems, cannot, without convicting themselves of Philistinism, deny that, however it may stand with philosophy as a revelation of eternal truths, it is tremendously significant as a revelation of the predicaments, protests and aspirations of humanity.

The two views of the history of thought are usually proffered as irreconcilable opposites. According to one, it is the record of the most profound dealings of the reason with ultimate being; according to the other, it is a scene of pretentious claims and ridiculous failures. Nevertheless, there is a point of view from which there is something common to the two notions, and this common denominator is more significant than the oppositions. Meaning is wider in scope as well as more precious in value than is truth, and philosophy is occupied with meaning rather than with truth. Making such a statement is dangerous; it is easily misconceived to signify that truth is of no great importance under any circumstances; while the fact is that truth is so infinitely important when it is important at all, namely, in records of events and descriptions of existences, that we extend its claims to regions where it has no jurisdiction. But even as respects truths, meaning is the wider category; truths are but one class of meanings, namely, those in which a claim to verifiability by their consequences is an intrinsic part of their meaning. Beyond this island of meanings which in their own nature are true or false lies the ocean of meanings to which truth and falsity are irrelevant. We do not inquire whether Greek civilization was true or false, but we are immensely concerned to penetrate its meaning. We may indeed ask for the truth of Shakespeare's *Hamlet* or Shelley's *Skylark*, but by truth we now signify something quite different from that of scientific statement and historical record.

In philosophy we are dealing with something comparable to the meaning of Athenian civilization or of a drama or a lyric. Significant history is lived in the imagination of man, and philosophy is a further excursion of the imagination into its own prior achievements. All that is distinctive of man, marking him off from the clay he walks upon or the potatoes he eats, occurs in his thought and emotions, in what we have agreed to call consciousness. Knowledge of the structure of sticks and stones, an enterprise in which, of course, truth is essential, apart from whatever added control it may yield, marks in the end but an enrichment of consciousness, of the area of meanings. Thus scientific thought itself is finally but a function of the imagination in enriching life with the significance of things; it is of its peculiar essence that it must also submit to certain tests of application and control. Were significance identical with existence, were values the same as events, idealism would be the only possible philosophy.

It is commonplace that physically and existentially man can but make a superficial and transient scratch upon the outermost rind of the world. It has become a cheap intellectual pastime to contrast the infinitesimal pettiness of man with the vastnesses of the stellar universes. Yet all such comparisons are illicit. We cannot compare existence and meaning; they are disparate. The characteristic life of man is itself the meaning of vast stretches of existences, and without it the latter have no value or significance. There is no common measure of physical existence and conscious experience because the latter is the only measure there is for the former. The significance of being, though not its existence, is the emotion it stirs, the thought it sustains.

It follows that there is no specifiable difference between philosophy and its role in the history of civilization. Discover and define the right characteristic and unique function in civilization, and you have defined philosophy itself. To try to define philosophy in any other way is to search for a will-of-the-wisp; the conceptions which result are of purely private interpretation, for they only exemplify the particular philosophies of their authorship and interpretation. Take the history of philosophy from whatever angle and in whatever cross-section you please, Indian, Chinese, Athenian, the Europe of the twelfth or the twentieth century, and you find a load of traditions proceeding from an immemorial past. You find certain preoccupying interests that appear hypnotic in their rigid hold upon imagination and you also find certain resistances, certain dawning rebellions, struggles to escape and to express some fresh value of life. The preoccupations may be political and artistic as in Athens; they may be economic and scientific as today. But in any case, there is a certain intellectual work to be done; the dominant interest working throughout the minds of masses of men has to be clarified, a result which can be accomplished only by selection, elimination, reduction and formulation; the interest has to be intellectually forced, exaggerated in order to be focused. Otherwise it is not intellectually in consciousness, since all clear consciousness by its very nature marks a wrenching of something from its subordinate place to confer upon it a centrality which is existentially absurd. Where there is sufficient depth and range of meanings for consciousness to arise at all, there is a function of adjustment, of reconciliation of the ruling interest of the period with preoccupations which had a different origin and an irrelevant meaning. Consider, for example, the uneasy, restless effort of Plato to adapt his new mathematical insights and his political aspirations to the traditional habits of Athens; the almost humorously complacent union of Christian supernaturalism in the middle ages with the naturalism of pagan Greece; the still fermenting effort of the recent age to unite the new science of nature with inherited classic and medieval institutions. The life of all thought is to effect a junction at some point of the new and the old, of deep-sunk customs and unconscious dispositions, that are brought to the light of attention by some conflict with newly emerging directions of activity. Philosophies which emerge at distinctive periods define the larger patterns of continuity which are woven in effecting the enduring junctions of a stubborn past and an insistent future.

Philosophy thus sustains the closest connection with the history of culture, with the succession of changes in civilization. It is fed by the streams of tradition, traced at critical moments to their sources in order that the current may receive a new direction; it is fertilized by the ferment of new inventions in industry, new explorations of the globe, new discoveries in science. But philosophy is not just a passive reflex of civilization that persists through changes, and that changes while persisting. It is itself a change; the patterns formed in this junction of the new and the old are prophecies rather than records; they are policies, attempts to forestall subsequent developments. The intellectual registrations which constitute a philosophy are generative just because they are selective and eliminative exaggerations. While purporting to say that such and such is and always *has* been the purport of the record of nature, in effect they proclaim that such and such *should* be the significant value to which mankind should loyally attach itself. Without evidence adduced in its behalf such a statement may seem groundless. But I invite you to examine for yourselves any philosophical idea which has had for any long period a significant career, and find therein your own evidence. Take, for example, the Platonic patterns of cosmic design and harmony; the Aristotelian perpetually recurrent ends and grooved potentialities; the Kantian fixed forms of intellectual synthesis; the conception of nature itself as it figured in seventeenth and eighteenth century thought. Discuss them as revelations of eternal truth, and something almost childlike or something beyond possibility of decision enters in; discuss them as selections from existing culture by means of which to articulate forces which the author believed should and would dominate the future, and they become preciously significant aspects of human history.

Thus philosophy marks a change of culture. In forming patterns to be conformed to in future thought and action, it is additive and transforming in its role in the history of civilization. Man states anything at his peril; once stated, it occupies a place in a new perspective; it attains a permanence which does not belong to its existence; it enters provokingly into wont and use; it points in a troubling way to need of new endeavors. I do not mean that the creative element in the role of philosophy is necessarily the dominant one; obviously its formulations have been often chiefly conservative, justificatory of selected elements of traditions and received institutions. But even these preservative systems have had a transforming if not exactly a creative effect; they have lent the factors which were selected a power over later human imagination and sentiment which they would otherwise have lacked. And there are other periods, such as those of the seventeenth and eighteenth centuries in Europe, when philosophy is overtly revolutionary in attitude. To their authors, the turn was just from complete error to complete truth; to later generations looking back, the alteration in strictly factual content does not compare with that in desire and direction of effort.

Of the many objections which may be brought against the conception that philosophy not only *has* a role, but that it *is* a specifiable role in the development of human culture, there are two misconceptions which I wish to touch upon. What has been said, taken without qualifying additions, might suggest a picture of a dominant system of philosophy at each historic period. In fact there are diverse currents and aspirations in almost every historic epoch; the divergence of philosophic systems instead of being a reproach (as of course it is from the standpoint of philosophy as a revelation of truth) is evidence of sincerity and vitality. If the ruling and the oppressed elements in a population, if those who wish to maintain the *status quo* and those concerned to make changes, had, when they became articulate, the same philosophy, one might well be skeptical of its intellectual integrity. The other point is much more important. In making a distinction between meaning and truth and asserting that the latter is but one type of meaning, important under definite conditions, I have expressed the idea as if there might be in the processes of human life meanings which are wholly cut off from the actual course of events. Such is not the intent; meanings are generated and in some degree sustained by existence. Hence they cannot be wholly irrelevant to the world of existence; they all have some revelatory office which should be apprehended as correctly as possible. This is true of politics, religion and art as well as of philosophy. They all tell something of the realm of existence. But in all of them there is an exuberance and fertility of meanings and values in comparison with which correctness of telling is a secondary affair, while in the function termed science accuracy of telling is the chief matter.

In the historic role of philosophy, the scientific factor, the element of correctness, of verifiable applicability, has a place, but it is a negative one. The meanings delivered by confirmed observation, experimentation and calculation, scientific facts and principles, serve as tests of the values which tradition transmits and of those which emotion suggests. Whatever is not compatible with them must be eliminated in any sincere philosophizing. This fact confers upon scientific knowledge an incalculably important office in philosophy. But the criterion is negative; the exclusion of the inconsistent is far from being identical with a positive test which demands that only what has been scientifically verifiable shall provide the entire content of philosophy. It is the difference between an imagination that acknowledges its responsibility to meet the logical demands of ascertained facts, and a complete abdication of all imagination in behalf of a prosy literalism.

Finally, it results from what has been said that the presence and absence of native born philosophies is a severe test of the depth of unconscious tradition and rooted institutions among any people, and of the productive force of their culture. For sake of brevity, I may be allowed to take our own case, the case of civilization in the United States. Philosophy, we have been saying, is a conversion of such culture as exists into consciousness, into an imagination which is logically coherent and is not incompatible with what is factually known. But this conversion is itself a further movement of civilization; it is not something performed upon the body of habits and tendencies from without, that is, miraculously. If American civilization does not eventuate in an imaginative formulation of itself, if it merely rearranges the figures already named and placed—in playing an inherited European game—that fact is itself the measure of the culture which we have achieved. A deliberate striving for an American Philosophy as such would be only another evidence of the same emptiness and impotency. There is energy and activity, among us, enough and to spare. Not an inconsiderable part of the vigor that once went into industrial accomplishment now finds its way into science; our scientific "plant" is coming in its way to rival our industrial plants. Especially in psychology and the social sciences an amount of effort is putting forth which is hardly equaled in any one other part of the world. He would be a shameless braggart who claimed that the result is as yet adequate to the activity. What is the matter? It lies, I think, with our lack of imagination in generating leading ideas. Because we are afraid of speculative ideas, we do, and do over and over again, an immense amount of dead, specialized work in the region of "facts." We forget that such facts are only data; that is, are only fragmentary, uncompleted meanings, and unless they are rounded out into complete ideas—a work which can only be done by hypotheses, by a free imagination of intellectual possibilities—they are as helpless as are all maimed things and as repellent as are needlessly thwarted ones.

Please do not imagine that this is a plea in disguise for any particular type of philosophizing. On the contrary, any philosophy which is a sincere outgrowth and expression of our own civilization is better than none, provided it speaks the authentic idiom of an enduring and dominating corporate experience. If we are really, for instance, a materialistic people, we are at least materialistic in a new fashion and on a new scale. I should welcome then a consistent materialistic philosophy, if only it were sufficiently bold. For in the degree in which, despite attendant esthetic repulsiveness, it marked the coming to consciousness of a group of ideas, it would formulate a coming to self-consciousness of our civilization. Thereby it would furnish ideas, supply an intellectual policy, direct further observations and experiments, and organize their results on a grand scale. As long as we worship science and are afraid of philosophy we shall have no great science; we shall have a lagging and halting continuation of what is thought and said elsewhere. As far as any plea is implicit in what has been said, it is, then, a plea for the casting off of that intellectual timidity which hampers the wings of imagination, a plea for speculative audacity, for more faith in ideas, sloughing off a cowardly reliance upon those partial ideas to which we are wont to give the name of facts. I have given to philosophy a more humble function than that which is often assigned it. But modesty as to its final place is not incompatible with boldness in the maintenance of that function, humble as it may be. A combination of such modesty and courage affords the only way I know of in which the philosopher can look his fellowman in the face with frankness and with humanity.

The Supremacy of Method *

Uncertainty is primarily a practical matter. It signifies uncertainty of the *issue* of present experiences; these are fraught with future peril as well as inherently objectionable. Action to get rid of the objectionable has no warrant of success and is itself perilous. The intrinsic troublesome and uncertain quality of situations lies in the fact that they hold outcomes in suspense; they move to evil or to good fortune. The natural tendency of man is to do something at once; there is impatience with suspense, and lust for immediate action. When action lacks means for control of external conditions, it takes the form of acts which are the prototypes of rite and cult. Intelligence signifies that direct action has become indirect. It continues to be overt, but it is directed into channels of examination of conditions, and doings that are tentative and preparatory. Instead of rushing to "do something about it," action centers upon finding out something about obstacles and resources and upon projecting inchoate later modes of definite response. Thinking has been well called deferred action. But not all action is deferred; only that which is final and in so far productive of irretrievable consequences. Deferred action is present exploratory action.

The first and most obvious effect of this change in the quality of action is that the dubious or problematic situation becomes *a* problem. The risky character that pervades a situation as a whole is translated into an object of inquiry that locates what the trouble is, and hence facilitates projection of methods and means of dealing with it. Only after expertness had been gained in special fields of inquiry does the mind set out at once from problems: even then in novel cases, there is a preliminary period of groping through a situation

* [From: John Dewey, *The Quest for Certainty*. New York: Minton, Balch and Co.; 1929. Pp. 223-8, 98-104, 234-44, 250-3. Copyright 1957 by Frederick A. Dewey. Reprinted by permission of G. P. Putnam's Sons.]

which is characterized throughout by confusion, instead of presenting a clear-cut problem for investigation.

Many definitions of mind and thinking have been given. I know of but one that goes to the heart of the matter—response to the doubtful as such. No inanimate thing reacts to things *as* problematic. Its behavior to other things is capable of description in terms of what is determinately there. Under given conditions, it just reacts or does not react. Its reactions merely enstate a new set of conditions, in which reactions continue without regard to the nature of their outcome. It makes no difference, so to say, to a stone what are the results of its interactions with other things. It enjoys the advantage that it makes no difference how it reacts, even if the effect is its own pulverization. It requires no argument to show that the case is different with a living organism. To live signifies that a connected continuity of acts is effected in which preceding ones prepare the conditions under which later ones occur. There is a chain of cause and effects, of course, in what happens with inanimate things. But for living creatures, the chain has a particular cumulative continuity, or else death ensues.

As organisms become more complex in structure and thus related to a more complex environment, the importance of a particular act in establishing conditions favorable to subsequent acts that sustain the continuity of the life process, becomes at once more difficult and more imperative. A juncture may be so critical that the right or wrong present move signifies life or death. Conditions of the environment become more ambivalent. It is more uncertain what sort of action they call for in the interests of living. Behavior is thus compelled to become more hesitant and wary, more expectant and preparatory. In the degree that responses take place to the doubtful *as* the doubtful, they acquire *mental* quality. If they are such as to have a directed tendency to change the precarious and problematic into the secure and resolved, they are *intellectual* as well as mental. Acts are then relatively more instrumental and less consummatory or final; even the latter are haunted by a sense of what may issue from them.

This conception of the mental brings to unity various modes of response; emotional, volitional and intellectual. It is usual to say that there is no fundamental difference among these activities—that they are all different phases or aspects of a common action of mind. But I know of but one way of making this assertion good: that in which they are seen to be distinctive modes of response to the uncertain. The emotional aspect of response behavior is its *immediate* quality. When we are confronted with the precarious, an ebb and flow of emotion marks a disturbance of the even tenor of existence. Emotions are conditioned by the indeterminateness of present situations with respect to their issue. Fear and hope, joy and sorrow, aversion and desire, as perturbations, are qualities of a divided response. They involve concern, solicitude, for what the present situation may *become.* "Care" signifies two quite different things: fret, worry and anxiety, and cherishing attention to that in whose potentialities we are interested. These two meanings represent different poles of reactive behavior to a present having a future which is ambiguous. Elation and depression, moreover, manifest themselves only under conditions wherein not everything from start to finish is completely determined and certain. They may occur at a final moment of triumph or defeat, but this moment is one of victory or frustration in connection with a previous course of affairs whose issue was in suspense. Love for a Being so perfect and complete that our regard for it can make no difference to it is not so much affection as (a fact which the scholastics saw) it is concern for the destiny of our own souls. Hate that is sheer antagonism without any element of uncertainty is not an emotion, but is an energy devoted to ruthless destruction. Aversion is a state of affectivity only in connection with an obstruction offered by the disliked object or person to an end made uncertain by it.

The volitional phase of mental life is notoriously connected with the emotional. The only difference is that the latter is the immediate, the cross-sectional, aspect of response to the uncertain and precarious, while the volitional phase is the tendency of the reaction to modify indeterminate, ambiguous conditions in the direction of a preferred and favored outcome; to actualize one of its possibilities rather than another. Emotion is a hindrance or an aid to resolute will according as it is overwhelming in its immediacy or as it marks a gathering together of energy to deal with the situation whose issue is in doubt. Desire, purpose, planning, choice, have no meaning save in conditions where something is at stake, and where action in one direction rather than another may eventuate in bringing into existence a new situation which fulfills a need.

The intellectual phase of mental action is identical with an *indirect* mode of response, one whose purpose is to locate the nature of the trouble and form an idea of how it may be dealt with—so that operations may be directed in view of an intended solution. Take any incident of experience you choose, seeing a color, reading a book, listening to conversation, manipulating apparatus, studying a lesson, and it has or has not intellectual, cognitive, quality according as there is de- liberative endeavor to deal with the indeterminate so as to dispose of it, to settle it. Anything that may be called knowl- edge, or a known object, marks a question answered, a diffi- culty disposed of, a confusion cleared up, an inconsistency reduced to coherence, a perplexity mastered. Without ref- erence to this mediating element, what is called knowledge is but direct and unswerving action or else a possessive enjoy- ment. Similarly, thinking is the actual transition from the problematic to the secure, as far as that is intentionally guided. There is no separate "mind" gifted in and of itself with a faculty of thought; such a conception of thought ends in postulating the mystery of a power outside of nature and yet able to intervene within it. Thinking is objectively discover- able as that mode of serial responsive behavior to a prob- lematic situation in which transition to the relatively settled and clear is effected.

The concrete pathologies of belief, its failures and per- versions, whether of defect or excess, spring from failure to observe and adhere to the principle that knowledge is the completed resolution of the inherently indeterminate or doubtful. The commonest fallacy is to suppose that since the state of doubt is accompanied by a feeling of uncertainty, knowledge arises when this feeling gives way to one of assur- ance. Thinking then ceases to be an effort to effect change in the objective situation and is replaced by various devices which generate a change in feeling or "consciousness." Tend- ency to premature judgment, jumping at conclusions, excessive love of simplicity, making over of evidence to suit desire, taking the familiar for the clear, etc., all spring from con- fusing the feeling of certitude with a certified situation. Thought hastens toward the settled and is only too likely to force the pace. The natural man dislikes the dis-ease which accompanies the doubtful and is ready to take almost any means to end it. Uncertainty is got rid of by fair means or foul. Long exposure to danger breeds an overpowering love of security. Love for security, translated into a desire not to be disturbed and unsettled, leads to dogmatism, to acceptance of beliefs upon authority, to intolerance and fanaticism on one side and to irresponsible dependence and sloth on the other.

Here is where ordinary thinking and thinking that is scrupulous diverge from each other. The natural man is impatient with doubt and suspense: he impatiently hurries to be shut of it. A disciplined mind takes delight in the problematic, and cherishes it until a way out is found that approves itself upon examination. The questionable becomes an active questioning, a search; desire for the emotion of certitude gives place to quest for the objects by which the obscure and unsettled may be developed into the stable and clear. The scientific attitude may almost be defined as that which is capable of enjoying the doubtful; scientific method is, in one aspect, a technique for making a productive use of doubt by converting it into operations of definite inquiry. . . .

Just what did the new experimental method do to the qualitative objects of ordinary experience? Forget the conclusions of Greek philosophy, put out of the mind all theories about knowledge and about reality. Take the simple direct facts: Here are the colored, resounding, fragrant, lovable, attractive, beautiful things of nature which we enjoy, and which we suffer when they are hateful, ugly, disgusting. Just what is the effect upon them wrought by physical science?

If we consent for the time being to denude the mind of philosophical and metaphysical presuppositions, and take the matter in the most simple and naïve way possible, I think our answer, stated in technical terms, will be that it *substitutes data for objects.* (It is not meant that this outcome is the whole effect of the experimental method; that as we saw at the outset is complex; but that the first effect as far as stripping away qualities is concerned is of this nature.) That Greek science operated with *objects* in the sense of the stars, rocks, trees, rain, warm and cold days of ordinary experience is evident enough. What is signified by saying that the first effect of experimentation was to reduce these things from the status of objects to that of data may not be so clear.• By data is signified subject-matter for *further* interpretation; something to be thought about. *Objects* are finalities; they are complete, finished; they call for thought only in the way of definition, classification, logical arrangement, subsumption in syllogisms,

• For this shift from objects to data see G. H. Mead's essay in the volume entitled *Creative Intelligence* (New York, 1917).

etc. But data signify "material to serve"; they are indications, evidence, signs, clues to and of something still to be reached; they are intermediate, not ultimate; means, not finalities.

In a less technical way the matter may be stated as follows: The subject-matter which had been taken as satisfying the demands of knowledge, as the material with which to frame solutions, became something which set *problems*. Hot and cold, wet and dry, light and heavy, instead of being self-evident matters with which to explain phenomena, were things to be investigated; they were "effects," not causal principles; they set question marks instead of supplying answers. The differences between the earth, the region of the planets, and the heavenly ether, instead of supplying ultimate principles which could be used to mark off and classify things, were something to be explained and to bring under identical principles. Greek and medieval science formed an art of accepting things as they are enjoyed and suffered. Modern experimental science is an art of control.

The remarkable difference between the attitude which accepts the objects of ordinary perception, use and enjoyment as final, as culminations of natural processes and that which takes them as starting points for reflection and investigation, is one which reaches far beyond the technicalities of science. It marks a revolution in the whole spirit of life, in the entire attitude taken toward whatever is found in existence. When the things which exist around us, which we touch, see, hear and taste are regarded as interrogations for which an answer must be sought (and must be sought by means of deliberate introduction of changes till they are reshaped into something different), nature as it already exists ceases to be something which must be accepted and submitted to, endured or enjoyed, just as it is. It is now something to be modified, to be intentionally controlled. It is material to act upon so as to transform it into new objects which better answer our needs. Nature as it exists at any particular time is a challenge, rather than a completion; it provides possible starting points and opportunities rather than final ends.

In short, there is a change from knowing as an esthetic enjoyment of the properties of nature regarded as a work of divine art, to knowing as a means of secular control—that is, a method of purposefully introducing changes which will alter the direction of the course of events. Nature as it exists at a given time is material for arts to be brought to bear upon it to reshape it, rather than already a finished work of art. Thus the changed attitude toward change to which reference was made has a much wider meaning than that which the new science offered as a technical pursuit. When correlations of changes are made the goal of knowledge, the fulfillment of its aim in discovery of these correlations, is equivalent to placing in our hands an instrument of control. When one change is given, and we know with measured accuracy its connection with another change, we have the potential means of producing or averting that other event. The esthetic attitude is of necessity directed to what is already there; to what is finished, complete. The attitude of control looks to the future, to production.

The same point is stated in another way in saying that the reduction of given objects to data for a knowing or an investigation still to be undertaken liberates man from subjection to the past. The scientific attitude, as an attitude of interest in change instead of interest in isolated and complete fixities, is necessarily alert for problems; every new question is an opportunity for further experimental inquiries—for effecting more directed change. There is nothing which a scientific mind would more regret than reaching a condition in which there were no more problems. That state would be the death of science, not its perfected life. We have only to contrast this disposition with that which prevails in morals and politics to realize the difference which has already been made, as well as to appreciate how limited its development still is. For in higher practical matters we still live in dread of change and of problems. Like men of olden time—with respect to natural phenomena—we prefer to accept and endure or to enjoy—as the case may happen to be—what is, what we find in possession of the field, and at most, to arrange it under concepts, and thus give it the form of rationality.

Before the rise of experimental method, change was simply an inevitable evil; the world of phenomenal existence, that is of change, while an inferior realm compared with the changeless, was nevertheless there and had to be accepted practically as it happened to occur. The wise man if he were sufficiently endowed by fortune would have as little to do with such things as possible, turning away from them to the rational realm. Qualitative forms and complete ends determined by nature are not amenable to human control. They are grateful when they happen to be enjoyed, but for human purposes nature means fortune, and fortune is the contrary of art. A good that happens is welcome. Goods, however, can be made secure in existence only through regulation of processes of change, a regulation dependent upon knowledge of their relations. While the abolition of fixed tendencies toward definite ends has been mourned by many as if it involved a despiritualization of nature, it is in fact a precondition of the projection of new ends and of the possibility of realizing them through intentional activity. Objects which are not fixed goals of nature and which have no inherent defining forms become candidates for receiving new qualities; means for serving new purposes. Until natural objects were denuded of determinate ends which were regarded as the proper outcome of the intrinsic tendency of nature's own operations, nature could not become a plastic material of human desires and purposes.

Such considerations as these are implicit in that changed attitude which by experimental analysis reduces objects to data: the aim of science becomes discovery of constant relations among changes in place of definition of objects immutable beyond the possibility of alteration. It is interested in the mechanism of occurrences instead of in final causes. In dealing with the proximate instead of with the ultimate, knowledge deals with the world in which we live, the world which is experienced, instead of attempting through the intellect to escape to a higher realm. Experimental knowledge is a mode of doing, and like all doing takes place at a time, in a place, and under specifiable conditions in connection with a definite problem.

The notion that the findings of science are a disclosure of the inherent properties of the ultimate real, of existence at large, is a survival of the older metaphysics. It is because of injection of an irrelevant philosophy into interpretation of the conclusions of science that the latter are thought to eliminate qualities and values from nature. Thus is created the standing problem of modern philosophy—the relation of science to the things we prize and love and which have authority in the direction of conduct. The same injection, in treating the results of mathematical-mechanistic science as a definition of natural reality in its own intrinsic nature, accounts for the antagonism shown to naturalism, and for the feeling that it is the business of philosophy to demonstrate the being of a realm beyond nature, one not subject to the conditions which mark all natural objects. Drop the conception that

knowledge is knowledge only when it is a disclosure and
definition of the properties of fixed and antecedent reality;
interpret the aim and test of knowing by what happens in the
actual procedures of scientific inquiry, and the supposed
need and problem vanish.

For scientific inquiry always starts from things of the environment experienced in our everyday life, with things we see,
handle, use, enjoy and suffer from. This is the ordinary qualitative world. But instead of accepting the qualities and values
—the ends and forms—of this world as providing the objects
of knowledge, subject to their being given a certain logical
arrangement, experimental inquiry treats them as offering a
challenge to thought. They are the materials of problems not
of solutions. They are *to be* known, rather than objects of
knowledge. The first step in knowing is to locate the problems
which need solution. This step is performed by altering obvious and given qualities. These are effects; they are things *to
be* understood, and they are understood in terms of their
generation. The search for "efficient causes" instead of for
final causes, for extrinsic relations instead of intrinsic forms,
constitutes the aim of science. But the search does not signify
a quest for reality in contrast with experience of the unreal
and phenomenal. It signifies a search for those relations upon
which the *occurrence* of real qualities and values depends, by
means of which we can regulate their occurrence. To call
existences as they are directly and qualitatively experienced
"phenomena" is not to assign to them a metaphysical status.
It is to indicate that they set the problem of ascertaining the
relations of interaction upon which their occurrence depends. . . .

We have seen that situations are precarious and perilous
because the persistence of life-activity depends upon the
influence which present acts have upon future acts. The continuity of a life-process is secured only as acts performed
render the environment favorable to subsequent organic acts.
The formal generalized statement of this fact is as follows:
The occurrence of problematic and unsettled situations is due
to the *characteristic union of the discrete or individual and
the continuous or relational.* All perceived objects are individualized. They are, as such, wholes complete in themselves. Everything directly experienced is qualitatively unique;
it has its own focus about which subject-matter is arranged,
and this focus never exactly recurs. While every such situa-

tion shades off indefinitely, or is not sharply marked off from others, yet the pattern of arrangement of content is never exactly twice alike.

If the interactions involved in having such an individualized situation in experience were wholly final or consummatory, there would be no such thing as a situation which is problematic. In being individual and complete in itself, just what it is and nothing else, it would be discrete in the sense in which discreteness signifies complete isolation. Obscurity, for example, would be a final quality, like any other quality and as good as any other—just as the dusk of twilight is enjoyed instead of being troublesome until we need to see something the dusk interferes with seeing. Every situation has vagueness attending it, as it shades off from a sharper focus into what is indefinite; for vagueness is added quality and not something objectionable except as it obstructs gaining an eventual object.

There are situations in which self-enclosed, discrete, individualized characters dominate. They constitute the subject-matter of esthetic experience; and every experience is esthetic in as far as it is final or arouses no search for some other experience. When this complete quality is conspicuous the experience is denominated esthetic. The fine arts have as their purpose the construction of objects of just such experiences; and under some conditions the completeness of the object enjoyed gives the experience a quality so intense that it is justly termed religious. Peace and harmony suffuse the entire universe gathered up into the situation having a particular focus and pattern. These qualities mark any experience in as far as its final character dominates; in so far a mystic experience is simply an accentuated intensification of a quality of experience repeatedly had in the rhythm of experiences.

Interactions, however, are not isolated. No experienced situation can retain indefinitely its character of finality, for the interrelations that constitute it are, because they are interactions, themselves changing. They produce a change in what is experienced. The effort to maintain directly a consummatory experience or to repeat it exactly is the source of unreal sentimentality and of insincerity. In the continuous ongoing of life, objects part with something of their final character and become conditions of subsequent experiences. There is regulation of the change in the degree in which a causal character is rendered preparatory and instrumental.

In other words, all experienced objects have a double status. They are individualized, consummatory, whether in the way of enjoyment or of suffering. They are also involved in a continuity of interactions and changes, and hence are causes and potential means of later experiences. Because of this dual capacity, they become problematic. Immediately and directly they are just what they are; but as transitions to and possibilities of later experiences they are uncertain. There is a divided response; part of the organic activity is directed to them for what they immediately are, and part to them as transitive means of other experienced objects. We react to them both as finalities and in preparatory ways, and the two reactions do not harmonize.

This two-fold character of experienced objects is the source of their problematic character. Each of us can recall many occasions when he has been perplexed by disagreement between things directly present and their potential value as signs and means; when he has been torn between absorption in what is now enjoyed and the need of altering it so as to prepare for something likely to come. If we state the point in a formal way, it is signified that there is an incompatibility between the traits of an object in its direct individual and unique nature and those traits that belong to it in its relations or continuities. This incompatibility can be removed only by actions which temporarily reconstruct what is given and constitute a new object having both individuality and the internal coherence of continuity in a series.

Previous discussion has been a statement of the chief factors that operate in bringing about this reconstruction—of resolving a problematic situation: Acts of analytic reduction of the gross total situation to determine data—qualities that locate the nature of the problem; formation of ideas or hypotheses to direct further operations that reveal new material; deductions and calculations that organize the new and old subject-matter together; operations that finally determine the existence of a new integrated situation with added meaning, and in so doing test or prove the ideas that have been employed.

Without retraversing that discussion, I wish to add a few words on one point involved in it. Nothing is more familiar than the standardized objects of reference designated by common nouns. Their distinction from proper names shows that they are not singular or individual, not existing things. Yet "*the* table" is both more familiar and seemingly more substantial than *this* table, the individual. "This" undergoes change all the time. It is interacting with other things and with me, who are not exactly the same person as when I last wrote upon it. "This" is an indefinitely multiple and varied series of "thises."

But save in extreme cases, these changes are indifferent, negligible, from the standpoint of means for consequences. *The* table is precisely the constancy among the serial "thises" of whatever serves as an instrument for a single end. *Knowledge* is concerned wholly with this constant, this standardized and averaged set of properties and relations—just as esthetic perception is occupied with "this" in its individuality, irrespective of value in use. In the degree in which reactions are inchoate and unformed, "this" tends to be the buzzing, blooming confusion of which James wrote. As habits form, action is stereotyped into a fairly constant series of acts having a common end in view; *the* table serves a single use, in spite of individual variations. A group of properties is set aside, corresponding to the abiding end and single mode of use which form *the* object, in distinction from "this" of unique experiences. *The* object is an abstraction, but unless it is hypostatized it is not a vicious abstraction. It designates selected relations of things which, with respect to their mode of operation, are constant within the limits practically important. Moreover, the abstracted object has a consequence *in* the individualized experiences, one that is immediate and not merely instrumental to them. It marks an ordering and organizing of responses in a single focused way in virtue of which the original blur is definitized and rendered significant. Without habits dealing with recurrent and constant uses of things for abiding purposes, immediate esthetic perception would have neither rich nor clear meanings immanent within it.

The scientific or physical object marks an extension of the same sort of operation. *The* table, as *not* a table but as a swarm of molecules in motions of specified velocities and accelerations, corresponds to a liberated generalization of the purposes which *the* object may serve. "Table" signifies a definite but restricted set of uses; stated in the physical terms of science it is thought of in a wider environment and free from any specified set of uses; out of relation to any particular individualized experience. The abstraction is as legitimate as is that which gives rise to the idea of *the* table, for it consists of standardized relations or interactions. It is even more useful or more widely instrumental. For it has connection with an indefinite variety of unspecified but possible consummatory individual observations and enjoyments. It waits like a servant, idle for a time, but ready to be called upon as special occasion arises. When this standardized constant, the result of series of operations and expressing an indefinite multitude of possible relations among concrete things, is treated as the reality of nature, an instrument made for a purpose is hypostatized into a substance complete and self-sufficient in isolation. Then the fullness of qualities present in individual situations have to be treated as subjective impressions mysteriously produced in mind by the real object or else as products of a mysterious creative faculty of consciousness.

The bearing of the conclusion upon the qualitative values of experienced objects is evident. Interactions of things with the organism eventuate in objects perceived to be colored and sonorous. They also result in qualities that make the object hateful or delightful. All these qualities, taken as directly perceived or enjoyed, are terminal effects of natural interactions. They are individualized culminations that give static quality to a network of changes. Thus "tertiary" qualities (as they have been happily termed by Mr. Santayana), those which, in psychological analysis, we call affectional and emotional, are as much products of the doings of nature as are color, sound, pressure, perceived size and distance. But their very consummatory quality stands in the way of using the things they qualify as signs of other things. Intellectually they are even more in the way than are "secondary" qualities. With respect to preparatory acts they are useless; when they are treated as signs and means they work injury to thought and discovery. When not experienced, they are projected in thought as ends to be reached and in that dependence upon thought they are felt to be peculiarly mental. But only if *the* object, the physical object, instrumental in character, is supposed to define "the real" in an exhaustive way, do they cease to be for the philosopher what they are for the common man—real qualities of natural objects. This view forms the only complete and unadulterated realism.

The problem which is supposed to exist between two tables, one that of direct perception and use and the other that of physics (to take the favorite illustration of recent discussion) is thus illusory. The perceived and used table is the only table, for it alone has both individuality of form—without which nothing can exist or be perceived, and also includes within itself a continuum of relations or interactions brought to a focus. We may perhaps employ more instructively an illustration derived from the supposed contrast between an object experienced in perception as it is rendered by a poet and the same object described by a physicist. There is the instance of a body of water where the movement of the wind over its surface is reflected in sunlight. As an object of science, it is reported as follows: "Etherial vibrations of various wave lengths, reflected at different angles from the disturbed interface between air and water, reached our eyes and by photoelectric action caused appropriate stimuli to travel along optic nerves to a brain center." Such a statement, however, includes ordinary objects of individual perceptions; water, air, brain and nerves. Consequently, it must be reduced still further; when so reduced it consists of mathematical functions between certain physical constants having no counterpart in ordinary perception.•

It is worth while at this point to recur to the metric character of the physical object. Defining metric traits are reached by a series of operations of which they express the statistically constant outcome; they are not the result of a single act. Hence the physical object cannot be taken to be a single or individual thing in existence. Metric definitions are also, in large measure, reached by indirect measurements, by calculation. In other words, the conception of the physical object is, in considerable degree, the outcome of complex operations of comparison and translation. In consequence, while the physical object is *not* any one of the things compared, it enables things qualitatively unlike and individual to be treated as if they were members of a comprehensive, homogeneous, or non-qualitative system. The possibility of control of the *occurrence* of individualized objects is thereby increased. At the same time, the latter gain added meaning, for the import of the scheme of continuity of relationships with other things is in-

• The illustration is borrowed from Eddington, *The Nature of the Physical World;* see pp. 316-19. It is indicative of the hold which the older tradition of knowledge as the exclusive revelation of reality has obtained, that Eddington finds no way to combine this account with the poetic account, save to suppose that while the scientific statement describes reality as it is "in itself," the creative activity of mind adds to this skeleton the qualities characterizing an object in direct experience.

corporated within them. The procedure of physics itself, not any metaphysical or epistemological theory, discloses that physical objects cannot be individual existential objects. In consequence, it is absurd to put them in opposition to the qualitatively individual objects of concrete experience.

The vogue of the philosophy that identifies the object of knowledge as such with the reality of the subject-matter of experience makes it advisable to carry the discussion further. Physical science submits the things of ordinary experience to specifiable operations. The result are objects of thought stated in numbers, where the numbers in question permit inclusion within complex systems of equations and other mathematical functions. In the physical object everything is ignored but the relations expressed by these numbers. It is safe to assert that no physicist *while at work* ever thought of denying the full reality of the things of ordinary, coarse experience. He pays no attention to their qualities except as they are signs of operations to be performed and of inference to relations to be drawn. But in these capacities he has to admit their full reality on pain of having, logically, to deny reality to the conclusions of his operative inferences. He takes the instruments he employs, including his own sensory-motor organs and measuring instruments, to be real in the ordinary sense of the word. If he denied the reality of these things as they are had in ordinary non-cognitive perceptual experience, the conclusions reached by them would be equally discredited. Moreover, the numbers which define his metric object are themselves results of noting interactions or connections among perceived things. It would be the height of absurdity to assert the reality of these relations while denying the reality of the things between which they hold. If the latter are "subjective" what becomes of the former? Finally, observation is resorted to for verification. It is a strange world in which the conception of the real has to be corroborated by reference to that the reality of which is made dubious by the conception. To common sense these comments may seem wholly superfluous. But since common sense may also hold the doctrine from which flow the conclusions to which the critical comments are apposite, common sense should first ask whether it holds that knowledge is a disclosure of the antecedently real? If it entertains this belief, then the dismissal by science of the experienced object to a limbo of unreality, or subjectivity or the phenomenal—whatever terms be used—results logically from his own position.

Our discussion involves a summary as well as some repetition of points previously made. Its significance lies in the liberation which comes when knowing, in all its phases, conditions and organs, is understood after the pattern provided by experimental inquiry, instead of upon the groundwork of ideas framed before such knowing had a systematic career opened to it. For according to the pattern set by the practice of knowing, knowledge is the fruit of the undertakings that transform a problematic situation into a resolved one. Its procedure is public, a part and partner of the Nature in which all interactions exist. But experienced situations come about in two ways and are of two distinct types. Some take place with only a minimum of regulation, with little foresight, preparation and intent. Others occur because, in part, of the prior occurrence of intelligent action. Both kinds are *had;* they are undergone, enjoyed or suffered. The first are not known; they are not understood; they are dispensations of fortune or providence. The second have, as they are experienced, meanings that present the funded outcome of operations that substitute definite continuity for experienced discontinuity and for the fragmentary quality due to isolation. Dream, insanity and fantasy are natural products, as "real" as anything else in the world. The acts of intentional regulation which constitute thinking are also natural developments, and so are the experienced things in which they eventuate. But the latter are resolutions of the problems set by objects experienced without intent and purpose; hence they have a security and fullness of meaning the first lack. Nothing happens, as Aristotle and the scholastics said, without an end—without a terminal effectuation. *Every* experienced object is, in some sense, such a closing and consummatory closing episode: alike the doubtful and secure, the trivial and significant, the true and mistaken, the confused and ordered. Only when the ends are closing termini of *intelligent operations* of thinking are they ends in the honorific sense. We always experience individual objects, but only the individual things which are fruits of intelligent action have in them intrinsic order and fullness of qualities.

The conditions and processes of nature generate uncertainty and its risks as truly as nature affords security and means of insurance against perils. Nature is characterized by a constant mixture of the precarious and the stable. This mixture gives poignancy to existence. If existence were either completely necessary or completely contingent, there would be neither comedy nor tragedy in life, nor need of the will to live. The significance of morals and politics, of the arts both technical and fine, of religion and of science itself as inquiry and discovery, all have their source and meaning in the union in Nature of the settled and the unsettled, the stable and the hazardous. Apart from this union, there are no such things as "ends," either as consummations or as those ends-in-view we call purposes. There is only a block universe, either something ended and admitting of no change, or else a predestined march of events. There is no such thing as fulfillment where there is no risk of failure, and no defeat where there is no promise of possible achievement. . . .

Physical inquiry has been taken as typical of the nature of knowing. The selection is justified because the operations of physical knowledge are so perfected and its scheme of symbols so well devised. But it would be misinterpreted if it were taken to mean that science is the only valid kind of knowledge; it is just an intensified form of knowing in which are written large the essential characters of any knowing. It is in addition the most powerful tool we possess for developing other modes of knowledge. But we know with respect to any subject-matter whatsoever in the degree in which we are able deliberately to transform doubtful situations into resolved ones. Physical knowledge has the advantage of its specialized character, its whole-hearted devotion to a single purpose. The attitude involved in it, its method, has not as yet gone far beyond its own precincts. Beliefs current in morals, politics and religion, are marked by dread of change and by the feeling that order and regulative authority can be had only through reference to fixed standards accepted as finalities, because referring to fixed antecedent realities. Outside of physical inquiry, we shy from problems; we dislike uncovering serious difficulties in their full depth and reach; we prefer to accept what is and muddle along. Hence our social and moral "sciences" consist largely in putting facts as they are into conceptual systems framed at large. Our logic in social and humane subjects is still largely that of definition and classification as until the seventeenth century it was in natural science. For the most part the lesson of experimental inquiry has still to be learned in the things of chief concern.

We are, socially, in a condition of division and confusion because our best authenticated knowledge is obtained by directed practice, while this method is still limited to things aloof from man or concerning him only in the technologies of industries. The rest of our practice in matters that come home to us most closely and deeply is regulated not by intelligent operation, but by tradition, self-interest and accidental circumstance. The most significant phase of physical science, that which concerns its method, is unapplied in social practice, while its technical results are utilized by those in positions of privileged advantage to serve their own private or class ends. Of the many consequences that result, the state of education is perhaps the most significant. As the means of the general institution of intelligent action, it holds the key to orderly social reconstruction. But inculcation of fixed conclusions rather than development of intelligence as a method of action still dominates its processes. Devotion to training in technical and mechanical skills on one hand and to laying in a store of abstract information on the other is to one who has the power to read the scene an almost perfect illustration of the significance of the historic separation of knowledge and action, theory and practice. As long as the isolation of knowledge and practice holds sway, this division of aims and dissipation of energy, of which the state of education is typical, will persist. The effective condition of the integration of all divided purposes and conflicts of belief is the realization that intelligent action is the sole ultimate resource of mankind in every field whatsoever.

It is not claimed, therefore, that there is *no* philosophical problem of the relation of physical science to the things of ordinary experience. It is asserted that the problem *in the form* in which it has chiefly occupied modern philosophy is an artificial one, due to the continued assumption of premises formed in an earlier period of history and now having no relevancy to the state of physical inquiry. Clearing the ground of this unreal problem, however, only imposes upon philosophy the consideration of a problem which is urgently practical, growing out of the conditions of contemporary life. What revisions and surrenders of current beliefs about authoritative ends and values are demanded by the method and conclusions of natural science? What possibilities of controlled transformation of the content of present belief and practice in human institutions and associations are indicated by the control of natural energies which natural science has effected? These questions are as genuine and imperative as the traditional problem is artificial and futile.

The Construction of Good •

We saw at the outset of our discussion that insecurity generates the quest for certainty. Consequences issue from every experience, and they are the source of our interest in what is present. Absence of arts of regulation diverted the search for security into irrelevant modes of practice, into rite and cult; thought was devoted to discovery of omens rather than of signs of what is to occur. Gradually there was differentiation of two realms, one higher, consisting of the powers which determine human destiny in all important affairs. With this religion was concerned. The other consisted of the prosaic matters in which man relied upon his own skill and his matter-of-fact insight. Philosophy inherited the idea of this division. Meanwhile in Greece many of the arts had attained a state of development which raised them above a merely routine state; there were intimations of measure, order and regularity in materials dealt with which give intimations of underlying rationality. Because of the growth of mathematics, there arose also the ideal of a purely rational knowledge, intrinsically solid and worthy and the means by which the intimations of rationality within changing phenomena could be comprehended within science. For the intellectual class the stay and consolation, the warrant of certainty, provided by religion was henceforth found in intellectual demonstration of the reality of the objects of an ideal realm.

With the expansion of Christianity, ethico-religious traits came to dominate the purely rational ones. The ultimate authoritative standards for regulation of the dispositions and purposes of the human will were fused with those which satisfied the demands for necessary and universal truth. The authority of ultimate Being was, moreover, represented on earth by the Church; that which in its nature transcended intellect was made known by a revelation of which the Church was

• [From: John Dewey, *The Quest for Certainty*. New York: Minton, Balch and Co.; 1929. Pp. 254-86. Copyright 1957 by Frederick A. Dewey. Reprinted by permission of G. P. Putnam's Sons.]

the interpreter and guardian. The system endured for centuries. While it endured, it provided an integration of belief and conduct for the western world. Unity of thought and practice extended down to every detail of the management of life; efficacy of its operation did not depend upon thought. It was guaranteed by the most powerful and authoritative of all social institutions.

Its seemingly solid foundation was, however, undermined by the conclusions of modern science. They effected, both in themselves and even more in the new interests and activities they generated, a breach between what man is concerned with here and now and the faith concerning ultimate reality which, in determining his ultimate and eternal destiny, had previously given regulation to his present life. The problem of restoring integration and coöperation between man's beliefs about the world in which he lives and his beliefs about the values and purposes that should direct his conduct is the deepest problem of modern lift. It is the problem of any philosophy that is not isolated from that life.

The attention which has been given to the fact that in its experimental procedure science has surrendered the separation between knowing and doing has its source in the fact that there is now provided within a limited, specialized and technical field the possibility and earnest, as far as theory is concerned, of effecting the needed integration in the wider field of collective human experience. Philosophy is called upon to be the theory of the practice, through ideas sufficiently definite to be operative in experimental endeavor, by which the integration may be made secure in actual experience. Its central problem is the relation that exists between the beliefs about the nature of things due to natural science and beliefs about values—using that word to designate whatever is taken to have rightful authority in the direction of conduct. A philosophy which should take up this problem is struck first of all by the fact that beliefs about values are pretty much in the position in which beliefs about nature were before the scientific revolution. There is either a basic distrust of the capacity of experience to develop its own regulative standards, and an appeal to what philosophers call eternal values, in order to ensure regulation of belief and action; or there is acceptance of enjoyments actually experienced irrespective of the method or operation by which they are brought into existence. Complete bifurcation between rationalistic method and an empirical method has its final and most deeply human significance in the ways in which good and bad are thought of and acted for and upon.

As far as technical philosophy reflects this situation, there is division of theories of values into two kinds. On the one hand, goods and evils, in every region of life, as they are concretely experienced, are regarded as characteristic of an inferior order of Being—intrinsically inferior. Just because they are things of human experience, their worth must be estimated by reference to standards and ideals derived from ultimate reality. Their defects and perversion are attributed to the same fact; they are to be corrected and controlled through adoption of methods of conduct derived from loyalty to the requirements of Supreme Being. This philosophic formulation gets actuality and force from the fact that it is a rendering of the beliefs of men in general as far as they have come under the influence of institutional religion. Just as rational conceptions were once superimposed upon observed and temporal phenomena, so eternal values are superimposed upon experienced goods. In one case as in the other, the alternative is supposed to be confusion and lawlessness. Philosophers suppose these eternal values are known by reason; the mass of persons that they are divinely revealed.

Nevertheless, with the expansion of secular interests, temporal values have enormously multiplied; they absorb more and more attention and energy. The sense of transcendent values has become enfeebled; instead of permeating all things in life, it is more and more restricted to special times and acts. The authority of the church to declare and impose divine will and purpose has narrowed. Whatever men say and profess, their tendency in the presence of actual evils is to resort to natural and empirical means to remedy them. But in formal belief, the old doctrine of the inherently disturbed and unworthy character of the goods and standards of ordinary experience persists. This divergence between what men do and what they nominally profess is closely connected with the confusions and conflicts of modern thought.

It is not meant to assert that no attempts have been made to replace the older theory regarding the authority of immutable and transcendent values by conceptions more congruous with the practices of daily life. The contrary is the case. The utilitarian theory, to take one instance, has had great power. The idealistic school is the only one in contemporary philosophies, with the exception of one form of neorealism, that makes much of the notion of a reality which is all one with ultimate moral and religious values. But this school is also the one most concerned with the conservation of "spiritual" life. Equally significant is the fact that empirical theories retain the notion that thought and judgment are concerned with values that are experienced independently of them. For these theories, emotional satisfactions occupy the same place that sensations hold in traditional empiricism. Values are constituted by liking and enjoyment; to be enjoyed and to be a value are two names for one and the same fact. Since science has extruded values from its objects, these empirical theories do everything possible to emphasize their purely subjective character of value. A psychological theory of desire and liking is supposed to cover the whole ground of the theory of values; in it, immediately feeling is the counterpart of immediate sensation.

I shall not object to this empirical theory as far as it connects the theory of values with concrete experiences of desire and satisfaction. The idea that there is such a connection is the only way known to me by which the pallid remoteness of the rationalistic theory, and the only too glaring presence of the institutional theory of transcendental values can be escaped. The objection is that the theory in question holds down value to objects *antecedently* enjoyed, apart from reference to the method by which they come into existence; it takes enjoyments which are casual because unregulated by intelligent operations to be values in and of themselves. Operational thinking needs to be applied to the judgment of values just as it has now finally been applied in conceptions of physical objects. Experimental empiricism in the field of ideas of good and bad is demanded to meet the conditions of the present situation.

The scientific revolution came about when material of direct and uncontrolled experience was taken as problematic; as supplying material to be transformed by reflective operations into known objects. The contrast between experienced and known objects was found to be a temporal one; namely, one between empirical subject-matters which were had or "given" prior to the acts of experimental variation and redisposition and those which succeeded these acts and issued from them. The notion of an act whether of sense or thought which supplied a valid measure of thought in immediate knowledge was discredited. Consequences of operations became the important thing. The suggestion almost imperatively follows that escape from the defects of transcendental absolutism is not to be had by setting up as values enjoyments that happen anyhow, but in defining value by enjoyments which are the consequences of intelligent action. Without the intervention of thought, enjoyments are not values but problematic goods, becoming values when they re-issue in a changed form from intelligent behavior. The fundamental trouble with the current empirical theory of values is that it merely formulates and justifies the socially prevailing habit of regarding enjoyments as they are actually experienced as values in and of themselves. It completely side-steps the question of regulation of these enjoyments. This issue involves nothing less than the problem of the directed reconstruction of economic political and religious institutions.

There was seemingly a paradox involved in the notion that if we turned our backs upon the immediately perceived qualities of things, we should be enabled to form valid conceptions of objects, and that these conceptions could be used to bring about a more secure and more significant experience of them. But the method terminated in disclosing the connections or interactions upon which perceived objects, viewed as events, depend. Formal analogy suggests that we regard our direct and original experience of things liked and enjoyed as only *possibilities* of values to be achieved; that enjoyment becomes a value when we discover the relations upon which its presence depends. Such a causal and operational definition gives only a conception of a value, not a value itself. But the utilization of the conception in action results in an object having secure and significant value.

The formal statement may be given concrete content by pointing to the difference between the enjoyed and the enjoyable, the desired and the desirable, the satisfy*ing* and the satis*factory*. To say that something is enjoyed is to make a statement about a fact, something already in existence; it is not to judge the value of that fact. There is no difference between such a proposition and one which says that something is sweet or sour, red or black. It is just correct or incorrect and that is the end of the matter. But to call an object a value is to assert that it satisfies or fulfills certain conditions. Function and status in meeting conditions is a different matter from bare existence. The fact that something is desired only raises the *question* of its desirability; it does not settle it. Only a child in the degree of his immaturity thinks to settle the question of desirability by reiterated proclamation: "I want it, I want it, I want it." What is objected to in the current empirical theory of values is not connection of them with desire and enjoyment but failure to distinguish between enjoyments of radically different sorts. There are many common expressions in which the difference of the two kinds is clearly recognized. Take for example the difference between the ideas of "satisfying" and "satisfactory." To say that something satisfies is to report something as an isolated finality. To assert that it is satisfactory is to define it in its connections and interactions. The fact that it pleases or is immediately congenial poses a problem to judgment. How shall the satisfaction be rated? Is it a value or is it not? Is it something to be prized and cherished, to be enjoyed? Not stern moralists alone but everyday experience informs us that finding satisfaction in a thing may be a warning, a summons to be on the lookout for consequences. To declare something satisfactory is to assert that it meets specifiable conditions. It is, in effect, a judgment that the thing "will do." It involves a prediction: it contemplates a future in which the thing will continue to serve; it will do. It asserts a consequence the thing will actively institute; it will do. That it is satisfying is the content of a proposition of fact; that it is satisfactory is a judgment, an estimate, an appraisal. It denotes an attitude to be taken, that of striving to perpetuate and to make secure.

It is worth notice that besides the instances given, there are many other recognitions in ordinary speech of the distinction. The endings "able," "worthy" and "ful" are cases in point. Noted and notable, noteworthy; remarked and remarkable; advised and advisable; wondered at and wonderful; pleasing and beautiful; loved and lovable; blamed and blameable, blameworthy; objected to and objectionable; esteemed and estimable; admired and admirable; shamed and shameful; honored and honorable; approved and approvable, worthy of approbation, etc. The multiplication of words adds nothing to the force of the distinction. But it aids in conveying a sense of the fundamental character of the distinction; of the difference between mere report of an already existent fact and judgment as to the importance and need of bringing a fact into existence; or, if it is already there, of sustaining it in existence. The latter is a genuine practical judgment, and marks the only type of judgment that has to do with the direction of action.

Whether or no we reserve the term "value" for the latter (as seems to me proper) is a minor matter; that the distinction be acknowledged as the key to understanding the relation of values to the direction of conduct is the important thing.

This element of direction by an idea of value applies to science as well as anywhere else. For in every scientific undertaking, there is passed a constant succession of estimates; such as "it is worth treating these facts as data or evidence; it is advisable to try this experiment; to make that observation; to entertain such and such a hypothesis; to perform this calculation," etc.

The word "taste" has perhaps got too completely associated with arbitrary liking to express the nature of judgments of value. But if the word be used in the sense of an appreciation at once cultivated and active, one may say that the formation of taste is the chief matter wherever values enter in, whether intellectual, esthetic or moral. Relatively immediate judgments, which we call tact or to which we give the name of intuition, do not precede reflective inquiry, but are the funded products of much thoughtful experience. Expertness of taste is at once the result and the reward of constant exercise of thinking. Instead of there being no disputing about tastes, they are the one thing worth disputing about, if by "dispute" is signified discussion involving reflective inquiry. Taste, if we use the word in its best sense, is the outcome of experience brought cumulatively to bear on the intelligent appreciation of the real worth of likings and enjoyments. There is nothing in which a person so completely reveals himself as in the things which he judges enjoyable and desirable. Such judgments are the sole alternative to the domination of belief by impulse, chance, blind habit and self-interest. The formation of a cultivated and effectively operative good judgment or taste with respect to what is esthetically admirable, intellectually acceptable and morally approvable is the supreme task set to human beings by the incidents of experience.

Propositions about what is or has been liked are of instrumental value in reaching judgments of value, in as far as the conditions and consequences of the thing liked are thought about. In themselves they make no claims; they put forth no demand upon subsequent attitudes and acts; they profess no authority to direct. If one likes a thing he likes it; that *is* a point about which there can be no dispute—although it is not so easy to state just *what* is liked as is frequently assumed. A judgment about what is *to be* desired and enjoyed is, on the other hand, a claim on future action; it possesses *de jure* and not merely *de facto* quality. It is a matter of frequent experience that likings and enjoyments are of all kinds, and that many are such as reflective judgments condemn. By way of self-justification and "rationalization," an enjoyment creates a tendency to assert that the thing enjoyed is a value. This assertion of validity adds authority to the fact. It is a decision that the object has a right to exist and hence a claim upon action to further its existence.

The analogy between the status of the theory of values and the theory of ideas about natural objects before the rise of experimental inquiry may be carried further. The sensationalistic theory of the origin and test of thought evoked, by way of reaction, the transcendental theory of *a priori* ideas. For it failed utterly to account for objective connection, order and regularity in objects observed. Similarly, any doctrine that identifies the mere fact of being liked with the value of the object liked so fails to give direction to conduct when direction is needed that it automatically calls forth the assertion that there are values eternally in Being that are the standards of all judgments and the obligatory ends of all action. Without the introduction of operational thinking, we oscillate between a theory that, in order to save the objectivity of judgments of values, isolates them from experience and nature, and a theory that, in order to save their concrete and human significance, reduces them to mere statements about our own feelings.

Not even the most devoted adherents of the notion that enjoyment and value are equivalent facts would venture to assert that because we have once liked a thing we should go on liking it; they are compelled to introduce the idea that *some* tastes are to be cultivated. Logically, there is no ground for introducing the idea of cultivation; liking is liking, and one is as good as another. If enjoyments *are* values, the judgment of value cannot regulate the form which liking takes; it cannot regulate its own conditions. Desire and purpose, and hence action, are left without guidance, although the question of regulation of their formation is the supreme problem of practical life. Values (to sum up) may be connected inherently with liking, and yet not with *every* liking but only with those that judgment has approved, after examination of the relation upon which the object liked depends. A casual liking is one that happens without knowledge of how it occurs nor to what effect. The difference between it and one which is sought because of a judgment that it is worth having and is to be striven for, makes just the difference between enjoyments which are accidental and enjoyments that have value and hence a claim upon our attitude and conduct.

In any case, the alternative rationalistic theory does not afford the guidance for the sake of which eternal and immutable norms are appealed to. The scientist finds no help in determining the probable truth of some proposed theory by comparing it with a standard of absolute truth and immutable being. He has to rely upon definite operations undertaken under definite conditions—upon method. We can hardly imagine an architect getting aid in the construction of a building from an ideal at large, though we can understand his framing an ideal on the basis of knowledge of actual conditions and needs. Nor does the ideal of perfect beauty in antecedent Being give direction to a painter in producing a particular work of art. In morals, absolute perfection does not seem to be more than a generalized hypostatization of the recognition that there is a good to be sought, an obligation to be met— both being concrete matters. Nor is the defect in this respect merely negative. An examination of history would reveal, I am confident, that these general and remote schemes of value actually obtain a content definite enough and near enough to concrete situations as to afford guidance in action only by consecrating some institution or dogma already having social currency. Concreteness is gained, but it is by protecting from inquiry some accepted standard which perhaps is outworn and in need of criticism.

When theories of values do not afford intellectual assistance in framing ideas and beliefs about values that are adequate to direct action, the gap must be filled by other means. If intelligent method is lacking, prejudice, the pressure of immediate circumstance, self-interest and class-interest, traditional customs, institutions of accidental historic origin, are *not* lacking, and they tend to take the place of intelligence. Thus we are led to our main proposition: *Judgments about values are judgments about the conditions and the results of experienced objects; judgments about that which should regulate the formation of our desires, affections and enjoyments.* For whatever decides their formation will determine the main course of our conduct, personal and social.

If it sounds strange to hear that we should frame our judgments as to what has value by considering the connections in existence of what we like and enjoy, the reply is not far to seek. As long as we do not engage in this inquiry enjoyments (values if we choose to apply that term) are casual; they are given by "nature," not constructed by art. Like natural objects in their qualitative existence, they at most only supply material for elaboration in rational discourse. A *feeling* of good or excellence is as far removed from goodness in fact as a feeling that objects are intellectually thus and so is removed from their being actually so. To recognize that the truth of natural objects can be reached only by the greatest care in selecting and arranging directed operations, and then to suppose that values can be truly determined by the mere fact of liking seems to leave us in an incredible position. All the serious perplexities of life come back to the genuine difficulty of forming a judgment as to the values of the situation; they come back to a conflict of goods. Only dogmatism can suppose that serious moral conflict is between something clearly bad and something known to be good, and that uncertainty lies wholly in the will of the one choosing. Most conflicts of importance are conflicts between things which are or have been satisfying, not between good and evil. And to suppose that we can make a hierarchical table of values at large once for all, a kind of catalogue in which they are arranged in an order of ascending or descending worth, is to indulge in a gloss on our inability to frame intelligent judgments in the concrete. Or else it is to dignify customary choice and prejudice by a title of honor.

The alternative to definition, classification and systematization of satisfactions just as they happen to occur is judgment of them by means of the relations under which they occur. If we know the conditions under which the act of liking, of desire and enjoyment, takes place, we are in a position to know what are the consequences of that act. The difference between the desired and the desirable, the admired and the admirable, becomes effective at just this point. Consider the difference between the proposition "That thing has been eaten," and the judgment "That thing is edible." The former statement involves no knowledge of any relation except the one stated; while we are able to judge of the edibility of anything only when we have a knowledge of its interactions with other things sufficient to enable us to foresee its probable effects when it is taken into the organism and produces effects there.

To assume that anything can be known in isolation from its connections with other things is to identify knowing with merely having some object before perception or in feeling, and is thus to lose the key to the traits that distinguish an object as known. It is futile, even silly, to suppose that some quality that is directly present constitutes the whole of the thing presenting the quality. It does not do so when the quality is that of being hot or fluid or heavy, and it does not when the quality is that of giving pleasure, or being enjoyed. Such qualities are, once more, effects, ends in the sense of closing termini of processes involving causal connections. They are something to be investigated, challenges to inquiry and judgment. The more connections and interactions we ascertain, the more we *know* the object in question. Thinking is search for these connections. Heat experienced as a consequence of directed operations has a meaning quite different from the heat that is casually experienced without knowledge of how it came about. The same is true of enjoyments. Enjoyments that issue from conduct directed by insight into relations have a meaning and a validity due to the way in which they are experienced. Such enjoyments are not repented of; they generate no after-taste of bitterness. Even in the midst of direct enjoyment, there is a sense of validity, of authorization, which intensifies the enjoyment. There is solicitude for perpetuation of the *object* having value which is radically different from mere anxiety to perpetuate the *feeling* of enjoyment.

Such statements as we have been making are, therefore, far from implying that there are values apart from things actually enjoyed as good. To find a thing enjoy*able* is, so to say, a *plus* enjoyment. We saw that it was foolish to treat the scientific object as a rival to or substitute for the perceived object, since the former is intermediate between uncertain and settled situations and those experienced under conditions of greater control. In the same way, judgment of the value of an object to be experienced is instrumental to appreciation of it when it is realized. But the notion that every object that happens to satisfy has an equal claim with every other to be a value is like supposing that every object of perception has the same cognitive force as every other. There is no knowledge without perception; but objects perceived are *known* only when they are determined as consequences of connective operations. There is no value except where there is satisfaction, but there have to be certain conditions fulfilled to transform a satisfaction into a value.

The time will come when it will be found passing strange that we of this age should take such pains to control by every means at command the formation of ideas of physical things, even those most remote from human concern, and yet are content with haphazard beliefs about the qualities of objects that regulate our deepest interests; that we are scrupulous as to methods of forming ideas of natural objects, and either dogmatic or else driven by immediate conditions in framing those about values. There is, by implication, if not explicitly, a prevalent notion that values are already well known and that all which is lacking is the will to cultivate them in the order of their worth. In fact the most profound lack is not the will to act upon goods already known but the will to know what they are.

It is not a dream that it is possible to exercise some degree of regulation of the occurrence of enjoyments which are of value. Realization of the possibility is exemplified, for example, in the technologies and arts of industrial life—that is, up to a definite limit. Men desired heat, light, and speed of transit and of communication beyond what nature provides of itself. These things have been attained not by lauding the enjoyment of these things and preaching their desirability, but by study of the conditions of their manifestation. Knowledge of relations having been obtained, ability to produce followed, and enjoyment ensued as a matter of course. It is, however, an old story that enjoyment of these things as goods is no warrant of their bringing only good in their train. As Plato was given to pointing out, the physician may know how to heal and the orator to persuade, but the ulterior knowledge of whether it is better for a man to be healed or to be persuaded to the orator's opinion remains unsettled. Here there appears the split between what are traditionally and conventionally called the values of the baser arts and the higher values of the truly personal and humane arts.

With respect to the former, there is no assumption that they can be had and enjoyed without definite operative knowledge. With respect to them it is also clear that the degree in which we value them is measurable by the pains taken to control the conditions of their occurrence. With respect to the latter, it is assumed that no one who is honest can be in doubt what they are; that by revelation, or conscience, or the instruction of others, or immediate feeling, they are clear beyond question. And instead of action in their behalf being taken to be a measure of the extent in which things *are* values to us, it is assumed that the difficulty is to persuade men to act upon what they already know to be good. Knowledge of conditions and consequences is regarded as wholly indifferent to judging what is of serious value, though it is useful in a prudential way in trying to actualize it. In consequence, the existence of values that are by common consent of a secondary and technical sort are under a fair degree of control, while those denominated supreme and imperative are subject to all the winds of impulse, custom and arbitrary authority.

This distinction between higher and lower types of value is itself something to be looked into. Why should there be a sharp division made between some goods as physical and material and others as ideal and "spiritual"? The question touches the whole dualism of the material and the ideal at its root. To denominate anything "matter" or "material" is not in truth to disparage it. It is, if the designation is correctly applied, a way of indicating that the thing in question is a condition or means of the existence of something else. And disparagement of effective means is practically synonymous with disregard of the things that are termed, in eulogistic fashion, ideal and spiritual. For the latter terms if they have any concrete application at all signify something which is a desirable consummation of conditions, a cherished fulfillment of means. The sharp separation between material and ideal good thus deprives the latter of the underpinning of effective support while it opens the way for treating things which should be employed as means as ends in themselves. For since men cannot after all live without some measure of possession of such matters as health and wealth, the latter things will be viewed as values and ends in isolation unless they are treated as integral constituents of the goods that are deemed supreme and final.

The relations that determine the occurrence of what human beings experience, especially when social connections are taken into account, are indefinitely wider and more complex than those that determine the events termed physical; the latter are the outcome of definite selective operations. This is the reason why we know something about remote objects like the stars better than we know significantly characteristic things about our own bodies and minds. We forget the infinite number of things we do not know about the stars, or rather that what we call a star is itself the product of the elimination, enforced and deliberate, of most of the traits that belong to an actual existence. The amount of knowledge we possess about stars would not seem very great or very important if it were carried over to human beings and exhausted our knowledge of them. It is inevitable that genuine knowledge of man and society should lag far behind physical knowledge.

But this difference is not a ground for making a sharp division between the two, nor does it account for the fact that we make so little use of the experimental method of forming our ideas and beliefs about the concerns of man in his characteristic social relations. For this separation religions and philosophies must admit some responsibility. They have erected a distinction between a narrower scope of relations and a wider and fuller one into a difference of kind, naming one kind material, and the other mental and moral. They have charged themselves gratuitously with the office of diffusing belief in the necessity of the division, and with instilling contempt for the material as something inferior in kind in its intrinsic nature and worth. Formal philosophies undergo evaporation of their technical solid contents; in a thinner and more viable form they find their way into the minds of those who know nothing of their original forms. When these diffuse and, so to say, airy emanations re-crystallize in the popular mind they form a hard deposit of opinion that alters slowly and with great difficulty.

What difference would it actually make in the arts of conduct, personal and social, if the experimental theory were adopted not as a mere theory, but as a part of the working equipment of habitual attitudes on the part of everyone? It would be impossible, even were time given, to answer the question in adequate detail, just as men could not foretell in advance the consequences for knowledge of adopting the experimental method. It is the nature of the method that it has to be tried. But there are generic lines of difference which, within the limits of time at disposal, may be sketched.

Change from forming ideas and judgments of value on the basis of conformity to antecedent objects, to constructing enjoyable objects directed by knowledge of consequences, is a change from looking to the past to looking to the future. I do not for a moment suppose that the experiences of the past, personal and social, are of no importance. For without them we should not be able to frame any ideas whatever of the conditions under which objects are enjoyed nor any estimate of the consequences of esteeming and liking them. But past experiences are significant in giving us intellectual instrumentalities of judging just these points. They are tools, not finalities. Reflection upon what we have liked and have enjoyed is a necessity. But it tells us nothing about the *value* of these things until enjoyments are themselves reflectively controlled, or, until, as they are now recalled, we form the best judgment possible about what led us to like this sort of thing and what has issued from the fact that we liked it.

We are not, then, to get away from enjoyments experienced in the past and from recall of them, but from the notion that they are the arbiters of things to be further enjoyed. At present, the arbiter is found in the past, although there are many ways of interpreting what in the past is authoritative. Nominally, the most influential conception doubtless is that of a revelation once had or a perfect life once lived. Reliance upon precedent, upon institutions created in the past, especially in law, upon rules of morals that have come to us through unexamined customs, upon uncriticized tradition, are other forms of dependence. It is not for a moment suggested that we can get away from customs and established institutions. A mere break would doubtless result simply in chaos. But there is no danger of such a break. Mankind is too inertly conservative both by constitution and by education to give the idea of this danger actuality. What there is genuine danger of is that the force of new conditions will produce disruption externally and mechanically: this is an ever present danger. The prospect is increased, not mitigated, by that conservatism which insists upon the adequacy of old standards to meet new conditions. What is needed is intelligent examination of the consequences that are actually effected by inherited institutions and customs, in order that there may be intelligent consideration of the ways in which they are to be intentionally modified in behalf of generation of different consequences.

This is the significant meaning of transfer of experimental method from the technical field of physical experience to the wider field of human life. We trust the method in forming our beliefs about things not directly connected with human life. In effect, we distrust it in moral, political and economic affairs. In the fine arts, there are many signs of a change. In the past, such a change has often been an omen and precursor of changes in other human attitudes. But, generally speaking, the idea of actively adopting experimental method in social affairs, in the matters deemed of most enduring and ultimate worth, strikes most persons as a surrender of all standards and regulative authority. But in principle, experimental method does not signify random and aimless action; it implies direction by ideas and knowledge. The question at issue is a practical one. Are there in existence the ideas and the knowledge that permit experimental method to be effectively used in social interests and affairs?

Where will regulation come from if we surrender familiar and traditionally prized values as our directive standards? Very largely from the findings of the natural sciences. For one of the effects of the separation drawn between knowledge and action is to deprive scientific knowledge of its proper service as a guide of conduct—except once more in those technological fields which have been degraded to an inferior rank. Of course, the complexity of the conditions upon which objects of human and liberal value depend is a great obstacle, and it would be too optimistic to say that we have as yet enough knowledge of the scientific type to enable us to regulate our judgments of value very extensively. But we have more knowledge than we try to put to use, and until we try more systematically we shall not know what are the important gaps in our sciences judged from the point of view of their moral and humane use.

For moralists usually draw a sharp line between the field of the natural sciences and the conduct that is regarded as moral. But a moral that frames its judgments of value on the basis of consequences must depend in a most intimate manner upon the conclusions of science. For the knowledge of the relations between changes which enable us to connect things as antecedents and consequences *is* science. The narrow scope which moralists often give to morals, their isolation of some conduct as virtuous and vicious from other large ranges of conduct, those having to do with health and vigor, business, education, with all the affairs in which desires and affection are implicated, is perpetuated by this habit of exclusion of the subject-matter of natural science from a role in formation of moral standards and ideals. The same attitude operates in the other direction to keep natural science a technical specialty, and it works unconsciously to encourage its use exclusively in regions where it can be turned to personal and class advantage, as in war and trade.

Another great difference to be made by carrying the experimental habit into all matter of practice is that it cuts the roots of what is often called subjectivism, but which is better termed egoism. The subjective attitude is much more widespread than would be inferred from the philosophies which have that label attached. It is as rampant in realistic philosophies as in any others, sometimes even more so, although disguised from those who hold these philosophies under the cover of reverence of and enjoyment of ultimate values. For the implication of placing the standard of thought and knowledge in antecedent existence is that our thought makes no difference in what is significantly real. It then affects only our own attitude toward it.

This constant throwing of emphasis back upon a change made in ourselves instead of one made in the world in which we live seems to me the essence of what is objectionable in "subjectivism." Its taint hangs about even Platonic realism with its insistent evangelical dwelling upon the change made within the mind by contemplation of the realm of essence, and its depreciation of action as transient and all but sordid—a concession to the necessities of organic existence. All the theories which put conversion "of the eye of the soul" in the place of a conversion of natural and social objects that modifies goods actually experienced, is a retreat and escape from existence—and this retraction into self is, once more, the heart of subjective egoisms. The typical example is perhaps the other-worldliness found in religions whose chief concern is with the salvation of the personal soul. But other-worldliness is found as well in estheticism and in all seclusion within ivory towers.

It is not in the least implied that change in personal attitudes, in the disposition of the "subject," is not of great importance. Such change, on the contrary, is involved in any attempt to modify the conditions of the environment. But there is a radical difference between a change in the self that is cultivated and valued as an end, and one that is a means to alteration, through action, of objective conditions. The Aristotelian-medieval conviction that highest bliss is found in contemplative possession of ultimate Being presents an ideal attractive to some types of mind; it sets forth a refined sort of enjoyment. It is a doctrine congenial to minds that despair of the effort involved in creation of a better world of daily experience. It is, apart from theological attachments, a doctrine sure to recur when social conditions are so troubled as to make actual endeavor seem hopeless. But the subjectivism so externally marked in modern thought as compared with ancient is either a development of the old doctrine under new conditions or is of merely technical import. The medieval version of the doctrine at least had the active support of a great social institution by means of which man could be brought into the state of mind that prepared him for ultimate enjoyment of eternal Being. It had a certain solidity and depth which is lacking in modern theories that would attain the result by merely emotional or speculative procedures, or by any means not demanding a change in objective existence so as to render objects of value more empirically secure.

The nature in detail of the revolution that would be wrought by carrying into the region of values the principle now embodied in scientific practice cannot be told; to attempt it would violate the fundamental idea that we know only after we have acted and in consequence of the outcome of action. But it would surely effect a transfer of attention and energy from the subjective to the objective. Men would think of themselves as agents not as ends; ends would be found in experienced enjoyment of the fruits of a transforming activity. In as far as the subjectivity of modern thought represents a discovery of the part played by personal responses, organic and acquired, in the causal production of the qualities and values of objects, it marks the possibility of a decisive gain. It puts us in possession of some of the conditions that control the occurrence of experienced objects, and thereby it supplies us with an instrument of regulation. There is something querulous in the sweeping denial that things as experienced, as perceived and enjoyed, in any way depend upon interaction with human selves. The error of doctrines that have exploited the part played by personal and subjective reactions in determining what is perceived and enjoyed lies either in exaggerating this factor of constitution into the sole condition —as happens in subjective idealism—or else in treating it as a finality instead of, as with all knowledge, an instrument in direction of further action.

A third significant change that would issue from carrying over experimental method from physics to man concerns the import of standards, principles, rules. With the transfer, these, and all tenets and creeds about good and goods, would be recognized to be hypotheses. Instead of being rigidly fixed, they would be treated as intellectual instruments to be tested and confirmed—and altered—through consequences effected by acting upon them. They would lose all pretence of finality —the ulterior source of dogmatism. It is both astonishing and depressing that so much of the energy of mankind has gone into fighting for (with weapons of the flesh as well as of the spirit) the truth of creeds, religions, moral and political, as distinct from what has gone into effort to try creeds by putting them to the test of acting upon them. The change would do away with the intolerance and fanaticism that attend the notion that beliefs and judgments are capable of inherent truth and authority; inherent in the sense of being independent of what they lead to when used as directive principles. The transformation does not imply merely that men are responsible for acting upon what they profess to believe; that is an old doctrine. It goes much further. Any belief as such is tentative, hypothetical; it is not just to be acted upon, but is to be *framed* with reference to its office as a guide to action. Consequently, it should be the last thing in the world to be picked up casually and then clung to rigidly. When it is apprehended as a tool and only a tool, an instrumentality of direction, the same scrupulous attention will go to its formation as now goes into the making of instruments of precision in technical fields. Men, instead of being proud of accepting and asserting beliefs and "principles" on the ground of loyalty, will be as ashamed of that procedure as they would now be to confess their assent to a scientific theory out of reverence for Newton or Helmholz or whomever, without regard to evidence.

If one stops to consider the matter, is there not something strange in the fact that men should consider loyalty to "laws," principles, standards, ideals to be an inherent virtue, accounted unto them for righteousness? It is as if they were making up for some secret sense of weakness by rigidity and intensity of insistent attachment. A moral law, like a law in physics, is not something to swear by and stick to at all hazards; it is a formula of the way to respond when specified conditions present themselves. Its soundness and pertinence are tested by what happens when it is acted upon. Its claim or authority rests finally upon the imperativeness of the situation that has to be dealt with, not upon its own intrinsic nature—as any tool achieves dignity in the measure of needs served by it. The idea that adherence to standards external to experienced objects is the only alternative to confusion and lawlessness was once held in science. But knowledge became steadily progressive when it was abandoned, and clews and tests found within concrete acts and objects were employed. The test of consequences is more exacting than that afforded by fixed general rules. In addition, it secures constant development, for when new acts are tried new results are experienced, while the lauded immutability of eternal ideals and norms is in itself a denial of the possibility of development and improvement.

The various modifications that would result from adoption in social and humane subjects of the experimental way of thinking are perhaps summed up in saying that it would place *method and means* upon the level of importance that has, in the past, been imputed exclusively to ends. Means have been regarded as menial, and the useful as the servile. Means have been treated as poor relations to be endured, but not inherently welcome. The very meaning of the word "ideals" is significant of the divorce which has obtained between means and ends. "Ideals" are thought to be remote and inaccessible of attainment; they are too high and fine to be sullied by realization. They serve vaguely to arouse "aspiration," but they do not evoke and direct strivings for embodiment in actual existence. They hover in an indefinite way over the actual scene; they are expiring ghosts of a once significant kingdom of divine reality whose rule penetrated to every detail of life.

It is impossible to form a just estimate of the paralysis of effort that has been produced by indifference to means. Logically, it is truistic that lack of consideration for means signifies that so-called ends are not taken seriously. It is as if one professed devotion to painting pictures conjoined with contempt for canvas, brush and paints; or love of music on condition that no instruments, whether the voice or something external, be used to make sounds. The good workman in the arts is known by his respect for his tools and by his interest in perfecting his technique. The glorification in the arts of ends at the expense of means would be taken to be a sign of complete insincerity or even insanity. Ends separated from means are either sentimental indulgences or if they happen to exist are merely accidental. The ineffectiveness in action of "ideals" is due precisely to the supposition that means and ends are not on exactly the same level with respect to the attention and care they demand.

It is, however, much easier to point out the formal contradiction implied in ideals that are professed without equal regard for the instruments and techniques of their realization, than it is to appreciate the concrete ways in which belief in their separation has found its way into life and borne corrupt and poisonous fruits. The separation marks the form in which the traditional divorce of theory and practice has expressed itself in actual life. It accounts for the relative impotency of arts concerned with enduring human welfare. Sentimental attachment and subjective eulogy take the place of action. For there is no art without tools and instrumental agencies. But it also explains the fact that in actual behavior, energies devoted to matters nominally thought to be inferior, material and sordid, engross attention and interest. After a polite and pious deference has been paid to "ideals," men feel free to devote themselves to matters which are more immediate and pressing.

It is usual to condemn the amount of attention paid by people in general to material ease, comfort, wealth, and success gained by competition, on the ground that they give to mere means the attention that ought to be given to ends, or that they have taken for ends things which in reality are only means. Criticisms of the place which economic interest and action occupy in present life are full of complaints that men allow lower aims to usurp the place that belongs to higher and ideal values. The final source of the trouble is, however, that moral and spiritual "leaders" have propagated the notion that ideal ends may be cultivated in isolation from "material" means, as if means and material were not synonymous. While they condemn men for giving to means the thought and energy that ought to go to ends, the condemnation should go to them. For they have not taught their followers to think of material and economic activities as *really* means. They have been unwilling to frame their conception of the values that should be regulative of human conduct on the basis of the actual conditions and operations by which alone values can be actualized.

Practical needs are imminent; with the mass of mankind they are imperative. Moreover, speaking generally, men are formed to act rather than to theorize. Since the ideal ends are so remotely and accidentally connected with immediate and urgent conditions that need attention, after lip service is given to them, men naturally devote themselves to the latter. If a bird in the hand is worth two in a neighboring bush, an actuality in hand is worth, for the direction of conduct, many ideals that are so remote as to be invisible and inaccessible. Men hoist the banner of the ideal, and then march in the direction that concrete conditions suggest and reward.

Deliberate insincerity and hypocrisy are rare. But the notion that action and sentiment are inherently unified in the constitution of human nature has nothing to justify it. Integration is something to be achieved. Division of attitudes and responses, compartmentalizing of interests, is easily acquired. It goes deep just because the acquisition is unconscious, a matter of habitual adaptation to conditions. Theory separated from concrete doing and making is empty and futile; practice then becomes an immediate seizure of opportunities and enjoyments which conditions afford without the direction which theory—knowledge and ideas—has power to supply. The problem of the relation of theory and practice is not a problem of theory alone; it is that, but it is also the most practical problem of life. For it is the question of how intelligence may inform action, and how action may bear the fruit of increased insight into meaning: a clear view of the values that are worth while and of the means by which they are to be made secure in experienced objects. Construction of ideals in general and their sentimental glorification are easy; the responsibilities both of studious thought and of action are shirked. Persons having the advantage of positions of leisure and who find pleasure in abstract theorizing—a most delightful indulgence to those to whom it appeals—have a large measure of liability for a cultivated diffusion of ideals and aims that are separated from the conditions which are the means of actualization. Then other persons who find themselves in positions of social power and authority readily claim to be the bearers and defenders of ideal ends in church and state. They then use the prestige and authority their representative capacity as guardians of the highest ends confers on them to cover actions taken in behalf of the harshest and narrowest of material ends.

The present state of industrial life seems to give a fair index of the existing separation of means and ends. Isolation of economics from ideal ends, whether of morals or of organized social life, was proclaimed by Aristotle. Certain things, he said, are conditions of a worthy life, personal and social, but are not constituents of it. The economic life of man, concerned with satisfaction of wants, is of this nature. Men have wants and they must be satisfied. But they are only prerequisites of a good life, not intrinsic elements in it. Most philosophers have not been so frank nor perhaps so logical. But upon the whole, economics has been treated as on a lower level than either morals or politics. Yet the life which men, women and children actually lead, the opportunities open to them, the values they are capable of enjoying, their education, their share in all the things of art and science, are mainly determined by economic conditions. Hence we can hardly expect a moral system which ignores economic conditions to be other than remote and empty.

Industrial life is correspondingly brutalized by failure to equate it as the means by which social and cultural values are realized. That the economic life, thus exiled from the pale of higher values, takes revenge by declaring that it is the only social reality, and by means of the doctrine of materialistic determination of institutions and conduct in all fields, denies to deliberate morals and politics any share of causal regulation, is not surprising.

When economists were told that their subject-matter was merely material, they naturally thought they could be "scientific" only by excluding all reference to distinctively human values. Material wants, efforts to satisfy them, even the scientifically regulated technologies highly developed in industrial activity, are then taken to form a complete and closed field. If any reference to social ends and values is introduced it is by way of an external addition, mainly hortatory. That economic life largely determines the conditions under which mankind has access to concrete values may be recognized or it may not be. In either case, the notion that it is the means to be utilized in order to secure significant values as the common and shared possession of mankind is alien and inoperative. To many persons, the idea that the ends professed by morals are impotent save as they are connected with the working machinery of economic life seems like deflowering the purity of moral values and obligations.

The social and moral effects of the separation of theory and practice have been merely hinted at. They are so manifold and so pervasive that an adequate consideration of them would involve nothing less than a survey of the whole field of morals, economics and politics. It cannot be justly stated that these effects are in fact direct consequences of the quest for certainty by thought and knowledge isolated from action. For, as we have seen, this quest was itself a reflex product of actual conditions. But it may be truly asserted that this quest, undertaken in religion and philosophy, has had results which have reinforced the conditions which originally brought it about. Moreover, search for safety and consolation amid the perils of life by means other than intelligent action, by feeling and thought alone, began when actual means of control were lacking, when arts were undeveloped. It had then a relative historic justification that is now lacking. The primary problem for thinking which lays claim to be philosophic in its breadth and depth is to assist in bringing about a reconstruction of all beliefs rooted in a basic separation of knowledge and action; to develop a system of operative ideas congruous with present knowledge and with present facilities of control over natural events and energies.

We have noted more than once how modern philosophy has been absorbed in the problem of affecting an adjustment between the conclusions of natural science and the beliefs and values that have authority in the direction of life. The genuine and poignant issue does not reside where philosophers for the most part have placed it. It does not consist in accommodation to each other of two realms, one physical and the other ideal and spiritual, nor in the reconciliation of the "categories" of theoretical and practical reason. It is found in that isolation of executive means and ideal interests which has grown up under the influence of the separation of theory and practice. For this, by nature, involves the separation of the material and the spiritual. Its solution, therefore, can be found only in action wherein the phenomena of material and economic life are equated with the purposes that command the loyalties of affection and purpose, and in which ends and ideals are framed in terms of the possibilities of actually experienced situations. But while the solution cannot be found in "thought" alone, it can be furthered by thinking which is operative—which frames and defines ideas in terms of what may be done, and which uses the conclusions of science as instrumentalities. William James was well within the bounds of moderation when he said that looking forward instead of backward, looking to what the world and life might become instead of to what they have been, is an alteration in the "seat of authority."

It was incidentally remarked earlier in our discussion that the serious defect in the current empirical philosophy of values, the one which identifies them with things actually enjoyed irrespective of the conditions upon which they depend, is that it formulates and in so far consecrates the conditions of our present social experience. Throughout these chapters, primary attention has perforce been given to the methods and statements of philosophic theories. But these statements are technical and specialized in formulation only. In origin, content and import they are reflections of some condition or some phase of concrete human experience. Just as the theory of the separation of theory and practice has a practical origin and a momentous practical consequence, so the empirical theory that values are identical with whatever men actually enjoy, no matter how or what, formulates an aspect, and an undesirable one, of the present social situation.

For while our discussion has given more attention to the other type of philosophical doctrine, that which holds that regulative and authoritative standards are found in transcendent eternal values, it has not passed in silence over the fact that actually the greater part of the activities of the greater number of human beings is spent in effort to seize upon and hold onto such enjoyments as the actual scene permits. Their energies and their enjoyments are controlled in fact, but they are controlled by external conditions rather than by intelligent judgment and endeavor. If philosophies have any influence over the thoughts and acts of men, it is a serious matter that the most widely held empirical theory should in effect justify this state of things by identifying values with the objects of any interest as such. As long as the only theories of value placed before us for intellectual assent alternate between sending us to a realm of eternal and fixed values and sending us to enjoyments such as actually obtain, the formulation, even as only a theory, of an experimental empiricism which finds values to be identical with goods that are the fruit of intelligently directed activity has its measure of practical significance.

Science
and Society •

The significant outward forms of the civilization of the western world are the product of the machine and its technology. Indirectly, they are the product of the scientific revolution which took place in the seventeenth century. In its effect upon men's external habits, dominant interests, the conditions under which they work and associate, whether in the family, the factory, the state, or internationally, science is by far the most potent social factor in the modern world. It operates, however, through its undesigned effects rather than as a transforming influence of men's thoughts and purposes. This contrast between outer and inner operation is the great contradiction in our lives. Habits of thought and desire remain in substance what they were before the rise of science, while the conditions under which they take effect have been radically altered by science.

When we look at the external social consequences of science, we find it impossible to apprehend the extent or gauge the rapidity of their occurrence. Alfred North Whitehead has recently called attention to the progressive shortening of the time-span of social change. That due to basic conditions seems to be of the order of half a million years; that due to lesser physical conditions, like alterations in climate, to be of the order of five thousand years. Until almost our own day the time-span of sporadic technological changes was of the order of five hundred years; according to him, no great technological changes took place between, say, 100 A.D. and 1400 A.D. With the introduction of steam-power, the fifty years from 1780 to 1830 were marked by more changes than are found in any previous thousand years. The advance of chemical techniques and in use of electricity and radio-energy in the last forty years makes even this last change seem slow and awkward.

• [From: John Dewey, *Philosophy and Civilization*. New York: Minton, Balch and Co.; 1931. Pp. 318-30. Copyright 1931 by John Dewey; copyright renewed 1959 by Roberta L. Dewey. Reprinted by permission of G. P. Putnam's Sons.]

Domestic life, political institutions, international relations and personal contacts are shifting with kaleidoscopic rapidity before our eyes. We cannot appreciate and weigh the changes; they occur too swiftly. We do not have time to take them in. No sooner do we begin to understand the meaning of one such change than another comes and displaces the former. Our minds are dulled by the sudden and repeated impacts. Externally, science through its applications is manufacturing the conditions of our institutions at such a speed that we are too bewildered to know what sort of civilization is in process of making.

Because of this confusion, we cannot even draw up a ledger account of social gains and losses due to the operation of science. But at least we know that the earlier optimism which thought that the advance of natural science was to dispel superstition, ignorance, and oppression, by placing reason on the throne, was unjustified. Some superstitions have given way, but the mechanical devices due to science have made it possible to spread new kinds of error and delusion among a larger multitude. The fact is that it is foolish to try to draw up a debit and credit account for science. To do so is to mythologize; it is to personify science and impute to it a will and an energy on its own account. In truth science is strictly impersonal; a method and a body of knowledge. It owes its operation and its consequences to the human beings who use it. It adapts itself passively to the purposes and desires which animate these human beings. It lends itself with equal impartiality to the kindly offices of medicine and hygiene and the destructive deeds of war. It elevates some through opening new horizons; it depresses others by making them slaves of machines operated for the pecuniary gain of owners.

The neutrality of science to the uses made of it renders it silly to talk about its bankruptcy, or to worship it as the usherer in of a new age. In the degree in which we realize this fact, we shall devote our attention to the human purposes and motives which control its application. Science is an instrument, a method, a body of technique. While it is an end for those inquirers who are engaged in its pursuit, in the large human sense it is a means, a tool. For what ends shall it be used? Shall it be used deliberately, systematically, for the promotion of social well-being, or shall it be employed primarily for private aggrandizement, leaving its larger social results to chance? Shall the scientific attitude be used to create new mental and moral attitudes, or shall it continue to be subordinated to service of desires, purposes and institutions which were formed before science came into existence? Can the attitudes which control the use of science be themselves so influenced by scientific technique that they will harmonize with its spirit?

The beginning of wisdom is, I repeat, the realization that science itself is an instrument which is indifferent to the external uses to which it is put. Steam and electricity remain natural forces when they operate through mechanisms; the only problem is the purposes for which men set the mechanisms to work. The essential technique of gunpowder is the same whether it be used to blast rocks from the quarry to build better human habitations, or to hurl death upon men at war with one another. The airplane binds men at a distance in closer bonds of intercourse and understanding, or it rains missiles of death upon hapless populations. We are forced to consider the relation of human ideas and ideals to the social consequences which are produced by science as an instrument.

The problem involved is the greatest which civilization has ever had to face. It is, without exaggeration, the most serious issue of contemporary life. Here is the instrumentality, the most powerful, for good and evil, the world has ever known. What are we going to do with it? Shall we leave our underlying aims unaffected by it, treating it merely as a means by which uncoöperative individuals may advance their own fortunes? Shall we try to improve the hearts of men without regard to the new methods which science puts at our disposal? There are those, men in high position in church and state, who urge this course. They trust to a transforming influence of a morals and religion which have not been affected by science to change human desire and purpose, so that they will employ science and machine technology for beneficent social ends. The recent Encyclical of the Pope is a classic document in expression of a point of view which would rely wholly upon inner regeneration to protect society from the injurious uses to which science may be put. Quite apart from any ecclesiastical connection, there are many "intellectuals" who appeal to inner "spiritual" concepts, totally divorced from scientific intelligence, to effect the needed work. But there is another alternative: to take the method of science home into our own controlling attitudes and dispositions, to employ the new techniques as means of directing our thoughts and efforts to a planned control of social forces.

Science and machine technology are young from the standpoint of human history. Though vast in stature, they are infants in age. Three hundred years are but a moment in comparison with thousands of centuries man has lived on the earth. In view of the inertia of institutions and of the mental habits they breed, it is not surprising that the new technique of apparatus and calculation, which is the essence of science, has made so little impression on underlying human attitudes. The momentum of traditions and purposes that preceded its rise took possession of the new instrument and turned it to their ends. Moreover, science had to struggle for existence. It had powerful enemies in church and state. It needed friends and it welcomed alliance with the rising capitalism which it so effectively promoted. If it tended to foster secularism and to create predominantly material interests, it could still be argued that it was in essential harmony with traditional morals and religion. But there were lacking the conditions which are indispensable to the serious application of scientific method in reconstruction of fundamental beliefs and attitudes. In addition, the development of the new science was attended with so many internal difficulties that energy had to go to perfecting the instrument just as an instrument. Because of all these circumstances the fact that science was used in behalf of old interests is nothing to be wondered at.

The conditions have now changed, radically so. The claims of natural science in the physical field are undisputed. Indeed, its prestige is so great that an almost superstitious aura gathers about its name and work. Its progress is no longer dependent upon the adventurous inquiry of a few untrammeled souls. Not only are universities organized to promote scientific research and learning, but one may almost imagine the university laboratories abolished and still feel confident of the continued advance of science. The development of industry has compelled the inclusion of scientific inquiry within the processes of production and distribution. We find in the public prints as many demonstrations of the benefits of science from a business point of view as there are proofs of its harmony with religion.

It is not possible that, under such conditions, the subordination of scientific techniques to purposes and institutions that flourished before its rise can indefinitely continue. In all affairs there comes a time when a cycle of growth reaches maturity. When this stage is reached, the period of protective nursing comes to an end. The problem of securing proper use succeeds to that of securing conditions of growth. Now that science has established itself and has created a new social environment, it has (if I may for the moment personify it) to face the issue of its social responsibilities. Speaking without personification, we who have a powerful and perfected instrument in our hands, one which is determining the quality of social changes, must ask what changes we want to see achieved and what we want to see averted. We must, in short, plan its social effects with the same care with which in the past we have planned its physical operation and consequences. Till now we have employed science absent-mindedly as far as its effects upon human beings are concerned. The present situation with its extraordinary control of natural energies and its totally unplanned and haphazard social economy is a dire demonstration of the folly of continuing this course.

The social effects of the application of science have been accidental, even though they are intrinsic to the private and unorganized motives which we have permitted to control that application. It would be hard to find a better proof that such is the fact than the vogue of the theory that such unregulated use of science is in accord with "natural law," and that all effort at planned control of its social effects is an interference with nature. The use which has been made of a peculiar idea of personal liberty to justify the dominion of accident in social affairs is another convincing proof. The doctrine that the most potent instrument of widespread, enduring, and objective social changes must be left at the mercy of purely private desires for purely personal gain is a doctrine of anarchy. Our present insecurity of life is the fruit of the adoption in practice of this anarchic doctrine.

The technologies of industry have flowed from the intrinsic nature of science. For that is itself essentially a technology of apparatus, materials and numbers. But the pecuniary aims which have decided the social results of the use of these technologies have not flowed from the inherent nature of science. They have been derived from institutions and attendant mental and moral habits which were entrenched before there was any such thing as science and the machine. In consequence, science has operated as a means for extending the influence of the institution of private property and connected legal relations far beyond their former limits. It has operated as a device to carry an enormous load of stocks and bonds and to make the reward of investment in the way of profit and power one out of all proportion to that accruing from actual work and service.

Here lies the heart of our present social problem. Science has hardly been used to modify men's fundamental acts and attitudes in social matters. It has been used to extend enormously the scope and power of interests and values which anteceded its rise. Here is the contradiction in our civilization. The potentiality of science as the most powerful instrument of control which has ever existed puts to mankind its one outstanding present challenge.

There is one field in which science has been somewhat systematically employed as an agent of social control. Condorcet, writing during the French Revolution in the prison from which he went to the guillotine, hailed the invention of the calculus of probabilities as the opening of a new era. He saw in this new mathematical technique the promise of methods of insurance which should distribute evenly and widely the impact of the disasters to which humanity is subject. Insurance against death, fire, hurricanes and so on have in a measure confirmed his prediction. Nevertheless, in large and important social areas, we have only made the merest beginning of the method of insurance against the hazards of life and death. Insurance against the risks of maternity, of sickness, old age, unemployment, is still rudimentary; its idea is fought by all reactionary forces. Witness the obstacles against which social insurance with respect to accidents incurred in industrial employment had to contend. The anarchy called natural law and personal liberty still operates with success against a planned social use of the resources of scientific knowledge.

Yet insurance against perils and hazards is the place where the application of science has gone the furthest, not the least, distance in present society. The fact that motor cars kill and maim more persons yearly than all factories, shops, and farms is a fair symbol of how backward we are in that province where we have done most. Here, however, is one field in which at least the idea of planned use of scientific knowledge for social welfare has received recognition. We no longer regard plagues, famine and disease as visitations of necessary "natural law" or of a power beyond nature. By preventive means of medicine and public hygiene as well as by various remedial measures we have in idea, if not in fact, placed technique in the stead of magic and chance and uncontrollable necessity in this one area of life. And yet, as I have said, here is where the socially planned use of science has made the most, not least, progress. Were it not for the youth of science and the historically demonstrated slowness of all basic mental and moral change, we could hardly find language to express astonishment at the situation in which we have an extensive and precise control of physical energies and conditions, and in which we leave the social consequences of their operation to chance, laissez-faire, privileged pecuniary status, and the inertia of tradition and old institutions.

Condorcet thought and worked in the Baconian strain. But the Baconian ideal of the systematic organization of all knowledge, the planned control of discovery and invention, for the relief and advancement of the human estate, remains almost as purely an ideal as when Francis Bacon put it forward centuries ago. And this is true in spite of the fact that the physical and mathematical technique upon which a planned control of social results depends has made in the meantime incalculable progress. The conclusion is inevitable. The outer arena of life has been transformed by science. The effectively working mind and character of man have hardly been touched.

Consider that phase of social action where science might theoretically be supposed to have taken effect most rapidly, namely, education. In dealing with the young, it would seem as if scientific methods might at once take effect in transformation of mental attitudes, without meeting the obstacles which have to be overcome in dealing with adults. In higher education, in universities and technical schools, a great amount of research is done and much scientific knowledge is imparted. But it is a principle of modern psychology that the basic attitudes of mind are formed in the earlier years. And I venture the assertion that for the most part the formation of intellectual habits in elementary education, in the home and school, is hardly affected by scientific method. Even in our so-called progressive schools, science is usually treated as a side line, an ornamental extra, not as the chief means of developing the right mental attitudes. It is treated generally as one more body of ready-made information to be acquired by traditional methods, or else as an occasional diversion. That it is the method of all effective mental approach and attack in all subjects has not gained even a foothold. Yet if scientific method is not something esoteric but is a realization of the most effective operation of intelligence, it should be axiomatic that the development of scientific attitudes of thought, observation, and inquiry is the chief business of study and learning.

Two phases of the contradiction inhering in our civilization may be especially mentioned. We have long been committed in theory and words to the principle of democracy. But criticism of democracy, assertions that it is failing to work and even to exist are everywhere rife. In the last few months we have become accustomed to similar assertions regarding our economic and industrial system. Mr. Ivy Lee for example, in a recent commencement address, entitled *This Hour of Bewilderment,* quoted from a representative clergyman, a railway president, and a publicist, to the effect that our capitalistic system is on trial. And yet the statements had to do with only one feature of that system: the prevalence of unemployment and attendant insecurity. It is not necessary for me to invade the territory of economics and politics. The essential fact is that if both democracy and capitalism are on trial, it is in reality our collective intelligence which is on trial. We have displayed enough intelligence in the physical field to create the new and powerful instrument of science and technology. We have not as yet had enough intelligence to use this instrument deliberately and systematically to control its social operations and consequences.

The first lesson which the use of scientific method teaches is that control is coördinate with knowledge and understanding. Where there is technique there is the possibility of administering forces and conditions in the region where the technique applies. Our lack of control in the sphere of human relations, national, domestic, international, requires no emphasis of notice. It is proof that we have not begun to operate scientifically in such matters. The public press is full of discussion of the five-year plan and the ten-year plan in Russia. But the fact that the plan is being tried by a country which has a dictatorship foreign to all our beliefs tends to divert attention from the fundamental consideration. The point for us is not this political setting nor its communistic context. It is that by the use of all available resources of knowledge and experts an attempt is being made at organized social planning and control. Were we to forget for the moment the special Russian political setting, we should see here an effort to use coördinated knowledge and technical skill to direct economic resources toward social order and stability.

To hold that such organized planning is possible only in a communistic society is to surrender the case to communism. Upon any other basis, the effort of Russia is a challenge and a warning to those who live under another political and economic regime. It is a call to use our more advanced knowledge and technology in scientific thinking about our own needs, problems, evils, and possibilities so as to achieve some degree of control of the social consequences which the application of science is, willy-nilly, bringing about. What stands in the way is a lot of outworn traditions, moth-eaten slogans and catchwords, that do substitute duty for thought, as well as our entrenched predatory self-interest. We shall only make a real beginning in intelligent thought when we cease mouthing platitudes; stop confining our ideas to antitheses of individualism and socialism, capitalism and communism, and realize that the issue is between chaos and order, chance and control: the haphazard use and the planned use of scientific techniques.

Thus the statement with which we began, namely, that we are living in a world of change extraordinary in range and speed, is only half true. It holds of the outward applications of science. It does not hold of our intellectual and moral attitudes. About physical conditions and energies we think scientifically; at least, some men do, and the results of their thinking enter into the experiences of all of us. But the entrenched and stubborn institutions of the past stand in the way of our thinking scientifically about human relations and social issues. Our mental habits in these respects are dominated by institutions of family, state, church, and business that were formed long before men had an effective technique of inquiry and validation. It is this contradiction from which we suffer today.

Disaster follows in its wake. It is impossible to overstate the mental confusion and the practical disorder which are bound to result when external and physical effects are planned and regulated, while the attitudes of mind upon which the direction of external results depends are left to the medley of chance, tradition, and dogma. It is a common saying that our physical science has far outrun our social knowledge; that our physical skill has become exact and comprehensive while our humane arts are vague, opinionated, and narrow. The fundamental trouble, however, is not lack of sufficient information about social facts, but unwillingness to adopt the scientific attitude in what we do know. Men floundered in a morass of opinion about physical matters for thousands of years. It was when they began to use their ideas experimentally and to create a technique or direction of experimentation that physical science advanced with system and surety. No amount of mere fact-finding develops science nor the scientific attitude in either physics or social affairs. Facts merely amassed and piled up are dead; a burden which only adds to confusion. When ideas, hypotheses, begin to play upon facts, when they are methods for experimental use in action, then light dawns; then it becomes possible to discriminate significant from trivial facts, and relations take the place of isolated scraps. Just as soon as we begin to use the knowledge and skills we have to control social consequences in the interest of shared abundant and secured life, we shall cease to complain of the backwardness of social knowledge. We shall take the road which leads to the assured building up of social science just as men built up physical science when they actively used the techniques of tools and numbers in physical experimentation.

In spite, then, of all the record of the past, the great scientific revolution is still to come. It will ensue when men collectively and coöperatively organize their knowledge for application to achieve and make secure social values; when they systematically use scientific procedures for the control of human relationships and the direction of the social effects of our vast technological machinery. Great as have been the social changes of the last century, they are not to be compared with those which will emerge when our faith in scientific method is made manifest in social works. We are living in a period of depression. The intellectual function of trouble is to lead men to think. The depression is a small price to pay if it induces us to think about the cause of the disorder, confusion, and insecurity which are the outstanding traits of our social life. If we do not go back to their cause, namely our half-way and accidental use of science, mankind will pass through depressions, for they are the graphic record of our unplanned social life. The story of the achievement of science in physical control is evidence of the possibility of control in social affairs. It is our human intelligence and human courage which are on trial; it is incredible that men who have brought the technique of physical discovery, invention, and use to such a pitch of perfection will abdicate in the face of the infinitely more important human problem.

Experience, Nature and Art •

In short, the history of human experience is a history of the development of arts. The history of science in its distinct emergence from religious, ceremonial and poetic arts is the record of a differentiation of arts, not a record of separation from art. The chief significance of the account just given, lies, for our present purpose, in its bearing upon the theory of experience and nature. It is not, however, without import for a theory of criticism. The present confusion, deemed chaos by some, in the fine arts and esthetic criticism seems to be an inevitable consequence of the underlying, even if unavowed, separation of the instrumental and the consummatory. The further men go in the concrete the more they are forced to recognize the logical consequence of their controlling assumptions. We owe it to theories of art prevalent to-day in one school of critics that certain implications, long obscured, of the traditional theory of art and nature have been brought to light. Gratitude for this debt should not be stinted because the adherents of the traditional theory regarding the newer views as capricious heresies, wild aberrations. For these critics, in proclaiming that esthetic qualities in works of fine art are unique, in asserting their separation from not only everything that is existential in nature but also from all other forms of good, in proclaiming that such arts as music, poetry, painting have characters unshared with any natural things whatsoever—in asserting such things the critics carry to its conclusion the isolation of fine art from the useful, of the final

• [From: John Dewey, *Experience and Nature.* Chicago: Open Court Publishing Co.; 1925. Pp. 388-93. Copyright 1925, 1929 by Open Court Publishing Co. Reprinted by permission of the publishers.]

from efficacious. They thus prove that the separation of the consummation from the instrumental makes art wholly esoteric.

There are substantially but two alternatives. Either art is a continuation, by means of intelligent selection and arrangement, of natural tendencies of natural events; or art is a peculiar addition to nature springing from something dwelling exclusively within the breast of man, whatever name be given the latter. In the former case, delightfully enhanced perception or esthetic appreciation is of the same nature as enjoyment of any object that is consummatory. It is the outcome of a skilled and intelligent art of dealing with natural things for the sake of intensifying, purifying, prolonging and deepening the satisfactions which they spontaneously afford. That, in this process, new meanings develop, and that these afford uniquely new traits and modes of enjoyment is but what happens everywhere in emergent growths.

But if fine art has nothing to do with other activities and products, then of course it has nothing inherently to do with the objects, physical and social, experienced in other situations. It has an occult source and an esoteric character. It makes little difference what the source and the character be called. By strict logic it makes literally no difference. For if the quality of the esthetic experience is by conception unique, then the words employed to describe it have no significance derived from or comparable to the qualities of other experiences; their signification is hidden and specialized to a degree. Consider some of the terms which are in more or less current use among the critics who carry the isolation of art and the esthetic to its limit. It is sometimes said that art is the expression of the emotions; with the implication that, because of this fact, subject-matter is of no significance except as material through which emotion is expressed. Hence art becomes unique. For in works of science, utility and morals the character of the objects forming this subject-matter is all-important. But by this definition, subject-matter is stripped of all its own inherent characters in art in the degree in which it is genuine art; since a truly artistic work is manifest in the reduction of subject-matter to a mere medium of expression of emotion.

In such a statement emotion either has no significance at all, and it is mere accident that this particular combination of letters is employed; or else, if by emotion is meant the same sort of thing that is called emotion in daily life, the statement is demonstrably false. For emotion in its ordinary sense is something called out *by* objects, physical and personal; it is response *to* an objective situation. It is not something existing somewhere by itself which then employs material through which to express itself. Emotion is an indication of intimate participation, in a more or less excited way in some scene of nature or life; it is, so to speak, an attitude or disposition which is a function of objective things. It is intelligible that art should select and assemble objective things in such ways as to evoke emotional response of a refined, sensitive and enduring kind; it is intelligible that the artist himself is one capable of sustaining these emotions, under whose temper and spirit he performs his compositions of objective materials. This procedure may indeed be carried to a point such that the use of objective materials is economized to the minimum, and the evocation of the emotional response carried to its relative maximum. But it still remains true that the origin of the art-process lay in emotional responses spontaneously called out by a situation occurring without any reference to art, and without "esthetic" quality save in the sense in which all immediate enjoyment and suffering is esthetic. Economy in use of objective subject-matter may with experienced and trained minds go so far that what is ordinarily called "representation" is much reduced. But what happens is a highly funded and generalized representation of the formal sources of ordinary emotional experience.

The same sort of remark is to be made concerning "significant form" as a definition of an esthetic object. Unless the meaning of the term is so isolated as to be wholly occult, it denotes a selection, for sake of emphasis, purity, subtlety, of those forms which give consummatory significance to everyday subject-matters of experience. "Forms" are not the peculiar property or creation of the esthetic and artistic; they are characters in virtue of which anything meets the requirements of an enjoyable perception. "Art" does not create the forms; it is their selection and organization in such ways as to enhance, prolong and purify the perceptual experience. It is not by accident that some objects and situations afford marked perceptual satisfactions; they do so because of their structural properties and relations. An artist may work with a minimum of analytic recognition of these structures or "forms"; he may select them chiefly by a kind of sympathetic vibration. But they may also be discriminatively ascertained;

and an artist may utilize his deliberate awareness of them to create works of art that are more formal and abstract than those to which the public is accustomed. Tendency to composition in terms of the formal characters marks much contemporary art, in poetry, painting, music, even sculpture and architecture. At their worst, these products are "scientific" rather than artistic; technical exercises, sterile and of a new kind of pedantry. At their best, they assist in ushering in new modes of art and by education of the organs of perception in new modes of consummatory objects: they enlarge and enrich the world of human vision.

Thus, by only a slight forcing of the argument, we reach a conclusion regarding the relations of instrumental and fine art which is precisely the opposite of that intended by seclusive estheticians; namely, that fine art *consciously* undertaken as such is peculiarly instrumental in quality. It is a device in experimentation carried on for the sake of education. It exists for the sake of a specialized use, use being a new training of modes of perception. The creators of such works of art are entitled, when successful, to the gratitude that we give to inventors of microscopes and microphones; in the end, they open new objects to be observed and enjoyed. This is a genuine service; but only an age of combined confusion and conceit will arrogate to works that perform this special utility the exclusive name of fine art.

Experience in the form of art, when reflected upon, we conclude by saying, solves more problems which have troubled philosophers and resolves more hard and fast dualisms than any other theme of thought. As the previous discussion has indicated, it demonstrates the intersection in nature of individual and generic; of chance and law, transforming one into opportunity and the other into liberation; of instrumental and final. More evidently still, it demonstrates the gratuitous falsity of notions that divide overt and executive activity from thought and feeling and thus separate mind and matter. In creative production, the external and physical world is more than a mere means or external condition of perceptions, ideas and emotions; it is subject-matter and sustainer of conscious activity; and thereby exhibits, so that he who runs may read, the fact that consciousness is not a separate realm of being, but is the manifest quality of existence when nature is most free and most active.

Religion versus the Religious *

Never before in history has mankind been so much of two minds, so divided into two camps, as it is today. Religions have traditionally been allied with ideas of the supernatural, and often have been based upon explicit beliefs about it. Today there are many who hold that nothing worthy of being called religious is possible apart from the supernatural. Those who hold this belief differ in many respects. They range from those who accept the dogmas and sacraments of the Greek and Roman Catholic church as the only sure means of access to the supernatural to the theist or mild deist. Between them are the many Protestant denominations who think the Scriptures, aided by a pure conscience, are adequate avenues to supernatural truth and power. But they agree in one point: the necessity for a Supernatural Being and for an immortality that is beyond the power of nature.

The opposed group consists of those who think the advance of culture and science has completely discredited the supernatural and with it all religions that were allied with belief in it. But they go beyond this point. The extremists in this group believe that with elimination of the supernatural not only must historic religions be dismissed but with them everything of a religious nature. When historical knowledge has discredited the claims made for the supernatural character of the persons said to have founded historic religions, when the supernatural inspiration attributed to literatures held sacred has been riddled, and when anthropological and psychological knowledge has disclosed the all-too-human source from which religious beliefs and practices have sprung, everything religious must, they say, also go.

There is one idea held in common by these two opposite groups: identification of the religious with the supernatural.

* [From: John Dewey, *A Common Faith*. New Haven: Yale University Press; 1934. Pp. 1-28. Copyright 1934 by Yale University Press. Reprinted by permission of the publishers.]

The question I shall raise in these chapters concerns the ground for and the consequences of this identification: its reasons and its value. In the discussion I shall develop another conception of the nature of the religious phase of experience, one that separates it from the supernatural and the things that have grown up about it. I shall try to show that these derivations are encumbrances and that what is genuinely religious will undergo an emancipation when it is relieved from them; that then, for the first time, the religious aspect of experience will be free to develop freely on its own account.

This view is exposed to attack from both the other camps. It goes contrary to traditional religions, including those that have the greatest hold upon the religiously minded today. The view announced will seem to them to cut the vital nerve of the religious element itself in taking away the basis upon which traditional religions and institutions have been founded. From the other side, the position I am taking seems like a timid halfway position, a concession and compromise unworthy of thought that is thoroughgoing. It is regarded as a view entertained from mere tendermindedness, as an emotional hangover from childhood indoctrination, or even as a manifestation of a desire to avoid disapproval and curry favor.

The heart of my point, as far as I shall develop it in this first section, is that there is a difference between religion, *a* religion, and the religious, between anything that may be denoted by a noun substantive and the quality of experience that is designated by an adjective. It is not easy to find a definition of religion in the substantive sense that wins general acceptance. However, in the *Oxford Dictionary* I find the following: "Recognition on the part of man of some unseen higher power as having control of his destiny and as being entitled to obedience, reverence and worship."

This particular definition is less explicit in assertion of the supernatural character of the higher unseen power than are others that might be cited. It is, however, surcharged with implications having their source in ideas connected with the belief in the supernatural, characteristic of historic religions. Let us suppose that one familiar with the history of religions, including those called primitive, compares the definition with the variety of known facts and by means of the comparison sets out to determine just what the definition means. I think he will be struck by three facts that reduce the terms of the definition to such a low common denominator that little meaning is left.

He will note that the "unseen powers" referred to have been conceived in a multitude of incompatible ways. Eliminating the differences, nothing is left beyond the bare reference to something unseen and powerful. This has been conceived as the vague and undefined Mana of the Melanesians; the Kami of primitive Shintoism; the fetish of the Africans; spirits, having some human properties, that pervade natural places and animate natural forces; the ultimate and impersonal principle of Buddhism; the unmoved mover of Greek thought; the gods and semidivine heroes of the Greek and Roman Pantheons; the personal and loving Providence of Christianity, omnipotent, and limited by a corresponding evil power, the arbitrary Will of Moslemism; the supreme legislator and judge of deism. And these are but a few of the outstanding varieties of ways in which the invisible power has been conceived.

There is no greater similarity in the ways in which obedience and reverence have been expressed. There has been worship of animals, of ghosts, of ancestors, phallic worship, as well as of a Being of dread power and of love and wisdom. Reverence has been expressed in the human sacrifices of the Peruvians and Aztecs; the sexual orgies of some Oriental religions; exorcisms and ablutions; the offering of the humble and contrite mind of the Hebrew prophet, the elaborate rituals of the Greek and Roman Churches. Not even sacrifice has been uniform; it is highly sublimated in Protestant denominations and in Moslemism. Where it has existed it has taken all kinds of forms and been directed to a great variety of powers and spirits. It has been used for expiation, for propitiation and for buying special favors. There is no conceivable purpose for which rites have not been employed.

Finally, there is no discernible unity in the moral motivations appealed to and utilized. They have been as far apart as fear of lasting torture, hope of enduring bliss in which sexual enjoyment has sometimes been a conspicuous element; mortification of the flesh and extreme asceticism; prostitution and chastity; wars to extirpate the unbeliever; persecution to convert or punish the unbeliever, and philanthropic zeal; servile acceptance of imposed dogma, along with brotherly love and aspiration for a reign of justice among men.

I have, of course, mentioned only a sparse number of the facts which fill volumes in any well-stocked library. It may be asked by those who do not like to look upon the darker side of the history of religions why the darker facts should be brought up. We all know that civilized man has a background of bestiality and superstition and that these elements are still with us. Indeed, have not some religions, including the most influential forms of Christianity, taught that the heart of man is totally corrupt? How could the course of religion in its entire sweep not be marked by practices that are shameful in their cruelty and lustfulness, and by beliefs that are degraded and intellectually incredible? What else than what we find could be expected, in the case of people having little knowledge and no secure method of knowing; with primitive institutions, and with so little control of natural forces that they lived in a constant state of fear?

I gladly admit that historic religions have been relative to the conditions of social culture in which peoples lived. Indeed, what I am concerned with is to press home the logic of this method of disposal of outgrown traits of past religions. Beliefs and practices in a religion that now prevails are by this logic relative to the present state of culture. If so much flexibility has obtained in the past regarding an unseen power, the way it affects human destiny, and the attitudes we are to take toward it, why should it be assumed that change in conception and action has now come to an end? The logic involved in getting rid of inconvenient aspects of past religions compels us to inquire how much in religions now accepted are survivals from outgrown cultures. It compels us to ask what conception of unseen powers and our relations to them would be consonant with the best achievements and aspirations of the present. It demands that in imagination we wipe the slate clean and start afresh by asking what would be the idea of the unseen, of the manner of its control over us and the ways in which reverence and obedience would be manifested, if whatever is basically religious in experience had the opportunity to express itself free from all historic encumbrances.

So we return to the elements of the definition that has been given. What boots it to accept, in defense of the universality of religion, a definition that applies equally to the most savage and degraded beliefs and practices that have related to unseen powers and to noble ideals of a religion having the greatest share of moral content? There are two points involved. One of them is that there is nothing left worth preserving in the notions of unseen powers, controlling human destiny to which obedience, reverence and worship are due, if we glide silently over the nature that has been attributed to the powers, the radically diverse ways in which they have been supposed to control human destiny, and in which submission and awe have been manifested. The other point is that when we begin to select, to choose, and say that some present ways of thinking about the unseen powers are better than others; that the reverence shown by a free and self-respecting human being is better than the servile obedience rendered to an arbitrary power by frightened men; that we should believe that control of human destiny is exercised by a wise and loving spirit rather than by madcap ghosts or sheer force—when I say, we begin to choose, we have entered upon a road that has not yet come to an end. We have reached a point that invites us to proceed farther.

For we are forced to acknowledge that concretely there is no such thing as religion in the singular. There is only a multitude of religions. "Religion" is a strictly collective term and the collection it stands for is not even of the kind illustrated in textbooks of logic. It has not the unity of a regiment or assembly but that of any miscellaneous aggregate. Attempts to prove the universality prove too much or too little. It is probable that religions have been universal in the sense that all the peoples we know anything about have had *a* religion. But the differences among them are so great and so shocking that any common element that can be extracted is meaningless. The idea that religion is universal proves too little in that the older apologists for Christianity seem to have been better advised than some modern ones in condemning every religion but one as an impostor, as at bottom some kind of demon worship or at any rate a superstitious figment. Choice among religions is imperative, and the necessity for choice leaves nothing of any force in the argument from universality. Moreover, when once we enter upon the road of choice, there is at once presented a possibility not yet generally realized.

For the historic increase of the ethical and ideal content of religions suggests that the process of purification may be carried further. It indicates that further choice is imminent in which certain values and functions in experience may be selected. This possibility is what I had in mind in speaking of the difference between the religious and a religion. I am not proposing a religion, but rather the emancipation of elements and outlooks that may be called religious. For the moment we have a religion, whether that of the Sioux Indian or of Judaism or of Christianity, that moment the ideal factors in experience that may be called religious take on a load that is not inherent in them, a load of current beliefs and of institutional practices that are irrelevant to them.

I can illustrate what I mean by a common phenomenon in contemporary life. It is widely supposed that a person who does not accept any religion is thereby shown to be a non-religious person. Yet it is conceivable that the present depression in religion is closely connected with the fact that religions now prevent, because of their weight of historic encumbrances, the religious quality of experience from coming to consciousness and finding the expression that is appropriate to present conditions, intellectual and moral. I believe that such is the case. I believe that many persons are so repelled from what exists as a religion by its intellectual and moral implications, that they are not even aware of attitudes in themselves that if they came to fruition would be genuinely religious. I hope that this remark may help make clear what I mean by the distinction between "religion" as a noun substantive and "religious" as adjectival.

To be somewhat more explicit, a religion (and as I have just said there is no such thing as religion in general) always signifies a special body of beliefs and practices having some kind of institutional organization, loose or tight. In contrast, the adjective "religious" denotes nothing in the way of a specifiable entity, either institutional or as a system of beliefs. It does not denote anything to which one can specifically point as one can point to this and that historic religion or existing church. For it does not denote anything that can exist by itself or that can be organized into a particular and distinctive form of existence. It denotes attitudes that may be taken toward every object and every proposed end or ideal.

Before, however, I develop my suggestion that realization of the distinction just made would operate to emancipate the religious quality from encumbrances that now smother or limit it, I must refer to a position that in some respects is similar in words to the position I have taken, but that in fact is a whole world removed from it. I have several times used the phrase "religious elements of experience." Now at present there is much talk, especially in liberal circles, of religious experience as vouching for the authenticity of certain beliefs and the desirability of certain practices, such as particular forms of prayer and worship. It is even asserted that religious experience is the ultimate basis of religion itself. The gulf between this position and that which I have taken is what I am now concerned to point out.

Those who hold to the notion that there is a definite kind of experience which is itself religious, by that very fact make out of it something specific, as a kind of experience that is marked off from experience as aesthetic, scientific, moral, political; from experience as companionship and friendship. But "religious" as a quality of experience signifies something that may belong to all these experiences. It is the polar opposite of some type of experience that can exist by itself. The distinction comes out clearly when it is noted that the concept of this distinct kind of experience is used to validate a belief in some special kind of object and also to justify some special kind of practice.

For there are many religionists who are now dissatisfied with the older "proofs" of the existence of God, those that go by the name of ontological, cosmological and teleological. The cause of the dissatisfaction is perhaps not so much the arguments that Kant used to show the insufficiency of these alleged proofs, as it is the growing feeling that they are too formal to offer any support to religion in action. Anyway, the dissatisfaction exists. Moreover, these religionists are moved by the rise of the experimental method in other fields. What is more natural and proper, accordingly, than that they should affirm they are just as good empiricists as anybody else—indeed, as good as the scientists themselves? As the latter rely upon certain kinds of experience to prove the existence of certain kinds of objects, so the religionists rely upon a certain kind of experience to prove the existence of the object of religion, especially the supreme object, God.

The discussion may be made more definite by introducing, at this point, a particular illustration of this type of reasoning. A writer says: "I broke down from overwork and soon came to the verge of nervous prostration. One morning after a long and sleepless night . . . I resolved to stop drawing upon myself so continuously and begin drawing upon God. I determined to set apart a quiet time every day in which I could relate my life to its ultimate source, regain the consciousness that in God I live, move and have my being. That was thirty years ago. Since then I have had literally not one hour of darkness or despair."

This is an impressive record. I do not doubt its authenticity nor that of the experience related. It illustrates a religious aspect of experience. But it illustrates also the use of that quality to carry a superimposed load of a particular religion. For having been brought up in the Christian religion, its subject interprets it in the terms of the personal God characteristic of that religion. Taoists, Buddhists, Moslems, persons of no religion including those who reject all supernatural influence and power, have had experiences similar in their effect. Yet another author commenting upon the passage says: "The religious expert can be more sure that this God exists than he can of either the cosmological God of speculative surmise or the Christlike God involved in the validity of moral optimism," and goes on to add that such experiences "mean that God the saviour, the power that gives victory over sin on certain conditions that man can fulfill, is an existent, accessible and scientifically knowable reality." It should be clear that this inference is sound only if the conditions, of whatever sort, that produce the effect are called "God." But most readers will take the inference to mean that the existence of a particular Being, of the type called "God" in the Christian religion, is proved by a method akin to that of experimental science.

In reality, the only thing that can be said to be "proved" is the existence of some complex of conditions that have operated to effect an adjustment in life, an orientation, that brings with it a sense of security and peace. The particular interpretation given to this complex of conditions is not inherent in the experience itself. It is derived from the culture with which a particular person has been imbued. A fatalist will give one name to it, a Christian Scientist another, and the one who rejects all supernatural being still another. The determining factor in the interpretation of the experience is the particular doctrinal apparatus into which a person has been inducted. The emotional deposit connected with prior teaching floods the whole situation. It may readily confer upon the experience such a peculiarly sacred preciousness that all inquiry into its causation is barred. The stable outcome is so invaluable that the cause to which it is referred is usually nothing but a reduplication of the thing that has occurred, plus some name that has acquired a deeply emotional quality.

The intent of this discussion is not to deny the genuineness of the result nor its importance in life. It is not, save incidentally, to point out the possibility of a purely naturalistic explanation of the event. My purpose is to indicate what happens when religious experience is already set aside as something *sui generis*. The actual religious quality in the experience described is the *effect* produced, the better adjustment in life and its conditions, not the manner and cause of its production. The way in which the experience operated, its function, determines its religious value. If the reorientation actually occurs, it, and the sense of security and stability accompanying it, are forces on their own account. It takes place in different persons in a multitude of ways. It is sometimes brought about by devotion to a cause; sometimes by a passage of poetry that opens a new perspective; sometimes as was the case with Spinoza—deemed an atheist in his day— through philosophical reflection.

The difference between an experience having a religious force because of what it does in and to the processes of living and religious experience as a separate kind of thing gives me occasion to refer to a previous remark. If this function were rescued through emancipation from dependence upon specific types of beliefs and practices, from those elements that constitute a religion, many individuals would find that experiences having the force of bringing about a better, deeper and enduring adjustment in life are not so rare and infrequent as they are commonly supposed to be. They occur frequently in connection with many significant moments of living. The idea of invisible powers would take on the meaning of all the conditions of nature and human association that support and deepen the sense of values which carry one through periods of darkness and despair to such an extent that they lose their usual depressive character.

I do not suppose for many minds the dislocation of the religious from a religion is easy to effect. Tradition and custom, especially when emotionally charged, are a part of the habits that have become one with our very being. But the possibility of the transfer is demonstrated by its actuality. Let us then for the moment drop the term "religious," and ask what are the attitudes that lend deep and enduring support to the processes of living. I have, for example, used the words "adjustment" and "orientation." What do they signify?

While the words "accommodation," "adaptation," and "adjustment" are frequently employed as synonyms, attitudes exist that are so different that for the sake of clear thought they should be discriminated. There are conditions we meet that cannot be changed. If they are particular and limited, we modify our own particular attitudes in accordance with them. Thus we accommodate ourselves to changes in weather, to alterations in income when we have no other recourse. When the external conditions are lasting we become inured, habituated, or, as the process is now often called, conditioned. The two main traits of this attitude, which I should like to call accommodation, are that it affects *particular* modes of conduct, not the entire self, and that the process is mainly *passive*. It may, however, become general and then it becomes fatalistic resignation or submission. There are other attitudes toward the environment that are also particular but that are more active. We re-act against conditions and endeavor to change them to meet our wants and demands. Plays in a foreign language are "adapted" to meet the needs of an American audience. A house is rebuilt to suit changed conditions of the household; the telephone is invented to serve the demand for speedy communication at a distance; dry soils are irrigated so that they may bear abundant crops. Instead of accommodating ourselves to conditions, we modify conditions so that they will be accommodated to our wants and purposes. This process may be called adaptation.

Now both of these processes are often called by the more general name of adjustment. But there are also changes in ourselves in relation to the world in which we live that are much more inclusive and deep seated. They relate not to this and that want in relation to this and that condition of our surroundings, but pertain to our being in its entirety. Because of their scope, this modification of ourselves is enduring. It lasts through any amount of vicissitude of circumstances, internal and external. There is a composing and harmonizing of the various elements of our being such that, in spite of changes in the special conditions that surround us, these conditions are also arranged, settled, in relation to us. This attitude includes a note of submission. But it is voluntary, not externally imposed; and as voluntary it is something more than a mere Stoical resolution to endure unperturbed throughout the buffetings of fortune. It is more outgoing, more ready and glad, than the latter attitude, and it is more active than the former. And in calling it voluntary, it is not meant that it depends upon a particular resolve or volition. It is a change *of* will conceived as the organic plenitude of our being, rather than any special change *in* will.

It is the claim of religions that they effect this generic and enduring change in attitude. I should like to turn the statement around and say that whenever this change takes place there is a definitely religious attitude. It is not *a* religion that brings it about, but when it occurs, from whatever cause and by whatever means, there is a religious outlook and function. As I have said before, the doctrinal or intellectual apparatus and the institutional accretions that grow up are, in a strict sense, adventitious to the intrinsic quality of such experiences. For they are affairs of the traditions of the culture with which individuals are inoculated. Mr. Santayana has connected the religious quality of experience with the imaginative, as that is expressed in poetry. "Religion and poetry," he says, "are identical in essence, and differ merely in the way in which they are attached to practical affairs. Poetry is called religion when it intervenes in life, and religion, when it merely supervenes upon life, is seen to be nothing but poetry." The difference between intervening *in* and supervening *upon* is as important as is the identity set forth. Imagination may play upon life or it may enter profoundly into it. As Mr. Santayana puts it, "poetry has a universal and a moral function," for "its highest power lies in its relevance to the ideals and purposes of life." Except as it intervenes, "all observation is observation of brute fact, all discipline is mere repression, until these facts digested and this discipline embodied in humane impulses become the starting point for a creative movement of the imagination, the firm basis for ideal constructions in society, religion, and art."

If I may make a comment upon this penetrating insight of Mr. Santayana, I would say that the difference between imagination that only supervenes and imagination that intervenes is the difference between one that completely interpenetrates all the elements of our being and one that is interwoven with only special and partial factors. There actually occurs extremely little observation of brute facts merely for the sake of the facts, just as there is little discipline that is repression and nothing but repression. Facts are usually observed with reference to some practical end and purpose, and that end is presented only imaginatively. The most repressive discipline has some end in view to which there is at least imputed an ideal quality; otherwise it is purely sadistic. But in such cases of observation and discipline imagination is limited and partial. It does not extend far; it does not permeate deeply and widely.

The connection between imagination and the harmonizing of the self is closer than is usually thought. The idea of a whole, whether of the whole personal being or of the world, is an imaginative, not a literal, idea. The limited world of our observation and reflection becomes the Universe only through imaginative extension. It cannot be apprehended in knowledge nor realized in reflection. Neither observation, thought, nor practical activity can attain that complete unification of the self which is called a whole. The *whole* self is an ideal, an imaginative projection. Hence the idea of a thoroughgoing and deep-seated harmonizing of the self with the Universe (as a name for the totality of conditions with which the self is connected) operates only through imagination—which is one reason why this composing of the self is not voluntary in the sense of an act of special volition or resolution. An "adjustment" possesses the will rather than is its express product. Religionists have been right in thinking of it as an influx from sources beyond conscious deliberation and purpose—a fact that helps explain, psychologically, why it has so generally been attributed to a supernatural source and that, perhaps, throws some light upon the reference of it by William James to unconscious factors. And it is pertinent to note that the unification of the self throughout the ceaseless flux of what it does, suffers, and achieves, cannot be attained in terms of itself. The self is always directed toward something beyond itself and so its own unification depends upon the idea of the integration of the shifting scenes of the world into that imaginative totality we call the Universe.

The intimate connection of imagination with ideal elements in experience is generally recognized. Such is not the case with respect to its connection with faith. The latter has been regarded as a substitute for knowledge, for sight. It is defined, in the Christian religion, as *evidence* of things not seen. The implication is that faith is a kind of anticipatory vision of things that are now invisible because of the limitations of our finite and erring nature. Because it is a substitute for knowledge, its material and object are intellectual in quality. As John Locke summed up the matter, faith is "assent to a proposition . . . on the credit of its proposer." Religious faith is then given to a body of propositions as true on the credit of their supernatural author, reason coming in to demonstrate the reasonableness of giving such credit. Of necessity there results the development of theologies, or bodies of systematic propositions, to make explicit in organized form the content of the propositions to which belief is attached and assent given. Given the point of view, those who hold that religion necessarily implies a theology are correct.

But belief or faith has also a moral and practical import. Even devils, according to the older theologians, believe—and tremble. A distinction was made, therefore, between "speculative" or intellectual belief and an act called "justifying" faith. Apart from any theological context, there is a difference between belief that is a conviction that some end should be supreme over conduct, and belief that some object or being exists as a truth for the intellect. Conviction in the moral sense signifies being conquered, vanquished, in our active nature by an ideal end; it signifies acknowledgment of its rightful claim over our desires and purposes. Such acknowledgment is practical, not primarily intellectual. It goes beyond evidence that can be presented to *any* possible observer. Reflection, often long and arduous, may be involved in arriving at the conviction, but the import of thought is not exhausted in discovery of evidence that can justify intellectual assent. The authority of an ideal over choice and conduct is the authority of an ideal, not of a fact, of a truth guaranteed to intellect, not of the status of the one who propounds the truth.

Such moral faith is not easy. It was questioned of old whether the Son of Man should find faith on the earth in his coming. Moral faith has been bolstered by all sorts of arguments intended to prove that its object is not ideal and that its claim upon us is not primarily moral or practical, since the ideal in question is already embedded in the existent frame of things. It is argued that the ideal is already the final reality at the heart of things that exist, and that only our senses or the corruption of our natures prevent us from apprehending its prior existential being. Starting, say, from such an idea as that justice is more than a moral ideal because it is embedded in the very make-up of the actually existent world, men have gone on to build up vast intellectual schemes, philosophies, and theologies, to prove that ideals are real not as ideals but as antecedently existing actualities

They have failed to see that in converting moral realities into matters of intellectual assent they have evinced lack of *moral* faith. Faith that something should be in existence as far as lies in our power is changed into the intellectual belief that it is already in existence. When physical existence does not bear out the assertion, the physical is subtly changed into the metaphysical. In this way, moral faith has been inextricably tied up with intellectual beliefs about the supernatural.

The tendency to convert ends of moral faith and action into articles of an intellectual creed has been furthered by a tendency of which psychologists are well aware. What we ardently desire to have thus and so, we tend to believe is already so. Desire has a powerful influence upon intellectual beliefs. Moreover, when conditions are adverse to realization of the objects of our desire—and in the case of significant ideals they are extremely adverse—it is an easy way out to assume that after all they are already embodied in the ultimate structure of what is, and that appearances to the contrary are *merely* appearances. Imagination then merely supervenes and is freed from the responsibility for intervening. Weak natures take to reverie as a refuge as strong ones do to fanaticism. Those who dissent are mourned over by the first class and converted through the use of force by the second.

What has been said does not imply that all moral faith in ideal ends is by virtue of that fact religious in quality. The religious is "morality touched by emotion" only when the ends of moral conviction arouse emotions that are not only intense but are actuated and supported by ends so inclusive that they unify the self. The inclusiveness of the end in relation to both self and the "universe" to which an inclusive self is related is indispensable. According to the best authorities, "religion" comes from a root that means being bound or tied. Originally, it meant being bound by vows to a particular way of life—as *les religieux* were monks and nuns who had assumed certain vows. The religious attitude signifies something that is bound through imagination to a general attitude. This comprehensive attitude, moreover, is much broader than anything indicated by "moral" in its usual sense. The quality of attitude is displayed in art, science and good citizenship.

If we apply the conception set forth to the terms of the definition earlier quoted, these terms take on a new significance. An unseen power controlling our destiny becomes the power of an ideal. All possibilities, as possibilities, are ideal in character. The artist, scientist, citizen, parent, as far as they are actuated by the spirit of their callings, are controlled by the unseen. For all endeavor for the better is moved by faith in what is possible, not by adherence to the actual. Nor does this faith depend for its moving power upon intellectual assurance or belief that the things worked for must surely prevail and come into embodied existence. For the authority of the object to determine our attitude and conduct, the right that is given it to claim our allegiance and devotion is based on the intrinsic nature of the ideal. The outcome, given our best endeavor, is not with us. The inherent vice of all intellectual schemes of idealism is that they convert the idealism of action into a system of beliefs about antecedent reality. The character assigned this reality is so different from that which observation and reflection lead to and support that these schemes inevitably glide into alliance with the supernatural.

All religions, marked by elevated ideal quality, have dwelt upon the power of religion to introduce perspective into the piecemeal and shifting episodes of existence. Here too we need to reverse the ordinary statement and say that whatever introduces genuine perspective is religious, not that religion is something that introduces it. There can be no doubt (referring to the second element of the definition) of our dependence upon forces beyond our control. Primitive man was so impotent in the face of these forces that, especially in an unfavorable natural environment, fear became a dominant attitude, and, as the old saying goes, fear created the gods.

With increase of mechanisms of control, the element of fear has, relatively speaking, subsided. Some optimistic souls have even concluded that the forces about us are on the whole essentially benign. But every crisis, whether of the individual or of the community, reminds man of the precarious and partial nature of the control he exercises. When man, individually and collectively, has done his uttermost, conditions that at different times and places have given rise to the ideas of Fate and Fortune, of Chance and Providence, remain. It is the part of manliness to insist upon the capacity of mankind to strive to direct natural and social forces to humane ends. But unqualified absolutistic statements about the omnipotence of such endeavors reflect egoism rather than intelligent courage.

The fact that human destiny is so interwoven with forces

beyond human control renders it unnecessary to suppose that dependence and the humility that accompanies it have to find the particular channel that is prescribed by traditional doctrines. What is especially significant is rather the form which the sense of dependence takes. Fear never gave stable perspective in the life of anyone. It is dispersive and withdrawing. Most religions have in fact added rites of communion to those of expiation and propitiation. For our dependence is manifested in those relations to the environment that support our undertakings and aspirations as much as it is in the defeats inflicted upon us. The essentially unreligious attitude is that which attributes human achievement and purpose to man in isolation from the world of physical nature and his fellows. Our successes are dependent upon the cooperation of nature. The sense of the dignity of human nature is as religious as is the sense of awe and reverence when it rests upon a sense of human nature as a cooperating part of a larger whole. Natural piety is not of necessity either a fatalistic acquiescence in natural happenings or a romantic idealization of the world. It may rest upon a just sense of nature as the whole of which we are parts, while it also recognizes that we are parts that are marked by intelligence and purpose, having the capacity to strive by their aid to bring conditions into greater consonance with what is humanly desirable. Such piety is an inherent constituent of a just perspective in life.

Understanding and knowledge also enter into a perspective that is religious in quality. Faith in the continued disclosing of truth through directed cooperative human endeavor is more religious in quality than is any faith in a completed revelation. It is of course now usual to hold that revelation is not completed in the sense of being ended. But religions hold that the essential framework is settled in its significant moral features at least, and that new elements that are offered must be judged by conformity to this framework. Some fixed doctrinal apparatus is necessary for *a* religion. But faith in the possibilities of continued and rigorous inquiry does not limit access to truth to any channel or scheme of things. It does not first say that truth is universal and then add there is but one road to it. It does not depend for assurance upon subjection to any dogma or item of doctrine. It trusts that the natural interactions between man and his environment will breed more intelligence and generate more knowledge provided the scientific methods that define intelligence in operation are pushed further into the mysteries of the world, being themselves promoted and improved in the operation. There is such a thing as faith in intelligence becoming religious in quality—a fact that perhaps explains the efforts of some religionists to disparage the possibilities of intelligence as a force. They properly feel such faith to be a dangerous rival.

Lives that are consciously inspired by loyalty to such ideals as have been mentioned are still comparatively infrequent to the extent of that comprehensiveness and intensity which arouse an ardor religious in function. But before we infer the incompetency of such ideals and of the actions they inspire, we should at least ask ourselves how much of the existing situation is due to the fact that the religious factors of experience have been drafted into supernatural channels and thereby loaded with irrelevant encumbrances. A body of beliefs and practices that are apart from the common and natural relations of mankind must, in the degree in which it is influential, weaken and sap the force of the possibilities inherent in such relations. Here lies one aspect of the emancipation of the religious from religion.

Any activity pursued in behalf of an ideal end against obstacles and in spite of threats of personal loss because of conviction of its general and enduring value is religious in quality. Many a person, inquirer, artist, philanthropist, citizen, men and women in the humblest walks of life, have achieved, without presumption and without display, such unification of themselves and of their relations to the conditions of existence. It remains to extend their spirit and inspiration to ever wider numbers. If I have said anything about religions and religion that seems harsh, I have said those things because of a firm belief that the claim on the part of religions to possess a monopoly of ideals and of the supernatural means by which alone, it is alleged, they can be furthered, stands in the way of the realization of distinctively religious values inherent in natural experience. For that reason, if for no other, I should be sorry if any were misled by the frequency with which I have employed the adjective "religious" to conceive of what I have said is a disguised apology for what have passed as religions. The opposition between religious values as I conceive them and religions is not to be bridged. Just because the release of these values is so important, their identification with the creeds and cults of religions must be dissolved.

George Herbert Mead

1863-1931

*George Herbert Mead, a colleague of Dewey's at Michigan
and at Chicago, had, like Peirce, a "seminal mind." Dewey
and Mead shared a common viewpoint and greatly influenced
one another. As was the case with Peirce, Mead worked
throughout his life on a comprehensive system of philosophy.
Unfortunately, he, also like Peirce, published only discrete
articles during his lifetime. It was left for his friends and
former pupils to assemble as best they could from his manuscripts and lecture notes a systematic exposition of his philosophy. The system that he partially completed is involved,
intricate, and, in parts, obscure.*

*Mead starts with a social conception of experience. Ex-
perience is not something isolated and subjective—on the
contrary, it occurs in a larger context—that of the live creature within his* WHOLE *environment. From this standpoint he
developed a bio-social behaviorism. For Mead, individual
minds and selves are emergents within a social matrix. They
are generated and sustained by those processes of interaction
which constitute modes of communication: "Mind" resides
not merely in individuals, it is also concretely embodied in
institutions, e.g., "science," as a process of co-operative inquiry. And it is the development of this sort of intelligence*

which will enable men to deliberately control their own future by giving them a means of guiding the course of social evolution.

The "social and psychological process is," Mead said, "but an instance of what takes place in nature, if nature is an evolution." Hence, experience affords a prototype for the general comprehension of natural events. By inference from what is GIVEN in our experience he worked out a theory of emergent evolution analogous to the theories of Bergson, Alexander, and Whitehead. In this system the basic problem is that of the relation between determinism and novelty. During his last years Mead was occupied with this problem. In attempting to solve it he developed a highly original theory of time. We regard as "common sense" the statement that the past is irrevocable and determinant of the present. Any sort of novelty is a "repugnant fact." By contrast, Mead's view is that as unpredictables (novelties) emerge in a present, ITS past must be reconstituted to account for them. This involves the paradox that every present must have, as it were, its own past. Past and present can have meaning, then, only as related in a complex system of "temporal perspectives." Mead tried to assimilate the results of modern physics, in particular the theory of relativity, to this system of perspectives, thus constructing on the basis of his radical empiricism a metaphysical framework for modern physics.

(The editors are indebted to Professor Maurice Natanson for suggesting several possible excerpts from the writings of George Herbert Mead.)

*The Genesis
of the Self
and Social Control* •

It is my desire to present an account of the appearance of the self **in** social behavior, and then to advert to some implica-

• [From: George Herbert Mead, "The Genesis of the Self and Social Control," 35 *The International Journal of Ethics* (1924-25), pp. 251-77. Reprinted by permission of the University of Chicago Press.]

tions of such an account in their bearings upon social control.

The term "behavior" indicates the standpoint of what follows, that of a behavioristic psychology. There is an aspect of this psychology that calls for an emphasis which I think has not been sufficiently given it. It is not simply the objectivity of this psychology which has commended it. All recent psychology, in so far as it lays claim to a scientific approach, considers itself objective. But behavioristic psychology, coming in by the door of the study of animals lower than man, has perforce shifted its interest from psychical states to external conduct. Even when this conduct is followed into the central nervous system, it is not to find the correlate of the neurosis in a psychosis, but to complete the act, however distant this may be in space and time. This doctrine finds itself in sympathetic accord with recent realism and pragmatism, which places the so-called sensa and the significances of things in the object. While psychology has been turning to the act as a process, philosophic thought has been transferring contents that had been the subject-matter of earlier psychology from the field of states of consciousness to the objective world. Prebehavioristic psychology had a foot in two worlds. Its material was found in consciousness and in the world of physiology and physics. As long, however, as psychology was occupied with states of consciousness which constituted objects, there was an inevitable duplication. The whole physiological and physical apparatus could be stated in terms of states of consciousness, and solipsism hovered in the background. A psychology that is called upon to analyze the object into the states of consciousness which it is studying may conceivably be an empirical science, but in so far its world is not the world of the other sciences. A behavioristic psychology, on the other hand, that is not responsible for the content of the object, becomes a science that is cognate with physiology and dynamics, and escapes the trail of the epistemological serpent.

I am not concerned with the philosophical justification of this attitude of behavioristic psychology; I merely wish to emphasize its inevitable tendency to deal with processes, that is, with acts, and to find its objects given in the world with which all science deals. From Descartes' time on, it has been a border state, lying between philosophy and the natural sciences, and has suffered the inconveniences which attend buffer states. Descartes' unambiguous and uncompromising division between an extended physical world, and an unextended world of thought, when it reached the pineal gland found itself in ambiguous territory, and only avoided compromise by leaving the relations of mind and body to the infinite power of his *deus ex machina*. The difficulties which have attended psychology's regulation of these relations have been only in part metaphysical. More fundamentally they have been logical. The natural sciences start pragmatically with a world that is there, within which a problem has arisen, and introduce hypothetical reconstructions only in so far as its solution demands them. They always have their feet upon the solid ground of unquestioned objects of observation and experiment, where Samuel Johnson placed his in his summary refutation of Berkeley's idealism. Speculative philosophy, beset with the problem of epistemology, found its problem in the nature and very existence of the world inside which the problems of the natural sciences appeared, and which furnished the test of its hypotheses. Thus psychology as a philosophic discipline carried the epistemological problem into the experience of the individual, but as a science located the problem in a given world which its epistemological problem could not accept as given. Between the two, its sympathies have always been with the presuppositions and method of the natural sciences. On the one hand, as empirical science it has sought to regard the so-called consciousness of the individual as merely given in the sense of the objects of the natural sciences, but as states of consciousness were still regarded as cognitive, they had inevitably inherited the epistemological diathesis. On the other hand, as experimental science it was forced to place states of consciousness within or without the processes it was studying. Placing them in interactionism within the natural processes ran counter to the presuppositions of its scientific procedure, so that the prevailing attitude has been that of epiphenomenalism, an adaptation of Leibnitz' pre-established harmony and Spinoza's parallel attributes. They ran as harmless conscious shadows beside the physical and physiological processes with which science could come to immediate terms. But this proved but an unstable compromise. The conscious streak that accompanied the neuroses could answer only to sensing and thinking as processes; as qualities and significance of things, states of consciousness became hardly tolerable reduplications of things, except in the case of the secondary qualities. The molecular structure of things seemed to remove these from the hypothetical objects of physical science, and consciousness proved a welcome dumping-ground for them. This bifurcation of nature proves equally unsatisfactory. The horns and the hoofs go with the hide. States of contact experience have no better right to objective existence than those of distance experience. Psychology, however, has not been interested in these epistemological and metaphysical riddles, it has been simply irritated by them. It has shifted its interest to the processes where phenomenalism is most harmless, appearing as physiological psychology, as functional psychology, as dynamic psychology, and has ignored the problems for which it had no care. The effect of this has been to give to the central nervous system a logical pre-eminence in the procedure and textbooks of psychology which is utterly unwarranted in the analysis of the experience of the individual. The central nervous system has been unwittingly assimilated to the logical position of consciousness. It occupies only an important stage in the act, but we find ourselves locating the whole environment of the individual in its convolutions. It is small wonder, then, that behaviorism has been welcomed with unmistakable relief, for it has studied the conduct of animals in necessary ignoration of consciousness, and it has been occupied with the act as a whole, not as a nervous arc.

But the relief with which one turns to conduct and away from states of consciousness has not disposed of the problems involved in the ambiguous term "consciousness," even for the psychologist. Bergson's theory of perception was at least a step toward the clarification of this ambiguity. It recognizes that in so far as the content of the percept can be termed consciousness, it indicates a diminution of the reality of the object rather than an addition, and this diminution answers to the active interests of the organism, which are represented in the central nervous system by paths of possible response. These co-ordinated paths in some sense cut out the object of perception. The percept is relative to the perceiving individual, but relative to his active interest, not relative in the sense that its content is a state of his consciousness. It is at least meaningless to lodge the so-called sensuous characters of things in the cortex. When, however, Bergson suggests that certain of these qualities may be the condensation of vibrations, we seem again to be in the presence of qualities that are states of consciousness. Presumably the condensations, e.g., the actual quality of color, do not exist in the object, but in the condensing mind. However, Bergson's statement at least placed the central nervous system in the world of things, of percepts, on the one hand, and on the other placed the characters of things in pure perception in the things themselves; but the divorce of duration, as psychical, from a static intellectualized spatial world left a dichotomy which was functional only from the standpoint of a Bergsonian metaphysics. Neo-realism undertook to return all the qualities of things to the things, over against a mind which was simply aware of the sensa. This simple, radical procedure left problems of a perception which was still cognitive in its nature, which a Critical Realism sought to solve by retreating to representative perception again. It remained for pragmatism to take the still more radical position that in immediate experience the percept stands over against the individual, not in a relation of awareness, but simply in that of conduct. Cognition is a process of finding out something that is problematical, not of entering into relation with a world that is there.

There is an ambiguity in the word "consciousness." We use it in the sense of "awareness," "consciousness of," and are apt to assume that in this sense it is coextensive with experience, that it covers the relation of the sentient organism to its environment in so far as the environment exists for the organism. We thus predicate of this existence of the environment for the organism the attitude of cognition on the part of the organism. The other use of consciousness to which I refer is in the sense of certain contents, to wit, the sense qualities of things, more especially the so-called secondary qualities, the affections of the body of the sentient organism, especially those that are pleasurable and painful, the contents of the images of memory and imagination, and of the activities of the organism, so far as they appear in its experience. There is another field, that of self-consciousness, to which I am not as yet referring. There is a common character which in varying degree belongs to all of these contents, that is, that these contents could not appear at all, or exactly as they do appear, in the experience of any other organism. They are in this sense private, though this privacy does not imply necessarily anything more than difference of access or of perspective on the part of the different organisms. If we take the pragmatic attitude, referred to above, consciousness in the first sense, that of awareness, would disappear from immediate experience, while the world that is there for the organism would still be there. A particular organism would become conscious from this standpoint, that is, there would be a world that would exist for the organism, when the organism marked or plotted or, to use Bergson's term, canalized its environment in terms of its future conduct. For Bergson, a percept is an object of possible action for an organism, and it is the active relationship of the organism to the distant object that constitutes it an object. Bergson meets the difficulty that the organism can exercise no physical influence upon the distant object by his assumption that consciousness in this sense is in reality not an addition to the object, but an abstraction from all in the relation of the organism to the object which does not bear upon this action. There arises, then, a selected series of objects, determined by the active interests of the organism.

An environment thus arises for an organism through the selective power of an attention that is determined by its impulses that are seeking expression. This peculiar environment does not exist in the consciousness of the form as a separate milieu, but the consciousness of the organism consists in the fact that its future conduct outlines and defines its objects. In so far as the organization of one individual differs from that of others, it will have a private environment, though these differences may be called those of standpoint. They are objective differences. They exist in nature. The most fundamental phase of these differences is found in the determination of what the relativist calls a "consentient set," i.e., the selection of those objects which may all be considered as "here" with reference to the individual. It is this set, which is co-gredient with the individual, that constitutes an environment within which motion may take place. These perspectives of nature exist in nature, not in the consciousness of the organism as a stuff. In this relation of a peculiar environment for an individual, there is no implication of an awareness. All that is implied is that the ongoing activity of the individual form marks and defines its world for the form, which thus exists for it as it does not for any other form. If this is called consciousness, a behavioristic psychology can state it in terms of conduct.

Consciousness in the second sense, that of a peculiar content or contents, implies relativity in another sense, in the sense of emergence, as this has been defined by Alexander, in *Space, Time and Deity*, and accepted by Lloyd Morgan, in *Emergent Evolution*. In evolution not only have new forms appeared, but new qualities or contents in experience. It is the sensitivities of forms that are the occasions for the appearance, in the worlds of these forms, of new characters of things, answering to all the senses, and new meanings answering to their new capacities for conduct. And these new characters and new meanings exist in nature as do the forms of physical objects, though they are relative to the sensitivities and capacities of the individual forms. If we drop awareness from immediate experience, Alexander's distinction between perception and enjoyment may be also dropped. This distinction lies between the awareness of perception of external objects and that of the experience of the individual in perception and his other processes. Pleased palates and irritated or suffering members are there in the same sense as other percepts or objects. And this is true also of straining muscles, of fearful objects, or a turned stomach, or an attractive thing, nor can we deny this sort of objectivity to imagery, because access to it is confined to the individual in whose world it appears. Part of this imagery fits into the world that is there, and is with great difficulty analyzed out. That which will not fit in becomes located in our pasts or in futures of varying degrees of definiteness.

If my friend enters the room, and I catch a glimpse of his face, the imagery of his face fills out the countenance, and I see him with his whole complement of features. The same imagery might have figured in my memory of last meeting him. Or it might have figured in the plan I entertained of calling, on the following evening. It belongs either to the passing present, or to the irrevocable past, or to the contingent future. This imagery is for the percipient as objective as the so-called sense object. It may enter that object and be indistinguishable from it. Where it can be distinguished, however, it is recognized as having this private character; that is, while we assume that the color of the object perceived, even if it vary from eye to eye, is in some respects identical for all eyes in so far as the organs are alike, it is not assumed that the image which one has is there for other eyes, or imaginations. While this sole accessibility of imagery to the individual does not in itself render it less objective, it places it at the disposal of the individual, when he attains to a mind which it can furnish. The same is true of the other class of objects which in his experience is accessible only to him. I refer to the objects which the individual possesses from the inside, so to speak, the parts of his organism, especially as they are painful or pleasurable. In the so-called lower animals, there is no evidence that this private field is organized and used as the possession of a self. The passing present is neither extended into a memory series, nor into an anticipated future.

Imagery is but one phase of the presence of the past in the passing present. In the living form it appears as facility in the response, and in the selection of the stimulus, in selective discrimination, in the stimulus. Imagery emerges, in the sense of Alexander, as the content of the past in the stimulus, and as meaning in the response. Imagery and meaning are there in the objects as contents, before they become material for the mind, before the mind appears in conduct.

I have referred to the doctrine of relativity. More specifically, my reference was to formulation of the doctrine given in Professor Whitehead's three books, *The Principles of Natural Knowledge, The Concept of Nature,* and *The Principle of Relativity.* What I have had particularly in mind is Whitehead's recognition, as over against current Einsteinian doctrine, that if motion is to be accepted as an objective fact, we must also accept the existence in nature of so-called consentient sets at rest, determined by their relation to so-called percipient events. The same events in nature appear in different consentient sets, as these events are ordered in different time systems, and this ordering in different time systems is dependent upon their relations to different percipient events. Motion in nature implies rest in nature. Rest in nature implies co-gredience, i.e., a persistent relation of here and there with reference to some individual, and it is this that determines the time system in accordance with which events are ordered. If rest is a fact in nature, we must conceive of it as stratified, to use Whitehead's term, by the different temporal perspectives of different individuals, though a group of individuals may have the same perspective; we must, however, remember that this is a stratification of nature not in a static space, but a nature whose extension is affected with a time dimension.

It is this conception of the existence in nature of consentient sets determined by their relations to percipient events that I wish to generalize so that it will cover the environment in relation to the living form, and the experienced world with reference to the experiencing individual. This is evidently only possible if we conceive life as a process and not a series of static physicochemical situations, and if we regard experience as conduct or behavior, not as a series of conscious states. This I take to be the essence of Bergson's philosophy of change, in accordance with which our perceptual world is determined by the actions that are taking place. Conduct does cut out and fashion the objects upon which action is directed. It is only with reference to life as an ongoing process that the animal determines his habitat. The most convincing illustration can be found in the different presentation of the life of a community, in terms of a social statics, the statistical data of population and occupations and the like, or in terms of the actual lives of the different individuals who make up the community. In the latter case we realize that each individual has a world that differs in some degree from that of any other member of the same community, that he slices the events of the community life that are common to all from a different angle from that of any other individual. In Whitehead's phrase, each individual stratifies the common life in a different manner, and the life of the community is the sum of all these stratifications, and all of these stratifications exist in nature. It is this recognition that takes psychology out of its isolation, as a science that deals with what is found in the mind of an individual, and makes of it the standpoint from which to approach reality as it is going on.

It is evident that a statement of the life of each individual in terms of the results of an analysis of that which is immediately experienced would offer a common plane of events, in which the experience of each would differ from the experiences of others only in their extent, and the completeness or incompleteness of their connections. These differences disappear in the generalized formulations of the social sciences. The experiences of the same individuals, in so far as each faces a world in which objects are plans of action, would implicate in each a different succession of events. In the simplest illustration, two persons approach a passing automobile. To one it is a moving object that he will pass before it reaches the portion of the street that is the meeting-place of their two paths. The other sees an object that will pass this meeting-point before he reaches it. Each slices the world from the standpoint of a different time system. Objects which in a thousand ways are identical for the two individuals, are yet fundamentally different through their location in one spatio-temporal plane, involving a certain succession of events, or in another. Eliminate the temporal dimension, and bring all events back to an instant that is timeless, and the individuality of these objects which belongs to them in behavior is lost, except in so far as they can represent the results of past conduct. But taking time seriously, we realize that the seemingly timeless character of our spatial world and its permanent objects is due to the consentient set which each one of us selects. We abstract time from this space for the purposes of our conduct. Certain objects cease to be events, cease to pass as they are in reality passing and in their permanence become the conditions of our action, and events take place with reference to them. Because a whole community selects the same consentient set does not make the selection less the attitude of each one of them. The life-process takes place in individual organisms, so that the psychology which studies that process in its creative determining function becomes a science of the objective world.

Looked at from the standpoint of an evolutionary history, not only have new forms with their different spatio-temporal environments and their objects arisen, but new characters have arisen answering to the sensitivities and capacities for response. In the terms of Alexander, they have become differently qualitied. It is as impossible to transfer these characters of the habitats to the consciousness of the forms as it is to transfer the spatio-temporal structure of the things to such a so-called consciousness. If we introduce a fictitious instantaneousness into a passing universe, things fall to pieces. Things that are spatio-temporally distant from us can be brought into this instant only in terms of our immediate contact experience. They are what they would be if we were there and had our hands upon them. They take on the character of tangible matter. This is the price of their being located at the moment of our bodies' existence. But this instantaneous view has the great advantage of giving to us a picture of what the contact experience will be when we reach the distant object, and of determining conditions under which the distance characters arise. If the world existed at an instant in experience, we should be forced to find some realm such as consciousness into which to transport the distance or so-called secondary qualities of things. If consciousness in evolutionary history, then, has an unambiguous significance, it refers to that stage in the development of life in which the conduct of the individual marks out and defines the future field and objects which make up its environment, and in which emerge characters in the objects and sensitivities in the individuals that answer to each other. There is a relativity of the living individual and its environment, both as to form and content.

What I wish to trace is the fashion in which self and the mind has arisen within this conduct.

It is the implication of this undertaking that only selves have minds, that is, that cognition only belongs to selves, even in the simplest expression of awareness. This, of course, does not imply that below the stage of self-consciousness sense characters and sensitivity do not exist. This obtains in our own immediate experience in so far as we are not self-conscious. It is further implied that this development has taken place only in a social group, for selves exist only in relation to other selves, as the organism as a physical object exists only in its relation to other physical objects. There have been two fields within which social groups have arisen which have determined their environment together with that of their members, and the individuality of its members. These lie in the realm of the invertebrates and in that of the vertebrates. Among the Hymenoptera and termites there are societies whose interests determine for the individuals their stimuli and habitats, and so differentiate the individuals themselves, mainly through the sexual and alimentary processes, that the individual is what he is because of his membership within those societies. In the complex life of the group, the acts of the individuals are completed only through the acts of other individuals, but the mediation of this complex conduct is found in the physiological differentiation of the different members of the society. As Bergson has remarked of the instincts, the implements by which a complex act is carried out are found in the differentiated structure of the form. There is no convincing evidence that an ant or a bee is obliged to anticipate the act of another ant or bee, by tending to respond in the fashion of the other, in order that it may integrate its activity into the common act. And by the same mark there is no evidence of the existence of any language in their societies. Nor do we need to go to the invertebrates to discover this type of social conduct. If one picks up a little child who has fallen, he adapts his arms and attitude to the attitude of the child, and the child adapts himself to the attitude of the other; or in boxing or fencing one responds to stimulus of the other, by acquired physiological adjustment.

Among the vertebrates, apart from the differentiation of the sexes and the nurture and care of infant forms, there is little or no inherited physiological differentiation to mediate the complexities of social conduct. If we are to co-operate successfully with others, we must in some manner get their on-going acts into ourselves to make the common act come off. As I have just indicated, there is a small range of social activity in which this is not necessary. The suckling of an infant form, or a dog fight, if this may be called a social activity, does not call for more than inherited physiological adjustment. Perhaps the so-called herding instinct should be added, but it hardly comes to more than the tendency of the herd to stick together in their various activities. The wooing and mating of forms, the care of the infant form, the bunching of animals in migrations, and fighting, about exhaust vertebrate social conduct, and beyond these seasonal processes vertebrate societies hardly exist till we reach man. They exhaust the possibilities in vertebrate structure of the mediation of social conduct, for the vertebrate organism has shown no such astonishing plasticity in physiological differentiation as that which we can trace among the insects, from isolated forms to members of the societies of the termites, the ants, and the bees.

A social act may be defined as one in which the occasion or stimulus which sets free an impulse is found in the character or conduct of a living form that belongs to the proper environment of the living form whose impulse it is. I wish, however, to restrict the social act to the class of acts which involve the co-operation of more than one individual, and whose object as defined by the act, in the sense of Bergson, is a social object. I mean by a social object one that answers to all the parts of the complex act, though these parts are found in the conduct of different individuals. The objective of the act is then found in the life-process of the group, not in those of the separate individuals alone. The full social object would not exist in the environments of the separate individuals of the societies of the Hymenoptera and termites, nor in the restricted societies of the vertebrates whose basis is found alone in physiological adjustment. A cow that licks the skin of a calf stuffed with hay, until the skin is worn away, and then eats the hay, or a woman who expends her parental impulse upon a poodle, cannot be said to have the full social object involved in the entire act in their environments. It would be necessary to piece together the environments of the different individuals or superimpose them upon each other to reach the environment and objects of the societies in question.

Where forms such as those of the Hymenoptera and the

termites exhibit great plasticity in development, social acts based on physiological adjustment, and corresponding societies, have reached astonishing complexity. But when the limit of that plasticity is reached, the limit of the social act and the society is reached also. Where, as among the vertebrates, that physiological adjustment which mediates a social act is limited and fixed, the societies of this type are correspondingly insignificant. But another type of social act, and its corresponding society and object, has been at least suggested by the description of the social act based upon physiological adjustment. Such an act would be one in which the different parts of the act which belong to different individuals should appear in the act of each individual. This cannot mean, however, that the single individual could carry out the entire act, for then, even if it were possible, it would cease to be a social act, nor could the stimulus which calls out his own part of the complex act be that which calls out the other parts of the act in so far as they appear in his conduct. If the social object is to appear in his experience, it must be that the stimuli which set free the responses of the others involved in the act should be present in his experience, not as stimuli to his response, but as stimuli for the responses of others; and this implies that the social situation which arises after the completion of one phase of the act, which serves as the stimulus for the next participant in the complex procedure, shall in some sense be in the experience of the first actor, tending to call out, not his own response, but that of the succeeding actor. Let us make the impossible assumption that the wasp, in stinging a spider which it stores with its egg, finds in the spider a social object in the sense which I have specified. The spider would have to exist in the experience of the wasp as live but quiescent food for the larva when it emerges from the egg. In order that the paralyzed spider should so appear to the wasp, the wasp would need to be subject to the same stimulus as that which sets free the response of the larva; in other words, the wasp would need to be able to respond in some degree as the larva. And of course the wasp would have to view the spider under the time dimension, grafting a hypothetical future onto its passing present, but the occasion for this would have to lie in the wasp's tending to respond in role of larva to the appropriate food which it is placing in storage. This, then, presents another possible principle of social organization, as distinguished from that of physiological differentiation. If the objects that answer to the complex social act can exist spatio-temporally in the experience of the different members of the society, as stimuli that set free not only their own responses, but also as stimuli to the responses of those who share in the composite act, a principle of co-ordination might be found which would not depend upon physiological differentiation. And one necessary psychological condition for this would be that the individual should have in some fashion present in his organism the tendencies to respond as the other participants in the act will respond. Much more than this would be involved, but this at least would be a necessary precondition. A social object answering to the responses of different individuals in a society could be conceived of as existing in the experiences of individuals in that society, if the different responses of these individuals in the complex acts could be found in sufficient degree in the natures of separate individuals to render them sensitive to the different values of the object answering to the parts of the act.

The cortex of the vertebrate central nervous system provides at least a part of the mechanism which might make this possible. The nervous currents from the column and the stem of the brain to the cortex can there bring the acts that go out from these lower centers into relation with each other so that more complex processes and adjustments can arise. The centers and paths of the cortex represent an indefinite number of possible actions; particularly they represent acts which, being in competition with each other, inhibit each other, and present the problem of organization and adjustment so that overt conduct may proceed. In the currents and cross-currents in the gray matter and its association fibers, there exist the tendencies to an indefinite number of responses. Answering to these adjustments are the objects organized into a field of action, not only spatially but temporally; for the tendency to grasp the distant object, while already excited, is so linked with the processes of approach that it does not get its overt expression till the intervening stretch is passed. In this vertebrate apparatus of conduct, then, the already excited predispositions to thousands of acts, that far transcend the outward accomplishments, furnish the inner attitudes implicating objects that are not immediate objectives of the individual's act.

But the cortex is not simply a mechanism. It is an organ that exists in fulfilling its function. If these tendencies to action which do not get immediate expression appear and persist, it is because they belong to the act that is going on. If, for example, property is a social object in the experience of men, as distinguished from the nut which the squirrel stores, it is because features of the food that one buys innervate the whole complex of responses by which property is not only acquired, but respected and protected, and this complex so innervated is an essential part of the act by which the man buys and stores his food. The point is not that buying food is a more complicated affair than picking it up from the ground, but that exchange is an act in which a man excites himself to give by making an offer. An offer is what it is because the presentation is a stimulus to give. One cannot exchange otherwise than by putting one's self in the attitude of the other party to the bargain. Property becomes a tangible object, because all essential phases of property appear in the actions of all those involved in exchange, and appear as essential features of the individual's action.

The individual in such an act is a self. If the cortex has become an organ of social conduct, and has made possible the appearance of social objects, it is because the individual has become a self, that is, an individual who organizes his own response by the tendencies on the part of others to respond to his act. He can do this because the mechanism of the vertebrate brain enables the individual to take these different attitudes in the formation of the act. But selves have appeared late in vertebrate evolution. The structure of the central nervous system is too minute to enable us to show the corresponding structural changes in the paths of the brain. It is only in the behavior of the human animal that we can trace this evolution. It has been customary to mark this stage in development by endowing man with a mind, or at least with a certain sort of mind. As long as consciousness is regarded as a sort of spiritual stuff out of which are fashioned sensations and affections and images and ideas or significances, a mind as a locus of these entities is an almost necessary assumption, but when these contents have been returned to things, the necessity of quarters for this furniture has disappeared also.

It lies beyond the bounds of this paper to follow out the implications of this shift for logic and epistemology, but there is one phase of all so-called mental processes which is central to this discussion, and that is self-consciousness. If the suggestions which I have made above should prove tenable, the self that is central to all so-called mental experience has appeared only in the social conduct of human vertebrates. It is just because the individual finds himself taking the attitudes of the others who are involved in his conduct that he becomes an object for himself. It is only by taking the roles of others that we have been able to come back to ourselves. We have seen above that the social object can exist for the individual only if the various parts of the whole social act carried out by other members of the society are in some fashion present in the conduct of the individual. It is further true that the self can exist for the individual only if he assumes the roles of the others. The presence in the conduct of the individual of the tendencies to act as others act may be, then, responsible for the appearance in the experience of the individual of a social object, i.e., an object answering to complex reactions of a number of individuals, and also for the appearance of the self. Indeed, these two appearances are correlative. Property can appear as an object only in so far as the individual stimulates himself to buy by a prospective offer to sell. Buying and selling are involved in each other. Something that can be exchanged can exist in the experience of the individual only in so far as he has in his own make-up the tendency to sell when he has also the tendency to buy. And he becomes a self in his experience only in so far as one attitude on his own part calls out the corresponding attitude in the social undertaking.

This is just what we imply in "self-consciousness." We appear as selves in our conduct in so far as we ourselves take the attitude that others take toward us, in these correlative activities. Perhaps as good an illustration of this as can be found is in a "right." Over against the protection of our lives or property, we assume the attitude of assent of all members in the community. We take the role of what may be called the "generalized other." And in doing this we appear as social objects, as selves. It is interesting to note that in the development of the individual child, there are two stages which present the two essential steps in attaining self-consciousness. The first stage is that of play, and the second that of the game, where these two are distinguished from each other. In play in this sense, the child is continually acting as a parent, a teacher, a preacher, a grocery man, a policeman, a pirate, or an Indian. It is the period of childish existence which Wordsworth has described as that of "endless imitation." It is the period of Froebel's kindergarten plays. In it, as Froebel recognized, the child is acquiring the roles of those who belong to his society. This takes place because the child is continually exciting in himself the responses to his own social acts. In his infant dependence upon the responses of others to his own social stimuli, he is peculiarly sensitive to this relation. Having in his own nature the beginning of the parental response, he calls it out by his own appeals. The doll is the universal type of this, but before he plays with a doll, he responds in tone of voice and in attitude as his parents respond to his own cries and chortles. This has been denominated imitation, but the psychologist now recognizes that one imitates only in so far as the so-called imitated act can be called out in the individual by his appropriate stimulation. That is, one calls or tends to call out in himself the same response that he calls out in the other.

The play antedates the game. For in a game there is a regulated procedure, and rules. The child must not only take the role of the other, as he does in the play, but he must assume the various roles of all the participants in the game, and govern his action accordingly. If he plays first base, it is as the one to whom the ball will be thrown from the field or from the catcher. Their organized reactions to him he has imbedded in his own playing of the different positions, and this organized reaction becomes what I have called the "generalized other" that accompanies and controls his conduct. And it is this generalized other in his experience which provides him with a self. I can only refer to the bearing of this childish play attitude upon so-called sympathetic magic. Primitive men call out in their own activity some simulacrum of the response which they are seeking from the world about. They are children crying in the night.

The mechanism of this implies that the individual who is stimulating others to response is at the same time arousing in himself the tendencies to the same reactions. Now, that in a complex social act which serves as the stimulus to another individual to his response is not as a rule fitted to call out the tendency to the same response in the individual himself. The hostile demeanor of one animal does not frighten the animal himself, presumably. Especially in the complex social reactions of the ants or termites or the bees, the part of the act of one form which does call out the appropriate reaction of another can hardly be conceived of as arousing a like reaction in the form in question, for here the complex social act is dependent upon physiological differentiation, such an unlikeness in structure exists that the same stimulus could not call out like responses. For such a mechanism as has been suggested, it is necessary to find first of all some stimulus in the social conduct of the members of an authentic group that can call out in the individual, that is responsible for it, the same response that it calls out in the other; and in the second place, the individuals in the group must be of such like structure that the stimulus will have the same value for one form that it has for the other. Such a type of social stimulus is found in the vocal gesture in a human society. The term gesture I am using to refer to that part of the act or attitude of one individual engaged in a social act which serves as the stimulus to another individual to carry out his part of the whole act. Illustrations of gestures, so defined, may be found in the attitudes and movements of others to which we respond in passing them in a crowd, in the turning of the head toward the glance of another's eye, in the hostile attitude assumed over against a threatening gesture, in the thousand and one different attitudes which we assume toward different modulations of the human voice, or in the attitudes and suggestions of movements in boxers or fencers, to which responses are so nicely adjusted. It is to be noted that the attitudes to which I have referred are but stages in the act as they appear to others, and include expressions of countenance, positions of the body, changes in breathing rhythm, outward evidence of circulatory changes, and vocal sounds. In general these so-called gestures belong to the beginning of the overt act, for the adjustments of others to the social process are best made early in the act. Gestures are, then, the early stages in the overt social act to which other forms involved in the same act respond. Our interest is in finding gestures which can affect the individual that is responsible for them in the same manner as that in which they affect other individuals. The vocal gesture is at least one that assails our ears who make it in the same physiological fashion as that in which it affects others. We hear our own vocal gestures as others hear them. We may see or feel movements of our hands as others see or feel them, and these sights and feels have served in the place of the vocal gestures in the case of those who are congenitally deaf or deaf and blind. But it has been the vocal gesture that has pre-eminently provided the medium of social organization in human society. It belongs historically to the beginning of the act, for it arises out of the change in breathing rhythm that accompanies the preparation for sudden action, those actions to which other forms must be nicely adjusted.

If, then, a vocal gesture arouses in the individual who makes it a tendency to the same response that it arouses in another, and this beginning of an act of the other in himself enters into his experience, he will find himself tending to act toward himself as the other acts toward him. In our self-conscious experience we understand what he does or says. The possibility of this entering into his experience we have found in the cortex of the human brain. There the co-ordinations answering to an indefinite number of acts may be excited, and while holding each other in check enter into the neural process of adjustment which leads to the final overt conduct. If one pronounces and hears himself pronounce the word "table," he has aroused in himself the organized attitudes of his response to that object, in the same fashion as that in which he has aroused it in another. We commonly call such an aroused organized attitude an idea, and the ideas of what we are saying accompany all of our significant speech. If we may trust to the statement in one of St. Paul's epistles, some of the saints spoke with tongues which had no significance to them. They made sounds which called out no response in those that made them. The sounds were without meaning. Where a vocal gesture uttered by one individual leads to a certain response in another, we may call it a symbol of that act; where it arouses in the man who makes it the tendency to the same response, we may call it a significant symbol. These organized attitudes which we arouse in ourselves when we talk to others are, then, the ideas which we say are in our minds, and in so far as they arouse the same attitudes in others, they are in their minds, in so far as they are self-conscious in the sense in which I have used that term. But it is not necessary that we should talk to another to have these ideas. We can talk to ourselves, and this we do in the inner forum of what we call thought. We are in possession of selves just in so far as we can and do take the attitudes of others toward ourselves and respond to those attitudes. We approve of ourselves and condemn ourselves. We pat ourselves upon the back and in blind fury attack ourselves. We assume the generalized attitude of the group, in the censor that stands at the door of our imagery and inner conversations, and in the affirmation of the laws and axioms of the universe of discourse. *Quod semper, quod ubique.* Our thinking is an inner conversation in which we may be taking the roles of specific acquaintances over against ourselves, but usually it is with what I have termed the "generalized other" that we converse, and so attain to the levels of abstract thinking, and that impersonality, that so-called objectivity that we cherish. In this fashion, I conceive, have selves arisen in human behavior and with the selves their minds. It is an interesting study, that of the manner in which the self and its mind arises in every child, and the indications of the corresponding manner in which it arose in primitive man. I cannot enter into a discussion of this. I do wish, however, to refer to some of the implications of this conception of the self for the theory of social control.

I wish to recur to the position, taken earlier in this paper, that, if we recognize that experience is a process continually passing into the future, objects exist in nature as the patterns of our actions. If we reduce the world to a fictitious instantaneous present, all objects fall to pieces. There is no reason to be found, except in an equally fictitious mind, why any lines should be drawn about any group of physical particles, constituting them objects. However, no such knife-edge present exists. Even in the so-called specious present there is a passage, in which there is succession, and both past and future are there, and the present is only that section in which, from the standpoint of action, both are involved. When we take this passage of nature seriously, we see that the object of perception is the existent future of the act. The food is what the animal will eat, and his refuge is the burrow where he will escape from his pursuer. Of course the future is, as future, contingent. He may not escape, but in nature it exists there as the counterpart of his act. So far as there are fixed relations there, they are of the past, and the object involves both, but the form that it has arises from the ongoing act. Evolutionary biology, in so far as it is not mere physics and chemistry, proceeds perhaps unwittingly upon this assumption, and so does social science in so far as it is not static. Its objects are in terms of the habitat, the environment. They are fashioned by reactions. I am merely affirming the existence of these objects, affirming them as existent in a passing universe answering to acts.

In so far as there are social acts, there are social objects, and I take it that social control is bringing the act of the individual into relation with this social object. With the control of the object over the act, we are abundantly familiar. Just because the object is the form of the act, in this character it controls the expression of the act. The vision of the distant object is not only the stimulus to movement toward it. It is also, in its changing distance values, a continual control of the act of approach. The contours of the object determine the organization of the act of its seizure, but in this case the whole act is in the individual and the object is in his field of experience. Barring a breakdown in the structure or function, the very existence of the object insures its control of the act. In the social act, however, the act is distributed among a number of individuals. While there is or may be an object answering to each part of the act, existing in the experience of each individual, in the case of societies dependent upon physiological differentiation the whole object does not exist in the experience of any individual. The control may be exercised through the survival of those physiological differentiations that still carry out the life-process involved in the complex act. No complication of the act which did not mediate this could survive. Or we may take refuge in a controlling factor in the act, as does Bergson, but this is not the situation that interests us. The human societies in which we are interested are societies of selves. The human individual is a self only in so far as he takes the attitude of another toward himself. In so far as this attitude is that of a number of others, and in so far as he can assume the organized attitudes of a number that are co-operating in a common activity, he takes the attitudes of the group toward himself, and in taking this or these attitudes he is defining the object of the group, that which defines and controls the response. Social control, then, will depend upon the degree to which the individual does assume the attitudes of those in the group who are involved with him in his social activities. In the illustration already used, the man who buys controls his purchase from the standpoint of a value in the object that exists for him only in so far as he takes the attitude of a seller as well as a buyer. Value exists as an object only for individuals within whose acts in exchange are present those attitudes which belong to the acts of the others who are essential to the exchange.

The act of exchange becomes very complicated; the degree to which all the essential acts involved in it enter into the acts of all those engaged therein varies enormously, and the control which the object, i.e., the value, exercises over the acts varies proportionately. The Marxian theory of state ownership of capital, i.e., of exclusive state production, is a striking illustration of the breakdown of such control. The social object, successful economic production, as presented in this theory, fails to assume the attitudes of individual initiative which successful economic production implies. Democratic government, on the theory of action through universal interest in the issues of a campaign, breaks down as a control, and surrenders the government largely to the political machine, whose object more nearly answers to the attitudes of the voters and the non-voters.

Social control depends, then, upon the degree to which the individuals in society are able to assume the attitudes of the others who are involved with them in common endeavor. For the social object will always answer to the act developing itself in self-consciousness. Besides property, all of the institutions are such objects, and serve to control individuals who find in them the organization of their own social responses.

The individual does not, of course, assume the attitudes of the numberless others who are in one way or another implicated in his social conduct, except in so far as the attitudes of others are uniform under like circumstances. One assumes, as I have said, the attitudes of generalized others. But even with this advantage of the universal over the multiplicity of its numberless instances, the number of different responses that enter into our social conduct seems to defy any capacity of any individual to assume the roles which would be essential to define our social objects. And yet, though modern life has become indefinitely more complex than it was in earlier periods of human history, it is far easier for the modern man than for his predecessor to put himself in the place of those who contribute to his necessities, who share with him the functions of government, or join with him in determining prices. It is not the number of participants, or even the number of different functions, that is of primary importance. The important question is whether these various forms of activities belong so naturally to the member of a human society that, in taking the role of another, his activities are found to belong to one's own nature. As long as the complexities of human society do not exceed those of the central nervous system, the problem of an adequate social object, which is identical with that of an adequate self-consciousness, is not that of becoming acquainted with the indefinite number of acts that are involved in social behavior, but that of so overcoming the distances in space and time, and the barriers of language and convention and social status, that we can converse with ourselves in the roles of those who are involved with us in the common undertaking of life. A journalism that is insatiably curious about the human attitudes of all of us is the sign of the times. The other curiosities as to the conditions under which other people live, and work, and fight each other, and love each other, follow from the fundamental curiosity which is the passion of self-consciousness. We must be others if we are to be ourselves. The modern realistic novel has done more than technical education in fashioning the social object that spells social control. If we can bring people together so that they can enter into each other's lives, they will inevitably have a common object, which will control their common conduct.

The task, however, is enormous enough, for it involves not simply breaking down passive barriers such as those of distance in space and time and vernacular, but those fixed attitudes of custom and status in which our selves are imbedded. Any self is a social self, but it is restricted to the group whose roles it assumes, and it will never abandon this self until it finds itself entering into the larger society and maintaining itself there. The whole history of warfare between societies and within societies shows how much more readily and with how much greater emotional thrill we realize our selves in opposition to common enemies than in collaboration with them. All over Europe, and more specifically at Geneva, we see nationals with great distrust and constant rebounds trying to put themselves in each other's places and still preserve the selves that have existed upon enmities, that they may reach the common ground where they may avoid the horror of war, and meliorate unendurable economic conditions. A Dawes Plan is such a social object, coming painfully into existence, that may control the conflicting interests of hostile communities, but only if each can in some degree put himself in the other's place in operating it. The World Court and the League of Nations are other such social objects that sketch out common plans of action if there are national selves that can realize themselves in the collaborating attitudes of others.

Percy W. Bridgman

1882-

Philosophy, Dewey asserted, does not have any specific sub-ject matter, but it does perform a function. That function is criticism. Wherever in any area of knowledge there is reflec-tion about the meaning of fundamental ideas, one's thinking is philosophical. Philosophy is always OF—*it is an activity into which one is forced whenever confronted in any field with problems on a high level of generality. Percy W. Bridgman exemplifies this conception. He is primarily a physicist who has devoted his life to research on the behavior of liquids, solids, and gases under high pressures. For this work he re-ceived the Nobel Prize in 1946. His excursions into philos-ophy have been the consequence of problems arising out of his scientific activities. In this respect he belongs to a dis-tinguished group, among such men as Mach, Poincaré, Ein-stein, and Born.*

Einstein once remarked that if you wish to understand their methods do not listen to what the scientists SAY, *but look at what they* DO. *It is in this spirit that Bridgman attempts to discern and to describe how an experimental scientist thinks about his problems. The scientist's mode of procedure Bridg-man calls "operational analysis." Operational analysis pre-*

sumes a definition of meaning which he states as follows: "In general, we mean by any concept nothing more than a set of operations: THE CONCEPT IS SYNONYMOUS WITH THE CORRE-SPONDING SET OF OPERATIONS." *This definition of meaning is related to the one given by Peirce: "Consider what effects, that might conceivably have practical bearings, we conceive the object of our conception to have. Then, our conception of these effects is the whole of our conception of the object." Now, Peirce states his definition in terms of the behavior of the object of our conception, while Bridgman, by formulating his as an activity of the subject who is doing the conceiving, in effect points out a necessary presupposition of Peirce's statement. The two definitions are complementary.*

In a series of books Bridgman has developed the application of operational analysis to problems of method in the physical sciences. This mode of analysis may be used, however, in any field of inquiry. His book THE INTELLIGENT IN-DIVIDUAL AND SOCIETY *(1938) is an attempt to apply it to social questions.*

Broad Points
of View●

Whatever may be one's opinion as to our permanent accept-ance of the analytical details of Einstein's restricted and general theories of relativity, there can be no doubt that through these theories physics is permanently changed. It was a great shock to discover that classical concepts, ac-cepted unquestioningly, were inadequate to meet the actual situation, and the shock of this discovery has resulted in a critical attitude toward our whole conceptual structure which must at least in part be permanent. Reflection on the situa-tion after the event shows that it should not have needed the new experimental facts which led to relativity to convince us of the inadequacy of our previous concepts, but that a

● [From: Percy W. Bridgman, *The Logic of Modern Physics.* New York: The Macmillan Company; 1927. Pp. 1-32. Copyright 1927 by The Macmillan Company; copyright renewed 1953. Reprinted by permission of the publishers.]

sufficiently shrewd analysis should have prepared us for at least the possibility of what Einstein did.

Looking now to the future, our ideas of what external nature is will always be subject to change as we gain new experimental knowledge, but there is a part of our attitude to nature which should not be subject to future change, namely that part which rests on the permanent basis of the character of our minds. It is precisely here, in an improved understanding of our mental relations to nature, that the permanent contribution of relativity is to be found. We should now make it our business to understand so thoroughly the character of our permanent mental relations to nature that another change in our attitude, such as that due to Einstein, shall be forever impossible. It was perhaps excusable that a revolution in mental attitude should occur once, because after all physics is a young science, and physicists have been very busy, but it would certainly be a reproach if such a revolution should ever prove necessary again.

NEW KINDS OF EXPERIENCE ALWAYS POSSIBLE

The first lesson of our recent experience with relativity is merely an intensification and emphasis of the lesson which all past experience has also taught, namely, that when experiment is pushed into new domains, we must be prepared for new facts, of an entirely different character from those of our former experience. This is taught not only by the discovery of those unsuspected properties of matter moving with high velocities, which inspired the theory of relativity, but also even more emphatically by the new facts in the quantum domain. To a certain extent, of course, the recognition of all this does not involve a change of former attitude; the *fact* has always been for the physicist the one ultimate thing from which there is no appeal, and in the face of which the only possible attitude is a humility almost religious. The new feature in the present situation is an intensified conviction that in reality new orders of experience do exist, and that we may expect to meet them continually. We have already encountered new phenomena in going to high velocities, and in going to small scales of magnitude: we may similarly expect to find them, for example, in dealing with relations of cosmic magnitudes, or in dealing with the properties of matter of enormous densities, such as is supposed to exist in the stars.

Implied in this recognition of the possibility of new experience beyond our present range, is the recognition that no element of a physical situation, no matter how apparently irrelevant or trivial, may be dismissed as without effect on the final result until proved to be without effect by actual experiment.

The attitude of the physicist must therefore be one of pure empiricism. He recognizes no *a priori* principles which determine or limit the possibilities of new experience. Experience is determined only by experience. This practically means that we must give up the demand that all nature be embraced in any formula, either simple or complicated. It may perhaps turn out eventually that as a matter of fact nature can be embraced in a formula, but we must so organize our thinking as not to demand it as a necessity.

THE OPERATIONAL CHARACTER OF CONCEPTS

Einstein's Contribution in Changing Our Attitude Toward Concepts

Recognizing the essential unpredictability of experiment beyond our present range, the physicist, if he is to escape continually revising his attitude, must use in describing and correlating nature concepts of such a character that our present experience does not exact hostages of the future. Now here it seems to me is the greatest contribution of Einstein. Although he himself does not explicitly state or emphasize it, I believe that a study of what he has done will show that he has essentially modified our view of what the concepts useful in physics are and should be. Hitherto many of the concepts of physics have been defined in terms of their properties. An excellent example is afforded by Newton's concept of absolute time. The following quotation from the Scholium in Book I of the *Principia* is illuminating:

> I do not define Time, Space, Place or Motion, as being well known to all. Only I must observe that the vulgar conceive those quantities under no other notions but from the relation they bear to sensible objects. And thence arise certain prejudices, for the removing of which, it will be convenient to distinguish them into Absolute and Relative, True and Apparent, Mathematical and Common.

> (1) Absolute, True, and Mathematical Time, of itself, and from its own nature flows equably without regard to anything external, and by another name is called Duration.

Now there is no assurance whatever that there exists in nature anything with properties like those assumed in the definition, and physics, when reduced to concepts of this character, becomes as purely an abstract science and as far removed from reality as the abstract geometry of the mathematicians, built on postulates. It is a task for experiment to discover whether concepts so defined correspond to anything in nature, and we must always be prepared to find that the concepts correspond to nothing or only partially correspond. In particular, if we examine the definition of absolute time in the light of experiment, we find nothing in nature with such properties.

The new attitude toward a concept is entirely different. We may illustrate by considering the concept of length: what do we mean by the length of an object? We evidently know what we mean by length if we can tell what the length of any and every object is, and for the physicist nothing more is required. To find the length of an object, we have to perform certain physical operations. The concept of length is therefore fixed when the operations by which length is measured are fixed: that is, the concept of length involves as much as and nothing more than the set of operations by which length is determined. In general, we mean by any concept nothing more than a set of operations; *the concept is synonymous with the corresponding set of operations.* If the concept is physical, as of length, the operations are actual physical operations, namely, those by which length is measured; or if the concept is mental, as of mathematical continuity, the operations are mental operations, namely those by which we determine whether a given aggregate of magnitudes is continuous. It is not intended to imply that there is a hard and fast division between physical and mental concepts, or that one kind of concept does not always contain an element of the other; this classification of concept is not important for our future considerations.

We must demand that the set of operations equivalent to any concept be a unique set, for otherwise there are possibilities of ambiguity in practical applications which we cannot admit.

Applying this idea of "concept" to absolute time, we do not understand the meaning of absolute time unless we can tell how to determine the absolute time of any concrete event, *i.e.,* unless we can measure absolute time. Now we merely have to examine any of the possible operations by which we measure time to see that all such operations are relative operations. Therefore the previous statement that absolute time does not exist is replaced by the statement that absolute time is meaningless. And in making this statement we are not saying something new about nature, but are merely bringing to light implications already contained in the physical operations used in measuring time.

It is evident that if we adopt this point of view toward concepts, namely that the proper definition of a concept is not in terms of its properties but in terms of actual operations, we need run no danger of having to revise our attitude toward nature. For if experience is always described in terms of experience, there must always be correspondence between experience and our description of it, and we need never be embarrassed, as we were in attempting to find in nature the prototype of Newton's absolute time. Furthermore, if we remember that the operations to which a physical concept are equivalent are actual physical operations, the concepts can be defined only in the range of actual experiment, and are undefined and meaningless in regions as yet untouched by experiment. It follows that strictly speaking we cannot make statements at all about regions as yet untouched, and that when we do make such statements, as we inevitably shall, we are making a conventionalized extrapolation, of the looseness of which we must be fully conscious, and the justification of which is in the experiment of the future.

There probably is no statement either in Einstein or other writers that the change described above in the use of "concept" has been self-consciously made, but that such is the case is proved, I believe, by an examination of the way concepts are now handled by Einstein and others. For of course the true meaning of a term is to be found by observing what a man does with it, not by what he says about it. We may show that this is the actual sense in which concept is coming to be used by examining in particular Einstein's treatment of simultaneity.

Before Einstein, the concept of simultaneity was defined

in terms of properties. It was a property of two events, when described with respect to their relation in time, that one event was either before the other, or after it, or simultaneous with it. Simultaneity was a property of the two events alone and nothing else; either two events were simultaneous or they were not. The justification for using this term in this way was that it seemed to describe the behavior of actual things. But of course experience then was restricted to a narrow range. When the range of experience was broadened, as by going to high velocities, it was found that the concepts no longer applied, because there was no counterpart in experience for this absolute relation between two events. Einstein now subjected the concept of simultaneity to a critique, which consisted essentially in showing that the operations which enable two events to be described as simultaneous involve measurements on the two events made by an observer, so that "simultaneity" is, therefore, not an absolute property of the two events and nothing else, but must also involve the relation of the events to the observer. Until therefore we have experimental proof to the contrary, we must be prepared to find that the simultaneity of two events depends on their relation to the observer, and in particular on their velocity. Einstein, in thus analyzing what is involved in making a judgment of simultaneity, and in seizing on the act of the observer as the essence of the situation, is actually adopting a new point of view as to what the concepts of physics should be, namely, the operational view.

Of course Einstein actually went much further than this, and found precisely how the operations for judging simultaneity change when the observer moves, and obtained quantitative expressions for the effect of the motion of the observer cn the relative time of two events. We may notice, parenthetically, that there is much freedom of choice in selecting the exact operations; those which Einstein chose were determined by convenience and simplicity with relation to light beams. Entirely apart from the precise quantitative relations of Einstein's theory, however, the important point for us is that if we had adopted the operational point of view, we would, before the discovery of the actual physical facts, have seen that simultaneity is essentially a relative concept, and would have left room in our thinking for the discovery of such effects as were later found.

Detailed Discussion of the Concept of Length

We may now gain further familiarity with the operational attitude toward a concept and some of its implications by examining from this point of view the concept of length. Our task is to find the operations by which we measure the length of any concrete physical object. We begin with objects of our commonest experience, such as a house or a house lot. What we do is sufficiently indicated by the following rough description. We start with a measuring rod, lay it on the object so that one of its ends coincides with one end of the object, mark on the object the position of the other end of the rod, then move the rod along in a straight line extension of its previous position until the first end coincides with the previous position of the second end, repeat this process as often as we can, and call the length the total number of times the rod was applied. This procedure, apparently so simple, is in practice exceedingly complicated, and doubtless a full description of all the precautions that must be taken would fill a large treatise. We must, for example, be sure that the temperature of the rod is the standard temperature at which its length is defined, or else we must make a correction for it; or we must correct for the gravitational distortion of the rod if we measure a vertical length; or we must be sure that the rod is not a magnet or is not subject to electrical forces. All these precautions would occur to every physicist. But we must also go further and specify all the details by which the rod is moved from one position to the next on the object—its precise path through space and its velocity and acceleration in getting from one position to another. Practically of course, precautions such as these are not mentioned, but the justification is in our experience that variations of procedure of this kind are without effect on the final result. But we always have to recognize that all our experience is subject to error, and that at some time in the future we may have to specify more carefully the acceleration, for example, of the rod in moving from one position to another, if experimental accuracy should be so increased as to show a measureable effect. In *principle* the operations by which length is measured should be *uniquely* specified. If we have more than one set of operations, we have more than one concept, and strictly there should be a separate name to correspond to each different set of operations.

So much for the length of a stationary object, which is complicated enough. Now suppose we have to measure a moving street car. The simplest, and what we may call the "naïve" procedure, is to board the car with our meter stick and repeat the operations we would apply to a stationary body. Notice that this procedure reduces to that already adopted in the limiting case when the velocity of the street car vanishes. But here there may be new questions of detail. How shall we jump on to the car with our stick in hand? Shall we run and jump on from behind, or shall we let it pick us up from in front? Or perhaps does now the material of which the stick is composed make a difference, although previously it did not? All these questions must be answered by experiment. We believe from present evidence that it makes no difference how we jump on to the car, or of what material the rod is made, and that the length of the car found in this way will be the same as if it were at rest. But the experiments are more difficult, and we are not so sure of our conclusions as before. Now there are very obvious limitations to the procedure just given. If the street car is going too fast, we can not board it directly, but must use devices, such as getting on from a moving automobile; and, more important still, there are limitations to the velocity that can be given to street cars or to meter sticks by any practical means in our control, so that the moving bodies which can be measured in this way are restricted to a low range of velocity. If we want to be able to measure the length of bodies moving with higher velocities such as we find existing in nature (stars or cathode particles), we must adopt another definition and other operations for measuring length, which also reduce to the operations already adopted in the static case. This is precisely what Einstein did. Since Einstein's operations were different from our operations above, *his "length" does not mean the same as our "length."* We must accordingly be prepared to find that the length of a moving body measured by the procedure of Einstein is not the same as that above; this of course is the fact, and the transformation formulas of relativity give the precise connection between the two lengths.

Einstein's procedure for measuring the length of bodies in motion was dictated not only by the consideration that it must be applicable to bodies with high velocities, but also by mathematical convenience, in that Einstein describes the world mathematically by a system of coördinate geometry, and the "length" of an object is connected simply with quantities in the analytic equations.

It is of interest to describe briefly Einstein's actual operations for measuring the length of a body in motion; it will show how operations which may be simple from a mathematical point of view may appear complicated from a physical viewpoint. The observer who is to measure the length of a moving object must first extend over his entire plane of reference (for simplicity the problem is considered two-dimensional) a system of time coördinates, *i.e.*, at each point of his plane of reference there must be a clock, and all these clocks must be synchronized. At each clock an observer must be situated. Now to find the length of the moving object at a specified instant of time (it is a subject for later investigation to find whether its length is a function of time), the two observers who happen to coincide in position with the two ends of the object at the specified time on their clocks are required to find the distance between their two positions by the procedure for measuring the length of a stationary object, and this distance is by definition the length of the moving object in the given reference system. This procedure for measuring the length of a body in motion hence involves the idea of simultaneity, through the simultaneous position of the two ends of the rod, and we have seen that the operations by which simultaneity are determined are relative, changing when the motion of the system changes. We hence are prepared to find a change in the length of a body when the velocity of the measuring system changes, and this in fact is what happens. The precise numerical dependence is worked out by Einstein, and involves other considerations, in which we are not interested at present.

The two sorts of length, the naïve one and that of Einstein, have certain features in common. In either case in the limit, as the velocity of the measuring system approaches zero, the operations approach those for measuring the length of a stationary object. This, of course, is a requirement in any good definition, imposed by considerations of convenience, and it is too obvious a matter to need elaboration. Another feature is that the operations equivalent to either concept both involve the motion of the system, so that we must recognize the possibility that the length of a moving object may be a function of its velocity. It is a matter of experiment, unpredictable until tried, that within the limits of present experimental error the naïve length is not affected by motion, and Einstein's length is.

So far, we have extended the concept of length in only one way beyond the range of ordinary experience, namely to high velocities. The extension may obviously be made in other directions. Let us inquire what are the operations by which we measure the length of a very large object. In practice we probably first meet the desirability of a change of procedure in measuring large pieces of land. Here our procedure depends on measurements with a surveyor's theodolite. This involves extending over the surface of the land a system of coördinates, starting from a base line measured with a tape in the conventional way, sighting on distant points from the extremities of the line, and measuring the angles. Now in this extension we have made one very essential change: the angles between the lines connecting distant points are now angles between beams of light. We assume that a beam of light travels in a straight line. Furthermore, we assume in extending our system of triangulation over the surface of the earth that the geometry of light beams is Euclidean. We do the best we can to check the assumptions, but at most can never get more than a partial check. Thus Gauss[•] checked whether the angles of a large terrestrial triangle add to two right angles and found agreement within experimental error. We now know from the experiments of Michelson[••] that if his measurements had been accurate enough he would not have got a check, but would have had an excess or defect according to the direction in which the beam of light travelled around the triangle with respect to the rotation of the earth. But if the geometry of light beams is Euclidean, then not only must the angles of a triangle add to two right angles, but there are definite relations between the lengths of the sides and the angles, and to check these relations the sides should be measured by the old procedure with a meter stick. Such a check on a large scale has never been attempted, and is not feasible. It seems, then, that our checks on the Euclidean character of optical space are all of restricted character. We have apparently proved that up to a certain scale of magnitude optical space is Euclidean with respect to measures of angle, but this may not necessarily involve that space is also Euclidean

• C. F. Gauss, *Gesammelte Werke*, especially vol. IV.
•• See a discussion of the theory of this experiment by L. Silberstein, *Jour. Opt. Soc. Amer.* 5, 291-307, 1921.

with respect to measures of length, so that space need not be completely Euclidean. There is a further most important restriction in that our studies of non-Euclidean geometry have shown that the *percentage* excess of the angles of a non-Euclidean triangle over 180° may depend on the magnitude of the triangle, so that it may well be that we have not detected the non-Euclidean character of space simply because our measurements have not been on a large enough scale.

We thus see that the concept of length has undergone a very essential change of character even within the range of terrestrial measurements, in that we have substituted for what I may call the tactual concept an optical concept, complicated by an assumption about the nature of our geometry. From a very direct concept we have come to a very indirect concept with a most complicated set of operations. Strictly speaking, length when measured in this way by light beams should be called by another name, since the operations are different. The practical justification for retaining the same name is that within our present experimental limits a numerical difference between the results of the two sorts of operations has not been detected.

We are still worse off when we make the extension to solar and stellar distances. Here space is entirely optical in character, and we never have an opportunity of even partially comparing tactual with optical space. No direct measures of length have ever been made, nor can we even measure the three angles of a triangle and so check our assumption that the use of Euclidean geometry in extending the concept of space is justified. We never have under observation more than two angles of a triangle, as when we measure the distance of the moon by observation from the two ends of the earth's diameter. To extend to still greater distance our measures of length, we have to make still further assumptions, such as that inferences from the Newtonian laws of mechanics are valid. The accuracy of our inferences about lengths from such measurements is not high. Astronomy is usually regarded as a science of extraordinarily high accuracy, but its accuracy is very restricted in character, namely to the measurement of angles. It is probably safe to say that no astronomical distance, except perhaps that of the moon, is known with an accuracy greater than 0.1%. When we push our estimates to distances beyond the confines of the solar system in which we are assisted by the laws of mechanics, we are reduced in the first place to measurements of parallax, which at best have a quite inferior accuracy, and which furthermore fail entirely outside a rather restricted range. For greater stellar distances we are driven to other and much rougher estimates, resting for instance on the extension to great distances of connections found within the range of parallax between brightness and spectral type of a star, or on such assumptions as that, because a group of stars looks as if it were all together in space and had a common origin, it actually is so. Thus at greater and greater distances not only does experimental accuracy become less, but the very nature of the operations by which length is to be determined becomes indefinite, so that the distances of the most remote stellar objects as estimated by different observers or by different methods may be very divergent. A particular consequence of the inaccuracy of the astronomical measures of great distances is that the question of whether large scale space is Euclidean or not is merely academic.

We thus see that in the extension from terrestrial to great stellar distances the concept of length has changed completely in character. To say that a certain star is 10^5 light years distance is actually and conceptually an entire different *kind* of thing from saying that a certain goal post is 100 meters distant. Because of our conviction that the character of our experience may change when the range of phenomena changes, we feel the importance of such a question as whether the space of distances of 10^5 light years is Euclidean or not, and are correspondingly dissatisfied that at present there seems no way of giving meaning to it.

We encounter difficulties similar to those above, and are also compelled to modify our procedures, when we go to small distances. Down to the scale of microscopic dimensions a fairly straightforward extension of the ordinary measuring procedure is sufficient, as when we measure a length in a micrometer eyepiece of a microscope. This is of course a combination of tactual and optical measurements, and certain assumptions, justified as far as possible by experience, have to be made about the behavior of light beams. These assumptions are of a quite different character from those which give us concern on the astronomical scale, because here we meet difficulty from interference effects due to the finite scale of the structure of light, and are not concerned with a possible curvature of light beams in the long reaches of space. Apart from the matter of convenience, we might also measure small distances by the tactual method.

As the dimensions become smaller, certain difficulties become increasingly important that were negligible on a larger scale. In carrying out physically the operations equivalent to our concepts, there are a host of practical precautions to be taken which could be explicitly enumerated with difficulty, but of which nevertheless any practical physicist is conscious. Suppose, for example, we measure length tactually by a combination of Johanssen gauges. In piling these together, we must be sure that they are clean, and are thus in actual contact. Particles of mechanical dirt first engage our attention. Then as we go to smaller dimensions we perhaps have to pay attention to adsorbed films of moisture, then at still smaller dimensions to adsorbed films of gas, until finally we have to work in a vacuum, which must be the more nearly complete the smaller the dimensions. About the time that we discover the necessity for a complete vacuum, we discover that the gauges themselves are atomic in structure, that they have no definite boundaries, and therefore no definite length, but that the length is a hazy thing, varying rapidly in time between certain limits. We treat this situation as best we can by taking a time average of the apparent positions of the boundaries, assuming that along with the decrease of dimensions we have acquired a corresponding extravagant increase in nimbleness. But as the dimensions get smaller continually, the difficulties due to this haziness increase indefinitely in percentage effect, and we are eventually driven to give up altogether. We have made the discovery that there are *essential* physical limitations to the operations which defined the concept of length. (We perhaps do not regard the substitution of optical for tactual space on the astronomical scale as compelled by the same sort of physical necessity, because I suppose the possible eventual landing of men in the moon will always be one of the dreams of humanity.) At the same time that we have come to the end of our rope with our Johanssen gauge procedure, our companion with the microscope has been encountering difficulties due to the finite wave length of light; this difficulty he has been able to minimize by using light of progressively shorter wave lengths, but he has eventually had to stop on reaching X-rays. Of course this optical procedure with the microscope is more convenient, and is therefore adopted in practice.

Let us now see what is implied in our concept of length extended to ultramicroscopic dimensions. What, for instance, is the meaning of the statement that the distance between the planes of atoms in a certain crystal is 3×10^8 cm.? What we would like to mean is that $\frac{1}{3} \times 10^8$ of these planes piled on top of each other give a thickness of 1 cm.; but of course such a meaning is not the actual one. The actual meaning may be found by examining the operations by which we arrived at the number 3×10^{-8}. As a matter of fact, 3×10^{-8} was the number obtained by solving a general equation derived from the wave theory of light, into which certain numerical data obtained by experiments with X-rays had been substituted. Thus not only has the character of the concept of length changed from tactual to optical, but we have gone much further in committing ourselves to a definite optical theory. If this were the whole story, we would be most uncomfortable with respect to this branch of physics, because we are so uncertain of the correctness of our optical theories, but actually a number of checks can be applied which greatly restore our confidence. For instance, from the density of the crystal and the grating space, the weight of the individual atoms may be computed, and these weights may then be combined with measurements of the dimensions of other sorts of crystal into which the same atoms enter to give values of the densities of these crystals, which may be checked against experiment. All such checks have succeeded within limits of accuracy which are fairly high. It is important to notice that, in spite of the checks, the character of the concept is changing, and begins to involve such things as the equations of optics and the assumption of the conservation of mass.

We are not content, however, to stop with dimensions of atomic order, but have to push on to the electron with a diameter of the order of 10^{-13} cm. What is the possible meaning of the statement that the diameter of an electron is 10^{-13} cm.? Again the only answer is found by examining the operations by which the number 10^{-13} was obtained. This number came by solving certain equations derived from the field equations of electrodynamics, into which certain numerical data obtained by experiment had been substituted. The concept of length has therefore now been so modified as to include that theory of electricity embodied in the field equations, and, most important, assumes the correctness of extending these equations from the dimensions in which they may be verified experimentally into a region in which their correctness is one of the most important and problematical of present-day questions in physics. To find whether the field equations are correct on a small scale, we must verify the relations demanded by the equations between the electric and magnetic forces and the space coördinates, to determine which involves measurement of lengths. But if these space coördinates cannot be given an independent meaning apart from the equations, not only is the attempted verification of the equations impossible, but the question itself is meaningless. If we stick to the concept of length by itself, we are landed in a vicious circle. As a matter of fact, the concept of length disappears as an independent thing, and fuses in a complicated way with other concepts, all of which are themselves altered thereby, with the result that the total number of concepts used in describing nature at this level is reduced in number. A precise analysis of the situation is difficult, and I suppose has never been attempted, but the general character of the situation is evident. Until at least a partial analysis is attempted, I do not see how any meaning can be attached to such questions as whether space is Euclidean in the small scale.

It is interesting to observe that any increased accuracy in knowledge of large scale phenomena must, as far as we now can see, arise from an increase in the accuracy of measurement of small things, that is, in the measurement of small angles or the analysis of minute differences of wave lengths in the spectra. To know the very large takes us into the same field of experiment as to know the very small, so that operationally the large and the small have features in common.

This somewhat detailed analysis of the concept of length brings out features common to all our concepts. If we deal with phenomena outside the domain in which we originally defined our concepts, we may find physical hindrances to performing the operations of the original definition, so that the original operations have to be replaced by others. These new operations are, of course, to be so chosen that they give, within experimental error, the same numerical results in the domain in which the two sets of operations may be both applied; but we must recognize in principle that in changing the operations we have really changed the concept, and that to use the same name for these different concepts over the entire range is dictated only by considerations of convenience, which may sometimes prove to have been purchased at too high a price in terms of unambiguity. We must always be prepared some day to find that an increase in experimental accuracy may show that the two different sets of operations which give the same results in the more ordinary part of the domain of experience, lead to measurably different results in the more unfamiliar parts of the domain. We must remain aware of these joints in our conceptual structure if we hope to render unnecessary the services of the unborn Einsteins.

The second feature common to all concepts brought out by the detailed discussion of length is that, as we approach the experimentally attainable limit, concepts lose their individuality, fuse together, and become fewer in number, as we have seen that at dimensions of the order of the diameter of an electron the concepts of length and the electric field vectors fuse into an amorphous whole. Not only does nature as experienced by us become different in character on its horizons, but it becomes simpler, and therefore our concepts, which are the building stones of our descriptions, become fewer in number. This seems to be an entirely natural state of affairs. How the number of concepts is often kept formally the same as we approach the horizon will be discussed later in special cases.

A precise analysis of our conceptual structure has never been attempted, except perhaps in very restricted domains, and it seems to me that there is room here for much important future work. Such an analysis is not to be attempted in this essay, but only some of the more important qualitative aspects are to be pointed out. It will never be possible to give a clean-cut logical analysis of the conceptual situation, for the nature of our concepts, according to our operational point of view, is the same as the nature of experimental knowledge, which is often hazy. Thus in the transition regions where nature is getting simpler and the number of operationally independent concepts changes, a certain haziness is inevitable, for the actual change in our conceptual structure in these transition regions is continuous, corresponding to the continuity of our experimental knowledge, whereas formally the number of concepts should be an integer.

The Relative Character of Knowledge

Two other consequences of the operational point of view must now be examined. First is the consequence that all our knowledge is relative. This may be understood in a general or a more particular sense. The general sense is illustrated in Haldane's book on the *Reign of Relativity*. Relativity in the general sense is the merest truism if the operational definition of concept is accepted, for experience is described in terms of concepts, and since our concepts are constructed of operations, all our knowledge must unescapably be relative to the operations selected. But knowledge is also relative in a narrower sense, as when we say there is no such thing as absolute rest (or motion) or absolute size, but rest and size are relative terms. Conclusions of this kind are involved in the specific character of the operations in terms of which rest or size are defined. An examination of the operations by which we determine whether a body is at rest or in motion shows that the operations are relative operations: rest or motion is determined with respect to some other body selected as the standard. In saying that there is no such thing as absolute rest or motion we are not making a statement about nature in the sense that might be supposed, but we are merely making a statement about the character of our descriptive processes. Similarly with regard to size: examination of the operations of the measuring process shows that size is measured relative to the fundamental measuring rod.

The "absolute" therefore disappears in the original meaning of the word. But the "absolute" may usefully return with an altered meaning, and we may say that a thing has absolute properties if the numerical magnitude is the same when measured with the same formal procedure by all observers. Whether a given property is absolute or not can be determined only by experiment, landing us in the paradoxical position that the absolute is absolute only relative to experiment. In some cases, the most superficial observation shows that a property is not absolute, as, for example, it is at once obvious that measured velocity changes with the motion of the observer. But in other cases the decision is more difficult. Thus Michelson thought he had an absolute procedure for measuring length, by referring to the wave length of the red cadmium line as standard;• it required difficult and accurate experi-

• A. A. Michelson, *Light Waves and Their Uses,* University of Chicago Press, 1903, Chap. V.

ment to show that this length varies with the motion of the observer. Even then, by changing the definition of the length of a moving object, we believe that length might be made to reassume its desired absolute character.

To stop the discussion at this point might leave the impression that this observation of the relative character of knowledge is of only a very tenuous and academic interest, since it appears to be concerned mostly with the character of our descriptive processes, and to say little about external nature. (What this means we leave to the metaphysician to decide.) But I believe there is a deeper significance to all this. It must be remembered that all our argument starts with the concepts as given. Now these concepts involve physical operations; in the discovery of what operations may be usefully employed in describing nature is buried almost all physical experience. In erecting our structure of physical science, we are building on the work of all the ages. There is then this purely physical significance in the statement that all motion is relative, namely that no operations of measuring motion have been found to be useful in describing simply the behavior of nature which are not operations relative to a single observer; in making this statement we are stating something about nature. It takes an enormous amount of real physical experience to discover relations of this sort. The discovery that the number obtained by counting the number of times a stick may be applied to an object can be simply used in describing natural phenomena was one of the most important and fundamental discoveries ever made by man.

Meaningless Questions

Another consequence of the operational character of our concepts, almost a corollary of that considered above, is that it is quite possible, nay even disquietingly easy, to invent expressions or to ask questions that are meaningless. It constitutes a great advance in our critical attitude toward nature to realize that a great many of the questions that we uncritically ask are without meaning. If a specific question has meaning, it must be possible to find operations by which an answer may be given to it. It will be found in many cases that the operations cannot exist, and the question therefore has no meaning. For instance, it means nothing to ask whether a star is at rest or not. Another example is a question proposed by Clifford, namely. whether it is not possible that as the solar system moves from one part of space to another the absolute scale of magnitude may be changing, but in such a way as to affect all things equally, so that the change of scale can never be detected. An examination of the operations by which length is measured in terms of measuring rods shows that the operations do not exist (because of the nature of our definition of length) for answering the question. The question can be given meaning only from the point of view of some imaginary superior being watching from an external point of vantage. But the operations by which such a being measures length are different from the operations of our definition of length, so that the question acquires meaning only by changing the significance of our terms—in the original sense the question means nothing.

To state that a certain question about nature is meaningless is to make a significant statement about nature itself, because the fundamental operations are determined by nature, and to state that nature cannot be described in terms of certain operations is a significant statement.

It must be recognized, however, that there is a sense in which no serious question is entirely without meaning, because doubtless the questioner had in mind some intention in asking the question. But to give meaning in this sense to a question, one must inquire into the meaning of the concepts as used by the questioner, and it will often be found that these concepts can be defined only in terms of fictitious properties, as Newton's absolute time was defined by its properties, so that the meaning to be ascribed to the question in this way has no connection with reality. I believe that it will enable us to make more significant and interesting statements, and therefore will be more useful, to adopt exclusively the operational view, and so admit the possibility of questions entirely without meaning.

This matter of meaningless questions is a very subtle thing which may poison much more of our thought than that dealing with purely physical phenomena. I believe that many of the questions asked about social and philosophical subjects will be found to be meaningless when examined from the point of view of operations. It would doubtless conduce greatly to clarity of thought if the operational mode of thinking were adopted in all fields of inquiry as well as in the physical. Just as in the physical domain, so in other domains, one is making a significant statement about his subject in stating that a certain question is meaningless.

In order to emphasize this matter of meaningless questions, I give here a list of questions, with which the reader may amuse himself by finding whether they have meaning or not.

(1) Was there ever a time when matter did not exist?

(2) May time have a beginning or an end?

(3) Why does time flow?

(4) May space be bounded?

(5) May space or time be discontinuous?

(6) May space have a fourth dimension, not directly detectible, but given indirectly by inference?

(7) Are there parts of nature forever beyond our detection?

(8) Is the sensation which I call blue really the *same* as that which my neighbor calls blue? Is it possible that a blue object may arouse in him the same sensation that a red object does in me and *vice versa?*

(9) May there be missing integers in the series of natural numbers as we know them?

(10) Is a universe possible in which $2 + 2 \neq 4$?

(11) Why does negative electricity attract positive?

(12) Why does nature obey laws?

(13) Is a universe possible in which the laws are different?

(14) If one part of our universe could be *completely* isolated from the rest, would it continue to obey the same laws?

(15) Can we be sure that our logical processes are valid?

GENERAL COMMENTS ON THE OPERATIONAL POINT OF VIEW

To adopt the operational point of view involves much more than a mere restriction of the sense in which we understand "concept," but means a far-reaching change in all our habits of thought, in that we shall no longer permit ourselves to use as tools in our thinking concepts of which we cannot give an adequate account in terms of operations. In some respects thinking becomes simpler, because certain old generalizations and idealizations become incapable of use; for instance, many of the speculations of the early natural philosophers become simply unreadable. In other respects, however, thinking becomes much more difficult, because the operational implications of a concept are often very involved. For example, it is most difficult to grasp adequately all that is contained in the apparently simple concept of "time," and requires the continual correction of mental tendencies which we have long unquestioningly accepted.

Operational thinking will at first prove to be an unsocial virtue; one will find oneself perpetually unable to understand the simplest conversation of one's friends, and will make oneself universally unpopular by demanding the meaning of apparently the simplest terms of every argument. Possibly after every one has schooled himself to this better way, there will remain a permanent unsocial tendency, because doubtless much of our present conversation will then become unnecessary. The socially optimistic may venture to hope, however, that the ultimate effect will be to release one's energies for more stimulating and interesting interchange of ideas.

Not only will operational thinking reform the social art of conversation, but all our social relations will be liable to reform. Let any one examine in operational terms any popular present-day discussion of religious or moral questions to realize the magnitude of the reformation awaiting us. Wherever we temporize or compromise in applying our theories of conduct to practical life we may suspect a failure of operational thinking.

C. I. Lewis

1883-

In their quest for certainty philosophers have traditionally clung to the exact sciences. From Plato through Descartes to Bertrand Russell this has been the main line in Western philosophy. The crucial argument against empiricism was that it could not explain the exact and universal knowledge given in logic and pure mathematics. Empirical generalizations, no matter how fundamental and pervasive they may be, are always fallible and they can never prejudge the future. There must, then, be an A PRIORI *element in knowledge. And Kant, it would seem, had shown that the* A PRIORI *is prescriptive. In order to know anything at all, we* MUST *apprehend it as coming under antecedent categories—to know is literally to* IN-FORM *whatever is given in experience. It is our own minds that impose a rational order upon the world.*

Against this rationalism the "left-wing" pragmatists, William James and F. C. S. Schiller, were in open revolt. In the last chapter of his PSYCHOLOGY, *"Necessary Truths and the Effects of Experience," James advanced the hypothesis that while our minds* DO *impose an order upon the outer world, this may be a congenial rather than a necessary way of organizing experience. And Schiller's first important piece of philosophical writing (as a pragmatist) was a long essay on the same theme entitled "Axioms as Postulates." This hypothesis, that reality is to some degree—determinable only by actual trial—plastic; that the world can, within limits, be interpreted and fashioned as we will; that the ways in which we think and act upon it do make a real difference in the eventual consequences of our thought and action—was elaborated and developed by Schiller, who gave it the name "humanism."*

James and Schiller thought that humanism was incompatible with formal logic. In consequence, Peirce's continual reminders to James that he ought to study logic, since pragmatism was above all a logical principle, were fruitless. If logic and the plasticity of immediate experience were in conflict, then so much the worse for logic! For it was the form and not the content of experience which he regarded as malleable. When, however, Peirce remarked to James's younger colleague, "Royce, you ought to study logic, you need it so much," the advice was heeded. One result was that C. I. Lewis, as a student at Harvard with a bent for symbolic logic, came predominantly under the influence of Royce. "His ponderous cogency kept my steady attention, even though I never followed to his metaphysical conclusions. James, I thought, had a swift way of being right, but how he reached his conclusions was his own secret." The study of exact logic convinced Lewis that there are alternative systems which are equally valid. How, then, does one choose between them? In answer to this question he concluded that "in every process of reasoning there is an extra-logical element." Lewis was thus led on to develop what Peirce had called a "conceptualistic pragmatism." Our decision to make use of one mode of reasoning rather than another is based upon our ends-in-view. "The difference between . . . prescriptive laws and empirical generalizations is one determined by pragmatic considerations of the particular interests our knowledge is to serve."

"Truth" is a correspondence of proposition to fact only in the way that a key fits a lock, and there MAY be different keys for the same lock—but not ANY key. Lewis would not follow Schiller in denying that "there is an objective world given independently of us and constraining us to recognize it." His own view is:

> *Pragmatism has sometimes been charged with oscillating between two contrary notions; the one, that*

experience is "through and through malleable to our purpose," the other, that facts are "hard" and un-created by the mind. We here offer a mediating con-ception: through all our knowledge runs the element of the A PRIORI. which is indeed malleable to our pur-pose and responsive to our need. But throughout, there is also that other element of experience which is "hard," "independent," and unalterable to our will.

From this it follows that mind "makes classifications and determines meanings; in so doing it creates that truth without which there could be no other truth." By one of those not infrequent paradoxes in the history of thought, Lewis uses the exact logic to which rationalists have always appealed to vindicate (within limits) the humanism of Schiller and James.

A Pragmatic
Conception of
the A Priori •

The conception of the *a priori* points two problems which are perennial in philosophy; the part played in knowledge by the mind itself, and the possibility of "necessary truth" or of knowledge "independent of experience." But traditional con-ceptions of the *a priori* have proved untenable. That the mind approaches the flux of immediacy with some godlike fore-knowledge of principles which are legislative for experience, that there is any natural light or any innate ideas, it is no longer possible to believe.

Nor shall we find the clue to the *a priori* in any compulsion of the mind to incontrovertible truth or any peculiar kind of demonstration which establishes first principles. All truth lays upon the rational mind the same compulsion to belief; as Mr. Bosanquet has pointed out, this character belongs to all prop-ositions or judgments once their truth is established.

The difficulties of the conception are due, I believe, to two mistakes: whatever is *a priori* is necessary, but we have mis-

• [From: C. I. Lewis, "A Pragmatic Conception of the *A Priori*," 20 *The Journal of Philosophy* (1923), pp. 169-77. Reprinted by permission of *The Journal of Philosophy* and the author.]

construed the relation of necessary truth to mind. And the *a priori* is independent of experience, but in so taking it, we have misunderstood its relation to empirical fact. What is *a priori* is necessary truth not because it compels the mind's acceptance, but precisely because it does not. It is given experience, brute fact, the *a posteriori* element in knowledge which the mind must accept willy-nilly. The *a priori* represents an attitude in some sense freely taken, a stipulation of the mind itself, and a stipulation which might be made in some other way if it suited our bent or need. Such truth is necessary as opposed to contingent, not as opposed to voluntary. And the *a priori* is independent of experience not because it prescribes a form which the data of sense must fit, or anticipates some preëstablished harmony of experience with the mind, but precisely because it prescribes nothing to experience. That is *a priori* which is true, *no matter what*. What it anticipates is not the given, but our attitude toward it: it concerns the uncompelled initiative of mind or, as Josiah Royce would say, our categorical ways of acting.

The traditional example of the *a priori* par excellence is the laws of logic. These can not be derived from experience since they must first be taken for granted in order to prove them. They make explicit our general modes of classification. And they impose upon experience no real limitation. Sometimes we are asked to tremble before the spectre of the "alogical," in order that we may thereafter rejoice that we are saved from this by the dependence of reality upon mind. But the "alogical" is pure bogey, a word without a meaning. What kind of experience could defy the principle that everything must either be or not be, that nothing can both be and not be, or that if x is y and y is z, then x is z? If anything imaginable or unimaginable could violate such laws, then the ever-present fact of change would do it every day. The laws of logic are purely formal; they forbid nothing but what concerns the use of terms and the corresponding modes of classification and analysis. The law of contradiction tells us that nothing can be both white and not-white, but it does not and can not tell us whether black is not-white, or soft or square is not-white. To discover *what contradicts what* we must always consult the character of experience. Similarly the law of the excluded middle formulates our decision that whatever is not designated by a certain term shall be designated by its negative. It declares our purpose to make, for every term, a complete dichot-

omy of experience, instead—as we might choose—of classifying on the basis of a tripartite division into opposites (as
black and white) and the middle ground between the two.
Our rejection of such tripartite division represents only our
penchant for simplicity.

Further laws of logic are of similar significance. They are
principles of procedure, the parliamentary rules of intelligent thought and speech. Such laws are independent of experience because they impose no limitations whatever upon
it. They are legislative because they are addressed to ourselves
—because definition, classification, and inference represent no
operations of the objective world, but only our own categorical attitudes of mind.

And further, the ultimate criteria of the laws of logic are
pragmatic. Those who suppose that there is, for example, *a*
logic which everyone would agree to if he understood it and
understood himself, are more optimistic than those versed
in the history of logical discussion have a right to be. The
fact is that there are several logics, markedly different, each
self-consistent in its own terms and such that whoever, using
it, avoids false premises, will never reach a false conclusion.
Mr. Russell, for example, bases *his* logic on an implication
relation such that if twenty sentences be cut from a newspaper and put in a hat, and then two of these be drawn at
random, one of them will certainly imply the other, and it
is an even bet that the implication will be mutual. Yet upon
a foundation so remote from ordinary modes of inference the
whole structure of *Principia Mathematica* is built. This logic
—and there are others even more strange—is utterly consistent and the results of it entirely valid. Over and above all
questions of consistency, there are issues of logic which can
not be determined—nay, can not even be argued—except on
pragmatic grounds of conformity to human bent and intellectual convenience. That we have been blind to this fact,
itself reflects traditional errors in the conception of the *a
priori*.

We may note in passing one less important illustration of
the *a priori*—the proposition "true by definition." Definitions
and their immediate consequences, analytic propositions generally, are necessarily true, true under all possible circumstances. Definition is legislative because it is in some sense
arbitrary. Not only is the meaning assigned to words more
or less a matter of choice—that consideration is relatively

trivial—but the manner in which the precise classifications which definition embodies shall be effected, is something not dictated by experience. If experience were other than it is, the definition and its corresponding classification might be inconvenient, fantastic, or useless, but it could not be false. Mind makes classifications and determines meanings; in so doing it creates the *a priori* truth of analytic judgments. But that the manner of this creation responds to pragmatic considerations, is so obvious that it hardly needs pointing out.

If the illustrations so far given seem trivial or verbal, that impression may be corrected by turning to the place which the *a priori* has in mathematics and in natural science. Arithmetic, for example, depends *in toto* upon the operation of counting or correlating, a procedure which can be carried out at will in any world containing identifiable things—even identifiable ideas—regardless of the further characters of experience. Mill challenged this *a priori* character of arithmetic. He asked us to suppose a demon sufficiently powerful and maleficent so that every time two things were brought together with two other things, this demon should always introduce a fifth. The implication which he supposed to follow is that under such circumstances $2 + 2 = 5$ would be a universal law of arithmetic. But Mill was quite mistaken. In such a world we should be obliged to become a little clearer than is usual about the distinction between arithmetic and physics, that is all. If two black marbles were put in the same urn with two white ones, the demon could take his choice of colors, but it would be evident that there were more black marbles or more white ones than were put in. The same would be true of all objects in any wise identifiable. We should simply find ourselves in the presence of an extraordinary physical law, which we should recognize as universal in our world, that whenever two things were brought into proximity with two others, an additional and similar thing was always created by the process. Mill's world would be physically most extraordinary. The world's work would be enormously facilitated if hats or locomotives or tons of coal could be thus multiplied by anyone possessed originally of two pairs. But the laws of mathematics would remain unaltered. It is because this is true that arithmetic is *a priori*. Its laws prevent *nothing;* they are compatible with anything which happens or could conceivably happen in nature. They would be true in any possible world. Mathematical addition is not a physical transformation. Physical changes which result in an increase or decrease of the countable things involved are matters of everyday occurrence. Such physical processes present us with phenomena in which the purely mathematical has to be separated out by abstraction. Those laws and those laws only have necessary truth which we are prepared to maintain, no matter what. It is because we shall always separate out that part of the phenomenon not in conformity with artihmetic and designate it by some other category—physical change, chemical reaction, optical illusion—that arithmetic is *a priori.*

The *a priori* element in science and in natural law is greater than might be supposed. In the first place, all science is based upon definitive concepts. The formulation of these concepts is, indeed, a matter determined by the commerce between our intellectual or our pragmatic interests and the nature of experience. Definition is classification. The scientific search is for such classification as will make it possible to correlate appearance and behavior, to discover law, to penetrate to the "essential nature" of things in order that behavior may become predictable. In other words, if definition is unsuccessful, as early scientific definitions mostly have been, it is because the classification thus set up corresponds with no natural cleavage and does not correlate with any important uniformity of behavior. A name itself must represent *some* uniformity in experience or it names nothing. What does not repeat itself or recur in intelligible fashion is not a thing. Where the definitive uniformity is a clue to other uniformities, we have successful scientific definition. Other definitions can not be said to be false; they are merely useless. In scientific classification the search is, thus, for *things worth naming.* But the naming, classifying, defining activity is essentially prior to investigation. We can not interrogate experience in general. Until our meaning is definite and our classification correspondingly exact, experience can not conceivably answer our questions.

In the second place, the fundamental laws of any science— or those treated as fundamental—are *a priori* because they formulate just such definitive concepts or categorical tests by which alone investigation becomes possible. If the lightning strikes the railroad track at two places, *A* and *B,* how shall we tell whether these events are simultaneous? "We . . . require a definition of simultaneity such that this definition supplies us with the method by means of which . . . we can decide whether or not both the lightning strokes occurred simultaneously. As long as this requirement is not satisfied, I allow myself to be deceived as a physicist (and of course the same applies if I am not a physicist), when I imagine that I am able to attach a meaning to the statement of simultaneity. . . .

"After thinking the matter over for some time you then offer the following suggestion with which to test simultaneity. By measuring along the rails, the connecting line AB should be measured up and an observer placed at the mid-point M of the distance AB. This observer should be supplied with an arrangement (e.g., two mirrors inclined at 90°) which allows him visually to observe both places A and B at the same time. If the observer perceives the two flashes at the same time, then they are simultaneous.

"I am very pleased with this suggestion, but for all that I can not regard the matter as quite settled, because I feel constrained to raise the following objection: 'Your definition would certainly be right, if I only knew that the light by means of which the observer at M perceives the lightning flashes travels along the length A—M with the same velocity as along the length B—M. But an examination of this supposition would only be possible if we already had at our disposal the means of measuring time. It would thus appear as though we were moving here in a logical circle.'

"After further consideration you cast a somewhat disdainful glance at me—and rightly so—and you declare: 'I maintain my previous definition nevertheless, because in reality it assumes absolutely nothing about light. There is only *one* demand to be made of the definition of simultaneity, namely, that in every real case it must supply us with an empirical decision as to whether or not the conception which has to be defined is fulfilled. That light requires the same time to traverse the path A—M as for the path B—M is in reality *neither a supposition nor a hypothesis* about the physical nature of light, but a *stipulation* which I can make of my own free-will in order to arrive at a definition of simultaneity.' . . . We are thus led also to a definition of 'time' in physics." •

As this example from the theory of relativity well illustrates, we can not even ask the questions which discovered law would answer until we have first by *a priori* stipulation formulated definitive criteria. Such concepts are not verbal

• Einstein, *Relativity*, pp. 26-8: italics are the author's.

definitions, nor classifications merely; they are themselves laws which prescribe a certain uniformity of behavior to whatever is thus named. Such definitive laws are *a priori;* only so can we enter upon the investigation by which further laws are sought. Yet it should also be pointed out that such *a priori* laws are subject to abandonment if the structure which is built upon them does not succeed in simplifying our interpretation of phenomena. If, in the illustration given, the relation "simultaneous with," as defined, should not prove transitive—if event *A* should prove simultaneous with *B,* and *B* with *C,* but not *A* with *C*—this definition would certainly be rejected.

And thirdly, there is that *a priori* element in science—as in other human affairs—which constitutes the criteria of the real as opposed to the unreal in experience. An object itself is a uniformity. Failure to behave in certain categorical ways marks it as unreal. Uniformities of the type called "natural law" are the clues to reality and unreality. A mouse which disappears where no hole is, is no real mouse; a landscape which recedes as we approach is but illusion. As the queen remarked in the episode of the wishing-carpet: "If this were real, then it would be a miracle. But miracles do not happen. Therefore I shall wake presently." That the uniformities of natural law are the only reliable criteria of the real, is inescapable. But such a criterion is *ipso facto a priori.* No conceivable experience could dictate the alteration of a law so long as failure to obey that law marked the content of experience as unreal.

This is one of the puzzles of empiricism. We deal with experience: what any reality may be which underlies experience, we have to learn. What we desire to discover is natural law, the formulation of those uniformities which obtain amongst the real. But experience as it comes to us contains not only the real but all the content of illusion, dream, hallucination, and mistake. The *given* contains both real and unreal, confusingly intermingled. If we ask for uniformities of this unsorted experience, we shall not find them. Laws which characterize all experience, of real and unreal both, are nonexistent and would in any case be worthless. What we seek 'are the uniformities of the *real;* but *until we have such laws, we can not sift experience and segregate the real.*

The obvious solution is that the enrichment of experience, the separation of the real from the illusory or meaningless, and the formulation of natural law, all grow up together. If the criteria of the real are *a priori,* that is not to say that no conceivable character of experience would lead to alteration of them. For example, spirits can not be photographed. But if photographs of spiritistic phenomena, taken under properly guarded conditions, should become sufficiently frequent, this *a priori* dictum would be called in question. What we should do would be to redefine our terms. Whether "spook" was spirit or matter, whether the definition of "spirit" or of "matter" should be changed; all this would constitute one interrelated problem. We should reopen together the question of definition or classification, of criteria for this sort of real, and of natural law. And the solution of one of these would mean the solution of all. Nothing could *force* a redefinition of spirit or of matter. A sufficiently fundamental relation to human bent, to human interests, would guarantee continuance unaltered even in the face of unintelligible and baffling experiences. In such problems, the mind finds itself uncompelled save by its own purposes and needs. I *may* categorize experience as I will; but *what* categorical distinctions will best serve my interests and objectify my own intelligence? What the mixed and troubled experience shall be—that is beyond me. But what I shall do with it—that is my own question, when the character of experience is sufficiently before me. I am coerced only by my own need to understand.

It would indeed be inappropriate to characterize as *a priori* a law which we are wholly prepared to alter in the light of further experience, even though in an isolated case we should discard as illusory any experience which failed to conform. But the crux of the situation lies in this; beyond such principles as those of logic, which we seem fully prepared to maintain no matter what, there must be further and more particular criteria of the real prior to any investigation of nature whatever. We can not even interrogate experience without a network of categories and definitive concepts. And we must further be prepared to say what experimental findings will answer what questions, and how. Without tests which represent anterior principle, there is no question which experience could answer at all. Thus the most fundamental laws in any category—or those which we regard as most fundamental—are *a priori,* even though continued failure to render experience intelligible in such terms might result eventually in the abandonment of that category altogether.

Matters so comparatively small as the behavior of Mercury and of starlight passing the sun's limb may, if there be persistent failure to bring them within the field of previously accepted modes of explanation, result in the abandonment of the independent categories of space and time. But without the definitions, fundamental principles, and tests, of the type which constitute such categories, no experience whatever could prove or disprove anything. And to that mind which should find independent space and time absolutely necessary conceptions, no possible experiment could prove the principles of relativity. "There must be some error in the experimental findings, or some law not yet discovered," represents an attitude which can never be rendered impossible. And the only sense in which it could be proved unreasonable would be the pragmatic one of comparison with another method of categorical analysis which more successfully reduced all such experience to order and law.

At the bottom of all science and all knowledge are categories and definitive concepts which represent fundamental habits of thought and deep-lying attitudes which the human mind has taken in the light of its total experience. But a new and wider experience may bring about some alteration of these attitudes, even though by themselves they dictate nothing as to the content of experience, and no experience can conceivably prove them invalid.

Perhaps some will object to this conception on the ground that only such principles should be designated *a priori* as the human mind *must* maintain, no matter what; that if, for example, it is shown possible to arrive at a consistent doctrine of physics in terms of relativity, even by the most arduous reconstruction of our fundamental notions, then the present conceptions are by that fact shown not to be *a priori*. Such objection is especially likely from those who would conceive the *a priori* in terms of an absolute mind or an absolutely universal human nature. We should readily agree that a decision by popular approval or a congress of scientists or anything short of such a test as would bring to bear the full weight of human capacity and interest, would be ill-considered as having to do with the *a priori*. But we wish to emphasize two facts: first, that in the field of those conceptions and principles which have altered in human history, there are those which could neither be proved nor disproved by any experience, but represent the uncompelled initiative of human thought—that without this uncompelled initiative no growth of science, nor any science at all, would be conceivable. And second, that the difference between such conceptions as are, for example, concerned in the decision of relativity versus absolute space and time, and those more permanent attitudes such as are vested in the laws of logic, there is only a difference of degree. The dividing line between the *a priori* and the *a posteriori* is that between principles and definitive concepts which *can* be maintained in the face of all experience and those genuinely empirical generalizations which *might* be proven flatly false. The thought which both rationalism and empiricism have missed is that there are principles, representing the initiative of mind, which impose upon experience no limitations whatever, but that such conceptions are still subject to alteration on pragmatic grounds when the expanding boundaries of experience reveal their infelicity as intellectual instruments.

Neither human experience nor the human mind has a character which is universal, fixed, and absolute. "The human mind" does not exist at all save in the sense that all humans are very much alike in fundamental respects, and that the language habit and the enormously important exchange of ideas has greatly increased our likeness in those respects which are here in question. Our categories and definitions are peculiarly social products, reached in the light of experiences which have much in common, and beaten out, like other pathways, by the coincidence of human purposes and the exigencies of human coöperation. Concerning the *a priori* there need be neither universal agreement nor complete historical continuity. Conceptions, such as those of logic, which are least likely to be affected by the opening of new ranges of experience, represent the most stable of our categories; but none of them is beyond the possibility of alteration.

Mind contributes to experience the element of order, of classification, categories, and definition. Without such, experience would be unintelligible. Our knowledge of the validity of these is simply consciousness of our own fundamental ways of acting and our own intellectual intent. Without this element, knowledge is impossible, and it is here that whatever truths are necessary and independent of experience must be found. But the commerce between our categorical ways of acting, our pragmatic interests, and the particular character of experience, is closer than we have realized. No explanation of any one of these can be complete without consideration of the other two.

Pragmatism has sometimes been charged with oscillating between two contrary notions; the one, that experience is "through and through malleable to our purpose," the other, that facts are "hard" and uncreated by the mind. We here offer a mediating conception: through all our knowledge runs the element of the *a priori,* which is indeed malleable to our purpose and responsive to our need. But throughout, there is also that other element of experience which is "hard," "independent," and unalterable to our will.

Horace M. Kallen

1882-

A friend of William James and John Dewey, Kallen has been a prolific writer whose philosophic position has been variously called pragmatism, humanism, cultural pluralism, or Hebraism. He has applied his philosophy to many aspects of human life and existence, among them the co-operative movement, civil liberties, art, education, Zionism, religion, science. Kallen's philosophy is first of all a category of thought which sees nature and life in perpetual flux, which sees all things under the aspect of time. It is a philosophy of existence in which time and change are real, in which history is significant, and in which biography is meaningful and precious. It rejects any form of predestination or any sense of immutable or inexorable destiny. It affirms freedom of the will and human responsibility for actions that follow from the reality and freedom of the will.

Reality is not made up of generalized forms of existence, such as Santayana's essences, or Plato's ideas, but of the things that come into being and pass away—things that are apprehended under the aspect of becoming more than under the aspect of being. These things, including specific human beings, have a right to be themselves, a right to be different.

It is difference that defines character and that identifies a person.

This means individualism: respect for the dignity of each human being and for his right to be different. This means freedom, radical liberty; it means a commitment to a maximum of democratic freedom—civil liberties, the preservation and strengthening of inherent, inalienable rights.

It means, too, a constant effort to bring about social justice and the securing of peace through cultivation of the intelligence and the methods of science in the interests of a furtherance of life and justice. Actions, values, tools, methods justify themselves as and when they "prove" themselves by contributing to the satisfaction of the heart's desire; and the heart learns what it desires and what it should desire as man works for and with humane ideals.

That You
Can Change
Human Nature •

In the history of teaching, such words as "indoctrination," "instruction," "inculcation" give away the persistent relation of teacher to pupil, of adult to child. It is a relation of superior to inferior power, of hardness to plasticity, of authority to dependence. The primary activities, upon which the later meanings of the words are variations, are activities of building in, stamping in, talking in. Among the armed forces "indoctrination" has been the word for all teachings of ideas, while the teaching of only actions is called training. Teachers tend automatically to resort to it when pupils appear unable or unwilling to learn that which teachers purport to teach. The component of force in the meaning of the terms points to a certain recalcitrance and aversion in the learner.

Yet commonly the doctrines of the indoctrinators are

• [From: Horace M. Kallen, *The Education of Free Men.* New York: Farrar, Straus and Company; 1949. Pp. 149-73. Copyright 1949 by Horace M. Kallen. Reprinted by permission of the publishers.]

presented as self-evident ineluctable truths. But it must be obvious that if they were such, indoctrination would be unnecessary. If indoctrination is necessary, the doctrines can be neither self-evident nor ineluctable. If indoctrination is necessary, it is necessary because the doctrines cannot come to acceptance on their competitive merits and need support from strengths other than their own. They need support against alternatives which dispute their claims upon the learner. The alternatives may be unconscious beliefs or conscious judgments. Their resistance may be active and deliberate or passive and automatic. But it is operative and it lays upon indoctrinators the burden of meeting and overcoming it. Wherever alternatives fight for place, wherever an issue is controversial and options are live, weighted and momentous, indoctrination becomes an applauded educational method, a pedagogic trouble-shooter which strips away the hesitancies and trials and errors of natural learning. Few people dispute about how to teach the multiplication table. So long as it is learned and used, *how* it is learned stays of little concern, although it is true that during more than a quarter of a century the teaching of all arithmetic has moved steadily away from indoctrination. Pass, however, from the multiplication table to statistics, to non-Euclidean geometries, to relativity, the quantum theory and biophysics, and you enter worlds of active controversy. Schools among the Communists, the Catholics, the Nazis, the Fascists will treat those as issues of doctrine. The dogmas and regulations of the churches, the mores directing the ways of a man with a maid, the professions and practices of war, the sanctions of property, are among the most notable of human interests and relations which societies tend to keep taboo against free inquiry and reserve for inculcation. Each society and each group within a society may have its own way of rationalizing these ultimately arbitrary preferences and decisions. Each employs a certain conception of the nature of man and of the world, and of man's place and destiny in the world. Each labors to hold its conception invariant against its own inner changes and against the outer impacts of the *libre examen*. Hence, although the schools have been considerably secularized and pedagogy makes large pretensions to science, education retains many of the traits of the religious establishment it was freed from. It also has its singular definitions of human nature, its diverse fixed techniques of faith and works, its salvational goals, some of them still for immortal souls at rendezvous with eternity. The argots and the procedures are different. The attitude remains. It ages but it does not change.

And perhaps this is why only something like a religious conversion can bring a professionally trained teacher to realize that pupils are people, that colleagues are people, that the living child is by no means the same as the classroom pupil and the human being as the classroom teacher. The latter are occupational fictions, artificial characters shaped to occupational ends by abstracting a few possibilities of behavior from the lasting *totum simul* of personality and by suppressing and ignoring the enormous organic residue whence the abstraction draws whatever life it may have. Even in the classroom, it is this residue which gives force to the interpersonal relations that the words *pupil, teacher, colleague,* enchannel or the bookkeeping of the school system can or does take account of. In the schoolroom also, pedagogy seems happy to forget that teachers and pupils are people, each different from the others and each under greater or less duress to live together with the others. By the acts of indoctrination the pedagogue weights and intensifies this initial duress; while the arts of the *libre examen* remove it from the spirit of the learner, converting compulsion into cooperation and authority into consent.

Which comes to prevail, indoctrination or *libre examen,* is largely a consequence of *how* people envisage each other, realize each other, understand each other. No living person can enter the perception of his fellow save as a body. This holds in the most spiritistic of systems. Even the bodyless dead must have a living body for a medium of their manifestation; nor can any event of heaven or hell make sense except by way of bodily reference. In a word, presence, existence, being *there,* always means some experience of seeing, hearing, smelling, tasting, touching, acting on, feeling, a something not the same as the sensori-motor adience which answers the thing's call. In the case of people, living or dead, this something is the body or some symbol or image of the body. But it is true that the bodies are not the people. By themselves alone, bodies, humanly speaking, are not human. By themselves alone bodies are only animal organisms reacting to stimuli. The humanity which attaches to them envelopes them like an atmosphere, radiates from them like an aura and illuminates them like an aureole. This effulgence is an added something, for which the name in any individual is personality, and which is the self that the individual struggles to preserve as he "struggles for self-preservation." Though we see people as bodies, we experience them as persons. Every person is a unique body which somehow is uniquely embodying a unique personality-image.

A clear, distinct, scientific definition of how personality and the personality-image relate themselves to the body is still out of my reach. There are many theories of what mind is and of how it is related to the body. I have received small aid and less comfort from any. There is only one thing on which all are agreed: this is that body is not mind and mind is not body. The recognition that the two are different may be as old as humanity itself. Certainly every known species of human culture builds a considerable part of its commonalty of organization upon or around this difference. And even sophisticated cultures with totally monistic philosophies, that make all different things modes or mutations of one thing and only one—one spirit or one matter—are compelled to employ the distinction in order to liquidate it.

In the prescientific world the most widespread as well as the most conventional equivalent for personality is "soul." Tradition is apt to designate education as the culture or discipline of the soul, and the soul as an immaterial simple entity, create or uncreate, having functions but no parts, but in any event immortal, receiving the body for a dwelling place at birth and moving from its ruinous shelter to another habitation at death. The soul's functions are to think, to will and to feel. Its career during life is an exercise of those functions which may require a warfare with the flesh in which it dwells, or with its own self as a being whose will is free. Its choices and decisions while it is in life will establish its fortunes when it is dead. The duty of education is to instruct in right doctrine and to inculcate right discipline. This will render any choice but the right choice and any decision but the right decision impossible. Education, that is, should be indoctrination in orthodoxy of thought, of judgment, and of conduct.• Different cultures cultivate different orthodoxies,

---

• The Democratic Revolution, with its faith in reason and progress, superseded this conception with another which has been winning an ever wider allegiance since the age of Jefferson and Condorcet. This other is intrinsic to the Jeffersonian philosophy of education. "We should be far, too," he wrote in 1811

but each develops as a variant upon this ground plan of belief relating body, soul and destiny. The multitudinous societies of mankind hold, each in its manner, to these beliefs. Their religious and political economies are addressed to enchanneling these beliefs in the conduct of life. Education, as we have seen, has been held internal to these economies, their instrument for transmitting their principles and practices to the generations. The personality into which any member of such an economy develops will absorb into his singularity at least the dominant features of this transmitted cultural inheritance. Willy-nilly he will pattern his works and ways to the lines of force which this projects.

That neither the conception of personality as "soul" nor the conception's implications—however widely and strongly they continue to be held—is acceptable to the modern spirit, need not be argued. The sciences of life and of man deny that personality is a lodger, or even a freeholder, in the body, that it is from the body detached or detachable, that it is independent and subject to the law of its own nature alone. In the light of these sciences, personality and body belong to one another. Their relationship is not external but internal, the first being a growth of the second, a sort of effulgence from its structure and activities. But concerning the *how* of this dynamic inwardness, the sciences provide no unambiguous deliverance. Analogies abound—analogies from ideas of force and field, of heat and light, channel and stream, sun and ray, and so on to no end. Nevertheless what is said of the relation between mind and body belongs rather to speculative than to experimental psychology. The latter assumes the relation, exploits it, but does not explain it. The former purports to explain it, but cannot exploit it; and when it can, turns out to have used in the explanation that

(The Rockfish Gap Report), "from the discouraging persuasion that man is fixed, by the law of his nature, at a given point; that his improvement is a chimaera, and the hope delusive of rendering ourselves wiser, happier or better than our forefathers were. . . . Education engrafts a new man on the native stock, and improves what in his nature was vicious and perverse into qualities of virtue and social worth. And it cannot be but that each generation succeeding to the knowledge acquired by those who preceded it, adding to it their own acquisitions and discoveries, and handing the mass down for successive and constant accumulation, must advance the knowledge and well-being of mankind, not infinitely, as some have said, but indefinitely, and to a term no one can fix and foresee."

which it undertook to explain. Faculty psychologists, psychoanalysts, behaviorists, connectionists, gestaltists, hormicists, topologists and all the rest; philosophers as diverse as Bergson and Russell and Dewey and Whitehead—each starts from assumptions only to return with that alone which they took with them. A consensus seems as remote as ever in these modern times.

This should cause a certain inconvenience to education, and certainly does when the educational establishment calls for a philosophy. And when, indeed, does the establishment not call for a philosophy? Being always, however, a pressing, present enterprise, education cannot wait for a consensus. It must act on working hypotheses, whatever at last may be the religious or scientific and philosophic ultimates regarding the mind-body relation, and whatever may be their bearing on the many devices of postulation, determination and measurement which make up so much of the educational psychology of our time. The schools avail themselves of whatever assumption and whatever devices and techniques authority sanctions or fashion suggests. And in using them they tend to exalt them from postulates into principles, from working hypotheses into infallible dogmas, from tools into idols. Because of their uses, these servants of education become its masters.

With this in mind, let us assume that personality is to the body as, say, music is to the violin. Obviously its music is not the same as the violin, nor as the moving bow that causes the fiddlestrings to vibrate. True, music is not until the bow strikes the strings; if the former should be called stimulus, the latter's vibration must be called response. Those vibrations are the immediate antecedents of music, and music ensues upon the sequence of the relationships to one another of the fiddle's parts and of the whole fiddle and the bow. That fiddle is a special, if you like, a singular, organization of stuffs which because thus patterned are able to respond, among others, to certain selected stimuli external and internal. The bow is but the stimulus acknowledged by convention. But the fiddle may also vibrate because of difference between its woods, of a step on the floor, a wind outside, and many other impacts which do not customarily figure in the formation of music. So it is also with body and personality. Personality is the vector relationship between a body and its environments. It is not actual until the diverse environment stimulates and the body responds. Its being is not however response merely, it is response impatterned, projected, changing, yet developing continuously. Aristotle was among the first to observe this fact of relationship. He noted that soul is to body as cutting is to an axe. Soul thus is an activity or "actualization" of the body. Aristotle also thought that the most human, the most rational part of the soul had no organ of which it was an activity, that it was actual of itself, in itself and for itself, an independent and autonomous power. We know that this is not the case, that personality and body belong together as field and magnet or music and instrument. We know that they affect each other as function affects structure and structure function.

Taking the analogy with music for a working hypothesis, how does any person realize his personality? • How does he

• We must always keep in mind that even the most perfect analogy is inadequate, and that every one of them can cause error. The music which comes from a violin is a terminal event for the violin. It figures as the final effect of a sequence of actions whose energies are used up in the music, as the force of a spring is consumed in the pattern which the water makes as it fountains into the air. The music might be compared to the incandescence of a tungsten filament in an electric light. Music is the goal and consumption to which all other operations of a musical performance lead. Although the fiddle does undergo structural and other modifications in the course of being played upon, it is generally believed that those modifications are mechanical only. The speculations that interpret them as a sort of learning are not many. To be genuinely learning, the violin's changes would have to resemble those of a singer learning to sing. Her vocalizations are also an incandescence, also the final term to which all her other activities are preliminaries, and in which they are at once spent and consummated. But if her singing were only that, she could no more learn her art than the violin. She would be to the music she produces what the violin is, or a record is—a mechanical occasion of a mechanical effect. Since the violin is not a living organism and she is, the violin does not remember, and she does. All her body remembers, her vocal chords remember. In minding the experiences to which her response is singing, she takes in some items, shuts out others; she so assimilates and compounds those she takes in, that her organs of musical perception and expression modify in form and diversity and expand in function. During each lesson, exercise or performance, her printed notes, her instrumental accompaniment, and other matters relevant and irrelevant, are contributing accessories to the functioning of those organs. The process is continuous, and it is such that each event of its compounds with its predecessors and all together exercise a shaping influence on the future ones still unformed. Currently, this process is declared to be "feedback," and to envisage and understand the selfhood of his self? Is it in the manner of the image that a snapshot catches or the pose a photographer arranges or the form and features that a mirror reflects? Every man knows that it cannot be any of these by itself nor all of them together, alone. They are events of a moment that passes and though they are substance of his substance and form of his form, the self he is not only passes but continues as it passes. The self endures. Images, postures, gestures, actions, expressions, like the notes of a tune, are passing events; what permanence they attain, they attain, again like the notes of a tune, when and as they have ceased to pass and become the past. The self's continuity and existence is the activity of passing; it is process; it is transition wherein somehow, as in a melody or other musical progression, the shifts of transit stay on as they disappear. Those that do so become the living past, the past out of which presently flows that next movement we call the future. They are biography that makes itself as the hours of the day and the days of the years and the years of the life, until the making stops and the personality does not even linger on. The composition has finished or is stopped. As Bergson wrote somewhere, the individual makes his own road as he travels, for none has traveled that road before. Though his body grows up, grows old and dies, the spirit of that body, his personality, lasts. The fiddle may wear out as the tunes played on it diversify and multiply and compound. And similarly every body sustains more than one personality, whose multiplicity nevertheless orchestrates into simplicity. The years do not diminish it, the years increase it. For its growing is learning and its living is remembering. There is more of it at the body's death than at the body's birth, and its nucleus is an organization of activities whose singularity is an orchestration of the body with the diversities of the world it has taken for field.

---

resemble the stimulus-response circle that the physiologist calls "homeostasis." This requires that the end-term of a given activity as an effect shall serve at the same time as an initiator of repetitions as well as new consequences until the action completes itself. Thus, the analogy between music and mind has its application limited by the fact that mind is not only terminal incandescence, but also consequential "feedback." Minding changes the organism which minds. So far as we know, music does not similarly change the violin. Mindful changes are fundamentally processes of remembering and constitute what is usually called learning.

Which diversities are largely matters of the Zeitgeist, of the "climate of opinion," of the "culture" patterns prevailing. One is born into a family, in a place, at a time, when people dress in a certain mode, do their hair in a certain style, carry themselves in a certain posture, make use of a certain vocabulary at a certain pitch with a certain rhythm and with certain gestures, prefer this music and not that, read these books and not those, eat these things in that way and not otherwise, and admire and emulate these contemporaries and those historic types but no others. And so on. Words like "Victorian," "Georgian," "Elizabethan," "pre-war," "post-war," signify such constellations of preferences and practices, of manners, morals, attitudes and judgments. They name a social and cultural atmosphere. They designate the traits which are common to its types. Their import is the characteristic of the age.

An age's philosophers, poets, novelists, painters and sculptors for the most part embody, and so conserve it, in types. The core of Aristotle's ethics is a delineation of Greek types. The brave man, the prudent man, the foolhardy man, the free man, the slavish man, the man of magnanimous mind, are each a type. Plato, Aristotle's teacher, began it by delineating types in his Republic, and Theophrastus, Aristotle's pupil, made of types or characters the explicit theme of his writing. And what else, for that matter, does Victorian Carlyle make of his heroes of history, with all their singularities on their heads, but types, or as Emerson would have them, "representative men"? These are first living men of blood and bone and brain, with all the juices of individuality in their veins. The image-maker abstracts from these singularities the delimiting shape, the gradient of form. The thinker breaks up the form into a collocation of traits and rules, recomposes them in a set of relationships exemplifying his "laws of thought" rather than the original's way of life, and thereby transmutes the whole into a system of abstractions which is called a philosophy of life and character. After the tongue has uttered what the eyes have seen, the ears have heard and the heart has felt, the head can transpose the utterance from empirical description into dialectical definition. But always the image of the Self begins in the direct impact of another person, in the form and feel of him as a living force, as a gradient of one's own growth toward freedom and fulfillment. The image begins as a recollection of something netted from that impact, as a dynamic line along which the imagist's energies readily flow, as a role to enact, a character to achieve, and as achieving to alter, even to outgrow.

Every soul, every personality, starts its life course upon a track thus chosen and thus followed. *Curriculum vitae* is more than a metaphor. Every personality is a manifold music which the fingerings and blowings and percussions of the world awaken from its body, and the diapason swells, with all the discords and dissonances that enter such harmonies, until the body dies and can no more respond. Psychologists will endeavor to reduce the aggregate event to a single dynamic. According to the dogmas or the postulates of their sects and schools, they will talk of extravert and introvert, eroticisms oral or anal, feelings of inferiority and masculine protests, behaviors, connections, frustrations, aggressions, vectors and *Gestalts,* and so on in ever-diversifying volume. But whatever its drives, how limited, how varied, how scattered or how concentrated, a life story is a succession of personality-images thus enacted, compenetrative or mutually exclusive, toned alike by irreducible conflicts or by ever-heightened orchestrations.

How an individual's personality-images relate to one another sustains the kind of person he is. And one's kind of person is always an event going on and never a static condition. It is the sustaining of a constellation of adiencies and withdrawals, a role maintained, a limit sought, surpassed or kept up to. Its dynamic is well exemplified in the expression "keeping up with the Joneses." This phrase, which significantly has become a part of our American idiom, is a title of a comic strip. The inward theme of the strip is how people choose and embody their ideals. "The Joneses" are a generic name for the ideal. They are neighbors. Where they live does not matter: they may be American Middletowners, Chinese in China, Gandhi's Hindus, Stalin's Communists, Main Street's "best people"—the local banker or businessman or minister or politician or woman's club leader. But wherever and whoever they are, they will impress the mind as figures of force, freedom and fulfillment, at once life's going and life's goal. They will be taken for objects of emulation and imitation, for characters to enact until habit makes the self-characterization the "second" nature which, as Pascal somewhere observes, is more primitively and expressively a person's self than the original nature of his birth and heritage. In the comic strip, the

Joneses embody the personal ideal. They set the standards and make the pace. What they are is good, how they act is right. They are both the measures and the measurement of all things. And so it is in the daily life. The persistent vogue of the comic strip rests upon the fact that it does bring out and 'up into the open, and does, under the guise of laughing at it, confess to the workings of this central drive in every man, at once his secret substance and his secret shame.

The range of emulation knows no limit, nothing is too strange, no item is too little, no principle too sweeping. Sometimes it will focus exclusively on Mrs. Jones's hat or tableware, or Mr. Jones's necktie or golf score or motor car. Often it will embrace the entire Jones career, again limit itself to his love-life, or his hobbies or his special abilities in sport or profession, or his ways of walking and talking, of eating and drinking and smoking, of sitting down and standing up. It will draw from comic strips like *Dick Tracy* or *Superman,* from motion pictures, from stage-plays, from novels, from newspaper reports and other more authentic forms of poetry, making of these emulative shapes that impattern for the individual the upkeep and enlargement of his life, liberty and happiness.

That children live and grow through such emulative embodiments is a commonplace observation. Their play is a make-believe. Whether they make-believe they are Orphan Annies, cops and robbers, Dick Tracys or Supermans, all the personalities that they enact live through adventure, channel love and hate, achieve the struggle and overcoming of misfortune, the war and the victory over poverty, wickedness and stupidity alike in the commonplaces of the daily round and in the deep fantasies of "escape" and "compensation" such as are Aladdin of the Arabian nights of old or Walter Mitty in the Thurberian nights of our new day.

The knowing explain this play in many ways and every single one of them may be right. But its dynamic reality is the embodiment of the succession of personality-images, each somehow impatterning energies, liberating and expressing powers, making over the players into something they are not. Such impersonation may also be called learning, and the learning even of the most abstract of abstractions calls for a modicum of some such impersonation. Not until powers have failed and stimulus no longer receives response does it come to a stop. In adults it goes by other names than make-believe and seeks other consequences than the consequences of play (which is supposed to be its own reward). As each new enactment becomes an old memory, it condenses into a vestige, a sign, a symbol of that richly diverse image whose present incarnation was freedom and fulfillment. It may condense into the potent ideo-motor tension we call habit. It may persist only as attitude, tonus, psychic timbre. In whatever form it continues, it is of the persistent stuff of personality.

The initiating model appears always to be some psychologically near exemplification of force, freedom and fulfillment. With children it is as a rule a parent, an elder brother, a playmate, whose form is directly perceived and whose power is directly felt. To this perceptual base are then assimilated the images supplied by the comic strips and other contemporary transpositions of ancient faerie; then there accrues the faerie land of tradition itself, and all the outlying kingdoms of make-believe. As children grow they change old images for new, and make all sorts of starts at new personalities with new careers. Those which they achieve are always, at the core, some hero of the place and time whose adventures among men and things and ideas sets before their attention and effort "the standard of living" of their aspiration, the image of the personality they would live into. They also become the prototypes of myth and tale as well. Miss Pyrtle's reference to Lindbergh signalized the beginning of one such mutation—"the lone eagle"—now forgotten, but the starting point for so many comic strips. The canonization of Henry Ford among the Soviets is another instance of the same process. The stories of the heroes' lives are first confronted, then confused, then compenetrated, with the life stories of other heroes from other times and other places, from history and legend, and from the artist's creation. The images do not serve as models to emulate only. Automatically they are taken as well for measures to appraise with. So in the eighteenth century the actual Indian of the North American continent was worked over into the child of nature whom Pope and Rousseau and Voltaire imagined; he became the personality whom Marie Antoinette and her ladies-in-waiting simulated in the Gardens of Versailles; and the Man Friday who served shipwrecked Robinson Crusoe on his desert island. Crusoe himself was a compounding and refinement of English "cits" whose powers of self-help and self-respect as colonials won them mastery and liberty. The Persians and Chinese in whose mouths Montesquieu or another put his judgments of the French were but costume versions of admired actual English ways and ideas. So "the man nobody knows" who is one of the twentieth century images named Christ, is more contemporary man of affairs and master of publicity assimilated to the reverence-evoking figure of the gospel legend.

Personalities who signalize to their neighbors concretions of the force, freedom and fulfillment they desire for themselves are, of course, not only admired, loved and emulated; they are also despised, hated and attacked. These very traits and attainments which exalt them into the Joneses men want to keep up with may affect other men not as configurations of liberty but as powers of oppression. The model, instead of being freely chosen from among alternatives present, may impose itself. To Hitler, for example, Kaiser Wilhelm II was so releasing an image, that like many other German-speaking males, he long wore his mustachios pointed up like horns, in emulation of his Jovian Kaiser. After the German defeat of World War I, the figure of the Kaiser could no longer symbolize a German dream of self-consummation. Hitler cut off the horns of his mustachios, and gave his upper lip the adornment of which the most widely recognizable wearer was Charles Chaplin's mirth-making, servile weakling, whose misadventures somehow make him stronger and freer than he was before. German mustaches ceased to be kingly horns and became the abrupt subnasal smears of the führer. But they signalized the same gradients of force, freedom and fulfillment that Wilhelm's horns had expressed, only loosed from the refinements, the politenesses and the punctilios that clothed the elder tradition, and with its tyranny, its sadism, its egomania and its stupidity stripped naked and exalted. The new version of the German Jones was made into a systematized image of the conqueror of the world. The schools, the press, the churches, the arts and sciences were ordered to project and inculcate and indoctrinate the image of this Jones by every means of communication in their power among Germans and everywhere in the world. Those Germans who despised, hated and would oust this image and its embodiment in works and ways for another were, however, estopped by the police power from modeling this other image upon the originals in other lands, as Voltaire and Montesquieu modeled upon the English, and Voltaire and Rousseau and Defoe upon the American Indians. They could turn only to figures of history and art, in so far as the latter might be envisaged and projected free from the moldings to the dominant image imposed by a teaching whose purpose is propaganda and whose method is indoctrination. Since only education could supply such a knowledge of the past, a primary duty of the educator would be to prevent or to pervert such knowledge. Whatever the images of record might be, the image to which the arch-educator permitted his pupil access would be his party's prescribed equivalent of Plato's "noble lies." Authority and its spiritual police—the teachers, the censors, the preachers—undertook to see that no aspiration of the heart should be unconformed to the dominant image. Hitlerism of course, has its antecedents as well as its successors. Stalinism is the most important, both as antecedent and successor. In matters of the personality-image it has a parallel history. Nor did Hitler Germany improve upon its initiating example.

Nevertheless, as the record sufficiently shows, for any individual to accept an image that he may grow into, imposition and coercion are rarely enough. Plastic as spirit may be, it has, we know, an ineffable limit, beyond which its individuality will not conform. The adiencies of curiosity are as diverse as they are numerous, and all are procedures of psychosomatic energies seeking free way and fulfillment. Commonly that channel is accepted which opposes the least obstruction and calls for the least effort, which is most congruous with the form and flow of the personal consciousness from its springs. Although our adiencies go in all directions and our curiosity reaches out to all things, we follow only those roads that enlarge and satisfy our being and get to grips with those things that nourish and advance our powers. These are countless, and which of them we take and follow is always, within the bounds set by our powers, more a personal option than a social or natural necessity. To experience, there is never one and only one road to Rome, or one Rome; one and only one nourishing stuff, one and only one personality-image. Alternatives continually present themselves simply or in multitude. There are not only planes and ships or trains to go to our Rome in. There are different companies traveling different roads. There are not only white breads and dark breads. There are breads of different bakings, different compositions, different forms. There are not only the career of engineer or poet, or what have you. There are different modes of each career, exemplified in different personalities between whose images we choose for our going and goal.

And as a rule, that which we freely choose must promise or possess congruity with our spontaneous powers. Our choices must offer fulfillment of our natures, not violations; liberations, not inhibitions. The once fashionable notion of the behaviorist school that the human organism is a plastic which that expert in human engineering, the psychologist, can mold as he chooses, has turned out a wistful postulate which the behaviorists' own experiments have falsified. Whatever may be done to us or by us in the making of our personalities, if the making is not to be a mere breaking, its events must be assimilable to the singularity of our organic becoming whose wholeness is our self. If this do not confirm the making, it remains alien, excremental.

There is, Edward Thorndike tells us, a "confirming reaction." It acts, he says, "biologically, not logically. It does not pick out infallibly the connections which the person wishes to strengthen, and confirm, that is, strengthen them. It strengthens primarily the connection that has just been acting, but may strengthen a neighboring connection in addition, or instead. It acts more like a hormone than a syllogism . . . is more like a knee jerk than like either a syllogism or a cash register." It goes on all the time and compounds. It sustains the skills and knowledge we have attained and are attaining. It applies, not to details, but "to 'large' trends and total thoughts." It "has its source in the over-all control of a person at the time. This over-all control may be any one of the numerous selves of a man. . . . [It] has its origin outside the situation—response unit upon which it acts . . . there is no simple opposite [of it]. . . . The confirming reaction may be the act of a free agent, a free will, in the most useful sense of those words. Science has hitherto denied this or seemed to deny it. Science commonly thinks of the modification in human beings as caused by the environment, including the social environment constituted by other living men and the intellectual and moral environment constituted by all surviving institutions of such men living or dead. The environment, in this very broad sense of the word with all its persons, customs, arts, religions, and sciences, undoubtedly determines most of what occurs in man and most of what is rewarded. Most, but not all.

"To some extent man modifies himself. The confirming

reaction is issued by a man when a man is satisfied. That man originates in a certain collection or battery or output of genes which is by definition apart from and contrasted with its environment. Day by day that man has changed his nature partly by the influence of his own confirmations of connections whose consequences satisfy him. Each person is to that extent an *imperium in imperio naturae*. Each person is a center of creative force modifying himself more or less to suit himself."

So Thorndike affirms by his lights what Bergson has declared by his. In the workings of "heredity and environment" which the conventions of science single out to be causes of personality, the "battery of genes" is assigned a certain autonomy with respect to which the geneticists and environmentalists invoke contradictory postulates. One is that we are that which we were born to be; in the last analysis, the world where we grow up and grow old and die can serve only to suppress, to release or to destroy our inborn powers, but cannot alter them; it can stop up the springs of ancestry or set them free, and that is all; heredity is destiny. The other postulate is that "the battery of genes" is but a collocation of plastic energies with no inevitable inner gradient, and that the world of their struggle, not the powers we inherit, makes us what we are today and is never satisfied; destiny is environment. In neither case is personality cause; in both, it is effect and only effect, a passive "this and no other" with no role and no influence on its own making.

A fundamental consequence of this position for the theory and practice of education is that "science" provides its own aid and comfort to the traditional conception of human nature as invariant, and its own justification of the Platonic notion that education is at best a kind of sorting machine—in military parlance, a "screening" device for separating and training according to their inalterable powers the generations of mankind. The good society, whose rule is justice, is a society with a place for everybody and everybody in his place, minding the business for which he was made and not sticking his nose into other people's business. Justice requires that those should rule who are born to rule, those watch and fight who are born to do so and those serve whose nature can no more exercise another function than a donkey can be an elephant. Slaves are such by nature, not by nurture; free men are born to freedom, and cannot owe their capacities and status to any institution or other environment. The evils of the common life ensue when society instead of perfecting confuses the natural order of things and slavish natures receive the power and prerogatives of freedom, while free men go in bonds. Servility is the true freedom of the slave—by nature but a tool with life in it, as a tool is a lifeless slave. Power and rule are the true service of the free man whose worth is in himself and whose self is the discipline wherewith his spontaneous powers are shaped toward perfection. Each form of government—the tyranny, the oligarchy, the polity, the aristocracy, the plutocracy, the ochlocracy, the timocracy and the democracy—imparts its own singularity to this general confusion. But the worst sinner is democracy, which enshrines the disorder of the social faculties at their height, with nobody in the place where by nature he belongs, and everybody in the place where by nature he does not belong.

This idea of human existence, of the relation of the individual to society and of the task of education in society, has never lost its hold on the power-holders among the peoples of mankind. The idea that nurture can transform nature, that education must provide nurture before it can discern and discipline nature, is its revolutionary counter. The idea's vogue began with the critique of the inequities of the social order that is one of the labors of the illuminati of the eighteenth century. It received a great increment of meaning from the ideas of the American Revolution and the French Bill of Rights, and the early essays of biological and social science were held to bring it confirmation. It is a dogma of the Marxist faith and a directive for biological research in the Russia of Stalin. But as both free biology and free psychology became more experimental and specific, evidence accumulated that seemed to give support to the older view. From the initiation of the Binet-Simon efforts to define and measure intelligence until this day and beyond into the indefinite dark future, schemes of accountancy of human traits follow one another, device upon device, formula upon formula, rule of interpretation upon rule. The distance from the first Binet-Simon test to the last Rorschach test is spanned by a succession of measuring gadgets and bookkeeping devices, each carefully called by the name of its inventor, to assure his immortality, and each purporting to be in its own way a demonstration of the fixity of human nature, enabling assurance in counseling and certainty in prediction. World War I gave the entrepreneurs of these devices an immense opportunity and established the devices as a permanent part of the schools' equipment. It opened up new careers in the domain of education—school psychologists, testers, counselors. In World War II all that had been brought to market since World War I was mobilized to the end of finding the right place for the right conscript in the hierarchical division of labor imposed by the requirements of a mechanized organization of the armed forces on the land, on the sea and in the air.

In the schools, especially in the overgrown urban schools, with their overlarge classes, their formal and passionally and practically irrelevant curricula, the measuring devices provided reliefs from the responsibilities of teaching. As the children are passed on from grade to grade, their I.Q.'s go with them. Those have ostensibly revealed in thirty minutes what it would have taken a teacher weeks to discover concerning her pupils as learners. They constitute a grid upon which the pupils may be ranked in a hierarchy from superior to dull and moronic, with a precise number for each—69 for the "feeble-minded," 90-109 for the "normal," 130 and over for the superior. The grid will compose a "normal distribution curve" with defectives at one end, 2 per cent of the whole, the borderline cases 6.7 per cent, the dull normal, 16.1 per cent, the average, 50 per cent, the bright normal, 16 per cent, the superior, 6 per cent, the very superior, 2.2 per cent. In the order set down, children of Jewish, English and Scotch extraction will outnumber all others among the superior and very superior; Germans, Norse, Bohemians, Chinese and Japanese will bulk large among the average, while the dull normal and the rest will be drawn from Italians, Poles, Portuguese, French, Canadians, Mexicans, Indians and Negroes. Pupils of private schools reveal higher I.Q.'s than public school pupils, city dwellers than country people; the city-slicker and the country hick, then, are born, not made.

And if these findings are taken for constants, in which the actualities of variation are so small as to be negligible, I.Q. foretells the destiny of each child. How can you make an intellectual silk purse out of an intellectual sow's ear? Knowing the limits of the pupil's capacity, the school's task then is to suit the curriculum to the capacity, to bring to the future citizen that personality-image and to train him for that station in life which his nature fits him for. Education becomes in modern practice the sorting or screening device that Plato held it must be. It accepts the existing hierarchical correlation of vocations and powers and inducts the growing American into that vocation best fitted to his inalterable powers. The school becomes a caste-ing device, an instrument of classification and distribution of the generations of Americans in the national economy, and thus the keystone of the arch of economy's continuing structure and operation. As a time-and-labor-saving tool in the management and instruction, the I.Q. and the other numbers produced by the other tests are a godsend alike to administrators and classroom teachers. They now truly know what their pupils can and can't do, and it saves them a lot of heartache and trouble. The measures determine for them what their educational ideals may not fail to be. Variation, and the practice called "enrichment" can have no place in those ideals. Wisdom points to a method more indoctrination than free inquiry, to a simple homogeneous content and discipline—a refinement and perfection of what exists, not a variation *from* what exists. The educational goal must needs be excellence, not growth.

Excellence accrues to a thought or an action or a personality when it reaches the optimum of economy, efficiency and order appropriate to its essence. Excellence is performance with the least material in the simplest and quickest way and the most suitable form. Machines, particularly scientific machines, are the usual models of such excellence. Human beings attain it through drill or practice. By dint of unrelaxing repetition they become virtuosos in some occupation, art or science, masters of a "mystery." The attainment of virtuosity would thus be the goal of education, general as well as special, and virtuosities would vary only with the invariant endowments of the men and women whose virtuosities they are. Business enterprise leaped at the idea. It would enable employers to choose employees that would produce the most with the least trouble. All over the land testing was taken for a trouble-and-money-saving device. The idea was taken to be true, as Mr. Hutchins asserts, that the poor truck driver does not need to learn physics, nor for that matter, the nuclear physicist how to drive a truck. The virtue of the former would be his virtuosity with trucks in motion; of the latter with protons and electrons in motion. The two would be organic parts of the same society as the wheels of a clock are organic parts of the same machine. Each would mind his own business utterly unaware of the business of the other, and the union of the two would be the care of some very superior I.Q. with a liberal education acquired through drill in the liberal arts; or else some divine overseer of a pre-established harmony by God's grace granted and God's grace maintained.

To the postulates upon which this image of human nature and of its education is grounded there have been counters from the very beginning, nor was their environmentalist form the most effective, though its force is undeniable. The other counters appeared early in the controversy over the level of American intelligence raised by the alarums of propagandists using inferences from the army Alpha and Beta tests of World War I as provocations to xenophobia. A number of studies were launched, a variety of experiments were initiated, to establish that, far from being constant, the I.Q. and other ratios stating the amounts and degrees of human quality vary with the environment. There were the studies of Burtt in England, during the early '20's. In America there were Freeman's studies of the late '20's. In the '30's there came from the Iowa Child Welfare Experiment Station the reports of Skeels and Fillmore, and of Stoddard and Wellman.• The studies dealt not only with young children. They investigated twins both fraternal and identical. They analyzed the effects of alterations of the same home and of changes from one home to another. They studied the workings of changes from homes to schools, and the like. The investigators found that changing conditions brought large changes in the I.Q., both up and down, average to genius and average to dull. An especially striking record of change was made by Miss Bernadine Schmidt, now of the State Teachers College at Terre Haute, Indiana. She had launched, when she graduated from the Chicago Teachers College at the onset of the Great De-

• Cf. Brigham, *American Intelligence* (Princeton: 1921); F. M. Freeman, "The Influence of Environment," *27th Yearbook, National Society for the Study of Education* (1928); H. M. Skeels, "Mental Development of Children in Foster Homes," *Journal of General Psychology* (1936); Beth L. Wellman, "The Role of Cultural Status in the Intelligence of Pre-school Children," "The Effect of Pre-school Attendance on the I.Q.," "Growth in Intelligence under Differing Pre-School Environments," *Journal of Experimental Education and of Genetic Psychology* (December 1937).

pression, a school of her own for feeble-minded children. In a loft above an undertaking establishment, she assembled 70 boys and girls, aged 7 to 16, with I.Q.'s from 40 to 70, and school grades corresponding. She taught these children for three years. Her idea was that all too often feeble mind is weak will, deficient initiative, not deficient intellect. And she set about developing initiative, by methods of self-help and self-orientation. Her projects were progressions from immediate to remoter needs and interests. Her results were such at the end of three years that she was put in charge of Chicago's Opportunity Center for Subnormal Children. There, the city sent her 254 boys and girls 12 to 14 years old, none with an I.Q. higher than 69, most lower, so that the average for the 254 children was 51.7. With eleven other teachers to help her, Miss Schmidt worked with these children for eight years in all. Standard tests given at the end of the third year showed them to have an average gain of four grades. During the next five years tests were given eighteen months apart. At the end of the eighth year the standard tests demonstrated that upward of 80 per cent of the children had gained 30 points, that only 7.2 per cent remained "feeble-minded." Even more recently, Irving Lorge, of Columbia University, reported upon comparative changes in the I.Q.'s of the schooled and the unschooled. His study covers a period of twenty years. It establishes that I.Q. varies as much as 15 to 20 points directly with the amount of schooling. "An adult's measured mental ability is related to his intelligence as a boy and to the extent of his subsequent schooling."

None of the studies in the variation of the I.Q., all of them controversial, convincingly separates hereditary endowment from environmental influence. All of them establish that change does take place and that the absence of any noticeable measure of change cannot be accounted for on the ground of biological necessity. Together, the studies establish that the constancy observed or inferred has been rather a consequence of the fact that the wish for constancy shaped inquiry and determined its assumptions and procedures, and that the latter could hardly fail to satisfy the wish that set them going. As soon as investigators began to look for variability, they saw it. Genius and feeble-mindedness can be made as well as found.

Now for democracy the observation that human traits can be made is of prime importance. For democracy rejects the idea that there is one place and only one place for each and every person, and that the good society must be one in which there is a place for everybody and everybody is in his place. Democracy assumes that people are free, that they have no sole inevitable place and function, but move from one to another as their hearts prompt and their powers carry. Democracy rejects social hierarchy for social mobility and invariant personality for changing personality. And the careful studies of such mobility and change bring democracy aid and comfort. But they are not enough. For the making here reported does not take into account the role of the individual in his own making. It pays no heed to that aspect of a life which Thorndike names "the confirming reaction" and Bergson *élan*, and which the tradition, perhaps less aptly, has called free will. The idea, that one's heredity or one's environment are causes external to the personality of which the personality is the effect, leaves no room for the most intimate and the most lasting of Everyman's experiences—the experience that he is, even at his most passive, diversely up and doing, selecting, rejecting, excreting, assimilating, from among the multitudinous alternatives which present themselves for his response, those that then and there engage and enchannel his powers most livingly and variedly. These he incorporates into his changing self with the "confirming reaction."

No such confirmation can be a repetition merely. Even the drill and repetitions that compound into excellence are not simply repetitive. The new event, identical as it may be with old, in so far as it *is not* the old, changes the latter. Every genuine repetition is alteration. The two together are a quality different from either alone. As in struggling to preserve ourselves we change ourselves, so in repeating a same, we alter it. As the study of human development becomes fuller, more detailed and more prolonged, there is a disposition among students such as Arnold Gesell to see development as a series of mutations, analogous to the form changes of insects from egg to adult, rather than as a continuous enlargement of childhood into maturity. The experts discriminate well-marked stages, each with its characteristic traits and preferences, with the antecedent surviving in the consequent, and altered by being suffused by the consequent. They do not take growth as a waxing of sames, but as diversification of the same into the different and a transformation of the same by the different.

This happens even with the born idiot, and an idiot is by definition a human animal incapable of acquiring a personality. He can repeat the past but he cannot differentiate and thus transform and enrich the past. He cannot learn as better-endowed creatures learn. But he, too, struggles to live and makes himself different if his struggle succeeds. He too has his confirming reactions, his life story singular to himself, whose plot he weaves as he lives, tomorrow, and tomorrow, and tomorrow, to the last syllable of his recorded time. No more for the idiot than for his *soi-disant* betters, can the life line be fixed by a cross-section of tests and a graph of measurements. These are to his personality what a frame from a motion-picture is to the whole event which is the picture's action, or a single tone to the whole event which is a melody. Neither the tone by itself nor the single frame by itself can make any revelation of the total past nor any prophecy of the future. The turn of events before either was reached was multitudinous, and multitudinous are the turns to follow. Of which were taken, of which will be taken, the present instance can give no unambiguous warning. Its best is like the Delphic oracles: the inquirer pays his money and takes his choice. Looking back he can always see true prophecy if he wishes. But as the present image or sound is different from all that went before, so those will vary that follow it.

The further a life grows from its starting point the more numerous and diverse are the differentiations its rocket-like energies shoot forth. In order to take a hold on it and harness it up we think the days of a life as repetitions of identicals. We separate out their compenetrations and measure their passage by that which they passed through. We restate the events of them in the categories of the psychologies and the other social sciences; we undertake to arrest them mid-passage in concepts they pass through and that are themselves a passage. As we struggle for self-preservation, and change the more because we struggle, so we struggle to hold in identity the diversifying multiplicities around us that alter as our concepts rein and check them. Their existence is not a rubber band that stretches, returns to its original form, and goes on as if it had never been stretched. In fact its every stretch is a transformation, into a different structure with an altering function. In fact heredity is not a force outside us, compelling us; in fact heredity is our past alive and present within us—in the ways and works of our organs, in the posture and patterns of our minds transformed by experience and transforming it, as new skills and new knowledge are learned, and being learned, suffuse the old and give them new characters and new meanings. It is a static illusion to hold we cannot change the past. What else is there *to* change? If the present is not the enduring consummation of all past, if the future is not the enduring diversification of the present, what can they be? Change is change of the past, from the past in the present; it is making the future. Heredity and the genes are to personality and memory what the atom is to the energy locked in it and released by it. As the atom is both particle and wave, so the personality is both soma and psyche, and the psyche is a continuous learning, a remembering thrusting forward into form. Let a man lose his memory and he loses himself. All of him that is not animal body is an orchestration of memories which are the continuing music of that body as its environments play upon it. The impacts from without are assimilated and digested into growth from within.

This is why the eugenists rest their case on a fallacy. They fancy that the qualities of men are ancestral constants like property in entail. They can little foretell what personality any body will enact from an examination of its parentage or a knowledge of its genes. Nor are the speculations of such investigators as Kretschmer and Sheldon, with their classification of human beings into constitutional types, any less ambiguous and retrospective. It is an ancient adage that you cannot argue a soul from a body, that you cannot deduce Socrates the personality from Socrates the pyknik or Socrates the athletic or Socrates the asthenic; nor Churchill, nor Roosevelt, nor Frank Sinatra, nor Jesus Christ. We are not born with souls, with personalities; we acquire them, and acquiring them alters the endowment we *are* born with. Personality is self or soul ever-in-the-making, a continuing embodiment of an image chosen from a multitude, nourished by contributions from every member and every institution of society that affects the image. The I.Q.'s and the other fractions number a point in its passage, not the force and figure of its going.

Take that number for inalterable and you take with it hierarchy, authority, indoctrination and all the other postulates of anti-democratic society as the latter cultivates the static illusion. Take that number for what in philosophic fact it is, for a starting point for new change, to be used in the process of accomplishing its own alteration, its own diversification, and you take with it the diversity and mobility intrinsic to the democratic way. I.Q.'s and other measurements need not be enclosures; they can be doors and gates. They need not be limits which teachers may only confirm and repeat; they can be taken for prisons whose doors teachers must open for pupils to pass through. They can be employed as indicators of the teacher's task of enabling her pupils to outgrow them. That which the pupils require from the teacher is not instruction in things, nor even perfection in skills; it is the facilitation of power, of growth in self-rule and self-help. Excellence is good, but not good enough. For excellence is a limitation of the static illusion. If excellence and growth were mutually exclusive alternatives, the democrat would be committed to growth. But they are not such alternatives. The records show that living men attain to both, with excellence as a phase in the initiations of growth. The possibilities are known to be far greater than the achievements. Long ago William James called attention to the fact that the energies of men appear to exceed every last demand ever made on them. And recently Dr. Howard Rusk deplored the fact that most human beings live far, far below their psychic income. They make the least effort they dare in order to exist, and even crises will not call forth all their available powers. Dr. Rusk has been looking at the rehabilitation of both disabled war veterans and civilian workers. He had come to the conclusion that few were disposed to exert more than one-tenth of the power they were capable of exerting and that the rest were a fair sample of mankind as a whole. Schoolmen educating free men for a free society could well study the arts of releasing the immense energies of the spirit and powers of reason locked up in each personality, so that each might enact many roles and live many lives so orchestrated to one another that they nevertheless compose one happy and abundant growth from birth to death.

The Esthetic Experience •

Although works of art are presumed to be the specific and particular fields of the esthetic experience, they are not often so, while the working of the artist is. The feel of mastery which any cumulative process brings when means compenetrate to become the ends they are means to, seems to pervade and sustain all modes of workmanship, all domains where materials assimilate and reshape forms and forms work out, use up and reshape materials. Veblen even thought that workmanship is an instinct, that sense for it pervades everything men do; and that the doings tend, hence, to be cumulative in elaboration and momentum. They become, in his view, dominant ways of life, not habits of mastery merely but pedantries and professionalisms nourishing themselves, compounding and stereotyping, in the law as technicality, in religion as ritual, in philosophy as dialectic, and so on to every human activity whatsoever. Instinctual or not, the elaborative and consummatory process is a fact of experience. With it goes a sense of progression, of ways opening, of freedom being achieved—which is so large a component of this feeling—that assimilates the warlike *To Kalon* of aristocracy to the beauty of action of the less domineering occupations. It is this sense of progression which, in the end, puts the craftsman and artist in the place of the warrior at the center of the social scene. Because of it, the esthetic experience comes, in any biography, first as play and then as an experience of creation; only much later as an experience of contemplation. It is owing to this sequence that we tend to name works of art for the operations which work them out and not for the forms which the operations work out. Are they not operas, sonatas, songs, symphonies, paintings, drawings, etchings, sculptures, plays, motion pictures—each and every one an act compenetrated into a fact, a procession of

• [From: Horace M. Kallen, *Art and Freedom*. New York: Duell, Sloan and Pearce; 1942. Vol. II, pp. 948-64. Copyright 1942 by Horace M. Kallen. Reprinted by permission of the publishers.]

consequences consummated as a pattern? The style of them is the mode in which they have been worked out—the manner of manipulating their matter into the shape which defines it as a work of art.

Style, then, is action-pattern. Style, it might be said, is operation dammed up in opera, formation in form, process in product, way-of-doing in thing done. Style is the process felt in the product, enfolded there, and perduring. Contemplation of the product is sometimes supposed to bring a repristination of the process to another mind, and often the study of art is designed to induct the other mind into the rituals of such contemplation, which should initiate the esthetic experience. It does not however appear that the scholar, the critic, the connoisseur is more privileged to receive the experience than the uninitiate. The formers' knowledge about art enlarges the field where the experience may come; it does not more surely bring the experience. That happens as readily in factories and office buildings as in museums and concert halls; in elevators and subways, on highways and streets, as among the mountains or on the sea; in mines as in motion-picture palaces; on dumps, by slagpiles and dungheaps, as in landscaped gardens or well-ordered groves.

The estheticians hardly realize how common is the experience, how frequent. Plain people are as surprised and pleased about it as was Molière's M. Jourdain when he learned that all his life he had been talking prose. It comes to them nameless, undefined by verbal markers and unaltered by estheticians' palaver, so that they live it through without classifying it, just as they breathe. For the most part it comes by way of a sudden redirection of their actions, a new enchannelment of their interests, a fresh orchestration of their passions, all mounting swiftly to the brief flood, and then falling, to leave them flat to the preoccupations from which it had translated them, their feelings heightened or diminished, and no notion why.

You can see it happen. Here on the street are a number of men with picks and shovels. They are unskilled laborers working at jobs. They are producers whose work is a step in the process of producing a new pavement.

Their behavior does not suggest that they have any inward concern in what they are doing. They do it, not because it is their way of living their lives, but because it is a way of earning their livings. They pick and they shovel intermittently, clumsily, slowly, without zest, without eagerness. The slightest occasion is enough to stop their work, and they return to it reluctantly, as if forced. They appear to be at once bound to it and in flight from it, like an animal tethered, and it seems to constrain them like a tether in painful effort. When the five-o'clock whistle blows they stop with an incomparable promptness, with every sign of bonds loosed, burdens dropped. They have stopped earning their livings and are ready now, perhaps, to begin living their lives. Their occupation serves them absolutely and exclusively as a means, a means as Aristotle understood means, having nothing in common with the end it is a means to; utterly distinct from it, sheerly external to it. Beside this incommensurable end for which the means is employed, the means is low and slavish, an instrument with no virtue or significance of its own, justified and justifiable only by its end. The end is not a consummation of the means but a discarding, a negation of the means, an experience of a different nature, in a different dimension. When the whistle blows, the workday is over. The laborers stop being merely producers and become consumers. They do not earn to earn; they earn to spend; they do not spend to earn; they spend to spend. Spending, they live their lives; earning, they work for a living, and between the two there is only the external relation that earning produces, and spending receives, the product.

And so you may see them day in and day out, doing things they have no heart for in the hope of getting things the heart is for. Yet every so often you will notice a change. Here a man with a pick, there a man with a shovel will begin to make his movements, you can't tell how or why, in a different way. The intermittency, the slowness, the clumsiness pass over into a smooth, continuous rhythm; tool and man seem no longer externally attached but inwardly confluent and shaping a melody of action-patterns between the pounding pavement and the sky. When the whistle blows, they do not stop. Interruptions are now interference, not relief; obstacles, not liberation. The swing of the pickax, the lift of the shovel has ceased to be a means to an alien end, and has become a means to an end of which it is a phase; earning one's living and living one's life have for the moment compenetrated and become one and the same. Here is no longer an end justifying the means, but a means justifying an end. The virtue and significance of the end is now the virtue and significance of the means which by compenetrating compose it. Its existence is their sequence, its import their value. Working to live and living to work are for this instant synonymous and equivalent. Look at the men thus engaged, compare them with their comrades servilely at work, and they stand out. Their personalities come to you as somehow stronger, intenser, of greater assurance and greater dignity. Their experience of their shovels and picks and of the pavement they break and scatter with those tools is now esthetic; the relation between them and those objects is beauty. It reaches a height of intensity, then the men fall back into usual modes of the daily task. The tools become tethers again; using them becomes the servile labor of earning a living; the pavement they are used on becomes once more repellent matter from which the personality again averts.

Now you turn from your contemplation of laborers in and out of an esthetic experience, to go about your own business. You have things to do, wants to satisfy, places to get to. You start on your way, intent on your ends, your attention playing on what you need to do and how you need to do it. On the sidewalks are pedestrians loitering, scurrying, going in every direction; in the street, motor cars and other vehicles. To make progress, you must keep changing course and pace, keep going now to the left, now to the right, now faster, now slower; stopping perhaps, for a person, a vehicle or a light. Your way down the street is a succession of stops, looks, and listens, a sequence of continuous alert adjustments to a dangerously mobile environment. Then, without notice or preparation, something turns your attention: a pastry or a poster in a shop window, an abstract idea or a flight of images in your head, a girl's profile, a man's pace, the silhouette of buildings against the sky, a drift of song, a philosophic argument perhaps about beauty itself, a gleam of light, a guttershine, a cookshop smell, anything. Your mind begins to go over it like the fingers of the blind over some dark thing. The motor cars, the pedestrians, the street lights, your desires and destination fall away. The new thing now impatterns your actions; your feelings gather about it, concentrically, convergently, and flow along it and over it; images and ideas vaguely constellate around it, your muscles take a new posture, the direction and pattern of your movements change, your body comes into a new ideo-motor set. The object grows ever more vivid, its parts and phases move into clearness, distinct but not separate, individual yet dynamically together, in the swelling tide of your attention, which reaches a climax, and lapses.

Your experience has been esthetic. All that you are, your purposes, your passions, your memories of the past, your present action, mind and body, have been set to that object, orchestrated to its go and form. At the flood of this fitting, you feel very freed and very alive. You and that object compose for the moment a completely co-ordinated team, function confluent with form, organ with action. There are no readjustments you are forced to make, no manipulations you need to perform. Desire passes to fulfillment without interval, activity into consequence without break, and each continues in the other. What you have is what you want; where you are at is where you are going and want to go. You don't need to do anything but just let yourself live. Your selfhood, heightened and concentrated, is entirely taken up with the object. When the bond breaks, and from another stance you judge the object, you say "It is beautiful." Encountering it the next day, you wonder whether it could possibly have been the same object. A relation once holding no longer holds.

Of course, Beauty was the relation. And of course, what you experienced was not the relation; it was the thing or event that it related you to; and what you responded to, afterward, was not the relation but the dynamic import of the event or thing. This relation happens to surgeons at the operating table, to chemists in their laboratories, to mathematicians at their desks, to anybody, to everybody. They pass into and out of it even as the day laborers at their picks, the pedestrians on their streets. In fact, its domain is as wide as experience itself. Anything may on occasion be beautiful, and again indifferent or ugly. Alike the most rigid abstractions of geometric order and the most turgid singularities of the excrements of human life may become terms in an esthetic experience. Here are two sonnets of Edna Millay's, glorifying the beauty of just such incommensurables.

> Euclid alone has looked on Beauty bare.
> Let all who prate of Beauty hold their peace,
> And lay them prone upon the earth and cease
> To ponder on themselves, the while they stare
> At nothing, intricately drawn nowhere
> In shapes of shifting lineage; let geese

Gabble and hiss, but heroes seek release
From dusty bondage into luminous air.

O blinding hour, O holy, terrible day,
When first the shaft into his vision shone
Of light anatomized! Euclid alone
Has looked on Beauty bare. Fortunate they
Who, though once only and then but far away,
Have heard her massive sandal set on stone.

Still will I harvest beauty where it grows:
In colored fungus and the spotted fog
Surprised on foods forgotten; in ditch and bog
Filmed brilliant with irregular rainbows
Of rust and oil, where half a city throws
Its empty tins; and in some spongy log
Whence headlong leaps the oozy emerald frog . . .
And a black pupil in the green scum shows.

Her the inhabiter of divers places
Surmising at all doors, I push them all.
Oh, you that fearful of a creaking hinge
Turn back forevermore with craven faces,
I tell you Beauty bears an ultra fringe
Unguessed of you upon her gossamer shawl.

Light anatomized, food forgotten, the empty tins of half a
city, things simple, things complex, ineffable order and equally
ineffable chaos it seems, may be objects in an esthetic experience. The experience appears, moreover, as undetermined
to any one state of the psychophysical organism as to any
one object or event. The record shows how depressed and
expansive emotion, daytime fantasies, dreams by night, conceptual abstractions or intricate dialectic may function sep-
arately or together as contact points with the object, or for
that matter be, on occasion, themselves the object. The experience is at least as common to diseased states as to healthy,
and the conventionally beautiful will go as often with the
physiologically distorted and pathological as with the physiologically healthy and well-ordered. Whenever any moment
or phase of the psychophysical personality becomes one
term in a relation with another person, or with a thing or an
event, which so conjoins the two that an esthetic experience
obtains, the relation is actual beauty. So long as the relation
holds the object of it works as the exclusive interest, the
ruling passion of the personality. Its holding is a process of

orchestration, a mounting quantum of activity with a beginning, a middle and an apex. It mounts to a climax, then lapses. While it lasts, the object gains vividness, intensity, reality; that which it uniquely is—be it uniquely disorder, uniquely confusion—comes home to the mind with an invincible clarity and distinctiveness. While it lasts, there is first a sort of ingathering and then an untrammeled discharge of all a person's diversities of feeling and purpose upon the object, in a new order. His sense of being deepens and swells; he feels freer and more alive. Sometimes, when the experience lapses, he feels spent and sad, as if he had ceased from a great effort on which his energies were poured out and consumed. What he feels, however, is less like the weary diminution that follows hard labor, less like the exhaustion and the strain, than like the restorative depletion of love spreading to the quiet places of the spirit. In this consequence, the esthetic experience has been a cleansing experience, a purification of the psyche. It is what makes beauty akin to tears, and sustains the esthetic of *lacrimae rerum*.

But this is a consequence of the esthetic experience, not the experience itself. In the experience itself the climactic progression is as nuclear as its transitiveness and tangency. Ultimately it is as this liberative progression that, chance and fate permitting, beauty generates use and use consummates itself as beauty.

USE IN THE ESTHETIC EXPERIENCE

The logic of classical esthetics cannot, of course, allow that beauty is a relation, that use is its consequential function and freedom its consummation. The dialecticians of the tradition maintain that if this be the case, there never can be a consensus regarding beauty and that since a consensus does exist, it cannot be the case. The fact is, however, that only if this be the case can any philosophy of art deal justly and according to reason with both diversity and agreement, both continuity and change.

Those who insist on the sheer inherence of beauty in things and on the unvarying and immediate self-identity of esthetic experience, do so partly because they are deluded by the dominant universalism of the philosophic tradition, partly because they identify the distinctions of analysis in discourse with the confluences of the subject of discourse. There is a sense in which every instant in a stretch of experience is immediate, mediation being itself such an instant. Equally with every meaningless presentation, each mediation, each symbol, each meaning presents to experience a cinematographic moment, a present surface, singular, definite, taken hold of directly. Analysis isolates this presence for discourse, and identifies it as the esthetic essence, *the* thing of beauty. But if the isolation in discourse is a prolongation of an actual isolation in the bulk of experience, no object could fail always to be an esthetic object and no experience an esthetic experience; everything would always be a thing of beauty. Existence would be beatitude and not adjustment, consciousness would be a passive, bergsonian contemplation and not an active response. The diversification of art from the rest of life would lapse.

That this is not the case is enough to signalize the fact that the attribution of beauty to a self-identical object as such only is due to an error of reference, involving a static illusion. When dealing with the esthetic experience and the nature of beauty, even so subtle and persuasive a philosopher of time and change as Henri Bergson came under the sway of this error and this illusion. Those of us who take time and change empirically enough, recognize that no experience whatsoever consists in fact of the self-same instancy which analysis ascribes to it. It stretches from a past which, however sharply it may differ from, it prolongs; and reaches into a future which prolongs it. How can esthetic experience not be like every other, a beat of time, a quantum of duration? If this quantum be an act of perception developing as a process of adjustment, is not its felt beginning a rise and new turn at the threshold of consciousness? Do not its growth and development achieve themselves by means of exploratory movements of the relevant organs of response under stimulation from the "aesthetic object"? And what does the sequence of these movements come out as, if not the form of adjustment? Does not the activity, when it prospers, when it overcomes blocking or frustration, compound and orchestrate more and more of the organism's functions? Does it not draw into collaboration the residual personality? Does it not orchestrate all other interests, wishes, impulses and memories to itself, including discordant and antagonistic ones? Observation of the esthetic experience shows that it does; that the powers and passions of the personality mount to a climax of mutual suffusion, the high point of which we conventionally identify as *the* esthetic experience. The personality's relation with the object during this process we now know, is what the word, beauty, names.

Analytically, it is this kind of happening which gives the primary meaning to the expression, use. It is the process of shaping an orchestrated response of the varied and often conflicting ideomotor sets of a living person to some identified external or internal stimulus. The shaping is such that the feeling of life and freedom is enhanced by the impact of the esthetic object, which operates as an intensifier and liberator of vital processes at the moment repressed, inhibited or obstructed.

Naturally, this primary and enduring private, personal significance of *use* occurs in a context of other persons and associations of persons. Industry, finance, religion, science, government, education, war, are its setting and enter into its ecology. As we know, each is an associational elaboration of devices working to facilitate and prolong one or another of the biopsychic processes of breathing, eating, drinking, seeing, hearing, touching, smelling, excreting, sweating, mating, fighting, sheltering, manipulating, imagining, thinking; working also to enchannel and reshape the action-patterns of our animal separateness *from* one another into the human configurations of our civilized association *with* one another. Sometimes, as with monastic societies or hermits, the intent may be separation or isolation. But in either case, so far as any one individual is concerned, each institution is an instrumentality to enhance and liberate personal existence. The entire institutional complex may enter, in part directly, and in the main representatively and symbolically, into the funded mentality of even the most isolated or brutalized individual growing up in a civilization. Each institution is in its own way an associative accumulation, summation and refinement of some consequences in the processes of history or biography; and a repression and elimination of others. And what are these processes but a compenetration and sublimation of uses, but the past, functioning *now,* now exfoliating the future? One or another phase of this living past cannot fail to be compounded into the awareness of any object called beautiful, and thus to count as an agency in developing and sustaining the free flow of feeling and the easement and satisfaction which distinguish otherwise identical experiences as "esthetic" in contrast with "intellectual" or "practical."

WHAT "NECESSARY, UNIVERSAL, DISINTERESTED" MEAN IN FREE ESTHETIC EXPERIENCE

Where these struggles, these often tangent and discordant sequences, set free and deepen the personality while their occasion grows ever more vivid and clearer, an esthetic experience is in process, and its object is appreciated as beautiful. The way in which it is beautiful is as singular and specific as personality itself, and is never quite the same two times running. The identity given to beauty in discourse is a consequence of an ingathering and overlapping of the relationships in perception, present and remembered; in actuality the identity is not an identity but an identification in a dimension different from the experience itself—an identification in a non-esthetic experience. Worked out by means of a word or other ideogram, the identification goes by the name of "concept."

Consequence of a wide-ranging give-and-take of memories and perceptions in personal experience, of free disputation and free accord between experiencing persons whose consensus it enchannels, this "concept" or idea expresses, while it lasts, the sense of beauty of its time. It is the esthetic norm shaped by the mood of the age. As such it operates like a dogma of religion, currently to settle doubts, to solve problems and to dissolve difficulties in its domain. The wider its field of operations, the more tenuous is its empire and immanent its rule, the more variegated and discordant are its instances. First on the margins, then at the center, something stands out and resists, not to be subordinated or reconciled, pressing counter-claims to the same dominion. But where faith cleaves to the norm and consensus-making consent sustains it, esthetic philosophy signalizes the norm's rule with Kantian attributes: *necessary, universal, disinterested.*

We now know that no norm owns such immortality, that most are like champions of the prize-ring; they have a life-story of birth and growth, of battle for place and power, of measure of victory and of final overthrow; that like others, they grow old and die a natural death. Their "necessity" is a transcendental compulsion from beyond experience, but working of consent within experience. At its most overwhelming, this necessity is the drive of personal impulse, the coercion of personal habit, both subject to check, abrogation, replacement, even liquidation: at its least potent, "necessity"

Which institutional complex, or which item of any complex is compounded, in any individual case, therefore in any *real* instance, is a contingency of personality, of luck and of circumstance. In the case of the community, as we have seen, specific individual differences tend to offset each other; what is common and confluent tends to overlay them, to become conventional and to present itself as folkways and mores. These folkways and mores then work as a frame of reference for esthetic judgments, bringing it about that in some places and times an expression such as "Madonna," with its context of meanings, institutional and personal, plays a far greater role in the composition of an esthetic experience than the most excellent achievement of the painter's art, while in others, the latter is more than sufficient. What else but analogous confluences maintain the distinction between, let us say, an archaeological museum and a garbage dump? In themselves, what are archaeological objects but the present existence of the material residue, of the excrementa, the waste, the ruins, the garbage, the dead actuality, of a once living present? How many European generations lived and labored in the presence of the relics of antiquity and saw in them nothing save brute stuff to stop holes with or line sewers? What transformed these relics from garbage into collector's items of fine art if not the suffusion of their immediacy by a context of historical meanings presently valuable for the intensification and liberation of personal consciousness? The conjugation of those residues with this use was the postulate on which was established—or if you prefer, re-established—the notion of their beauty as a convention of the mentality of cultured Europeans. And is not our own generation now doing with our steamcars, automobiles, airplanes and the like what our forebears had done with the gods and goddesses and temples of the ancients? Thrown on the garbage heap because they had been superseded as instruments of a living function by others held fitter and to be preferred, and left to become culture's fossils, they are transferred to the museum to serve as symbols of the changing phases of this function. Their past use is their present meaning, and *in hoc signo* they are lifted from the status of refuse in a junk pile to that of a significant form for contemplation in a museum. It is the past use which renders them esthetically significant, which sets them up as favored candidates for beauty.

And what else is being done with the sketches, the cartoons, the experiments and the mere atelier products of master painters, as the market finds their authentic works scarcer? Does not the garbage heap become a treasure-house, the dump a holy place, and are not objects that had hitherto not received a second glance glorified as avatars of beauty? If it is true that existence is a process and consciousness a stream, it is also true that the distinctions which make themselves between immediacy and the mediate are functional and not constitutive; that they are relations generated *ad hoc;* distinctions of movement within movement; distinctions of phase and tempo, of movements we seek to hurry up and make over and movements we seek to hold on to and stretch out. But, however else they are distinguished, both mediate and immediate movements are consequential emergences of events whose successive phases either conflict, diverge and cut each other off, or compound and compenetrate. In the personality, the marks of beauty in *any* experience are liberation, are the orchestration and free flow of its manifold conflicting and centrifugal movements into an ensemble whose concords and dissonances make up the feel and form of its conjunctive team-play with the object. The object, whatever that may be, in whose felt presence these occur we then call beautiful. If the function of the object in this liberating process is *Use*—and what else can it be?—then beauty is the relationship initiating and sustaining the function. Whether as release and gratification, unintended and unintentional, of reflex biological drives or spontaneous spiritual passions, or as the volitional employment of instrumentalities to gain foreseen satisfactions, *use* is an art of passing from a terminus *a quo* to a terminus *ad quem* in which consequences compenetrate, accumulate and mount. Where there are no consequences there is no *use.*

When a free flow of feeling and a sentiment of satisfaction become functions of such a climactic accumulation and compenetration, the personality is related to the object in the way of beauty, beauty that stays its brief moment and vanishes. The object is succeeded by another and forgotten; or, an item in the living past, continues in a museum, a library or some such place, sustained by the disputations of the cults and the ratiocinations of the critics as a sign, a token, a convention in discourse of a consensus once attained, on beauty. To the man who made or found or interpreted this object, its import may have been anything but beauty: its

import may have been relief from boredom or inner conflict; or pleasing a woman; or earnin communicating attitudes, ideas, feelings; or ge talked about; or winning over a rival; or feeding solving a material or an intellectual problem. these uses may have come into the making of th Each of them works out into a freeing of ene up, of aspirations kept shut from fulfillments, wishes held back from satisfaction by inner outer obstruction. For the maker called artist, beauty, are his work's enduring core of meani vival value.

After he has produced it, his work may be in another man's experience. When it does so its own, with no tie to its maker's uses. It con as distinct and detached from that maker as comes to his woman distinct and detached f Except to the biographer or art historian, th in the new experience is not its causes in the c quences in the new; its meaning and value d the motivations or inventions of the maker of the user. How many and how differen know from the record. Among the collectiv individual uses, we have counted: to serve a common emotion; to be the symbol of a co or the expression of a common purpose; image a general vision or common ideal; and agency of adjustment; to be a road o chalice of cleansing and purgation; to be imprisoned powers and dispositions; to pi gratification of suppressed desires; to enab satisfaction of real, unrepressed hungers intensify lust of conflict, inner division and enabling, as Nietzsche said of tragedy, th celebrate his Saturnalia . . .

And this is why it is mistaken to hold, as the work of art neither predicts nor int only. This was why it was mistaken on J consequences to scientific perception a esthetic. Both, if they are to survive, tha alike struggle toward a congruency with well as a harmony with our inner drives, a no less to the divisive than the associati within and the world without.

is the pretension of a formula, the implication of a symbol. The "universality" of norms is similarly statutory, a consequence of choice within and a claim to coercion without. The scope of a judgment of beauty is no greater than the range of the individuals who freely acquiesce in it and freely employ it. Their consent establishes its boundary. Only the arts of trade or the art of war can carry it beyond this boundary. Its champions are condemned either to persuade dissenters, to compel them, to destroy them, or to leave them to their own esthetic devices.

As for its disinterestedness—in view of what happens in the esthetic experience, no illusion of esthetic philosophers could be stranger or more fatuous. The customary assignment of disinterestedness to delight follows from the fancy that esthetic pleasure in no way depends on possessing the pleasing object. In how many ways has the idea not been restated and justified, since Kant! Yet in its Kantian form it is flatly false; in the others, simply not true. Sometimes ownership of the thing of beauty is an item indispensable to initiating the beauty-relation; sometimes it is irrelevant. When ownership shall be the one or the other submits to no determination in advance. Certainly the emulative struggle for ownership which contributes so long a chapter to the history of the arts cannot be said to be entirely unmoved by the idea that the objects of possessive rivalry are beautiful. Though he often reasoned otherwise, Goethe, for example, knew this well. He knew that Beauty could be an object of passionate and exclusive desire to possess which men fight one another to death. Some there are, Goethe knew, who would rather destroy Beauty than share it. As he had Mephisto-Phorkyas tell Helen: "Beauty is indivisible; who once possessed Her wholly, would rather slay than only share in part." Even the most generous and high-principled of men—John Ruskin, to take another example—may on occasion acknowledge a dynamic intimacy between esthetic pleasure and personal possession. In his apostolic ardor on behalf of the right practice of art, Ruskin had given forty of his drawings by Turner to Oxford University, twenty-five to Cambridge, for students to study. Soon thereafter, he wrote, "When I gave my Loire series of Turner drawings to Oxford, I thought I was rational enough to enjoy them as much in the University Gallery as in my own study. But not at all! I find I can't bear to look at them in the gallery because they are 'mine' no more." Of the writers who make much of the role of disinterestedness in the esthetic experience, very few have been collectors or owners of *objets d'art;* very few have had any to give away or have been known to give away any; very few have paid any attention to the consequence, in terms of beauty, from acquiring or losing possession of a work of art. Of necessity, their esthetic experiences, if any ever did come to them, came noticeably with objects and events they did not possess and could hardly hope to possess. Possession could not figure in their lives as an issue of practical esthetic import. Nevertheless, the sigh, "I wish it were mine" on more than one occasion breathes over the Eden of objects felt to be beautiful.

That initial identification of disinterestedness with an unconcern about ownership, moreover, has diverted philosophers of art from attending to realities of the esthetic experience. Looked at as it occurs, people to whom it comes are far less disinterested than during any other experience. Every act of attention, in that it brings the powers of the personality to bear on one particular object chosen from others, at the same time withdraws them from those others. Interest is redirected; transferred, not suspended. Interest is concentrated, intensified, swung to a climax, not dissipated; not dispersed but gathered up toward ecstasy. In such a situation, nothing could be less unselfish or impersonal. For in such a situation selfhood is for the moment at its maximum of concentration and vitality. If, in such a situation, the thing of beauty is not desired, it is because it is already a thing wholly and utterly possessed. While legal ownership often surely does contribute to such psychological possession, legal ownership is a relation from a very different dimension of experience, far short of the consummation which, now heedless of true and false and good and evil, cuts off and shuts out from the personality's attention all the world but the thing of beauty, at the moment its joy forever. Sometimes esthetic possession is so entire and so intense, that others, beholding how the personality is concentrated on its object, may say that possession is its passion, not its action; that instead of possessing, the personality is possessed.

Here the relational state, as we already know, is a quantum of activity, a process lasting a limited stretch of time, which carries its termination in itself. How egocentric is the absorption that the psyche sustains may be inferred from the angry responses which meet any attempt to interrupt an esthetic experience before it ends of itself. The intensity of these responses is a measure of the possessive affinity which the interruption loosens, of the free flow of feeling which it arrests and of the personal enlargement which it compresses.

Such compressions, stoppages and loosenings happen to esthetic experience even more frequently as acts of God than by the hand of man. Whatever they be in themselves, or to the manless world, to man they come as irruptions of evil, and the story of his labor and his thought suggests that they are more expressive of the nature of things than the arts and the sciences wherewith his spirit endeavors to humanize that nature, turning its inhuman diversities to human uses, consummating the uses as the beauty which frees him from his compelled adjustments to the fearful unhomeliness of the multitudinous universe. Perhaps the image of all art and of all science, of the entirety of civilization, the shining symbol of the first luster and the last of the human spirit, is Sisyphus, invincible, defying all necessity, refusing to let his freedom be denied; Sisyphus, everlastingly rerolling his stone up life's everlasting hill. Or perhaps an even nearer image is the man of Uz named Job, confronting the infinite and infinitely heedless Power which to him is God, to others Nature, declaring: "Behold, he will slay me; I have no hope. Nevertheless will I maintain my ways before him."

Of man's ways before God art is the bravest, the truest; the way in which man uses nature to consummate beauty and thereby to affirm his freedom within, establish it without. If man be slain maintaining these ways of his in his everlasting struggle with God, still God has won no victory. For God's victory cannot be that man should die, but that man should surrender, that he should repent his ways and submit his soul to the omnipresent yoke. In that man maintains his ways, that science as art and art as science flourish in his spirit, then, though death be his destiny, he conquers Fate and defeats God. He has not yielded his humanity; and his humanism stands, untaken. In its deepest, its broadest sense, Art, thus conquering Fate, conforms Nature to man, sets a bound to God's power and advances a frontier of freedom against the compulsions of the cosmos. Also at death, Art is Victory, Art is Freedom.

Sidney Hook

1902-

In a book published in 1959, Sidney Hook, who had been a student and close friend of John Dewey, wrote that one of the most significant facets of our cultural tradition is "the development of the experimental, empirical attitude—which, were it not for the inevitable misunderstandings that attend the phrase, I should like to call 'the pragmatic temper.'" He defines the "experimental, empirical attitude" as one that "assesses the truth of assertions and claims, both of fact and value, in terms of relevant results and consequences. It judges profession by consequences. It looks upon principles as rules of action. Without eschewing abstractions—for no one can think without abstractions—it relates them to what is observed or observable in public experience. It does not denigrate appearances in behalf of a reality with a higher claim to truth; the appearances are always part of reality and the real is rational only to the extent that the appearances are, while a reality that makes no difference to appearances is a chimera. This attitude is tentative in its judgments but, because it makes judgments, it is not irresolute. It is initially skeptical of all large claims, but by admitting that some are better guides to conduct than others, it is not cynical. It is profane, common-sensical, open-minded about possibilities, but tough-minded about evidence."

This attitude, Hook said, is "the dominant philosophic genius of the English-speaking peoples," and it accounts for the fact that Americans have developed a consensus of agreement on basic political institutions "without an OFFICIAL metaphysics or theology." We are attentive to what is done "in the name of principles rather than to what is said or written, to the public behavior to which [principles] lead rather than to the personal emotion overtones they arouse." We are not, he said, indifferent to principles, but we interpret them as "operating guides to actions."

Hook has also spoken of his position as "naturalism," which he has defined as "the systematization of what is involved in the scientific method of inquiry." There is reason for believing that "there is only one reliable method of reaching the truth about the nature of things anywhere and at any time, that this reliable method comes to full fruition in the methods of science, and that a man's normal behavior in adopting means to ends belies his work whenever he denies it. . . . IF we want to acquire new knowledge, the naturalist asserts, we should follow the basic pattern of inquiry— recognize the problem, state the hypotheses, draw the inferences, perform the experiment, and make the observation. There is no logical necessity or guarantee that we will achieve new knowledge this way but it is reasonable to act on the assumption."

One may call this faith, but Hook's comment on this kind of faith would be that "no faith has truth value or even a high survival value unless it is based on a prior faith in intelligence."

Sidney Hook's books, articles, and lectures provide many illustrations of the application of the "pragmatic temper" to democracy, civil liberties, socialism, Marxism, educational philosophy and methods, metaphysical problems, and scientific method.

The Centrality of Method *

The science and art of democratic education treats it as a continuing process from birth to death, subordinates transmitting the past to creating a future different from the past, makes precept a function of practice, exalts variation over repetition and encourages the free co-operation of differences to displace the regimented reproduction of identicals, prefers the doubt, the enquiry, the experiment of competitive co-operation and co-operative competition of the sciences of the obedient credulity and unquestioning rehearsals of dogmatic faiths.

—*Horace M. Kallen*

From the point of view of content, the focal problems of our age cannot be isolated in one compartment of studies. All studies of the required area, in varying degrees of relevance, will be concerned with them. Similarly from the point of view of method. Although in certain fields the subject matter itself may be methods of thinking, the importance of the attitude of critical evaluation must not be lost sight of in any field. It must pervade the curriculum as the fundamental allegiance of both teacher and student. Every other commitment must be prepared to accept its challenge and undergo trial by careful scrutiny before it can be responsibly held.

A great gap has always existed between talk about critical method and its practice. Many who spoke in the past about the importance of critical method tacitly assumed that it would strengthen belief in "the truths" they inherited and weaken "the prejudices" of those who disagreed with them. But, as events put cherished beliefs into doubt, and as spokesmen for pernicious errors also invoked the shibboleths of criticism, a reaction set in. One of the noteworthy features of the "new failure of nerve" in contemporary American life is fervent *dispraise* of critical methods and attitudes towards the dominant ideals of our culture. Criticism is now often

* [From: Sidney Hook, *Education for Modern Man.* New York: The Dial Press, Inc.; 1946. Pp. 112-38. Copyright 1946 by Sidney Hook. Reprinted by permission of the publishers.]

equated with negativism and defeatism. It is selling America short. From the most disparate quarters the charge has been made that the weaknesses of American education, even of American democracy, are in large measure to be laid at the door of American teachers. They are guilty of having adopted the attitude of critical objectivity in the classroom and consequently of disarming their students before the onslaught of enemies of democracy. They are guilty of having "taught contempt and fear of truth" to an entire generation of students by insisting upon the distinction between "fact and opinion."

To some extent this criticism of criticism expresses the typical war mentality observable in all countries of the world. But its roots go much deeper. Where people feel secure about their values they are less likely to be nervous when critical appraisal is made of them. The vogue of the critical attitude in some areas of American culture, literature, biography, history, reflected the degree of assurance with which the American community accepted its values. The more imperiled these values became by developments abroad and at home, the more urgent became the need for clarification, restatement and rededication. Unfortunately, this need was met by dogmatic and hysterical reaffirmation of slogans whose vagueness had been a target of previous attack. The earlier critics began to be blamed for the conditions they described. In a prolonged spell of bad weather, people become irritated by the weatherman. Under social conditions of tension and conflict, uncertainty often provokes a response of fear rather than of inquiry.

For present purposes, I am not concerned with the cause of the distrust of criticism but with the validity of the current arguments against it, and against the alleged over-emphasis on *methods* of thinking in education. For reasons that will soon appear, I shall use the terms "critical method" and "scientific method" interchangeably. I shall consider four general lines of argument that have been advanced against the view that scientific method should be central in the modern educational curriculum. (1) Concern with scientific method tends to create a mood of wholesale skepticism, of exaggerated distrust and cynical debunking. (2) Sensitiveness to the continuity of scientific inquiry, to the tentative and probable character of conclusions won by it, begets an indifference to programs of action: it is incompatible with a firm stand on basic problems of our culture whose consideration we have been urging as subject matter of the modern curriculum. (3) Preoccupation with method spells the death of vision and a creeping paralysis of the creative centers of mental life: it may inspire a passion for clarity but, in the words of a French critic, it is "the shining clarity of empty glasses." (4) Truth has many mansions, and scientific truth is one of its lowliest stories: there is some knowledge which is not accessible to scientific method and to deny this is to become victimized by the unintelligent cult of "scientism."

1. The attack upon critical or scientific method as making for skepticism derives whatever plausibility it has by confusing skepticism or rejection of *specific* conclusions with skepticism of "things in general"—where the latter phrase stands for all beliefs which are precious to the person making the charge. Scientific method is then conceived as a threat to those private or collective sanctities of faith, hope and wish which depend on belief. The prospect of an education which would make the use of scientific method habitual induces a pervasive sense of uneasiness, a fear of an intellectual anarchy or nihilism that would call all things into question. And yet it should be plain that scientific method cannot establish any attitude of wholesale skepticism. For, whenever it doubts, denies or rejects a belief, it must have *positive* grounds for the doubt, denial or rejection. We cannot doubt all our beliefs at once, although no particular belief is beyond doubt. Charles Peirce's criticism of Descartes on this point is definitive.

What has sometimes been called skepticism is a demand for further analysis, and a confession of uncertainty as to whether a customarily accepted analysis is correct. In one sense we know that one proposition is true and another false, that one act is better than another, that one woman is more beautiful than another, without knowing the correct analysis of "truth," "goodness" and "beauty." To infer that, because we regard some particular analysis of the *concept* of truth or justice inadequate, we are therefore calling into question the existence of truths and just actions, is preposterous. One of the ways of determining the adequacy of any such analysis is whether it squares with what we can observe by close study of judgments and actions which are warranted true and just by evidence at hand.

No one resents demands for evidence concerning matters about which he cares little. And one positively welcomes them in fields in which he is confident that he has knowledge. But it is quite different when we are challenged about precious beliefs to which we are emotionally wedded and for which rational grounds are not easy to find. Everyone holds some beliefs for which no rational grounds can be given. But few are willing to admit that they do—particularly when these beliefs are regarded as important. This reluctance is the unconscious tribute that men pay to their own rationality—acquired though it be.

The comforting assurance which fundamental beliefs give us is derived from their sway as familiar habits. To rest such beliefs on logical grounds, especially when we have not previously sought or formulated these grounds, is to place them on something precarious. It is to put in risk something which because of habit we do not feel is a risk. But the consequence of putting them in risk may be to weaken the passional force of belief and introduce an uneasiness whose edge may gradually weaken our emotional certainties. There is, for example, an important strand in the Christian tradition from St. Augustine down, which is suspicious of any attempt to base belief in the existence of God on logical reasons alone. God's existence seems more incontrovertible to some believers than the reasons which would justify their belief in Him. Since no one grasps all the implications of reasons, he cannot be safeguarded from surprises—among which may be some that would testify *against* the belief in God.

The current dispraise of criticism is born out of the fear that it imperils not the existence of God but the validity of democracy. Yet it is clear that most current theoretical criticisms of democracy are as old as Plato. What gave these criticisms force in the eyes of many were not additional arguments but the threatening practical successes of totalitarianism. Faint hearts and weak minds in democratic countries were impressed by triumphant power in the most vulgar way. They attributed this power in large measure to the absence of criticism, and imagined that existing democracies could become just as powerful as their rivals if all tendencies towards criticism were burned away in a faith every whit as fanatical as those of the enemies of democracy.

It was this superficial assumption—and one actually incompatible with the rationale and spirit of democracy—that accounted for a misunderstanding of the whole drift of criticism in the few regions of American culture in which it appeared. Criticisms were rarely launched against democracy but against practices and conditions that belied the democratic ideal. Criticism was directed against the duplicity of slogans, the miscarriage of justice and the cruelties of unnecessary poverty. In the nature of the case, such criticism could have no sustained force unless it was based on fact rather than skepticism, and a commitment to some values rather than others. A mood of general skepticism would have blunted its impact. There may have been disproportions of emphasis, lack of historical perspective and balance. *There were cases in which criticism was dishonest; particularly when American democracy was damned for its slightest lapse while critics ignored by discreet silence, when they did not praise, monstrous crimes in their favorite dictatorship.* But this was not skepticism—rather a mixture of credulity and duplicity. On the whole, criticism was motivated by a desire to achieve clarity, consistency and truth.

The discomfiture produced by critical analysis and "exposures" arose from a fear that what was said about the deficiencies of American democracy, and about the gap between professions and performance, might be true. The *existence* of these truths might give aid and comfort to the enemies of democracy. But the *recognition* of these truths by democrats could have no such effect, particularly when coupled with a recognition of the truths about totalitarian countries.

No one has presented convincing evidence that American students were indifferent to democratic ideals because of their addiction to critical methods of thought. For one thing, this would be difficult to do until we had some evidence that more than a small number of students had actually acquired the habits of critical thought. What is called "debunking" is a substitution of one form of dogmatism for another. It substitutes for the notion that some men are angelic mutants the notion that all men are but ignoble variants of one type. It has nothing to do with criticism which consists of the attempt to distinguish between what makes sense and what not, and of the examination of evidence to determine whether what makes sense is true or false, and *how* true or false.

The belief that faith in democracy can be instilled by the same methods as faiths in other forms of society overlooks the distinctive character of the democratic faith. This lies in its assumption that the reasonableness of the democratic way of life may be established by open, critical inquiry of its consequences. The *initial* loyalty to democracy, like the initial loyalty to anything else, arises from social atmosphere and practice. *Rational* loyalty results from a critical consideration of the claims, achievements and shortcomings of democracy compared to those of its rivals. The practice of democracy comes first in the order of time; the justification of democracy comes first in the order of logic. By training its students to think critically, a democracy gives them the power and the right to evaluate democracy, confident that its claims will withstand the analysis—that initial loyalties will become transformed into rational loyalties. No other form of society dares to chance this.

This means that ultimately a democracy is committed to facing the truth about itself. Preaching and edification have their holiday uses but they do not inspire initial loyalty— only practice does—nor do they sustain loyalty against critical doubts, for they present no rational grounds. It is in the very process of public, critical thinking that the democratic community and scientific community meet. Whoever introduces a breach in this process offends against both. Scientific skepticism in any specific situation flowers from a seed which is love of truth. A democracy is the only society which in principle believes that men can accept the truth in every realm of thought, and live with it.

2. The purpose of thinking is to reach conclusions. The validity of any specific conclusion depends upon the methods by which it is reached. Upon what does the validity of the methods depend? Without fear of circularity, we can say that these methods are justified by their historical fruitfulness in the solution of problems. That is why in any specific inquiry we are more likely to judge whether a problem is truly solved by reference to the methods of inquiry that have been followed, than we are to evaluate these methods by a *specific* result. This explains why we do not abandon the methods of scientific medicine when confronted by a patient who has been cured by an incantation after he has been given up by the physicians.

It also illumines the familiar contrast between "*how* we think" and "*what* we think." The *how* of thinking is more important than the *what* of thinking, not because the two are separable, for the *how* refers to the *what* in a class of cases or situations, but because it stresses the habits and morals of thought upon which the quest for truth and its successive corrections depend. Nonetheless, despite the self-corrective procedure of science, it always gives us a conclusion to a *specific* problem even if it is no more than that no warranted conclusion can be drawn. Many who complain about the footlessness of thought would do well to ascertain first whether thinking is going on.

The fear that stress upon critical methods of thinking will weaken desire to reach positive conclusions often reflects the failure to understand that genuine thinking is not a process of free association but departs fom a specific problem that controls it. The solution of the problem is the goal even when the means at hand are not adequate or when its low degree of urgency allows the quest for a solution to be postponed. Nor is there any ground for the assumption that, because scientific method does not warrant solutions that are certain, they do not warrant solutions that are *sufficient* for action, resolute action. The quaintness of this assumption is apparent not only in the light of the revolutionary achievements of science, which makes no claim to certainty, but in the light of every practical art, from medicine to military welfare, where resoluteness of action often goes hand in hand with a conclusion whose probabilities just shade those of its alternative.

There is nothing in the emphasis on scientific method in education which forbids reaching conclusions or making recommendations. There are occasions when *not* to do so would betray its spirit. The refusal to assert conclusions as warranted or to take a pragmatic stand on controversial issues is sometimes justified because of the necessity of avoiding "indoctrination" in the classroom. This subject calls for a few words.

Any discussion of indoctrination, if it is to avoid confusion and interminable verbalism, must distinguish between the nature of indoctrination and its justification. By "indoctrination" I mean the process of teaching through which acceptance of belief is induced by nonrational or irrational means, or both.

Nonrational methods of inducing belief involve the use of the technique of conditioning. Since it is necessary for human beings when they are young to act upon beliefs long before they can possibly understand or justify them, indoctrination is insofar unavoidable. Since this is not a controversial point, the issue must be sought elsewhere. Children will be indoctrinated in *some* specific beliefs, but the relevant questions are *which* beliefs and *who* is to determine them. To take the last question first: are these beliefs to depend exclusively on the authority of the community or also on that of educators? We have already indicated our answer: in a democracy the social and moral ideals of the community are filtered through the critical consciousness of its educators. This provides a clue to the distinctive quality of the beliefs and habits, like kindness, cleanliness, etc., in which children are to be "indoctrinated": they are to be such that a rational justification of them *can* be given on another level. But at *every* level the individual's power of reflective thought is to be encouraged and developed, so that when he reaches intellectual maturity he will be able to assess for himself the validity of the beliefs and habits in which he has been indoctrinated. *In the educational system of a democracy, the authority of method must ultimately replace the authority of persons and institutions in the determination of truth.* "Ultimately" here suggests not the postponement of critical education to some fixed period but the continuation of a process begun as the child's intelligence emerges, and develops in power.

Indoctrination by *irrational means,* as distinct from non-rational means, is the art of inducing consent, not by the techniques of conditioning, but by "argument" that has the appearance of reason. The objection to indoctrination of this kind is not that it reaches conclusions. The conclusions may be true. It is to the methods by which they are reached. But it is an insuperable objection. Even if a conclusion is known to be true on other grounds, there is no justification for "putting it over" by sophism, one-sided presentation, or cooked evidence. The enormity of the offence in teaching of this kind is not mitigated by the sincerity of the person indoctrinating or by the fact that he may be unconscious of what he is doing. It is bad teaching and no one who persists in it belongs in the classroom.

It is sometimes asked: how is indoctrination to be recognized? In general by the same tokens by which we recognize propaganda. The most obvious sign of indoctrination, as of propaganda which professes to reach conclusions by argument, is not outright invention but suppression of evidence that tends to invalidate or weaken a favored conclusion. No one objects to the teachers of natural science reaching and defending conclusions in class. Indeed, it would be ridiculous if they did not. We do not fear indoctrination here. We are confident that if the teacher employs scientific methods, students will be apprised of whatever evidence exists that testifies against the hypothesis under consideration.

The social sciences are different. Their subject matter is so loaded with value judgments, they engage such strong emotions, that we cannot rely on the automatic operation of the method of disinterested inquiry. Even the well-intentioned teacher may not be aware he is indoctrinating, or prejudicing the analysis. The best working rule here is for the teacher to deliberately build up the case for the position he is arguing against or cannot himself accept. He should strive to do it in such a way that reasonable proponents of the position will accept it as a fair exposition of their views—and then, and only then, let loose his critical shafts against it. It requires pedagogic skill to do this, but nothing less will insure the students against a pet phobia or enthusiasm. *No matter how controversial a subject may be, the teacher is justified in reaching or stating conclusions provided he has honestly made accessible to students the relevant data and arguments of the conflicting positions.* This is a permissive not a compulsive condition, of course. If he is interested in teaching, as well as in the promulgation of what he believes to be the truth, he will make the discussion of a controversial subject an occasion for cooperative thinking. Where there is a danger that students may make the teacher's position their own because of the prestige he enjoys, or where students are apparently shopping around for something consoling to believe no matter what its source or validity, the teacher does well *not* to express his personal stand—convinced as he may be of it.

Each generation of students has its own dogmas which it takes for granted. Whatever else a teacher does, he must make his students aware of these dogmas, that there are alternatives to them, and that they must assume an intellectual and moral responsibility for their first principles.

But if among these first principles there are value judgments, how is it possible to avoid on the one hand indoctrination, and on the other a pallid neutrality—or, what is worse, uneasy silence before the earnest questions of life? The detailed answer must be reserved until we consider the question of value judgments in education. It is sufficient here to say that, except for those who are prepared to acknowledge that their value judgments are arbitrary, it is possible to show that value judgments like other judgments may be reached without indoctrination.

3. Perhaps the most widespread objection against emphasis on critical method in education, and culture generally, is that it militates against vision. To stop up the organs of vision is really sinning against the light. If critical education resulted in turning the intelligence merely into an efficient cleanser, it would soon have nothing left to work on. As Whitehead has put it, "If men cannot live on bread alone, still less can they do so on disinfectants."

The seer of true visions, like the moral prophet, cannot be honored too much. He is always in the forefront of a new intellectual movement. An attitude that would silence him or give his pronouncements anything less than a respectful hearing condemns itself. But we honor the seer not for his vision but for the truth of his vision, and truth is often hidden at the bottom of a well. There has never been a time in which there has been a dearth of visionaries. Almost always, their visions are used as evidence for views about man and society which are incompatible with each other. Seers and prophets are notoriously at odds with their predecessors and contemporaries. To discover which is the trustworthy vision is therefore an absolute necessity for those who would put their faith in true vision. This can only be done by applying critical method to vision. To turn around at this juncture and accuse those who employ such methods of being hostile to vision is hardly just.

Criticism that is unwise, criticism that is fierce and tendentious, criticism that has the impact of a physical assault, that is commanded by a party line or is a tactic in the strategy of an intellectual pogrom, can choke off the sources of vision in others. Not all seers and prophets are tough, and in a time of troubles we hear only of those who are capable of martyrdom. But such criticism is *bad* criticism—in one sense, not criticism at all. Its proper alternative is not the absence of criticism but criticism appropriate to its subject, and guided primarily by love of truth.

The point of the objection to the educational emphasis on

criticism is that it tends to make those who employ it infertile. The eye for weaknesses in other people's creations turns inward and like a lethal x-ray kills the fancies and hunches and vague perceptions struggling to be born. The result of an educational program that strengthened critical faculties might be the generation of a pack of watchdogs who frightened one another from taking the ventures and risks without which we have no use for watchdogs.

It is an open question whether the *cultivation* of critical methods has a tendency to paralyze vision and creative effort. There are, of course, great creative minds who are also masters of criticism. Almost every great creative figure in the history of philosophy has been a penetrating critic of the ideas of other philosophers. Among lesser figures, it is true that some men of great critical gifts have had very little to say in constructive solutions of philosophical problems. But in such cases it would be very difficult to establish that the weakness of constructive vision has been a *consequence* of cultivation of criticism. Those who lie in wait merely in order to pounce upon the shortcomings of other people's visions, have been cursed by nature not by their critical art. Either they lack the power of vision or the courage to back their visions, and so are reduced to perpetual exercises in immediate inferences. They are critical only because they are barren: they are not barren because they are critical. And like trainers who cannot themselves fight, like art critics who cannot paint and teachers who cannot sing—by their critical insight they can often be of great help to those who can.

That a good critic discourages himself and others from attempting creation is dubious. That he has an encouraging effect in deepening perception and insight, and indirectly affecting the standards of creation, is less dubious. That nonsense is less likely to get itself accepted as truth where the critical spirit flourishes is not dubious at all. And it remains true that good criticism must nourish itself on the existing models of excellence in thought and expression. If it does not know the labors and joys of creation, it can at least savor to the full the pleasure of understanding.

4. The charge that reliance upon scientific method is a cult of "scientism" which impoverishes human experience by stripping it of all save quantitative dimensions, treats human beings as if they were inanimate things, and systemati-

cally obscures the difference between ends and means, values and facts, derives whatever force it has from a double confusion. It confuses scientific method as a general pattern of inquiry whenever we seek knowledge, with scientific method as the procedures pursued in the study of nature, and confuses these procedures with the specific methods and techniques employed in physics.

Scientific method was not discovered in the modern world. It was implicitly followed wherever men were able to distinguish between effective and ineffective means for the accomplishment of their daily tasks. Its systematic application to nature, the formulation of its rationale, and the program of its extension to society and man—these are the distinctive contributions of the modern world. Far from imperilling human values, scientific method enables us to give them a more effective status in experience. It is not the whole of life, but in its broadest sense it encompasses the whole intellectual enterprise of man. Those who urge its centrality in the educational curriculum do not seek to narrow the course of studies to the natural or social sciences but to enrich it by bringing the method to bear on all subject matters. Nor do they rule out or disparage the experiences of appreciation of color, sound, form and feeling. They assume that the more we understand, the more we appreciate; and that *tested* understanding always reveals the *pattern* of scientific method. It is not fortuitous that the author of *Logic: The Theory of Inquiry* is the author of *Art as Experience* and *Democracy and Education,* and that he has unweariedly insisted upon distinguishing between the general scientific method or handling subject matter, and some specific subject matter which illustrates the method in a particular way.

> There are those who would restrict the term [science] to mathematics or to disciplines in which exact results can be determined by rigorous methods of demonstration. Such a conception limits even the claims of physics and chemistry to be sciences, for according to it, the only scientific portion of these subjects is the strictly mathematical. The position of what are ordinarily termed the biological sciences is even more dubious, while social subjects and psychology would hardly rank as sciences at all, when measured by this definition. Clearly we must take the idea of science with some latitude. The important thing is to discover those traits in virtue of which

various fields are called scientific. When we raise the question in this way we are led to put emphasis upon *methods of dealing* with subject-matter rather than to look for uniform objective traits in subject-matter. From this point of view science signifies . . . the existence of systematic methods of inquiry, which when they are brought to bear on a range of facts, enables us to understand them better and to control them more intelligently, less haphazardly, and with less routine.

The chief features of the scientific method of dealing with subject matter are well known. They are the recognition and definition of a problem, the formulation of an hypothesis, the elaboration of its logical implications, the performance of an experimental act and the observation of its consequences. The experimental act does not necessarily mean a laboratory experiment. It may involve no more than the use of a tool, a change in the position of the body, or just looking—*all under critical controls*—depending upon the character of the problem. The observation does not have to be quantitatively measurable in any exact way. Even in many of the sciences, observation contents itself with gross occurrence and in ordinary affairs this is usually sufficient. Every step in the pattern of inquiry may be an occasion for special analysis. Dialectic, analysis of meaning, and what is usually designated by formal logic are here conceived as part of the pattern— an indispensable part but one which by itself does not suffice to give us knowledge of fact.

To many there seems to be something awkward about the term "scientific" when used to describe a method applied to humanistic or literary subject matter, but the exact equivalent of the term in these fields is "critical." An historian, for example, may deny that there is any such thing as "scientific" history or that there can be. But no historian will admit that he is writing fiction, or deny that some historical accounts are more warranted than others, or fail to repudiate the notion that he is writing uncritically. Yet precisely those features in an historical account which distinguish it from fiction, which make it more or less warranted than another account, which testify to its critical rather than uncritical nature, are features that will be found to be part of the general pattern of scientific inquiry. The same is true for anything put forth as a valid interpretation of a work of art or a correct explication of a text, without in any way denying that different qualities of experience are present, and that the critical or scientific approach has additional functions quite different in deciphering the meanings of a poem from, say, reconstructing the skeleton of a prehistoric animal from a few fragments of bone.

The great challenge to the centrality of scientific method in the process of education arises from the presence of values. How, on this view, are they to be approached? Can they be understood, can they be evaluated, without breaking free from the general pattern of inquiry? To this I now turn.

No matter what his *theory* of value is, every educator is committed to the proposition that one of the tasks of education is to teach values. Since not all values can be taught, and some selection must be made, every educator assumes that some values are better than others. What does it mean to teach values? What does it mean to teach that some values are better than others?

To teach values properly is to do a variety of related things. First, it is to make students *aware* of their attitudes of preference expressed in their choices and organized in their habits. By the time an individual reaches the stage when he can differentiate between himself and others he already has acquired a whole set of values. Every child imbibes values as he learns how to speak; and he learns how to speak before he learns how to think. By the time he is confronted by an experience that provokes moral doubt he is already in possession of many values. He does not start from scratch. He is committed to many values that may be more eloquently attested in his behavior than in his speech. These values are rarely organized and even their conflicts seldom lead to clear articulation unless certain intellectual habits have already been acquired. The existence of these values, rather than their source, is the important thing to note for our subsequent analysis.

To teach values is not only to make students aware of their commitments. It is also to make them aware of attitudes of evaluation to which not they but *others* are committed. This is not easily done. For it requires more than the realization that their own value commitment formally excludes its opposite. If they recognize themselves as ambitious, they must, of course, also be capable of formally recognizing what it means to be not ambitious. But this is not enough by far. For to be properly aware of what it means to be not ambitious is to understand it in relation to the psychological, historical, social or other contexts which make *that* commitment as natural or plausible to the person who holds it as being ambitious is to oneself. Here a good teacher working with good books in the fields of literature and history can make the value commitments of others appear as vital options, actively competing with the students' own, instead of abstract negations. If we want to understand what "intolerance" means, we must make some historical or literary character who was self-righteously intolerant come alive. Assuming for the moment that our values are "goods"—I am trying to use language innocently—we must make the "bads" credible in the sense that imaginatively we can conceive ourselves holding them.

Finally, to teach values means to develop within students a willingness to commit themselves to new values, and to reaffirm or to reject the values to which they find themselves previously committed. When this is done after the value alternatives which are being excluded have been presented, then it can be said we are teaching that some values are better than others. When this willingness is developed by rhetoric and the hortatory arts, by promises of personal reward or fear of punishment, we have indoctrination. When this willingness results from a rational consideration of the evidence for one or the other commitment, then we have scientific determination of value judgments.

The retort comes at once: then in either case indoctrination is unavoidable, for there is no way of establishing scientifically that one judgment of value is better or truer than another without circularity. Only judgments of fact can be established scientifically.

The view that what is generically called scientific method, as distinct from the specific techniques of the special sciences, is irrelevant in establishing the validity of judgments of value, is what unites all philosophers—whether Thomist or narrow positivist, whether intuitionist or reductive materialist—against the experimentalist philosophy. To do justice to the claims and criticisms of these various schools of ethical thought would require a treatise. But I propose in lieu of this to outline in a positive way an experimental approach to value judgments insofar as they enter into the content of education, and to see how far it will carry us before differences in philosophical theory obtrude.

A scientific or rational approach to judgments of value consists in (a) the investigation of the causes of such judgment, (b) their logical implications, and (c) their probable consequences. This investigation is always to be undertaken in relation to alternative values which limit freedom of choice.

(a) That judgments of value have histories, that they are related to interests, that they grow out of *problems* of valuation and appraisal are truths that no one denies. What is often denied is the relevance of these factors to the specific quality of value in any situation. Yet we are all aware of the simple fact that knowledge of the causes of value judgment often aids us in understanding what we are valuing. All who are not theoretically doctrinaire will grant that our knowledge that this man is starving makes some difference to our understanding of the good and bad quality of an action that flows from his acute need.

To discover why a man comes to value what he does, does not necessarily lead us to justify his value, but it enables us to be more intelligent about its character. What is true for individual values is true for group values. The whole of modern anthropology consists in removing the shock of difference, when one value system is confronted with another, by providing the cultural and historical perspectives within which both are surveyed—not rationalized—as responses to some need. One of the differences between moral insularity and parochialism on the one hand, and moral sophistication and wisdom on the other, is that the latter is aware of the conditions out of which values grow. We may not countenance these values when we have such knowledge; but we at least are not completely baffled by them. We know what they are an outgrowth of and response to.

(b) Value judgments are understood not only through knowledge of their origins and causes but through knowledge of their structural interrelations. What does it mean to say that an action is "courageous," "loyal" or "just"? Each value has a quality that we experience as specifically its own, but the meaning of the quality is enriched by the perception of the relations it bears to other values. Values come in clusters and constellations. They supplement and complement each other like colors. The *interpretation* of the nature of the relations between values may depend upon conflicting theories of their ontological, psychological and social status. But the *existence* of these relations has been recognized by thinkers as far apart as Aristotle and Pascal, Scheler and Dewey. Because these relationships are general, they are never sufficient in enabling us to grasp the meaning of the value qualities in any specific situation. Nonetheless, they contribute to enlarging our understanding and sharpening our perceptions in particular cases. When we are familiar with the ways in which values call to values, we know what to look for, what to reinforce or guard against, what to affirm or reject.

We have called this immanent relationship between values logical. It might just as well be called dramatic. For it involves the conflict and clash or reinforcement and support of human attitudes as they develop in time. This development is funded in the meanings of the values. The analysis of value relations therefore discloses something significant about the history and nature of men.

(c) The third avenue to an understanding of values is perhaps the most important. It consists in grasping the consequences of judgments proposing that something should be done, anticipating their effects on the original difficulties which set the problem of moral choice, and noting their bearing upon other values to which we are implicitly committed. To ignore or discount the consequences of a proposed course of conduct is the mark of fanaticism. And even fanatics often pretend that they have taken the costs of their actions into consideration. But these other values to which we are committed—are they not finally valid independent of consequences? No—they can be challenged, too, if a problem arises about them. And if we take our problems, as we should, one at a time, and remember that a moral problem is created not merely by asking a question but by discovering an objective difficulty in a concrete situation, we avoid narrow circularity and a vicious infinite regress. Whether life is worth living is a serious and legitimate question under certain circumstances when honor or health are at stake, but it is frivolous to introduce it as if it were necessarily involved in every moral problem that arises. Those who believe that all value deliberation *must* at some point anchor itself to ultimate or intrinsic values which are beyond all possibility of scientific validation are as mistaken as those who hold that scientific judgments of fact *must* be based upon incontrovertible first truths for which no evidence can be given.

The advantages of this approach to value judgments are independent of the specific analysis of the nature of value judgments. Whether we consider them as descriptions in the indicative mood, or commands in the imperative mood, or wishes in the optative mood is not as important as that we should be able to answer the question *"Why?"* about them and uncover the nexus of relations, of causes and consequences, which makes one judgment, command or wish more reasonable than another.

This does not in the least deny that there is a distinction between our knowledge of what it is right to do and our attitude towards the doing of it. Many who are aware of the injustice of racial discrimination are unable to liberate themselves from what they admit to be unfounded prejudice. The problem of inducing a change in attitude, of bridging the gap between recognition of moral truth and practical acceptance, is a perennial and basic educational task. Modern psychology has contributed powerful techniques of effecting voluntary persuasion that bear on this problem. But the point I wish to stress is that the transformation of attitude, no matter how subtly undertaken, is logically completely subordinate to the discovery of moral truth. Otherwise we have not risen above the level of nonrational indoctrination.

Nor am I denying that a legitimate distinction can be drawn between the judgments of fact and the judgments of value based upon them. But the stress should be placed upon their interrelation in any specific problem of evaluation, and above all on the method by which evaluations are justified. Whether this method is called "critical," "scientific," "experimental" or "rational" is a matter of indifference. The significant issue is whether in reaching conclusions regarded as true in considering questions of value we depart from the basic pattern observable in reaching conclusions regarded as true in considering questions of fact.

One fundamental cleavage on this point is between those who believe that moral statements are really not cognitive assertions at all and those who believe they are. The first denies that the term "truth" has any intelligible meaning when applied to moral statements. But they exempt all moral judgments which can be construed as instrumental or purposive and limit their taboo only to statements concerning "ultimate" or "intrinsic" values. For educational uses there is a sufficient margin of agreement between these two philosophical schools as to what can be investigated and what not, to justify a common procedure. For it is one of the hypotheses of the experimentalists that all statements which invoke "ultimate" values will be found to be instrumental or purposive in concrete situations involving other values.

Another fundamental cleavage divides those who believe that value statements are cognitive. The first maintain that the pattern of confirmation is, in essentials, the same as that which obtains in scientific inquiry. The second asserts that the pattern is different, that "scientific" inquiry into values is relevant only to the contexts of values not to their essential qualities, and that these are authenticated by a direct intuitive grasp. The opposition between these two approaches is unbridgeable on a theoretical level. Nonetheless, here, too, a theoretical impasse need not hold up educational cooperation. Practice can be based on a minimum agreement. Supernaturalists, traditionalists and a priorists in insisting that *something more* is required than investigation into causes, structure and consequences of values need not necessarily be opposed to such investigation. If it doesn't take us far enough there will be sufficient opportunity to try other methods. But a *beginning* can be made with such investigation without prejudging the theoretical issue. Those who believe that one common pattern of inquiry operates in all fields of investigation will be content to abide by the educative effects of the investigation they propose. All they ask is that the obstacles to such investigation be removed, and that it be wholeheartedly undertaken in fields in which it has hitherto been taboo.

It must be frankly recognized that this proposal is not innocent and that it will be fought tooth and nail by groups who hold to beliefs that are allegedly inaccessible to investigation by critical method but which in actuality may be affected once the authority of method replaces the authority of creed—religious, social or political. Surely there is an inconsistency in maintaining that certain truths are beyond reach of, or comparison with, truths established by scientific method, and refusing to permit them to be investigated scientifically. For by definition they cannot be imperilled by this approach. Such opposition raises the suspicion that these beliefs may in fact be invalid and that those who are fearful of the *attempt* to approach them scientifically are fearful of their possible invalidity.

If we conceive of science, as John Dewey has suggested, in terms of methods of dealing with subject matter instead of uniform traits of subject matter, we can establish the living bond between the scientific and liberal spirit. This lies not in the methods of physics, or the methods of the humanities, but in the method of intelligence which uses the devices and techniques appropriate to specific subject matters. Method is central in a liberal philosophy as in science because it undercuts the absolutisms that would arrest the flow of new knowledge and new insights. Method should be central in educational activity because it not only evaluates the funded tradition of the past but enhances the capacity to enrich it. This is the meaning of liberalism in education. "Like science," writes Morris R. Cohen, "liberalism insists on a critical examination of the content of all our beliefs, principles, or initial hypotheses and on submitting them to a continuous process of verification so that they will be progressively better founded in experience and reason."

The Justifications of Democracy •

The successful defense of democracy does not rest primarily upon the analysis of its nature and presuppositions. Nonetheless, some clarification of the meaning of democracy, of the ground upon which we hold our beliefs, and of the procedure by which we arrive at conclusions for the class of problems and decisions of this kind is necessary if our choice to defend democracy is to be an intelligent one. Insofar as intelligent choice makes a difference to events, analysis is not without ultimate bearing upon conduct. Particularly today, when the

• [From: Sidney Hook, *Political Power and Personal Freedom.* New York: Criterion Books, Inc.; 1959. Pp. 36-57. Copyright 1959 by Criterion Books, Inc. Reprinted by permission of the publishers.]

allegiances of large numbers of people have become un-hinged, and when even larger numbers are more certain of what they want to believe than of the reasons for their belief, the answers to our questions may be of some practical mo-ment. It is noteworthy that, in an age not conspicuous for its appeal to reason, few will give assent to doctrines which they admit to be demonstrably false or out of line with verifiable fact.

Perhaps more dangerous to democracy than arguments against it is the feeling that analysis or reflection is irrelevant to those "beliefs" for which we are prepared to suffer, to fight, and sometimes to die. They are then regarded either as automatic consequences of conditioning—social or biologi-cal—or as sacred commands from a divine source or as the irresistible cry of conscience. Once the rational nerve of belief is paralyzed, action in behalf of expressed goals may still be vigorous, but it cannot be intelligent. For whatever else intelligence is, it is sensitiveness to, and awareness of, the presence of *alternate means* which in fact determine the real-ized content of the goals we profess. Belief without reasons blinds us to the presence of alternate means. That is why the action it inspires is so often self-defeating. There are many causes in history of which we can say that they have been betrayed by their own successes.

It is hard to separate a discussion of democracy from a dis-cussion of its alleged philosophical presuppositions, for the nature of democracy is itself often in dispute. In addition, the meaning of the word "presuppositions" is not unequivocal. Its customary usage includes "consequences" and "implica-tions" as well as "assumptions." What I propose to do, there-fore, in order to facilitate the joining of issues, is to ask and answer three generic questions. The first is: What is democ-racy? The second: What are the grounds on or reasons by which we can justify our belief in democracy? The third: Are there any facts of a cosmic, historical, or psychological kind which stand in the way of our acceptance of democracy, i.e., which make democracy an impracticable ideal? It is apparent that these last two questions are related, since if any ideal is demonstrably impracticable, in a sense other than completely realizable (for no ideal can be completely real-ized) this would have some bearing on its desirability or on the grounds of our choice.

I

Any adequate description of the nature of democracy must at the very least do justice to customary usage, which distinguishes between democratic and nondemocratic societies and among historic phases within any one society, regarded as more or less democratic in relation to each other. Although for propaganda purposes even totalitarian states claim to be democratic "in a higher sense," their canonic writings recognize the differences between the structure of these states and those considered democratic in a less esoteric sense. This is often betrayed in such adjectives prefixed to the latter as "so-called," "alleged," "parliamentary," or "bourgeois." Historically, Spain and Russia and China are not democratic states; England and the United States are. And when historians examine the development of English and American society they unanimously acknowledge (although they evaluate the fact differently) that these societies were less democratic when property, racial, or religious qualifications were set for citizenship than they are today when these qualifications have been eliminated or reduced.

What principle is expressed in these customary distinctions? The principle may be stated in various ways, but for our purposes we may say that a democratic state is one in which the basic decisions of government rest upon the freely given consent of the governed. This obviously is only a beginning. For just as soon as we begin to investigate the conditions which must be present before we grant that a state lives up to this principle, we are carried beyond the sphere of political considerations into the domain of ethics. Thus, if information has been withheld or withdrawn before consent is assessed; if the opposition is muzzled or suppressed so that consent is as unanimous as a totalitarian plebiscite; or if economic sanctions are threatened against a section of the community in the event that consent takes one form or another, we declare that the "spirit" or "logic" or "rationale" of democracy is absent from its political forms. If birth does not give divine right, neither do numbers. We are all acquainted with situations in which we say that a political democracy has traduced its own ideals. Whenever we criticize existing states which conform to the political definition of democracy on the ground that they are not democratic enough; whenever we point out that Athenian democracy was limited only to free men, or that in some parts of the American South it is limited only to white men, or in some countries it is limited only to men—we are invoking a broader principle of democracy as a controlling reference in our judgments of comparison. This principle is an ethical one.

What is this principle of ethical democracy? It is a principle of equality—an equality not of status or origin but of opportunity, relevant functions, and social participation. The enormous literature and bitter controversy which center around the concept of equality indicate that it is only a little less ambiguous than the concept of democracy. It is necessary, therefore, to block it off from some current notions before developing the argument.

(*A*) The principle of equality is not a *description* of fact about men's physical or intellectual natures. It is a *prescription* or policy of treating men.

(*B*) It is not a prescription to treat in identical ways men who are unequal in their physical or intellectual nature. It is a policy of equality of concern or consideration for men whose different needs may require differential treatment.

(*C*) It is not a mechanical policy of equal opportunity for everyone at *any* time and in *all* respects. A musical genius is entitled to greater opportunities for developing his musical talents than someone who is tone deaf. It is equality of opportunity for all individuals to develop whatever personal and socially desirable talents they possess and to make whatever unique contributions their capacities permit.

(*D*) It is not a demand for absolute uniformity of living conditions or even for arithmetically equal compensation for socially useful work. It demands that, when the productive forces of a society make possible the gratification of basic human needs (which are, of course, historical variables), no one should be deprived of necessities in order to provide others with luxuries.

(*E*) It is not a policy of restricting the freedom of being different or becoming different. It is a policy of *encouraging* the freedom to be different, restricting only that exercise of freedom which converts talents or possessions into a monopoly that frustrates the emergence of other free personalities.

(*F*) It is not a demand that all people be leaders or that none should be. It does demand that the career of leadership,

I can see there are five generic types of justification which have been or can be offered. And by justification here I do not mean "proof," but the offering of valid reasons.

The first asserts that the rational foundation of democratic belief consists in a set of supernatural religious truths, in the sense that there can be no intelligent ground for choosing between democracy and other forms of society which does not logically commit us to some kind of theology.

The second asserts the same thing about metaphysics understood as a theory of "reality." Usually these two approaches go hand in hand.

The third attempts to derive democracy from natural law, leaving aside the origin of this law. It is a cross between metaphysics and theology, but important enough to consider by itself.

The fourth maintains that the choice of democracy is a nonrational preference rooted in the constitution of our natures and brought to flower by nurture and education.

The fifth affirms that the belief in democracy is a hypothesis controlled by the same general pattern of inquiry which we apply to any scientific hypothesis but referring to different subject matter, i.e., our evaluations.

(1) Democracy and religion. Does democracy as a way of life rest upon belief in supernatural religious truths in the sense that, if the latter are denied, the former must necessarily be denied? It is becoming increasingly fashionable to maintain this. Were historical considerations relevant here, I think it could be conclusively established that the great institutional religions, with the possible exception of some forms of Protestantism, have tended in fact to support theocratic forms of government. Nor is this surprising if the Kingdom of Heaven be taken as a model or inspiration for the Kingdom of Earth. Whoever heard of a democratically organized Paradise? Walt Whitman in heaven would meet with the same fate as Lucifer, but for different reasons. Not only is the notion of a democratically organized heaven blasphemous, but the proposal to reform along democratic lines a hierarchically organized church would lead to excommunication. If we examine the actual behavior which has been sanctified by the maxim, "Render unto Caesar what is Caesar's and to God what is God's," we will discover that historically institutional

like all other careers, be open to all whose natural or acquired talents qualify them; that everyone have a say in the process of selecting leaders; that the initiative of leaders operate within a framework of basic laws; and that these laws in turn ultimately rest upon the freely given consent of the persons who constitute the community.

(G) It does not make the assumption of sentimental humanitarianism that all men are naturally good. It does assume that men, treated as equals in a community of persons, may become better. The emphasis upon respect for the personality of all individuals, the attitude which treats the personality not as something fixed but as a growing, developing pattern, is unique to the philosophy of democracy.

What I have been trying to show is that the logic of the democrat's position compels him to go beyond the limited conception of political democracy—the equality of freedom—to a broader attitude extending to those other phases of social existence that bear upon the effective exercise of equality of freedom. This in fact has been the historical tendency observable wherever democratic principles and programs are permitted to operate. Perhaps the synoptic phrase "social equality," whose connotations encompass political, educational, and economic democracy, may be taken as the most appropriate expression of the meaning of democracy in the broadest sense.

It is clear that the principle of equality, like any principle of justice, cannot by itself determine what is specifically right or good in each concrete case. But whatever the right is discovered to be, from the point of view of democracy it is the result of an analysis which considers equally the needs of all the persons involved in the situation; and, further, whatever the good is, it becomes better to the extent that it is shared among other members of the community. It is also clear that in concrete situations there will be conflicts among various demands for equality, and that in negotiating these conflicts the methods of intelligence are indispensable to a functioning democracy. If empiricism is a generic term for the philosophic attitude which submits *all* claims of fact and value to test by experience, then empiricism as a philosophy is more congenial to a democratic than to an antidemocratic community, for it brings into the open light of criticism the interests in which moral values and social institutions are rooted. Empiricism so conceived is commitment to a procedure, not to a theory of metaphysics.

In this brief account of the nature of democracy as a way of life I have not aimed at an exhaustive analysis of the *forms* in which it may be expressed, but have tried to indicate the basic ideals which are involved in the customary usage of the term and in the implications of that usage.

Before proceeding to the question of the justification of democracy I wish to discuss briefly two points of possible criticism. The first takes issue with the conception of democracy as equality of concern, concretized above; the second believes that if democracy is not defined as the rule of law, at least the recognition of the primacy of law must be given a high order of priority in the democratic community.

From the point of view of democracy as purely and only a form of government, reference to equality of concern is indeed irrelevant. Theoretically, and sometimes even historically, democratic governments have shown less equality of concern for all members of the community than have some benevolent, or even feudal, despots. But if we broaden the term to speak of democracy as an ethical way of life then we would deny that equality of concern can be manifested by a master or ruler or despot without equality of power. A master who has no more power than a slave is not a master, and a ruler or despot whose interest counts for one and no more than one is not likely to hold on to his power without being forced to share it. Whatever designation we give the term, its meaning is the one intended when we charge that a democratic state, government, or community has acted undemocratically. If anyone bogs at the expression "democracy," let him substitute for it the phrase "social justice."

It is sometimes said that the distinguishing feature of democratic government is that it represents the rule of laws, not of men. This emphasis upon laws, unless qualified by reference to the kind of laws and how they are adopted, seems to me to miss the essential point. It describes not what is distinctive of democratic society but of *any stable society,* with definite laws, traditions, and procedures, whether democratic or not. The rule of law holds for slave societies and feudal societies as well as for democratic societies—perhaps more so in virtue of the complexity of the social relationships involved. In slave and feudal societies differences of interest are usually settled by an appeal to principles and customs which

define rights and duties. Even tyrants to the extent that they are rational creatures lay down rules, so that their subjects will know what to do or avoid, and try to follow them. Even in abandoning them, they enunciate new rules. At most the rule of law differentiates between societies in a state of anarchy and societies in a state of stability. But there are many different ways of being stable, and many different types of law regulating stability.

A democratic society is one ordered by laws; but the laws in such a society must be made or interpreted by individuals who, ultimately, are responsible to (and removable by) the community. The community must be one in which equality of civic status obtains, in which the laws ultimately rest upon the freely given consent of the adult population. For certain purposes the contrast between the rule of laws and the rule of men is legitimate, but very often it has deceptive connotations. For laws do not rule by themselves; they must always be interpreted and administered by men. And these men, no matter how august their robes or presence, are fallible human beings who read their different, and often conflicting, meanings into the same set of laws. The diverse meanings judges can torture out of apparently plain texts constitute a large part of the history of Anglo-American law, as precedent is stretched to meet new cases never even envisaged by legislatures and courts. The arbitrary nature of judicial interpretation of law finds its most notorious illustration perhaps in some of the decisions of the United States Supreme Court. In the light of the history of that court, its reversals of judgment as the composition of the court changes, its interpretations of the meaning of words by thought processes compared to which the derivation of the name of Middletown from the name of Moses is a straightforward inference, the belief that the United States is ruled by laws rather than by men is untenable. In many areas, it is easier to predict what the decision of the Supreme Court will be from the composition of the Court than from the existence of the basic law which presumably guides its decision.

II

We now come to the problem which is of primary concern to philosophers, and not only to philosophers. What are the grounds on which we can justify our acceptance of democracy in contradistinction to other modes of social life? So far as

religion has always been able to adapt itself to any form of government or society that will tolerate its existence.

But our concern is not with historical questions, fascinating as they are, but with the logic of the position. We must consequently rephrase the question to read: Does belief in democracy logically rest upon any theological propositions in the sense that the denial of the second entails the denial of the first? And for this discussion I shall take as illustrative of theological propositions the two cardinal propositions of natural theology, viz., "God exists" and "Man has an immortal soul." To assert that whoever has no grounds for affirming the existence of God and immortality has no ground for affirming the validity of democracy is to claim that the former are at least necessary conditions of the latter. I shall argue that they constitute neither necessary nor sufficient conditions.

(*a*) Before examining this claim, let us note the tremendous risk it involves. Were those who advance it ever compelled to admit that these theological propositions are undemonstrable or false, they would have to surrender their belief in democracy. But this, I submit, very few of them are prepared to do. They would search for other reasons and grounds. Like those who would make the validity of moral judgments dependent upon the existence of God and immortality, the theological defenders of democracy shift from a problem in which, although difficult, it is possible to reach an agreement on the basis of some empirical evidence to one in which the nature of the terms and sphere of discourse makes such agreement much more difficult. Confirmed democrats, it seems to me, are much more convinced of the validity of the democratic ideal than they are of the theological propositions upon which it presumably depends. They would no more exonerate an atheist or agnostic who pleaded that he had no reason to believe in God and the hereafter from the obligation of accepting the democatic ideal than they would from the obligation of living honestly.

(*b*) Aside from the difficulties of establishing God's existence, how can we get from the fact of his existence to the desirability of the democratic way of life? None of the attributes of God, save the moral attributes, can serve as a premise justifying one way of life rather than another. And if the moral attributes of God can serve as premises, necessary or sufficient, for the democratic way of life, it is only because *we* regard them as worthy, i.e. as truly moral. Obviously any theology which makes God's power the justification or source of his goodness is worse than useless for purposes of deriving democracy. The attribution of moral qualities to God is an expression of what we think his qualities ought to be. And this is a problem of precisely the same order as we are called upon to answer when we ask for the grounds of our democratic allegiance.

(*c*) The situation is the same if we grant that human beings have immortal souls. In what way is this a necessary or sufficient presupposition of democracy? The brotherhood of man may be a theological fact as it is a biological fact, but that which makes it wrong for Cain to kill his brother Abel and right, under certain circumstances, for us to kill Cain, and noble for Jonathan to lay down his life for David who was *not* his brother, is a moral principle which can no more be derived from theology than from biology—unless, of course, the moral principle is one of the premises of our theological (or biological) system. In which case we are no further along than we were when we raised the question about the democratic way of life. In passing it should be observed that belief in the immortality of the soul can be, and has been, used (in the Hindu doctrines of *Samsara* and *Karma*) to sanctify the tightest system of antidemocratic social stratification the world has ever seen.•

(2) *Democracy and metaphysics.* The problem of the metaphysical foundations of democracy is more difficult because of the varying conceptions of metaphysics. By metaphysics I shall understand the discipline designated by the term "ontology" or any theory of "being *überhaupt.*" The evidence seems to me to be overwhelming that there is a definite historical connection between the social movements of any period and its dominant metaphysical teachings; further, I am prepared to defend as historically true the proposition that systems of idealistic metaphysics, because of the semi-official roles they have played in their respective cultures,

---

• Cf. Max Weber, *Religionssoziologie,* II, 119-20. The lot of the Hindu in this life is a consequence of his sins or virtues in a previous life. Therefore, he cannot complain about the injustice of any "accident of birth" or station. But, no matter how unclean his caste, he has the hope that, by exemplary observance of the caste rituals and cheerful acceptance of his present lot, he may improve his social position in the next cycle of rebirth.

have been more generally employed to bolster antidemocratic social movements than have systems of empirical or materialistic metaphysics. Whether there is always an intrinsic personal or psychological relation between a philosopher's metaphysics and his ethics or politics is a more difficult question, but one which seems to me to require an answer in the negative. But more germane to our present concern is my contention that there is no necessary logical connection between a theory of being or becoming and any particular theory of ethics or politics. Stated more accurately, it seems to me demonstrable that no system of metaphysics unequivocally determines a system of ethics or politics. There may be certain facts about man and nature which might have a bearing upon our judgment about what social system is of the highest worth, but these are facts concerning which the empirical sciences are qualified to report without benefit of metaphysics.

Two species of metaphysics are most often invoked on behalf of democracy. One asserts that the value of democracy or the values from which it may be derived are "grounded in reality," a phrase which is interpreted to mean that the universe "justifies" or "guarantees" both the validity and the ultimate supremacy of basic human ideals. I must confess that it is difficult for me to understand this view except as a shamefaced kind of theology. But however that may be, there is no agreed-upon denotation of *the* universe; there are many universes. Nor is there any one basic human ideal, but many human ideals which are often in conflict with one another, even though they all invoke the universe as a ground of their validity and as a guarantee of their triumph. Finally, and most important, no matter what character the universe is alleged to have, no matter what the nature of the far-off event toward which it is moving, no matter who wins or loses, nothing logically compelling in the way of judgment follows unless *we* have already morally evaluated the character of events. For most metaphysicians the very word "reality" is an implicit value term. To be sure, history may be conceived as a struggle between the Prince of Darkness and the Prince of Light, but the latter is so named because he carries *our* moral flag.

The second metaphysical view to which resort is often made is at the same time a kind of rejoinder to our position. It distinguishes between a metaphysical realm of being and a metaphysical realm of values, and grounds the democratic way of life in the latter. Just as the spectrum of colors is there to be beheld by all who are not color blind and would still be there even if man's ancestors had climbed no higher than the mole in the tree of evolution, so the spectrum of values is there to be beheld by all who are not value blind and would still be there even if human beings had never existed at all. The view that colors would still be there even if human beings had no eyes is not without its difficulties. But they do not begin to compare in difficulty with the view that values are essentially unrelated to an evaluator and his interests. Santayana has quite aptly remarked of this doctrine that there is as much sense in saying that whiskey "is pervaded as it were, by an inherent intoxication, and stands dead drunk in its bottle."

The subject is vast, but it is enough to show that this view begs the question in precisely the same way as do other theological and metaphysical derivations. The existence of these absolute norms is presumably certified or authenticated at some point by an act of immediate intuition. If the testimony of the intuition is construed not merely from what individuals *say* they intuit but from the conduct that flows from their intuition—and in any moral scheme conduct counts for more than mere words—then it is clear that individuals intuit or "see" *different* values. The "great" visions are not at all compatible with one another in what they command, not to mention the visions which we do not call great. Which visions are the authentic ones? Prior to every conclusion that these are the objective values of all eternity, or even of all time and existence, is the assumption that *this* is the trustworthy seer. In a dispute between two men, one of whom asserts that the other is color blind and the other that the first is "just seeing things," there are definite ways of determining who is right. In a dispute between two seers whose immediate intuitions report conflicting news about the nature and hierarchy of absolute values, there is no rational way of reaching a consensus. The true prophet cannot be distinguished from the false by invoking absolute values whose validity depends upon a prior assumption of the reliability of prophetic testimony. The complacency with which some writers have cut the Gordian knot by introducing reference to the intuitions of "the best people" or "the most cultured people" or "the saving remnant" is evidence either of parochialism or of snobbery.

The record of human error and cruelty shows what ghastly consequences often result from the conviction that one's moral insight cannot possibly be wrong and that it needs no further justification than its own incandescent purity. No more than a solipsist can make plausible on his own assumptions the existence of another solipsist, can an absolutist find a rightful place for another absolutist who disagrees with him. Absolutists face each other over an abyss which cannot be bridged even by their weapons of war.

(3) Democracy and natural law. The attempt to justify democracy on the basis of "natural law" suffers from root ambiguities in the conception of natural law. There is a threefold confusion between the physical conception of law, the legal conception of law, and the conception of moral laws as laws of what should be.

The physical or scientific conception of law is descriptive, not prescriptive. It tells us how events of different kinds are in fact related. It cannot serve as a basis for an unequivocal judgment of what we should do. It is the nature of chickens to lay eggs and of fertilized eggs to become chickens. But this law of nature does not tell us whether we should permit chickens to lay eggs or put them in the pot, or whether we should permit eggs to hatch instead of making omelets of them. Further confusion is produced by the ambiguity of the term "natural." Sometimes it is taken to mean "normal"; sometimes merely "existent." The confusion is confounded when "normal" is given the connotation of "good" or "desirable" and "abnormal" is given the connotation of "bad" or "undesirable." Obviously "the abnormal" is just as natural as the normal though less frequent, and the "unnatural" unfortunately exists just as much as the natural, as when we speak of "the unnatural vices." This does not mean that the natural vices are desirable because they may be normal. And great courage and unselfishness are also abnormal without being undesirable.

Whatever the natural laws of physics or biology, they cannot by themselves serve as legitimate justifying premises of democracy. At most one can argue that the order a democratic society seeks to build is rendered impossible by such natural laws. But even if laws of nature make certain social arrangements impossible, this would not make the attempt to achieve them impossible, only foolish. It is obvious that the laws of physics are irrelevant to, or equally compatible with, any proposal to organize government or society on democratic or undemocratic lines. The same is true of the laws of biology. Even if it were a biological law that all animals love one another and live at peace with each other, it would not follow that men should do so. And if the opposite view were held that "nature is red in tooth and claw," it would not follow that because dog eats dog, man should eat man.

Natural law, in ordinary contexts, refers to connections or relations which cannot be violated. A violation of a natural law is an exception to a natural law and by definition an exception to a natural law is evidence that it is not a law and that the statement asserting that it holds is false. If the natural law of gravitation or cell division is violated there is no law. But the natural law upon which democracy presumably rests is violable. We are told that we "should" follow it and are condemned for not following it. This indicates that the natural law is neither "natural" or "a law" in the ordinary sense of these terms.

Those who speak of a conception of immutable, universal, and rational order which should serve as a model for human behavior cannot sensibly mean that it is a legal order, for all sorts of legal systems exist—some just, some unjust, some rational, some unrational. The problem is to make the legal order a moral one and, in part, to develop legal sanctions for some of our moral values.

This indicates that those who speak of natural law as a basis for democracy really have in mind some transcendent metaphysical or theological principle as a basis for human institution, to which they misleadingly refer as natural law. They should claim either that it is a law of God or that it is a metaphysical law of being which even God, if he exists, cannot alter. In either case, however, the difficulties in connection with these themes remain.

For purposes of summary let us examine a recent and eloquent claim to derive democracy from natural law.

> The human person possesses rights because of the very fact that it is a person, a whole, master of itself and of its acts, and which consequently is not merely a means to an end, but an end, an end which must be treated as such. The dignity of the human person? The expression means nothing if it does not signify that by virtue of natural law, the human person has

the right to be respected, is the subject of rights, possesses rights. There are things which are owed to man because of the very fact that he is man. The notion of right and the notion of moral obligation are correlative. They are both founded on the freedom proper to spiritual agents. If man is morally bound to the things which are necessary to the fulfillment of his destiny; and if he has the right to fulfill his destiny he has the right to the things necessary for this purpose.•

To begin with, we note that those who have held this view in the past have not been outstanding for their defense of democracy. On the contrary, they have defended on the basis of natural law undemocratic systems. Secondly, although we are told that the human being possesses rights and that things are owed him "because of the very fact that he is a man" we are not told specifically what those rights and what those things are. Is there any specific right that an individual human has which is absolute and inalienable? Is it the right to life? If an individual has an absolute and inalienable right to life, he has a right to what makes that life possible. But suppose he can only survive, as sometimes happens, by taking the life of another? Do both have an absolute right to live when the destruction of one is a condition for the survival of the other? Has an individual criminal a right to life independently of the character and frequency of his crimes? Had Hitler or Stalin, moral monsters both, more of a natural right to life than some innocent animal who never harmed anyone? Has any man a natural and absolute right to refuse to bear arms in the service of his country on the ground that he has a natural right to life—a right which is owed him merely because he is a man? M. Maritain and his ideological forebears would hardly grant this.

Is there, then, a natural, absolute, and inalienable right to liberty? Of speech? But what of the laws which punish criminal libel and the treason of betraying the secrets of national defense to an enemy? A right of action? But what of the laws which define the conditions under which our behavior is a nuisance, if not worse? Right of assembly? Surely not when traffic is obstructed or an emergency conveyance must have the right of way?

• Jacques Maritain, *The Rights of Man and Natural Law*. New York: Charles Scribner's Sons. 1943. P. 65. Used with permission.

Is there, then, a natural, absolute, and inalienable right to property, as Locke believed? But what if the things I make as a result of "mixing" my own labor with it are necessary for the safety and security of the community whose traditions and schools provided me with the skills and knowledge required to produce the "property"? What of "property" in land to which the community claims the right of eminent domain?

Is there, then, a natural, absolute, and inalienable right to happiness, as Jefferson claimed? What, then, shall we answer the young man who claimed the right to kidnap his beloved on the ground that she was absolutely necessary to his happiness? If we took seriously this assertion of the absolute right to the pursuit of happiness the world would be a much more unhappy place than it is.

And finally, what of the conflicts between these natural rights? Every difficult moral situation can be construed in terms of such a conflict. Our own time has spawned a whole series of moral problems in which the right to security conflicts with the right to liberty and which challenges us to fruitful and creative devices that aim at giving us as much as possible of both but must on occasion risk our security or curb our freedom. The theory of natural law does not take us an inch forward in negotiating such conflicts.

Even if all of these difficulties were met it would still be necessary to show in what way this theory of natural law, which some of its devotees call integral humanism or integral liberalism, justifies democracy rather than benevolent despotism. One modern exponent of natural law who attributes the decline of liberalism to a point of view which rejects metaphysical premises accepted on faith explicitly cites the following lines from Goethe, that consummate dabbler in politics, as "capturing the essential spirit of integral liberalism."

> Es ist kein schoen'rer Anblick in der Welt,
> Als einen Fuersten seh'n, der klug regieret,
> Das Reich zu seh'n, wo jeder stolz gehorcht,
> Wo jeder sich nur selbst zu diene glaubt,
> Weil ihm das Rechte nur befohlen wird.●

● Hallowel, "The Decline of Liberalism," *Ethics* (1942), p. 336. Freely translated the passage runs: "There is no more beautiful sight in the world than to observe a Prince who rules wisely and to see a country where everyone proudly obeys, and where everyone believes that he is serving his own interest because he is commanded to do only what is just."

The failure of the theory of natural law and natural rights to further the solution of any specific problem suggests that in the past it served as a rhetorical expression of man's sense of injustice against the *status quo*. Taken literally it was not credible. Taken with the saving grace of intellectual sophistication it was an appeal to reason, to the arts of intelligence, to make social life more humane and just. This made it often a linguistic preface to a more empirical approach.

(*4*) *Democracy and preferences*. The view that an acceptance of democracy is an expression of a preference does not carry us far until the kind of preference is indicated. A preference may express a passing whim or a deep natural bent; it may be impulsive or reflective. Preferences are rooted in our natures. Their forms, occasions, and objects are supplied by education, i.e., broadly speaking, by social habits and intelligence. But either our natures can be changed or the educators re-educated. If neither is possible, then the fact of moral choice becomes unintelligible. If we can offer no justification of a preference except that it is ours, obviously no point of intellectual or moral issue is raised, nor, *a fortiori*, can any be settled by the trial of arms. If we offer a justification of a preference, it will take one of the other four generic forms.

(*5*) *Democracy as a hypothesis*. When democracy is taken strictly as a form of political government, its superiority over other forms of government can be established to the extent that it achieves more security, freedom, and cooperative diversity than any of its alternatives. If we test the workings of political democracy by Paul's scheme of virtues or by Nietzsche's, we may perhaps reach another conclusion. So long as there is no dispute about observable effects and so long as we raise no question about the moral ideals by which we evaluate these effects, we have clear sailing.

But, as has already been made plain, by democracy as a way of life we mean a way of organizing human relationships which embodies a certain complex of moral ideals. Can these ideals be treated as hypotheses? The conventional reply has always been that no moral principle can be regarded as a hypothesis, for we must already have certain knowledge of what is good before we can evaluate the consequences of acting upon it. If any position is question-begging, surely this seems to be!

Were this a symposium on value theory, I would devote all my time to developing the general theory of moral ideals as hypotheses. But here I can only barely indicate that the notion is not viciously circular. A moral ideal is a prescription to act in a certain situation or class of situations in determinate ways that will organize the human needs and wants involved so as to fulfil a set of *other* values which are *postulated* as binding in relation to the problem in hand. No more than in other cases of inquiry do we start with an empty head. The cluster of values we bring to the situation is the result of prior experience and reflection. They are not arbitrarily postulated. The consequences of acting upon the hypothesis may lead us to challenge a postulated or assumed value. This in turn can become the subject of a similar investigation. Terminal values are always related to specific contexts; there is no absolute terminal value which is either self-evident or beyond the necessity of justifying itself if its credentials are challenged. There is no vicious infinite regress involved if we take our problems concretely and one at a time. Nor is the procedure narrowly circular. For if, in a long history of raising and solving moral problems, we postulate as a value in solving a later problem a value which had itself to be certified in an earlier problem, this would testify to the presence of a fruitful set of systematically related values in the structure of our moral behavior. New values would emerge, or be discovered, in the course of our attempt to act upon our ideals and from the necessity of mediating the conflict between the postulated values as they bear on concrete human needs in specific situations.

I should like, however, to make the general position take form out of the discussion of the theme before us. That theme is: Why should we treat individuals of unequal talents and endowments as persons who are equally entitled to relevant consideration and care? Short of a treatise I can state only the reasons, without amplification of the concrete needs of the social situation which democracy seeks to meet and the institutional practices by which it must meet them.

(*a*) This method of treating human beings is more successful than any other in evoking a maximum of creative, voluntary effort from all members of the community. Properly implemented it gives all persons a stake in the community and elicits a maximum of intelligent loyalty.

(*b*) It enlarges the scope of our experience by enabling

us to acquire insight into the needs, drives, and aspirations of others. Learning to understand how life is organized by other centers of experience is both a challenge and a discipline for our imagination. In aiding the growth of others, we aid our own growth.

(c) The willingness to understand another man's point of view without necessarily surrendering to it makes it more likely that different points of view may negotiate their differences and learn to live peacefully with one another. A democratic community cannot be free from strife in a world where inequalities will always exist, but its ethics when intelligently acted upon make more likely the diminution of strife or its transference to socially harmless forms than is the case when the principle of equality is denied. In consequence there is less toadying, less fear, and less duplicity in the equalitarian community than in the nonequalitarian society.

(d) In nurturing the capacities of each individual so that they may come to their greatest fulfillment, we can best share our existing stores of truth and beauty and uncover new dimensions in these realms. How can anyone dedicated to the values of science and art consistently oppose a policy which maximizes the possibility of the discovery and widest dispersion of scientific truths and artistic meanings?

(e) Regard for the potentialities of all individuals makes for less cruelty of man toward man, especially where cruelty is the result of blindness to, or ignorance of, others' needs. A community organized along democratic lines is guilty of cruelty only at those points where it has failed to live up to its own ideals. A totalitarian community is systematically insensitive to the personal needs not only of members of the outlawed scapegoat group but of the majority of its subjects who are excluded from policy-making discussions. At best, there is no way of determining these personal needs except by the interpretation of the dictator and his experts who operate with the dogma that they know the true interests of their subjects better than the subjects themselves. At worst, the dictator assumes not only that he speaks for his subjects but that in some mystic way he feels and thinks for them too. Despite the great limitations—limitations from the point of view of their own ideals—under which the nineteenth- and twentieth-century democracies of the Western world suffered, I think it is indisputable, on the evidence, that by and large their social life, insofar as this was the consequence of policy, displayed less cruelty than the social life of any other historical period.

(f) Reasonableness of conclusions, where attitudes and interests conflict, depends upon the degree of mutual consultation and free intellectual communication between the principals involved. The democratic way of life makes possible the widest forms of mutual consultation and communication. Conclusions reached by these processes have a quality that can never be found where conclusions are imposed by force or authority—even if they are our own. Who among us would forego the methods of public discussion, criticism, argument, and rejoinder for a philosophical consensus imposed by a Gestapo or a G.P.U., even if by a strange quirk of affairs it was *our* philosophic position that the goon squads of orthodoxy sought to make the way of salvation? Who among us, knowing that outside the door stood an individual of a strange country, color, or faith, capable of making a contribution to our lives, would not open the door to him? These are not rhetorical questions framed to discover philosophical fifth columnists. They are designed to show that the procedures of critical discussion and discovery, which are pre-eminently exhibited in the work of a scientific community, take for granted that national, racial, or religious origins are irrelevant to the logic of the method by which reasonable conclusions are reached. Democracy as a way of life differs from its alternatives in that it makes possible the extension of these methods of reaching reasonable conclusions from the fields of professional science and philosophy to all areas of human experience in which genuine problems arise.

There are other grounds that may be offered in justification of democracy as the most adequate social philosophy for our times. Every one of them postulates implicitly or explicitly values or desiderata. But I repeat: these postulates are ultimate only for the problem in hand. They may require justification. When we undertake such justification, we have undertaken a new inquiry into a new problem.

There are two important consequences of approaching democracy in this way. The first is that we avoid the temptation, which is rapidly gaining vogue, of making democracy absolutely valid in and for itself. There are many today who write as if they believe that democracy should prevail even though the heavens fall, and who say in so many words that "to question the validity of democracy is to disbelieve in it" and that we can meet the blind fanatical faith of fascism only with a faith in democracy which is at least just as fanatical. This temptation, it seems to me, must be avoided because, by counterposing subrational dogma to subrational dogma, it prepares the ground for an acceptance of a might-makes-right morality. Second, those who make of democracy an absolute value, which requires no justification but its inherent rightness, tend to identify this absolute democracy with whatever particular democratic *status quo* exists. On the other hand, among those who cannot distinguish between social philosophies on the ground of their inherent rightness, the natural tendency is to test a social philosophy by the social institutions in which it is embodied. They are, therefore, more attentive to the actual workings and effects of democracy, more historically minded, and less likely to gloss over existing imperfections.

To those who say that human beings will not fight wholeheartedly except for certainties, and emphatically not for a hypothesis which is only probable, the reply must be made that this empirical proposition is highly dubious. Men have fought and do fight vigorously for causes on the basis of preponderant evidence. Vigorous action, indeed, is only desirable when we have first decided what is intelligent action. And intelligent action does not result when we assume that our ideas or ideals simply cannot be wrong. That both intelligence and resoluteness are compatible is clear in fields as far apart as military science and medicine. Once it is decided that the chances of one action are relatively better than another, once it is decided that an operation gives a patient a better chance of surviving than no operation, wisdom demands that the best-warranted alternative be pursued with all our hearts and souls. Let us remember that when we fight for democracy we are not fighting for an ideal which has just been proposed as a merely possible valid ideal for our times; we already have considerable evidence in its behalf, the weight of which, unfortunately too often, is properly evaluated only when democracy is lost or imperiled.

III

We now turn to the question of the feasibility of democracy. We can imagine someone, who has accepted the tentative ends by which we evaluate ways of life, criticizing us as follows: "If only the assertions made in the previous section could be established as true, the case for democracy would be convincing. But the nature of man as we know him, of history as scientifically understood, and of the larger world we live in precludes the possibility of ever achieving democracy. It runs counter to the facts. Although you may still choose to live or die for democracy, the attempt to realize it, like any attempt to realize an ideal which has no natural basis, will be a ghastly failure. Its natural consequences will be worse than the evils it sets out to cure, and it will subvert the very ideals to which you have appealed in your argument. Democracy is an infirmity of noble but innocent minds who have never understood the world. It is not an intelligent option."

I will consider briefly three types of objection to the feasibility of the democratic ideal.

(*1*) The first is based upon its alleged psychological impossibility. It maintains that democracy is too good for men who are essentially evil, fallen creatures, dominated by lust for power, property, and self. In less theological form it asserts that democracy makes too high a call upon human intelligence and disinterestedness.

It is true that the psychological nature of man is quite relevant to our problem. If most human beings were idiots or infantile or permanently incapable of self-development, the democratic ideal could hardly be defended on plausible grounds. But there is no evidence that most human beings are such, and an intelligent attempt to find out whether they are would require that equalization of social opportunity which is of the essence of democracy. Even without such an experiment, if we surrender the utopian expectation of the complete realization of the democratic ideal and bear in mind that the forms of democracy may be direct as well as indirect and that democracy is compatible with the delegation of powers and responsibilities, the evidence at hand could hardly justify the belief either in universal cretinism or in man's permanent ineducability. Nor do we have to counter with the assertion that men are *infinitely* perfectible to make our option for democracy reasonable. We require merely that they be sufficiently plastic, sufficiently capable of learning, criticism, and improvement, to choose responsibly between alternatives of action whenever—and here lies the crux— they have alternatives of choice. It is only the democratic community which will systematically give them the alternatives of choice on basic decisions. It is not without significance that no free people has ever voluntarily relinquished its democratic forms for a government which openly proclaimed as its aim the establishment of a permanent dictatorship. Principled dictatorships, as distinct from those that come in through the unguarded doors of democracy, always triumph by usurpation. As low as the human estate is today, there is no reason to believe that human beings belong to a psychological species inferior to that of their ancestors. Although history is rich in human stupidities and lost opportunities, in the face of men's achievements in the arts and sciences it would be simply foolish to read history as nothing but the record of human error.

The theological doctrine of man's essentially evil nature metaphorically expresses the truth that he is always limited, always tempted, and never free of his animal origins. But, taken literally, it makes any kind of moral virtue inconceivable except by interposition of divine grace or mystery. Here, too, we do not have to counter with a contrary theological proposition that man is essentially good. He is neither one nor the other but becomes good or evil depending upon his society, his habits, and his intelligence.

(2) The most powerful arguments against the feasibility of democracy, strangely enough, have been neglected by most social philosophers. These are developed in the writings of Gaetano Mosca, Vilfredo Pareto, and Roberto Michels. Their common thesis, formulated on the basis of vast, detailed studies of political and social history, is that all historical change, whether reform or revolution, consists of the substitution of one ruling minority for another. This rule rests upon three pillars: vital myths which cement human relationships and conceal differences of interests; fraud or chicanery which prevent conflicting interests from becoming articulate when myths lose their vitality; and force which ultimately settles differences of interest. The nature of social organization, they claim, is such that democrats may be victorious but democracy never. So it has been, so it is, and so it will be.

Here I content myself with one consideration which points to the self-confessed inadequacy of their position. Despite this alleged law, every one of them admits, explicitly or implicitly, that some forms of society are better than others—and in every case it is the society which has a greater degree of democracy than the others. Thus Mosca, after maintaining the inescapability of minority rule, pays strong tribute to the superiority of parliamentary democracy over all other alternatives.

Three basic errors, it seems to me, vitiate their conclusion. The first is that the amount of freedom and democracy in a society is determined by a law *already known* or, as some would say today, by a historical wave. The truth is that the amount of freedom and democracy in the present and future depends as much upon human willingness to fight for them as upon anything else. The second error is the belief, common not only to these thinkers but to countless others, that human nature is unchangeable. Insofar as this is neither a proposition of biology or of theology nor a logical tautology, but refers to psychological and social traits, it can be shown to be false. The third is their confusion between an organizing principle and the individual members of the series organized. Since no identification is possible between the principle of democracy and any one member of the series, they go from the true conclusion that the principle is incompletely realized in any one case to the false conclusion that there are no degrees of realization in the series of cases.

(3) The third class of objections to the feasibility of the democratic ideal is derived from alleged cosmic or physico-chemical laws which contain the equations of doom for man and all his works. Even granting the validity of such laws, they would hold no matter what society exists, and, therefore, they establish nothing about the relative superiority of one form of society over another. Such laws, as William James already pointed out in a definitive refutation of all views of this type, tell us about the *size* of "energy-rills," not their *significance.*••

That the cosmic home of man limits his power, if not his dreams, is of course true. It is a perennial source of his humility before the intractabilities of things and the transient character of what he builds. But it is also true that this limitation is the source of his opportunities and a necessary condition for all achievement. From these truths we cannot infer that nature is the guarantor of man's ideals, certainly not of the democratic ideal. But neither is it the enemy of

• *The Ruling Classes* (Eng. trans.), p. 256.
•• See his reply to Henry Adams, who tried to draw social and historical implications from the second law of thermodynamics (*The Letters of William James,* II, 344-7).

human ideals. Man's friends and enemies are other men. To forget this is to go from natural piety to superstition. The cosmic scene against which men live out their lives will not be affected by the victory or defeat of a Hitler or Napoleon. Democracy needs no cosmic support other than the *chance* to make good. That chance it has, because man is part of nature. To ask for more is unreasonable as well as unworthy. The way in which man acts upon his chances is additional evidence of the objective possibilities and novelties of existence. Insofar as he is caught in the flux of things, the intelligent democratic man honestly confronts the potentialities of existence, its futurities, its openness, its indeterminateness. He is free of the romantic madness which would seek to outlaw the truths of science and of the quaint conceit, permissible only as poetry, that nature is a democratic republic. He takes the world as science describes it. He employs his knowledge of the world to achieve a more just and happier society.

Bibliography

RALPH WALDO EMERSON

Frederic Ives Carpenter, *Emerson Handbook* (1953).

Ralph L. Rusk, *Life of Ralph Waldo Emerson* (1949).

William James, "Address at the Emerson Centenary in Concord," in *Memories and Studies* (1911).

John Dewey, "Ralph Waldo Emerson," in *Characters and Events*, edited by Joseph Ratner (1929).

For bibliography, see Carpenter, *Emerson Handbook, supra.*

WILLIAM JAMES

Ralph Barton Perry, *The Thought and Character of William James* (1935). *In the Spirit of William James* (1938).

Horace M. Kallen, *Introduction to the Philosophy of William James Selected from His Chief Works* (1925). *William James and Henri Bergson* (1914).

Lloyd R. Morris, *William James, Message of a Modern Mind* (1950).

For bibliographies, see Ralph Barton Perry, *Annotated Bibliography of Writings of William James* (1920), and Morris, *William James, Message of a Modern Mind, supra.*

CHARLES S. PEIRCE

The Collected Papers of Charles Sanders Peirce, Vols. I-VI, edited by Charles Hartshorne and Paul Weiss (1931-1935); Vols. VII-VIII edited by Arthur W. Burks (1958).

Justus Buchler, *Charles Peirce's Empiricism* (1939).

W. B. Gallie, *Peirce and Pragmatism* (1952).

P. P. Wiener and F. H. Young, editors, *Studies in the Philosophy of C. S. Peirce* (1952).

John Dewey, "The Pragmatism of Peirce," *The Journal of Philosophy,* 13 (1916), 709-15.

Gail Kennedy, "Pragmatism, Pragmaticism and the Will to Believe—A Reconsideration," *The Journal of Philosophy,* 55 (1958), 578-88.

For bibliographies, see *Collected Papers,* Vol. VIII and *Studies in the Philosophy of C. S. Peirce, supra.*

OLIVER WENDELL HOLMES, JR.

Max Lerner, *Mind and Faith of Justice Holmes* (1943).

Felix Frankfurter, editor, *Mr. Justice Holmes* (1931). *Mr. Justice Holmes and the Supreme Court* (1938).

Mark De Wolfe Howe, *Justice Oliver Wendell Holmes* (1957).

Samuel Konefsky, *Legacy of Holmes and Brandeis* (1956).

Jerome Hall, *Readings in Jurisprudence* (1938), Chapter 6.

Morris R. Cohen, "Justice Holmes and the Nature of Law," in *Law and the Social Order* (1933).

Bibliography in Lerner, *Mind and Faith of Justice Holmes, supra.*

JOHN DEWEY

John Dewey, "From Absolutism to Experimentalism," in *Contemporary American Philosophy: Personal Statements,* Vol. II, edited by George P. Adams and William P. Montague (1930).

Sidney Hook, *John Dewey: An Intellectual Portrait* (1939).

George R. Geiger, *John Dewey in Perspective* (1958).

Gail Kennedy, four articles in *The Journal of Philosophy:* "Science and the Transformation of Common Sense: The Basic Problem of Dewey's Philosophy," 51 (1954), 313-26. "The Hidden Link in Dewey's Theory of Evaluation," 52 (1955), 85-94. "The Process of Evaluation in a Democratic Community," 56 (1959), 253-63. "Dewey's Concept of Experience: Determinate, Indeterminate, and Problematic," 56 (1959), 801-14.

Milton R. Konvitz, "On Jefferson and Dewey," in *John Dewey: Philosopher of Science and Freedom,* edited by Sidney Hook (1950).

For bibliographies, see Milton H. Thomas, *A Bibliography of John Dewey* (1939), and P. A. Schilpp, editor, *The Philosophy of John Dewey* (1939).

GEORGE HERBERT MEAD

George Herbert Mead, *Mind, Self, and Society from the Standpoint of a Social Behaviorist,* edited by Charles W. Morris (1934). *The Philosophy of the Present,* edited by A. E. Murphy (1932). *Movements of Thought in the Nineteenth Century* (1936). *The Philosophy of the Act* (1938).

Maurice Natanson, *The Social Dynamics of George H. Mead* (1956).

For analytic studies of Mead's philosophy, see the introductions to the works edited by Professor Morris and Professor Murphy. For bibliographies, see Maurice Natanson, *The Social Dynamics of George H. Mead,* and *Mind, Self, and Society from the Standpoint of a Social Behaviorist, supra.*

PERCY W. BRIDGMAN

Percy W. Bridgman, *The Logic of Modern Physics* (1927); reprinted in Macmillan paperback (1960). *The Nature of Physical Theory* (1936). *The Intelligent Individual and Society* (1938). *Reflections of a Physicist* (1950). *The Nature of Some of Our Physical Concepts* (1952). *The Way Things Are* (1959).

Symposium on "The Present State of Operationalism," by Bridgman, et al. In Philipp G. Frank, editor, *The Validation of Scientific Theories* (1956).

C. I. LEWIS

Clarence Irving Lewis, *Mind and the World Order* (1929); reprinted in Dover Books series (1956). *An Analysis of Knowledge and Valuation* (1946). *The Ground and Nature of the Right* (1955). *Our Social Inheritance* (1957).

Alice Ambrose Lazerowitz, "A Critical Discussion of *Mind and the World Order,*" *The Journal of Philosophy* 28 (1931), 365-81.

Paul Henle, review of "An Analysis of Knowledge and Valuation," *The Journal of Philosophy* 45 (1948), 524-32.

HORACE M. KALLEN

Sidney Ratner, "Some Central Themes in Horace Kallen's Philosophy," in *Vision and Action: Essays in Honor of Horace M. Kallen on His 70th Birthday,* edited by Sidney Ratner (1953).

Milton R. Konvitz, Foreword to *Of Them Which Say They Are Jews,* by Horace M. Kallen, edited by Judah Pilch (1954).

Bibliographies in *Vision and Action, supra,* and in Sidney Hook and Milton R. Konvitz, editors, *Freedom and Experience, Essays Presented to Horace M. Kallen* (1947).

SIDNEY HOOK

Sidney Hook, "Experimental Naturalism," in *American Philosophy Today and Tomorrow*, edited by Horace M. Kallen and Sidney Hook (1935). "Naturalism and First Principles," in *American Philosophers at Work*, edited by Sidney Hook (1956). *Political Power and Personal Freedom* (1959).

For bibliography, see Milton R. Konvitz, "Sidney Hook, Thinker in Action," 35 *New Leader* No. 51 (1952).

Index

scientific method, 94-7; data
and objects, 187-8; attack
on, 361-4; "scientism,"
371-3; and values, 374-9
self: and community, 266f.;
emergence of, 268; the
generalized other, 272-3;
play v. game, 273-5; character of, 324; and patterns
of culture, 325; personality
images, 326f.; center of
creative force, 331-3
situations: problematic, 183,
191-2; aesthetic, 192; two
types, 198
skepticism, 362
social planning, 233f.; acts
and objects, 269f.; 280;
significant symbols, 276-7;
control, 277-80
society, 268f.
space, 291f.
Spencer, 153
Stoicism, 128
Stout, G. F., 64
style, 343

Tarde, G., 155
theism: and moral principles,
387-8
theories: as instruments, 32
theory and practice: separation of, 222f.
Thorndike, E., 331
thought: and action, 105;
function of, 107

time, 124, 248f.
torts, 150, 154
Townsend, H. G., 11
transubstantiation, 107
truth: growth of, 35-6; and
the good, 42; defined, 46;
practical function, 46-7;
unverified, 48-9; and mental relations, 50; and correspondence, 51-3; as ex-
pedient, 55; as absolute,
55-6; rationalist's fallacy,
58; relative, 70-1; how v.
what, 70-2; and reality,
116; test of, 170-1; and
definition, 307-8; value
judgments, 377-8

values: and fact, 174; eternal, 203; rationalist and
empirical theories, 203f.;
desired v. desirable, 205f.;
judgments about, 209-10;
regulation of, 212; higher
and lower, 212-14; ante-
cedent and eventual 214f.;
and experimental method,
215f.; as hypotheses, 218-
19; means and ends, 220-1;
and scientific method,
374f.; value judgments,
377-8

Weber, M., 388
Whitehead, 265
wisdom, 25

MILTON R. KONVITZ
Milton R. Konvitz is Professor
of Industrial and Labor Relations
and Professor of Law at Cornell University.
He is the author of a number of books,
among them FUNDAMENTAL LIBERTIES
OF A FREE PEOPLE, and a contributor
to periodicals.

GAIL KENNEDY
Gail Kennedy is Professor of Philosophy
at Amherst College. Among his published
books are EVOLUTION AND RELIGION:
THE CONFLICT BETWEEN SCIENCE
AND THEOLOGY IN MODERN AMERICA
and PRAGMATISM AND AMERICAN CULTURE.